GLOBAL ISSUES

NATURAL RESOURCES AND SUSTAINABLE DEVELOPMENT

Kathy Wilson Peacock

Foreword by Jeremy Carl

Research Fellow,
Program on Energy and Sustainable Development
Stanford University

Viva Books

New Delhi | Mumbai | Chennai | Kolkata | Bangalore | Hyderabad | Kochi | Guwahati

First Indian Edition 2010

VIVA BOOKS PRIVATE LIMITED

- 4737/23 Ansari Road, Daryaganj, New Delhi 110 002
  E-mail: vivadelhi@vivagroupindia.net, Tel. 42242200
- 76, Service Industries, Shirvane, Sector 1, Nerul, Navi Mumbai 400 706
  E-mail: vivamumbai@vivagroupindia.net, Tel. 27721273, 27721274
- Jamals Fazal Chambers, 26 Greams Road, Chennai 600 006
  E-mail: vivachennai@vivagroupindia.net, Tel. 28290304, 28294241
- B-103, Jindal Towers, 21/1A/3 Darga Road, Kolkata 700 017
  E-mail: vivakolkata@vivagroupindia.net, Tel. 22836381, 22816713
- 7, Sovereign Park Apartments, 56-58, K. R. Road, Basavanagudi, Bangalore 560 004
  E-mail: vivabangalore@vivagroupindia.net, Tel. 26607409, 26607410
- 101-102 Mughal Marc Apartments, 3-4-637 to 641, Narayanguda, Hyderabad 500 029
  E-mail: vivahyderabad@vivagroupindia.net, Tel. 27564481, 27564482
- First Floor, Beevi Towers, SRM Road, Kaloor, Kochi 682 018, Kerala
  E-mail: vivakochi@vivagroupindia.net, Tel: 0484-2403055, 2403056
- 232, GNB Road, Beside UCO Bank, Silpukhuri, Guwahati 781 003
  E-mail: vivaguwahati@vivagroupindia.net, Tel: 0361-2666386

www.vivagroupindia.com

Published by arrangement with

Facts on File, Inc.
132 West 31st Street
New York 10001
USA

ISBN 978-81-309-1422-0

Published by Vinod Vasishtha for Viva Books Private Limited, 4737/23, Ansari Road, Daryaganj, New Delhi-110 002. Printed and bound by Anand Sons, Delhi - 110 092.

Contents

Foreword

What is sustainable development? Coming up with a comprehensive book about such an elusive subject presents a number of difficulties. The most well-known and widely cited definition of sustainable development comes from the 1987 World Commission on Environment and Development of the United Nations commonly known as the Brundtland Commission after its chair, former Norwegian prime minister Gro Harlem Brundtland. The Brundtland Commission defined sustainable development as "meeting the needs of the present without compromising the ability of future generations to meet their own needs."

And, while the Brundtland Commission's definition is the most famous, it is far from the only definition of sustainable development that is publicly cited. Another definition of sustainable development states that "humanity must take no more from nature than nature can replenish" and yet another that sustainable development is "achieving economic and social development in ways that do not exhaust a country's natural resources." A final commonly offered perspective considers not just human needs but the needs of nature as well: It argues that "sustainable development should include preserving the environment for other species as well as for people." Overall, more than 100 different definitions of the terms *sustainability* and *sustainable development* have been publicly cited.

If you read each of the previous definitions carefully, you will see that while they share a certain common core idea, they also differ from each other in important ways. Does sustainable development refer only to meeting human needs or should we consider the needs of other species? Does sustainable development exist as a concept only with reference to specific countries or is it a global concept? And most fundamentally, how do we know what the needs of future generations will be and what tools and resources they will use to supply them?

Sustainable development is obviously a worthy goal, but, like so many other complex issues, the devil is in the details. Depending on how sustainable development is defined, we may be seen as developing less sustainably or more sustainably. This book explores what those details are and what they mean for us as we attempt to sustain both our economic and planetary health in the 21st century.

Of course, as with any contentious issue, sustainable development has its extremists on both sides. Some skeptics dismiss the concept of sustainable development entirely, arguing that our current development trajectory is already sustainable and criticizing the sometimes exaggerated claims of some sustainable development advocates. At the other extreme, some advocates claim that development is inherently unsustainable and that if we are to preserve the planet, we must go back to a simpler, less resource-intensive lifestyle with far fewer modern conveniences. In reality, neither of these extreme views is indicative of the complicated reality of sustainable development.

While it is certainly true that some sustainable development boosters have exaggerated their cause for political effect, using misleading or scientifically unsupported numbers to bolster their argument, there is also little question that in several areas, such as fisheries, fossil fuel usage, or tropical forest protection, our development has been very unsustainable, with potentially serious long-term economic and environmental consequences that can be observed around us every day.

At the same time, there is also little question that those who claim that we must somehow retreat back into more primitive lifestyles in order to develop sustainably are incorrect. When regulations and goals were set appropriately, and full environmental costs were included in economic decision-making, societies have been outstanding innovators and experts at getting more and more benefits out of fewer resources. Similarly, ecosystems often can prove surprisingly resilient even when badly damaged, provided they are eventually given time to fully recover undisturbed. Nonetheless, some of the harm we have done developing unsustainably is irreversible, a sobering thought for those who care about the future of our planet.

While extremists on both sides often receive a great deal of media attention, once we move beyond the extremes of the debate, the world of policy becomes murkier. How much should we spend on alternative energy in order to reduce the environmental damage from fossil fuel use? Are treaties like the Kyoto Protocol the most effective way to reduce CO_2 emissions? How useful are concepts like the "ecological footprint" in determining the sustainability of our current lifestyles? How should we value the ecosystem services provided by a healthy forest?

Foreword

Kathy Wilson Peacock's book, written specifically with today's high school students in mind, provides an excellent introduction to these difficult questions. Unlike a textbook in a subject such as mathematics, it does not pretend to have all of the answers, but it hopes to teach you how to begin to understand the issues so that you can ask the right questions. In many ways, you are the ideal audience for such material. For the sustainability or lack of sustainability of our current lifestyles will affect you much more than it will affect your parents or your grandparents.

This book is also unique in that the author does not just tell you her opinions on sustainable development. Instead, she provides dozens of primary source documents from treaties to scientific reports to newspaper articles in order to provide a wide variety of perspectives on the issue.

It includes not just a wide variety of texts, but, more important, a wide variety of perspectives—from governments to businesses to NGOs. It considers not just the opinions of Americans, but also the views of Europeans, Asians, Africans, and others. It examines our collective experience with sustainable and unsustainable development through the experiences of key countries, both in developed economies such as Germany and the developing world of China, Nigeria, and India. It looks at the challenges that face these countries in implementing policies that consider sustainability while at the same time seeking to grow their economies and lead their citizens to more prosperous lifestyles. And, of course, it devotes substantial space to the United States, as an understanding of sustainable development around the world requires us to understand what is going on in our homes, schools, communities, and country as a whole. Within the United States, it looks at efforts that the federal government as well as state and local governments have made toward sustainability.

While the material in this book is complex, the style is clear and straightforward—terms are clearly defined and opposing points of view are fairly presented. Additional sources are provided so that students may learn more about topics of particular interest on their own. While this book quite correctly celebrates the concept and goal of sustainable development, it does not shy away from discussing past failures in which some previous prophets of "sustainable development" were exposed as unduly alarmist. When it comes to the future, especially the future of something as complex as the interaction between our economy and our planet, everyone has a cloudy crystal ball. Keeping in mind that no one can forecast the future and our tools for understanding sustainable development are still in their infancy, one should read this book with a modest approach and recognition that no one has all of the answers to such difficult and important questions.

While we may not know all of the answers, this book provides you with a number of useful tools to better understand sustainable development as a scientific concept. It introduces you to the important measurement techniques we use to define sustainable development, and it discusses the challenges of developing and using these techniques. Controversial topics such as peak oil and carbon capture are introduced and contrasting perspectives on these subjects are offered. Controversies over nuclear power and population growth have caused hot debate since before the concept of sustainable development existed are also discussed.

Sustainable development is sure to be one of the most important social, political, and environmental concepts of the 21st century. You hold in your hands an ideal introduction to this vital and important subject. We hope you will use this introduction either as a springboard for further study in a university or professional setting or simply to make yourself a more informed global citizen.

— Jeremy Carl
Research Fellow
Program on Energy and Sustainable Development
Stanford University

PART I

At Issue

1

Introduction

Hurricane Katrina was the costliest natural disaster in U.S. history, with damage to infrastructure and the economy estimated at $100 billion.[1] When the Category 3 storm made landfall in late August 2005, it did not hit New Orleans directly, but its storm surges broke through the levees that held back Lake Pontchartrain. Eighty percent of the city flooded, and more than 1,800 people died; hundreds of thousands of people were displaced. Devastation lined the coast for hundreds of miles, obliterating entire towns from Alabama to Mississippi. More than a half million homes were destroyed, and oil production was interrupted in the Gulf of Mexico, causing a spike in gasoline prices felt throughout the country. The landscape, population, and economy of the region may have been permanently altered.

Much of the media attention surrounding Hurricane Katrina focused on the government's slow and inadequate response to the human crisis, and the underlying causes of the crisis received much less attention. Apart from the storm itself, several environmental factors contributed to the loss of life and property. First among them was the fact that large portions of New Orleans were technically below sea level, making those areas—and the citizens who lived in them—extremely vulnerable to flooding. The city's system of levees and canals, an engineering marvel responsible for its initial economic prosperity, destroyed wetlands that served as a natural barrier that could have absorbed much of the storm's impact. Much of New Orleans was built on land that was not suitable for urban development. Hurricane Katrina illustrates what happens when population growth leads to increased development that has a negative impact on natural resources. The wetlands destroyed by urbanization limited the city's ability to sustain its residents in the face of a natural disaster.

Dire warnings of overpopulation, dwindling supplies of fossil fuels, and increasing energy consumption are repeated often in the media. These statements are symptoms of a larger phenomenon—lack of sustainability.

Sustainable development is the idea that economic growth and consumption should be planned in order to minimize negative ecological impact. The concept was first defined and outlined in the 1987 United Nations Report of the World Commission on Environment and Development, titled "Our Common Future," but better known as the Brundtland Report.[2] The report highlights the interdependence of economic, social, and environmental factors at the global level and presents a plan for enacting policies that would lift the developing world out of poverty while preserving each country's natural resources for future generations. Issues as varied as poverty, AIDS, air pollution, biodiversity, water rights, and birth control overlap and influence the planet's carrying capacity and humanity's ecological footprint. *Carrying capacity* refers to the number of people an environment can support without suffering negative effects, and a country's *ecological footprint* is the total area of land and water needed to support a given population with food and energy and to absorb its waste. If the total area of land and water needed to support the world's population is greater than the total area of the planet, then the human population is in ecological overshoot, and the Earth's carrying capacity has been surpassed.

Ecological footprinting has become a widely accepted concept in many scientific and political circles, but it is not without its critics. Several sources note potentially serious problems with the quality and methodology of the underlying data, the fact that footprint size does not accurately reflect water, waste, and non-CO_2 pollutant statistics, and the elasticity of carrying capacity due to international trade.[3] Neverthless, the *Living Planet Report 2006*, published by the Global Footprint Network and the World Wildlife Fund (WWF), states that the world is already operating in ecological overshoot.[4] According to their measurements, the world's ecological footprint comprises more global hectares than exist on the planet. (A hectare is a metric unit of land measurement that is equal to 2.47 acres.) If left unchecked, ecological overshoot jeopardizes the ability of future generations to meet their needs. The solution is to change the way people consume the natural resources of the planet, including fuel, water, and land. It is important to note that if a population limits its ecological footprint, the planet's carrying capacity can rise. Thus, the number of people the Earth can support is variable and depends on how those people use the Earth's resources.

When the builders and developers of New Orleans created the levee system out of a muddy wetlands at the mouth of the Mississippi River in the 19th century, they were interested in holding back the water, keeping commerce flowing, and providing new land for the city's growing population. They acted in response to the needs of the population. However, when Hurricane Katrina struck at the beginning of the 21st century, it became clear that their actions had compromised the ability of New Orleans's residents to meet their future needs. The reasons why are numerous, interdependent, and important to understand in order to prevent further tragedies.

HISTORICAL OVERVIEW

The Mayans, the Vikings, and Easter Island

Unsustainable development is nothing new. Throughout the ages, flourishing cultures have come to quick and brutal ends once they depleted their natural resources. Easter Island, for example, is a small, volcanic outpost in the middle of the Pacific Ocean, 1,000 miles off the west coast of Chile. It is one of the most remote regions of the world ever to be colonized by humans. Around 1600 C.E., it was home to as many as 15,000 people, descendants of settlers who arrived on the island somewhere between 300 and 800 C.E. As part of their culture, the residents of the island cleared the forests and built stone *moari*—giant, monolithic statues of heads that are still intact today. The civilization collapsed, many theorize, when the islanders cut down all their trees to make rails to transport their large statues.[5] Without trees, inhabitants had no seeds to plant new trees and no wood to construct fishing boats. The birds had no trees in which to nest, and so they left the island. The lack of trees led to soil erosion, which further reduced the number and types of plants and wildlife available to the inhabitants. This loss in biodiversity left the inhabitants with little food to eat. Archaeological evidence suggests the dwindling population may have resorted to cannibalism. When Western explorers landed on the island in 1722 (on Easter Sunday), they found only 2,000 to 3,000 inhabitants. Whether or not this example provides valid corollaries for today's world is a matter of debate.

Norse Viking immigrants settled on the temperate shores of what is now Greenland in 1261 and proceeded to organize their colony by the Scandinavian traditions with which they were familiar. Their longhouses required substantial amounts of wood to build, more wood to heat, and the livestock they raised depleted the limited arable land available along the coast. When the livestock overgrazed the land and died out, the land was no longer good for farming. Having isolated themselves from the more adaptable Inuit natives, the Vikings had developed no system of bartering or trading that would have allowed them to obtain food and fuel. Thus, the Vikings became vulnerable to disease and starvation—a fate not suffered by the Inuit because they lived a drastically different, seminomadic lifestyle. The Inuit fished and hunted whales and were able to cover large areas with their dogsleds, allowing their ecological footprint to be spread over many miles. They did not deplete the soil through overfarming or cut down trees to build houses or heat them. Lacking similar strategies, the Vikings reached the tipping point of unsustainability shortly after 1400, and their settlements died out. The longhouses and the other buildings of their community still stand, indicating that the end came suddenly.[6]

The Maya of the Yucatán Peninsula in what is now Mexico were an advanced, thriving people settled in a rich, agriculturally diverse region. They built large cities, developed a written language, exercised wide cultural influence, and designed grand architectural wonders that flourished from 250 to 900 C.E. However, many Mayan towns were placed at relatively high altitudes, making the underground aquifers difficult to access because the water table remained close to sea level. They dug wells up to 75 feet deep to obtain their water supply, but the soil surrounding their cities absorbed rain quickly, making it difficult to capture. So they built huge cisterns and reservoirs to hold their water reserves. The reservoir at Tikal was large enough to provide adequate drinking water for 10,000 people for up to 18 months.[7] However, a drought shorter than that would have a grave impact on agriculture, and a drought longer than that would be catastrophic.

Maya culture was unique because of its high population density—a remarkable 250 to 750 people per square mile. Because of this, any disruption in the food supply had huge consequences. Their chief crop was corn (they ate very little meat), and high humidity in the region shortened the storage period for grain. Their diet was low in protein and did not offer much variety, making them vulnerable if the corn crop failed. Finally, the Maya did not use domesticated animals in farming or transportation, making those tasks severely inefficient. Because they had to carry their food with them and because walking was their only transportation, they remained isolated. In the event of drought or another catastrophe, they could not easily obtain resources from nearby settlements or towns. The Classic Maya Collapse was, according to many scientists, precipitated by overpopulation and a period of drought that peaked in the year 800 C.E. As much as 99 percent of the population may have perished. The Central Petén region at its peak had a population of anywhere from 3 million to 14 million, but, when Hernán Cortés and the Spanish conquistadors arrived in 1524, only 30,000 people remained, and none of them knew anything about the great stone ruins built by their ancestors in the nearby forest.[8]

Evidence points to violent struggles as resources became scarce; people were killed and those who remained had fewer children. It may have been an extremely rapid depopulation caused by a simultaneous high death rate and low birthrate. Lack of written records makes facts scarce, and many scientists disagree on the specifics of the decline. Regardless of the details, the circumstances point to unsustainable development of one form or another. The Maya no longer had the resources to maintain their way of life.

Biologist Jared Diamond believes that civilizations decline for five reasons: human-caused environmental damage, climate change, violence, political and cultural factors, and cessation of trade.[9] In the examples cited above, politics enters into the fray in the sense that all these societies were hierarchical, and the prevailing rulers were concerned with only what happened during their reign, not with what would happen afterward. Leaders did not address what must have been obvious problems; instead they were consumed with short-term goals that underscored their power, such as hosting elaborate ceremonies and building grand monuments. Though the variations are endless, cultures as wide-ranging as the Vikings, the Maya, and the Anasazi—even the bastions of Western civilization, the Greek and Roman Empires—suffered declines for the same reason. Their way of life had become unsustainable.

From Malthus to the Population Bomb

In 1798, the English Episcopalian minister Thomas Malthus wrote *Essay on the Principle of Population,* an influential treatise on the dangers of unrestrained population growth. Malthus witnessed firsthand the Industrial Revolution as it transformed London from a city of 700,000 people in 1750 to more than 1 million in 1800 and 2 million by 1850. This skyrocketing population was accompanied by disease, crime, and poverty. Based on his observations, Malthus believed that soon there would not be enough food to feed everyone. Mass starvation and death would ensue. His solution, as outlined in his essay, was population control. People must resist having so many children, he stated, or all of humanity could be threatened. His ideas attracted much attention, and soon the term "Malthusian" came to describe someone who is pessimistic about the long-term growth and survival of humanity.

In 1968, Stanford University biologist Paul R. Ehrlich published *The Population Bomb,* in which he predicted impending mass starvation due to skyrocketing world population and resource mismanagement. "The battle to feed all of humanity is over. In the 1970s and 1980s hundreds of millions of people will starve to death in spite of any crash programs embarked upon now," he wrote.[10] The book was a best seller and introduced millions of readers to the population issue. After the book's publication, he founded the influential group Zero Population Growth (ZPG), whose goal was to lower fertility rates around the world. Some experts called Ehrlich a modern-day Malthus for his dire, doomsday predictions—especially when they did not come to pass (Malthus's had not either). But Ehrlich was right about the first part of the equation: World population surged as he predicted. However, catastrophic famine did not follow. One major reason was the Green Revolution.

The Green Revolution

In the 1960s, new agricultural technology drastically increased the world food supply. This change was dubbed the Green Revolution. Scientists engineered varieties of rice and other grains that yielded harvests vastly larger than what was previously possible. Widespread cultivation of these grains, especially in underdeveloped countries such as India, provided sustenance for surging populations and averted worldwide famine. Additionally, new sources of oil were discovered, and improvements in mining and refinery operations kept the price of oil and other nonrenewable energy sources low and the supply steady. Food and other necessities were shipped around the world to wherever they were needed.

The downside of the Green Revolution was that these new, improved grains required more water than previous grains. Rice, which is the most water-intensive grain of all, became a staple crop in many areas of the world where water supplies were dangerously low. In Beijing, China, the water table dropped 200 feet in 20 years.[11] By the year 2000 in India, lack of governmental water policies encouraged farmers to "steal" water from their neighbors by digging ever deeper wells. Agricultural irrigation siphoned off the lion's share of the water, leaving some urban populations without sufficient access.

Although worldwide famine as Ehrlich forecasted in *The Population Bomb* was averted, many regions have suffered horrible periods of drought and starvation resulting in hundreds of thousands of deaths, such as China in the 1950s and Africa in the 1980s. But analysts believe these famines were caused by political events, bad agricultural policies, or problems in food distribution, not lack of food per se.

Industrial Revolution and the Demand for Fossil Fuels

Wood has been the main source of energy for most of human history. Oil, gas, wind, and water power have been used as well, but to a lesser extent. That changed after Scottish inventor James Watt improved the steam engine in 1765 and set the stage for the Industrial Revolution, which ushered in the era of coal, a combustible rock comprised primarily of carbon and sulfur. Coal was plentiful in England, where the revolution took hold, and large-scale mining operations allowed the country to prosper. By the middle of the 19th century, industry in Britain and elsewhere was increasingly mechanized, and wood remained the fuel of choice only for rural and underdeveloped countries.

In the 1830s, Scotsman Robert Anderson built the first battery-powered horseless carriage, and in 1835 the world's first electric car rolled down the streets of the Netherlands. As the automobile age took its first baby steps, electric battery vehicles dominated the miniscule market; they were quiet, ran smoothly, and provided enough power to satisfy novice expectations. A number of companies began to manufacture electric cars, and by 1900 they outsold gasoline-powered vehicles. Advances in the internal combustion engine, however, began to turn the tide. By the time Henry Ford launched the Model T in 1908 and made automobiles affordable to the middle class, the race was over. Almost overnight, a vast infrastructure of oil wells, refineries, distribution systems, gas stations, and roads arose to support the booming industry.

Coal and oil are the titans of fossil fuels. Coal, from whose soot the Industrial Revolution rose, remains the world's primary source of energy for generating electricity. Unlike oil, worldwide supplies of coal seem sufficient for the coming generations. The United States in particular has generous reserves of coal, as do Russia and China. However, coal is far from an ideal energy source. First of all, coal-fired power plants are inefficient. In the process of burning coal, nearly two-thirds of its energy goes up in smoke, leaving only one-third to be converted into usable power. Second, it releases vast quantities of carbon dioxide and methane, both greenhouse gases, into the atmosphere. Third, mining is a hazardous business. Miners routinely die underground, and they suffer extremely high rates of lung disease. Also, strip mines obliterate environments wholesale, poison nearby water supplies, and turn vibrant ecosystems into acidic wastelands, particularly in poorly regulated developing countries.

In 1973, the Organization of the Petroleum Exporting Countries (OPEC), the Saudi Arabian–led consortium that controls the Middle East oil supply on which the United States and other countries depend, embargoed oil that was destined for the United States. The result was an energy crisis. Motorists encountered higher prices for gasoline and long lines at the pump. Though the crisis was short lived, it prompted individuals and lawmakers alike to make changes. Many consumers traded in their big cars for smaller, more fuel-efficient vehicles, and the government lowered the national speed limit and extended Daylight Savings Time. Within 20 years, however, the lessons of the crisis were largely forgotten. Energy prices plummeted, urban sprawl increased the number of cars on the road and the number of miles they were driven, mass transportation became largely irrelevant outside of a few major cities, and drivers whiled away hours stuck in traffic jams from the comfort of their sport utility vehicles—heavy cars built on truck chassis that got poor gas mileage. Drivers enjoyed low gas prices and higher speed limits, and automakers repeatedly blocked all efforts to increase fuel efficiency standards. Simultaneously, American oil production declined (very modestly), and imports from the Middle East increased. Even political skirmishes and wars—such as the Persian Gulf War of 1991 and the Iraq War that began in 2003—failed to interfere with United States–bound oil tankers. Though some energy analysts forecasted an impending oil shortage for the 1980s and beyond, like Ehrlich's predictions of worldwide famine, they did not come to pass and were for the most part dismissed.

THE HUBBERT CURVE

In 1956, M. King Hubbert, a geophysicist for Shell Oil, was in charge of discovering new oil fields for the company. His expertise in the field of oil exploration led him to declare that U.S. oil production would peak in 1970 and decline thereafter. He plotted the history and future of U.S. oil production on a graph and came up with a steep bell shape, later dubbed the Hubbert Curve, that represented the sudden rise in oil production beginning around 1870, peaking between 1970 and 1975, and then declining just as sharply thereafter.[12] The implication was clear: All existing U.S. oil fields had been discovered and would soon be drained. In an era of low gas prices and big cars, few took notice of Hubbert's prediction. Oil industry insiders believed new oil fields would be discovered and future technology would increase output of existing oil fields. Hubbert was dismissed as a modern-day Malthus.

However, U.S. oil production did indeed peak in 1970 at 11 million barrels a day.[13] Now Hubbert's Curve has been extrapolated in the concept of Peak Oil, the year in which worldwide oil production will crest. Although such a point can only be determined in hindsight and production statistics from foreign countries are often elusive, some oil industry experts believe that Peak Oil may have occurred in 2007[14] though such predictions have been made erroneously in the past. Oil will continue to be produced and sold at millions of barrels a day, but it will become much harder to obtain and most likely more expensive. Surpassing Peak Oil means the world has run out of the easily obtainable oil that fueled the explosive economic growth of the 20th century. Others maintain that the data and logic behind Hubbert's Curve are not appropriate for making such predictions; oil industry expert Michael C. Lynch believes that Hubbert theorists have misinterpreted and drawn erroneous conclusions from mathematical data.[15]

Some believe that new technology will enable oil companies to expand supplies by harvesting untraditional oil reserves, such as that which is trapped in shale and tar sands or in deep, offshore areas that will require advances in ocean-mounted rigs.[16] Worldwide reserves of oil shale are estimated to be at least 2.6 trillion barrels.[17] Tar sands, also known as oil sands, exist in quantities in Alberta, Canada, great enough to meet world oil demand for the next 100 years.[18] As of 2004, only 2 percent of the oil sands had been produced into petroleum products, but Canadian companies had invested more than $10 billion in developing the technology to further extract the oil.

Acid Rain

The Industrial Revolution generated widespread air and water pollution from unregulated factories and the burning of coal. One of the first measurable environmental results was acid rain, a startling but scientifically accurate term. Acid rain is precipitation that contains a pH level of less than 5.6, making it more acidic than alkaline. Such precipitation occurs when high levels of sulfur dioxide and nitrogen oxide are emitted into the atmosphere and then absorbed into the water vapor comprising the clouds. Acid rain prematurely weathers buildings, dissolves stones and rocks, kills trees, and acidifies both soil and water, making them hostile environments for some species of plant and animal life. Sulfur dioxide, the main component of acid rain, is a waste product of the coal-fired power plant.

The phenomenon of acid rain was first measured and reported by Robert Angus Smith in his 1872 book, *Air and Rain,* after observing the sky in Manchester, England, a highly industrialized city noted for its coal industry. But it was only in the 1960s that scientists began to understand it in a global sense and study its long-term effects. Since then, some countries have passed laws to combat the problem and instituted emissions trading programs. In emissions trading, or cap-and-trade programs as they are sometimes called, factories that generate pollution are issued licenses that allow them to emit a certain amount of pollutants into the atmosphere. If they install pollution-control devices or otherwise lower their emissions, they can sell the remaining portion of their license to another factory that wants to increase its emissions. However, even in the 21st century, the governments of many countries do not require coal-fired power plants to install pollution-control devices or limit their emissions in any way. Acid rain continues to be a problem, particularly in the fragile ecosystems of the Northern Hemisphere.

Nuclear Power

Beginning in the 1960s, the push toward nuclear energy resulted in a building boom that brought a total of 430 nuclear power plants online worldwide by 1993. However, disasters at Pennsylvania's Three Mile Island nuclear power plant in 1979 and the Chernobyl nuclear reactor in the Soviet Union in 1986 caused faith in nuclear power to plummet. By the 21st century, many of the earliest nuclear power plants had been shut down, resulting in a net loss of nuclear energy. Asian countries, particularly China, continued to build nuclear reactors, but even so the world's total nuclear power capacity falls far short of the 4.5 million megawatts that the International Atomic Energy Agency once forecasted the world supply to be in 2000.[19] Besides their image problems, nuclear power plants are expensive to build and require safety measures that make them economically unattractive compared to coal- and natural gas–fired power plants. Some believe that safety measures and waste regulations place a burden on builders of nuclear reactors that builders of other types of power plants do not have to share. While the percentage of electricity generated by nuclear power continues to decline in the United States, Japan produces 35 percent of its electricity from its nuclear power and France 75 percent, reflecting each country's policy of energy security and their lack of domestic fossil fuels.

However, growing concern over global climate change has revived interest in nuclear power, and many of those who once protested against it now hail it as a more sustainable alternative to oil.[20] Nuclear power plants emit no greenhouse gases and thus represent a source of zero-carbon energy. But nuclear waste, which contains spent fuel, is radioactive and remains harmful to humans for thousands of years. Developing a safe way to dispose of this waste has long been a sticking point between those who advocate nuclear power and those who rally against it. The U. S. Department of Energy, in compliance with the Nuclear Waste Policy Act of 1982, has begun building a permanent repository for high-level nuclear waste at Yucca Mountain in Nevada, which is scheduled to open in 2017. The facility has already been delayed numerous times and will no doubt remain controversial as that date draws near. In light of this, United States–based nuclear power companies have reached out to developing countries such as Brazil and China in an attempt to expand their businesses.

In terms of safety, some claim that one fatal accident—Chernobyl—in over 40 years of commercial nuclear power is a good track record. Moreover, that one accident happened under a system of corruption, insufficient regulations and safety measures, and poor personnel training. If these issues are addressed and the remaining reactors of the Chernobyl design are shut down, nuclear proponents argue, nuclear power may yet prove to be the carbon-free alternative to polluting coal-fired power plants.[21]

Nuclear Weapons

During the cold war, many people feared the nuclear arms race between the United States and the Soviet Union would end in nuclear annihilation. By the 1970s, many scientists who had helped develop nuclear weapons or laid the mathematical groundwork for them (including Albert Einstein and Robert Oppenheimer, director of the Manhattan Project) vocally opposed nuclear weapons. The concept of mutually assured destruction (MAD), government officials said, was our best defense against nuclear war as long as the only powers to have such weapons on a large scale were the United States and the Soviet Union.

MAD can be viewed as a small-scale study in sustainable development. The United States and the Soviet Union diverted ever greater amounts of resources to building weapons until the Soviet Union could no longer sustain itself and imploded under the strain in 1991, thus ending the cold war. A superpower that had maintained a solid grasp over much of the world for several generations became a nonentity almost overnight.

As political power shifted following the cold war, the vacuum left by the end of the arms race was quickly filled by the challenges facing second- and third-world countries. War and poverty led to widespread transmigration from rural areas to urban areas as people sought jobs and opportunities in regions of economic growth. Many of these urban areas, particularly those in underdeveloped nations, grew exponentially to become megacities.

The Rise of the Megacity

As of 2007, the largest metropolitan area in the world was Greater Tokyo, home to 35.53 million residents. The next most populous areas are Mexico City (19.24 million), Mumbai (18.84 million), New York City (18.65 million), and São Paulo (18.61 million). In 1950, only New York City had more than 10 million residents (the definition of a megacity), but now there are more than 25 such cities. Many of them, including Mumbai (India), Jakarta (Indonesia), Shanghai (China), Lagos (Nigeria), Dhaka (Bangladesh), Beijing (China), Kolkata (India), Cairo (Egypt), Manila (Philippines), and Karachi (Pakistan), are in underdeveloped countries. Megacities present unique problems when it comes to resources, law enforcement, public health and safety, employment, and risk of natural disasters. In many cases, the city population has risen faster than public services can provide for them, resulting in strains on the water supply, food supply, sanitation, and housing. These cities often experience high levels of air and water pollution, leading to widespread health problems that overwhelm existing services. Because of high population densities and socioeconomic differences among residents of megacities, they are at high risk of social disorganization and civil strife. Rampant poverty creates vast slum areas of substandard housing not serviced by existing water or sewage systems, where millions of people, many of them migrants from rural areas who have no jobs or skills, scavenge for food in garbage dumps. Slum residents are particularly vulnerable to natural disasters; often they live in coastal areas prone to flooding or in housing that cannot withstand even a moderate earthquake. Opportunities for economic improvement are virtually nonexistent, and local governments often do not have the resources to employ proper urban planning strategies. In brief, many megacities have exceeded their carrying capacity.

THE CHALLENGES

In 1992, Canadian ecologist William Rees created the concept of the ecological footprint, defined as the total area of land and water needed to support a given population with food and energy and to absorb its waste. According to his estimates, a world population of 6 billion allows each person a ration ("footprint") of 1.9 global hectares (gha) to maintain environmental equilibrium.[22]

Calculating an ecological footprint requires knowing how much of what types of resources an individual uses. Factors include how much meat and locally grown versus processed food a person eats, how often a person drives a car and what that car's gas mileage is, how much waste a person generates, the size of the house a person lives in, and the number of people he or she lives with. A small footprint would be consistent with eating mostly locally grown, unprocessed food and little meat, living in a small house with other people in a climate that does not require huge amounts of energy to make it comfortable, taking public transportation, or driving as little as possible and doing so in a fuel-efficient car.

According to the *Living Planet Report 2006*, published by the nonprofit organizations Global Footprint Network and WWF, by 2003 humanity's footprint was 25 percent larger than what the Earth could sustain.[23] That means it took 14 months for the Earth to regenerate the resources used by people in the previous 12 months. Factors contributing to the overshoot included overpopulation, water usage, carbon emissions, agricultural practices, and overuse of petroleum and minerals leading to pollution, climate change, loss of biodiversity, deforestation, desertification, depletion of fisheries, and depletion of groundwater.

China, at over 1 billion people, and India, at just under a billion, are the world's two most populous nations. The United States comes in a distant third at just over 300 million. Yet population alone does not tell the whole story. The United States has a much larger ecological footprint than do India and China, because both are still primarily impoverished and underdeveloped. The United States is home to 4 percent of the world's population but uses 25 percent of the world's natural resources.[24] According to Rees, the average citizen in the United States had an ecological footprint of 9.5 gha, versus 1.5 gha for the average Chinese citizen, in 2002.[25]

The statistics developed by Rees and others do a good job of highlighting the problems as well as consumption differences worldwide, but they are controversial. While some scientists cite footprint statistics as evidence that humankind has reached ecological overshoot, others say the idea of the footprint is flawed. For instance, the model is weighted in favor of large households, because in large families each person takes up less space and requires fewer resources than a single person living alone. Yet a family with 10 children uses more resources and contributes to overpopulation more than a person who chooses not to have any children. Similarly, the countries with the smallest ecological footprints (i.e., Malawi, Bangladesh, Somalia, and Afghanistan) suffer intense poverty, indicating that the footprint theory may oversimplify relationships between people and their environment.

Limiting Population

World population impacts the use of natural resources in many ways. As of 2008, world population stood at nearly 6.7 billion people, a number expected to rise to about 9 billion by 2050. Scientists for the Global Footprint Network calculate that the planet reached ecological overshoot at around 4 billion people, sometime around 1986.[26] For this reason alone, policymakers include population control as a component in all sustainable development programs. Despite this, many scientists (foremost among them the late economist Julian Simon) believe that overpopulation is not necessarily a harbinger of unsustainability.

Throughout human history, the size of the world population has remained relatively constant and well below 1 billion people. In fact, the 1 billion benchmark was reached as recently as 1800, when the first glimmers of European industrialization resulted in shifting patterns of urbanization and increased consumption of resources. By 1900, well after the Industrial Revolution had taken hold of much of the Western world, the global population reached 1.7 billion—a remarkable increase of 70 percent in just 100 years. Moreover, because population growth is exponential, it gathered momentum as it began to climb due to the increasing size of each generation. Thus, *doubling time* (the number of years it takes for a population to double) was shortened dramatically. Between 1900 and 2000, world population increased by 4.3 billion, despite record numbers of wars, genocides, famines, and epidemics that killed many millions.

Poverty is a key factor in high birthrates. Consequently, efforts by the United Nations and other organizations to limit world population often focus on eliminating poverty and improving education in developing countries, because higher levels of education correlate to lower levels of poverty. Indeed, the countries with the lowest birthrates are those with relatively low poverty rates, high education rates, and high rates of urbanization. Europe is actually experiencing a negative growth rate; women in European Union (EU) countries average 1.47 children, fewer than the 2.1 births necessary to maintain current population levels.[27] The United States, a wealthy country with high education levels, is still experiencing population growth, but it is due primarily to immigration rates, not birthrates. Given current economic conditions, some population experts believe the world's population will peak at 9 billion in the year 2050 and then slowly decline thereafter.[28]

While proponents of sustainable development believe that lowering fertility rates in underdeveloped countries is a key factor in stabilizing world population, other policy experts are concerned about the flip side of the coin: developed countries that have birthrates too low to maintain current standards of living. That is the issue of *global aging*. Global aging is a problem because if birthrates drop below replacement level, the population distribution of a country will become unbalanced, creating a surge of older people and not enough young, working people to support them.

The economic implications of global aging are enormous. As a society's dependency ratio becomes unbalanced, there are more people forced to rely on workers for support and care than there are workers to care for them. Many pension programs rely on having more workers paying into the system than retirees receiving disbursements, but the equation is quickly reversing itself in the United States, Germany, Italy, France, and elsewhere. In China, the situation is particularly dire. A "silver tsunami," the phenomenon of a large generation of senior citizens and a much smaller generation of workers, was created by the country's one-child policy that was instituted in the 1970s. As only children move to urban areas to take part in the country's industrial transformation, older parents are left behind in rural areas without any means of financial and social support and without adequate access to health care. In Japan, politicians have raised the idea of encouraging retirees to emigrate to the Philippines, where a large workforce could provide care for them. In the United States, corporations such as General Motors are facing economic collapse because the ratio of workers to retirees has been reversed following a generation of downsizing.

Protecting the Earth's Water

More than 1 billion people on the planet lack access to safe drinking water, and nearly 5,000 children in underdeveloped countries die every day of diarrhea, cholera, and typhoid contracted through contaminated water.[29] Water shortages are often a problem of distribution rather than supply. Some people do not live near sources of freshwater and must rely on well water that has become poisoned with arsenic or has been diverted for agriculture, or they live in a slum area of a large city that has no municipal water or sewage service. Others, such as the millions who live along the Ganges River in India and the Yangtze River in China, live in the midst of water that has become polluted beyond potability with raw sewage and chemicals.

Most water withdrawn from surface sources (lakes and rivers) and underground aquifers (wells) is used for agriculture. Industry consumes the second largest amount, and the remaining water is used for drinking and household needs. In many countries, much of the water used for agricultural irrigation is wasted, pirated, or used to grow crops on land that is unsuitable for agriculture. For example, rice requires more irrigation than almost any other grain, and yet it is the basic crop of China, India, and other countries that suffer from desertification, deforestation, soil erosion, a declining water table, increasing salinity, and other problems stemming from unsustainable agricultural practices. An area that requires more freshwater than it can obtain without depleting its groundwater supply is said to be suffering from water stress. The most water-stressed countries in the world are Kuwait, Syria, Israel, and Nepal.[30]

The major rivers of the planet—including the Nile, Mississippi, Amazon, Yangtze, Danube, Thames, Rhône, and Huang (Yellow) Rivers—have been intentionally altered by dams and other engineering projects and unintentionally altered through drought, pollution, urban growth, global warming, and unrestricted irrigation. The result is that the ecosystems of these waterways have been damaged, and the symbiosis between the rivers and the people who rely on them has become unbalanced. For example, the Huang He is the lifeline for 140 million people in China, but global warming has resulted in less rain and hotter temperatures in the Qinghai-Tibet plateau, the source of the river. The plateau's glaciers are melting at a rate of 7 percent a year. Because the permafrost is also melting, water that would normally flow into the Huang He is now seeping deeper into the ground where it is inaccessible.[31] The remaining water has been polluted far beyond potability by rampant industrialization since the 1990s. In an effort to stem overgrazing of the river's highlands near Tibet, which is a factor in the depletion of the headwaters, the government has offered to buy out the nomads who herd yaks on the land. In return for abandoning the land and their way of life, the nomads received free housing and a small annual stipend from the government, but no assistance in helping them sustain their culture.[32]

SECURING NEW WATER SOURCES

Desalination, the process by which salt is removed from salt water, is becoming a more feasible way to obtain freshwater than it was in the past, due to improvements that have made it more cost effective. In the 1980s, for instance, a cubic meter of water cost $2.50 to desalinate, but by the early 21st century that price had dropped to $.70 per cubic meter.[33] By 2004, the Persian Gulf region, led by Saudi Arabia and the United Arab Emirates, produced 16 million cubic meters per day of desalinated water—half of the world's total. Bahrain, Kuwait, Oman, Qatar, and Yemen are expected to bring more of their own desalination plants online soon.[34] This water will be used not only for drinking, but also for agricultural irrigation. Like many environmental resource solutions, however, desalination is not the panacea it first appears to be. It remains expensive and thus generally an option for wealthy countries; the process is energy intensive and results in significant greenhouse gas emissions; it may harm marine ecosystems; and it removes the focus on the need to establish better water management policies worldwide.[35]

A NEW FORM OF WATER POLLUTION

Some developed nations that have long had a good record of clean water, including the United States, now face a new kind of pollution. Their municipal water supplies now contain measurable amounts of antibiotics and other drugs, which have been introduced into the supply through wastewater. Antibiotics often come from livestock, which are given huge doses to ensure the safety of the meat supply. As livestock excrete the drugs, they leak into agricultural runoff and groundwater. The antibiotics then enter the food chain, where their pervasiveness results in their decreased effectiveness as bacteria become resistant to them.[36] Other pharmaceutical substances introduced into the water supply include estrogen from birth control pills, antidepressants, painkillers, and tranquilizers. Unregulated substances, including caffeine and nicotine, are also present in measurable amounts in sludge produced by wastewater treatment plants. These substances, when introduced to the water cycle at large, can affect marine life and people. In particular, antidepressants may lower sperm levels in some fish, which has a negative effect on the species' population. High levels of estrogen can interfere with the development of the reproductive system of some fish, in effect giving males female characteristics. A decreasing number of male fish reduces spawning and could ultimately threaten the survival of the species.[37]

Protecting the Earth's Land

Apart from water, land is the Earth's most valuable resource, and land use planning is a vital component of any sustainable development plan. Land use encompasses urban planning, deforestation, desertification, soil degradation, agricultural practices, biodiversity, and a host of other issues of local and global importance. Furthermore, land issues are inextricably linked to water issues: Whatever affects the land ultimately has an effect on the water. For instance, clear-cutting the rain forest increases soil runoff into water and eliminates protective wetlands. The lack of wetlands increases flooding in coastal areas and reduces biodiversity. Or, urban sprawl leads to a building boom of factories and power plants that discharge pollutants into the air and water, further intensifying the cycle of desertification and soil degradation. In rural areas, short-term gains of land for cattle grazing and farming are offset by long-term degradation of soil quality, a reduction in biodiversity, and the inability of the ecosystem to renew itself. Without strong land use laws and regulations, the immediate needs of a local population often take precedence over the long-term needs of a wider region. In the 21st century, much desertification and deforestation are the direct result of humanity's need to feed itself.

THE NEW FOOD REVOLUTION

Apart from clean water, food is the most important resource needed to sustain a projected global population of 9 billion. According to United Nations statistics, 36 million people die each year due to malnourishment and starvation.[38] The death toll is not due to lack of food per se (as Ehrlich had predicted), but rather to distribution problems in which food is disproportionately available to some populations (such as in developed nations where cheap, plentiful food has resulted in an epidemic of obesity) and not to others (such as African nations in which civil and political strife have resulted in blocked shipments of grain). There are also big problems internally in poor countries due to ineffective socialist planning mechanisms. In 2004 India had a record grain surplus rotting in storage while extreme malnutrition ran rampant. Some scientists believe that lack of food will become inevitable in the future and that the issue requires a valiant effort on par with the Green Revolution that prevented widespread world starvation in the 1960s and 1970s. One answer is genetically modified food (GMF).

Many people object to GMF on religious, moral, or environmental grounds, but proponents state that GMF "may be more resistant to pests, heat, cold, and drought. They also help the environment by reducing pesticide and herbicide use."[39] Crops that have been genetically modified to grow with less water and in greater salinity than unmodified versions include soybeans, maize, canola, rapeseed, and cotton. Engineered foods such as so-called "golden rice," which contains more iron and vitamins than other strains of rice, may help boost the health of people in underdeveloped nations and even help prevent dehydration due to severe diarrhea. By 2006, GMF accounted for more than 252 million acres of agricultural land worldwide, with more than 50 percent of that within the United States.[40] Brazil grows GM soybeans, and India is increasing the size of its GM cotton harvest.

Critics of the rapid rise of GM crops warn that the long-term effects of such products are unknown. Some claim that widespread GM agriculture will lead to a loss of biodiversity or that consumption of GMF may lead to allergies, kidney problems, or suppressed immune systems.[41] Proponents claim it is an ideal way to offer healthier and less expensive food to people throughout the world while using less land.

Maintaining Biodiversity

Biodiversity refers to the number of plant and animal species existing within a given region as well as the genetic variety within each species. Ecosystems containing a multitude of species and varieties of species are considered healthier and more sustainable than those containing limited numbers of species. Biodiversity is a main component of sustainable development, because it is an indication of a region's ability to renew its natural resources.

Seemingly insignificant changes in biodiversity can have wide-ranging consequences. For instance, when the bison of the American West were hunted nearly to extinction in the 18th and 19th centuries, the California condor, which fed primarily on the flesh of dead bison, lost its food source and became threatened with extinction as well. Even though humans stepped in and saved the handful of remaining condors and bred them in captivity beginning in 1987, their existence as a species is still precarious. Only 273 condors existed in 2007, and less than half lived in the wild.[42]

Agricultural practices, deforestation, desertification, destruction of wetlands, climate change, and introduction of nonnative species have all drastically reduced the biodiversity of many regions throughout the world.[43] Lack of biodiversity stresses the remaining resources of a region, making sustainable development difficult to achieve. In general, biodiversity is threatened by overconsumption in developed nations and by poverty in underdeveloped nations. To address this issue, several organizations, including the World Bank and Conservation International, formed the Critical Ecosystem Partnership Fund, which aims to maintain sustainability in biodiversity "hotspots" around the world.

Protecting the Earth's Energy Resources

Energy is generated from natural resources. Food generates muscle power; wood generates heat; water, coal, and natural gas generate electricity; oil and biomass materials such as corn and sugarcane are turned into gasoline for cars; uranium is used to generate nuclear power. The challenge is to meet the ever-growing demand for energy without jeopardizing reserves of natural resources that future generations will require to maintain their own way of life.

Natural resources are often grouped into two broad categories: renewable and nonrenewable. Renewable resources are those that are so abundant they cannot be depleted. Renewable energy resources include solar power, wind power, geothermal power, biomass power, and, to some extent, hydropower and nuclear power. Nonrenewable resources—those that exist on the planet in finite amounts—can be depleted completely or beyond economic feasibility. Nonrenewable energy resources include fossil fuels: oil, coal, and natural gas—currently the world's major sources of energy for transportation and electricity. Oil and petroleum corporations, in fact, are the world's largest and most profitable companies.[44]

NONRENEWABLE SOURCES OF ENERGY

Energy generated from nonrenewable resources is considered by some to be unsustainable. Once extracted from the Earth, fossil fuels are gone forever. Additionally, the burning of fossil fuels releases carbon dioxide and other harmful substances into the Earth's atmosphere. Carbon dioxide is the primary greenhouse gas responsible for global climate change; it also contributes to acid rain. Thus, not only do nonrenewable resources present a threat to sustainability because their use reduces the amount of energy available to people in the future, but also their use results in damage to the environment that will have cumulative negative effects on the food, water, and land people require to live.

The internal combustion engine altered human civilization in less than 100 years. Gasoline-powered cars, trucks, and other vehicles have transformed the way people live, where people live, and how people interact with their environment. But oil is a finite resource. In 2007, the world used approximately 84 million barrels of oil per day.[45] This number is expected to grow steadily as China and India aggressively pursue industrialization. Concurrently, new oil field discoveries are dwindling and known reserves are becoming more difficult (and expensive) to recover.

Not far behind oil in terms of popularity as an energy source is coal, which fuels a majority of the electricity-generating power plants in the

United States and the world. Though it is the world's most plentiful fossil fuel and supplies are still considered abundant—especially in the United States—coal is an inefficient and highly polluting energy source.

For this reason, natural gas has become a more popular fuel for generating electricity and heat since the 1970s. Natural gas is a fossil fuel comprised primarily of methane gas and is often found in conjunction with oil and coal. Methane gas releases carbon dioxide into the atmosphere too, but at lower levels than coal. That makes natural gas an attractive energy source, although difficulties in transporting it temper enthusiasm somewhat. Natural gas is a plentiful resource and is emitted from the Earth's crust by natural processes and geological features, such as anaerobic digestion (decomposition of organic material, often aided by microorganisms), biogas processes, and mud volcanoes.

One way to reduce the impact of these energy sources on the environment is to employ *carbon sequestration* to trap and store greenhouse gases underground instead of dispersing them into the atmosphere. Research and development of several different carbon capture and storage processes are promising, including implementation in coal-fired power plants, although many regulatory and safety issues need to be hammered out before large-scale operations can begin. Additionally, carbon capture beneath the ocean, carbon transport via pipelines, and carbon compression technology—all areas of much research—may have yet-to-be-determined environmental ramifications.[46]

RENEWABLE SOURCES OF ENERGY

Green energy refers to nonpolluting, renewable sources of energy. These include solar, wind, geothermal, tidal, and hydrogen energy, among others. The great attraction of renewable resources is that they generate power without releasing carbon dioxide or other greenhouse gases into the atmosphere. The downside is that the energy they produce can be intermittent, expensive, hard to distribute, and difficult to generate on a massive scale. However, since the 1980s, renewable energy resources have become increasingly efficient and economically viable in some situations. Technological advances have lowered the price and increased the performance of some infrastructure basics, such as wind turbines and photovoltaic films, making them more attractive to consumers. Fuel cells may prove to be efficient enough to implement in some instances; stationary fuel cell systems may provide power assists for many devices and possibly even fuel whole power plants, for example, but the dream of hydrogen-powered fuel cell vehicles cruising down the freeway emitting only a few drops of water from their tail pipes is likely to remain just that—a dream—without a breakthrough in technology.[47]

Wind Power

Wind power has been used for centuries. Some claim that the Netherlands's 18th-century windmill district was the world's first industrial park, predating the Industrial Revolution by 100 years. Old-fashioned windmills that pumped water or milled grain have been replaced by networks of wind turbines, which generate electricity rather than mechanical power. As of 2005, world wind power capacity stood at 59,000 megawatts, less than 1 percent of the world's electricity.[48] Denmark leads the world in generating 20 percent of its total electricity demand from wind turbines; Spain is second at 8 percent, and Germany is third with 6 percent. In these countries and some others, many wind farms, each comprised of hundreds of turbines, have been built offshore in order to take advantage of steady breezes and minimize the environmental impact on nearby residents. Wind turbines are most feasible in areas where the average wind speed is 10 MPH or higher and where temperatures do not often fall below freezing. Because wind patterns across the Earth are fairly constant, scientists can determine the best locations for wind farms. Despite this, wind power remains fairly inefficient. Most plants that generate electricity from wind turbines operate at about 35 percent capacity, a fraction of the capacity for nuclear and coal power plants, which typically operate at 90 percent and 70 percent respectively.

Ironically, objections to wind power often come from environmentalists who believe that large turbines ruin the aesthetics of the landscape and interfere with local bird populations.[49] Some people object to the large swaths of land (often many square miles) that wind farms require and the noise they make. For example, the Cape Wind Project proposed for Nantucket Sound off the coast of Cape Cod would be the world's largest wind park if built. The project proposes a total of 130 turbines, each 426 feet tall, covering an area of five square miles, generating 420 megawatts—enough electricity for 420,000 homes—and offsetting 1 million tons of greenhouse gases annually.[50] However, the project has met steep opposition from activists who believe that the park would cause interference with nearby military radar systems and bird migrations and would mar the area's natural beauty. Others like the idea that the farm would reduce the number of oil tankers present in the region, thereby lowering the possibility of future oil spills such as those Nantucket Sound has suffered in the past.

Solar Power

The Earth receives more energy from the Sun in one minute than the world consumes via fossil fuels each year.[51] Solar energy is plentiful, inexhaustible, and can be harnessed and used in a number of ways. It can heat houses and water, cook food, generate electricity, and even power cars. Yet the solar industry has not lived up to the hype it initially generated in the 1970s. Following the OPEC oil embargo of 1973, it was hailed as the alternative energy of the future. Solar panels were installed on houses and office buildings, and consumers were promised savings on their energy bills. But popular enthusiasm quickly waned when the technology was revealed to be weak, bulky, and inefficient. When energy prices receded, solar power was largely abandoned in favor of plentiful, cheap fossil fuels.

By the 21st century, however, private companies had vastly improved photovoltaic (PV) cells and other solar technologies, once again making the Sun an attractive energy source. Thin PV films captured solar energy, replacing the bulky, expensive solar panels of the 1970s. Solar power has proved especially effective in home water-heating systems, which were widely installed in China and other developing nations in the 1990s and 2000s.

Solar power is a broad term that encompasses passive and active systems, as well as concentrated and non-concentrated systems. Concentrated solar power systems contain a network of small solar panels and cells that funnel energy to a central tower, where it is then converted into electricity. Experimental PV solar cells convert the Sun's energy into direct current electricity. Several connected PV cells make up a PV module, and several connected modules make up a solar array, which produces even more power. Satellites and spacecraft often employ solar arrays as their main power source. Non-concentrated solar power is generated without the use of aggregated cells and is used on a small scale, such as in calculators, water heaters, and cookers. Passive solar systems are those that use solar energy without the help of additional devices, including greenhouses, solar water heaters, and green buildings that place windows in strategic locations to take advantage of the sun for light and heat. Active solar systems employ mechanical means to transform solar energy into electricity.

Germany leads the world in the amount of grid-connected PV power produced annually, with Japan coming in a close second. The world's largest PV power plant is Solarpark Gut Erlasee in Arnstein, Germany, which produces 12 megawatts, enough for several thousand customers.[52] A typical coal-fired power plant, by contrast, may generate around 1,000 megawatts and serve many thousands more customers.

When it comes to powering transportation, solar energy has many limitations. Hundreds of PV cells are needed on the surface of a vehicle to produce enough electricity to power the vehicle, resulting in large and awkward designs. A typical PV cell produces only one-half volt of electricity. In addition, commercial solar vehicles would require an energy storage system so they could operate at night or in cloudy weather. These limitations have not stopped enthusiasts from improving technology. Many "rayces" are sponsored each year for those who design and build experimental solar vehicles. One of the largest is the World Solar Challenge, a road race that takes place in Australia. University and corporate teams race their self-designed solar-powered vehicles from Darwin to Adelaide, a distance of more than 1,800 miles. By the early 2000s, the average speed of the top experimental vehicles was about 60 MPH.[53] Designs resemble spacecraft more than typical automobiles, with driver comfort mostly an afterthought. Solar-powered vehicles for the consumer market remain strictly theoretical.

Geothermal Power

Geothermal power is derived from the heat inside the Earth's core. As heat radiates through the Earth's mantle, some of the rock melts into magma and rises close enough to the surface of the Earth to heat the water that creates hot springs or geysers. Much of the time, however, the heat is retained in underground geothermal reservoirs that can be tapped for power by drilling into the rock. These reservoirs can reach 700°F; when holes are drilled into the reservoir, steam or hot water bursts through to the surface, where it powers large turbines that generate electricity. The primary emission is water vapor.

The first geothermal power plant was built in Larderello, Italy, in 1904. The largest geothermal power plant in the world is the Geysers in northern California, which has been operating since 1960 and produces enough electricity to power a city of more than 1 million people. According to the Geothermal Education Office, by the turn of the 21st century, 250 geothermal plants were operating worldwide, providing power to more than 60 million people; Iceland alone generates over 50 percent of its energy from geothermal sources. In the United States, geothermal power is concentrated in California, Nevada, and Utah and produces more electricity in those states than solar and wind power combined.[54]

Areas lacking in geothermal reservoirs may still be able to use geothermal heat pumps, which take advantage of an area's constant underground temperature. For example, fluid is pumped through a system of pipes from a building to an underground area and back again. In the summertime, the fluid is heated by the outside air and then pumped underground, where it is cooled by the Earth's steady temperature (usually 45–55° F). In the winter, the process is reversed using a system of compressors and refrigerants. The heat pumps still rely on conventional sources of electricity to move the fluid through the pipes, but they require less than half the energy it takes to generate the heat solely through electricity and can reduce energy costs by 50 percent.[55]

The downside of geothermal energy is that current technology limits geothermal power plants to areas with accessible steam fields. Additionally, the plants emit carbon dioxide, nitric oxide, and sulfur into the atmosphere, although the levels are much lower than coal-fired power plants. Finally, there is some risk of increased seismic activity and land instability in geothermal drilling areas, and over time some reservoirs may cool down causing the surrounding area to become unstable.

Tidal Power

Naturally occurring ocean tides can be harnessed as a nonpolluting source of energy. In such a system, a body of water surges inland at high tide and is retained in an artificially created lagoon until the tide goes out again. Then a dam releases the water, and, as it rushes through the sluice gates back to the sea, it powers turbines that produce electricity. Some modern tidal power plants are capable of generating power at both high tide and low tide. Tidal power has an advantage over wind and solar power because tides are predictable and reliable, while sunlight and wind are not. Tide mills, precursors to tidal power plants, have been used since the Middle Ages in Europe, and some still exist today in England. A tidal power plant on the Rance River in France opened in 1966 on a site that had been used as a tidal mill for hundreds of years and generates an average of 68 megawatts.

Tidal power plants are limited to certain geographical locations; they must be built in areas with large disparities between high and low tides and situated at the mouth of a river that can be successfully dammed. Tidal power plants are costly to construct, while conventional hydroelectric power is cheap and plentiful; this fact alone accounts for their scarcity. Additionally, many people object to them because they interfere with the habitat of local wildlife. Because of these circumstances, tidal power plants will most likely continue to be rare. China has eight and Canada has one. Scotland, England, Russia, Argentina, and South Africa have considered tidal power plants, but with the understanding that such plants would fulfill only a fraction of their energy needs.

Hydrogen Power, Fuel Cells, Flex-Fuel Vehicles, and Ethanol

Hydrogen is the most common element on Earth and currently considered the energy source with the most potential to change the way we live. The automobile industry has been trying to design a vehicle powered by a zero-emissions hydrogen fuel cell, which would drastically reduce greenhouse gas emissions and free the United States from foreign oil dependency. But is this idea too good to be true? In the 1990s, most major automakers predicted they would have a fuel cell vehicle on the market by the first decade of the 21st century. That did not happen, primarily due to cost and logistical problems.

Hydrogen is unstable, heavy, hard to compress, and even harder to transport, and fuel cells are expensive to produce. Creating a fuel distribution infrastructure is a huge challenge—one that must be conquered before fuel cell vehicles reach their tipping point and become the wave of the future.

Proton Exchange Membrane (PEM) fuel cells (also called Polymer Electrolyte Membrane fuel cells) were developed in the 1960s and first used by NASA to power the Gemini series of spacecraft.[56] Inside a PEM fuel cell, hydrogen is introduced to oxygen, creating energy to propel the vehicle. The hydrogen then combines with the oxygen to produce water, which is the PEM fuel cell's only by-product. The PEM fuel cell requires no fossil fuels to run (as opposed to electric vehicles, which are usually charged with electricity generated from coal-fired power plants). The cells used in hydrogen vehicles produce just over one volt of electricity, which means that many cells must be stacked together in order to produce enough electricity to power the vehicle. Cell stacks are heavy and take up a lot of space, making hydrogen-powered vehicles much heavier than a typical gasoline-powered car. Despite this, many believe that some form of PEM fuel cell will eventually replace the internal combustion engine.[57]

More likely to gain popularity in the short term are flex-fuel vehicles, which run on either traditional gasoline, ethanol (grain alcohol), or a blend of gasoline and ethanol. Flex-fuel vehicles have been around a long time. Henry Ford's original Model T was designed to run on ethanol, because he intended rural Midwestern farmers (who often lived miles away from the nearest gas station) to generate their own fuel and remain self-sufficient.[58]

In the United States, most ethanol is made from corn, but in other countries it is made from sugarcane, cassava, sugar beets, sweet potatoes, and many other crops. Not all these crops generate the same volume of ethanol. Miscanthus and switchgrass can produce up to five times as many gallons of ethanol per acre as corn, and sugarcane generates twice as many gallons per acre as corn.[59] The advantages of ethanol over gasoline are that it is renewable and burns cleaner. But many experts take issue with ethanol's supposed advantages because they believe that the immense amount of land, water, and energy needed to grow enough corn to fuel significant numbers of ethanol vehicles would cost just as much and generate similar amounts of pollution as do the processes to refine petroleum for gasoline-powered vehicles. Also, the fermentation of grain to produce ethanol emits carbon dioxide, although it may be offset by the oxygen emitted by the crops themselves. Additionally, ethanol contains about 34 percent less energy than gasoline, which makes it 34 percent less efficient.[60] This means that a car running on 100 percent ethanol may get only 20 miles per gallon, while a similar gasoline-powered vehicle may get 30 miles per gallon. Thus, even though ethanol and gasoline are often equivalent in price, ethanol will cost a motorist more money because the gas tank will need to be filled more often. Ultimately, the fate of flex-fuel vehicles may rest with whether or not the energy derived from ethanol is sufficiently greater than the energy it requires to produce—a factor known as energy balance.

Many cars produced in the United States since 1995 can run on ethanol, but ethanol is not widely available to consumers. E85, a blend of 15 percent gasoline and 85 percent ethanol, was available at only 900 service stations nationwide in 2007.[61] Flex-fuel vehicles have become the norm in Brazil and Sweden, but they have been slow to catch on in the United States. Some believe this is because gas stations owners have no incentive to offer ethanol at the pump.

One alternative to ethanol that has gained acceptance in recent years is natural gas. Natural gas burns cleaner than other fossil fuels, and although it does emit carbon dioxide—the primary greenhouse gas—it emits much less than conventional fuels. It is also readily available within the United States, which means it could ease some of the problems associated with a dependency on foreign oil. Natural gas also requires less processing and refining than gasoline, which means it costs less. It can be used in existing vehicle designs with few changes, and, because it burns so cleanly, engines last longer and require fewer repairs. The natural gas–powered 2007 Honda Civic GX was the cleanest internal-combustion car ever mass-produced at the time it was introduced.[62] In 2006, 150,000 natural gas–powered vehicles (NGVs) were on the road in the United States, most of them commercial vehicles, such as buses, delivery vehicles, and municipal vehicles, and more than 1,500 gas stations offered natural gas.[63]

Flex-fuel vehicles and NGVs should not be confused with hybrid vehicles. Hybrid electric vehicles (HEVs) are those that use two power sources, usually an electric battery and an internal combustion engine, as a way to improve fuel efficiency. Such vehicles rely on a rechargeable energy storage system (RESS) that assists the engine with propulsion over long distances and high speeds or is able to propel the vehicle on its own over short distances at moderate speeds. Such vehicles still use gasoline, but they get significantly better gas mileage than traditional vehicles. Plug-in hybrid vehicles (PHEVs) are another variation in which power is generated either solely by electricity (over a short distance) or by gasoline. Cars can be charged up at home, obtain 100 MPG, and save consumers significant costs in fuel and maintenance.

WISE ENERGY USE AND ENERGY SECURITY

As the world becomes increasingly reliant on automobiles, electricity, and consumer goods, the demand for energy will continue to rise. Many highly populated, developing nations, led by China and India, are scrambling to attain a level of prosperity enjoyed by more industrialized nations. Such unprecedented growth pushes the envelope of what is sustainable. From 1950 to 2000, the world's population grew 140 percent, but consumption of fossil fuels grew 400 percent.[64] Energy security is the ability of a country to generate or obtain as much energy as its population requires to sustain its needs and provide for further development, without endangering its political or economic stability. Energy security can be jeopardized by a sudden change in foreign relations, economic recession, acts of terrorism and war, and even natural disasters such as a hurricane or an earthquake. Countries that rely heavily on nonrenewable resources or who import more energy than they generate may not have sufficient energy security if they are at the mercy of other governments to keep their economy running smoothly. Obtaining energy security often entails diversifying energy sources and increasing efficiency. Most countries address the issue of energy security in their national energy policy, but continue to obtain energy on the world market.

FOSTERING SUSTAINABLE DEVELOPMENT

One of the first attempts to broker international cooperation on environmental issues came in 1987 when the United Nations created the World Commission on Environment and Development, which issued the report "Our Common Future." Better known as the Brundtland Report (after its chair, Gro Harlem Brundtland), the document was the first to define the concept of sustainable development and to recognize that it is in the best interests of developed nations to assist underdeveloped nations in achieving such development. The Brundtland Report defined sustainable development as "meeting the needs of the present without compromising the ability of future generations to meet their own needs."[65] The list of issues related to sustainable development is lengthy and includes traditional environmental issues ranging from agriculture, energy, sanitation, water, and land management to more social concerns, such as consumption and production patterns, human settlements, integrated decision making, poverty, and trade. Some charge that the definition of sustainable development is so broad and ambiguous as to be meaningless, or that continued, unending growth cannot be sustainable any more than oil can continue to be pumped out of the ground indefinitely. Also complicating sustainable development is that initiatives often place equal value on "ecocentrist" (nature-centered) and "anthropocentric" (human-centered) views, which are often at odds with one another.

The United Nations has brokered other conferences charged with tackling issues of sustainable development. When the seasonal hole in the Earth's ozone layer over Antarctica was discovered to be caused by chlorofluorocarbons (CFCs) in the 1980s, the United Nations in 1987 drafted the Montreal Protocol on Substances That Deplete the Ozone Layer, which was signed by many countries that agreed to ban CFCs. As a result, levels of CFCs in the atmosphere have largely leveled off, and the hole in the ozone layer, which reached its largest size in 2000, has been shrinking ever since. Advocates have hailed the Montreal Protocol as one of the most successful international treaties ever, due to its high level of participation and quick, measurable results.[66]

The United Nations also sponsored the 1992 Earth Summit in Rio de Janeiro, at which 172 nations participated. The conference focused on water issues, mass transportation, alternative fuels, pollution control, global warming, sustainable economic growth, and the need to protect the land of indigenous peoples from adverse development. Its leaders signed the Convention on Climate Change and the Convention on Biological Diversity. They endorsed the Rio Declaration and the Forest Principles. They adopted Agenda 21, a 300-page plan for achieving sustainable development. Agenda 21 is overseen by the UN's Commission on Sustainable Development, created to monitor and report on these agreements. Progress has been formally assessed several times, including in 1997 and 2002. Many countries have adapted Agenda 21 to their own specific needs; such a document is known as a Local Agenda 21.[67]

Buoyed by these successes, the United Nations continued to foster an international dialogue on issues relating to the environment and sustainable development. The Kyoto Protocol, which opened for signature in 1997, is an amendment to the Convention on Climate Change and formally addresses the issue of global warming by prompting signatory countries to limit their greenhouse gas emissions (mainly carbon dioxide) and engage in emissions trading to help stave off climate change. The treaty was greeted enthusiastically by a number of nations, but the United States refused to sign it, stating that it placed an unfair burden on the United States and gave a free ride to major polluters such as India and China. Additionally, many scholars have claimed that the actual changes in core energy deployments as a result of Kyoto have been modest to nonexistent.

The Millennium Summit in September 2000 was a historic convention of world leaders at the United Nations headquarters in New York for the purpose of mapping a strategy for dealing with the world's most pressing issues. The summit resulted in the adoption of the UN Millennium Development Goals (MDG) and set 2015 as the target date for achieving them. Environmental sustainability, including issues pertaining to wise use of natural resources, is a primary goal, along with developing a global partnership for development. The MDG incorporates many of the goals outlined in Agenda 21.

Many universities have formed academic institutes to promote the nascent field of sustainability science. The Center for International Earth Science Information Network at Columbia University in New York and the Yale Center for Environmental Law and Policy in Connecticut have collaborated with the World Economic Forum and the Joint Research Centre of the European Commission to create the Environmental Sustainability Index, a report ranking each country in the world on a multitude of variables. The variables, 76 in all, are grouped into 21 indicators and then further categorized into five components. The main components are:

1) environmental systems, which include indicators of air quality, water quality, and biodiversity, and variables of sulfur dioxide emissions and freshwater availability;
2) reducing environmental stresses, which include indicators of population growth and natural resource management and variables of overfishing, water salination, size of ecological footprint, and coal consumption;
3) reducing human vulnerability, which includes indicators of natural disaster vulnerability and environmental health and variables of child mortality and safe drinking water availability;
4) social and institutional capacity, which includes indicators of environmental governance and eco-efficiency and variables of female education, democracy, and renewable energy production; and
5) global stewardship, which includes indicators of greenhouse gas emissions, international cooperation, and variables of participation in international agreements and transboundary sulfur dioxide spillovers.[68]

According to these criteria, the 2005 Environmental Sustainability Index ranked Finland, Norway, Uruguay, Sweden, and Iceland as the top five most sustainable countries. The bottom five were Uzbekistan, Iraq, Turkmenistan, Taiwan, and North Korea. Out of 146 countries, the United States ranked 45th. The rankings are intended as a tool to identify areas for policy improvements and for comparative analysis.

[1] David L. Johnson. "Hurricane Katrina Service Assessment Report." United States Department of Commerce. June 2006. Available online. URL: http://www.weather.gov/om/assessments/pdfs/Katrina.pdf. Posted June 2006.

[2] Gro Harlem Brundtland. "Our Common Future." Report, World Commission on Environment and Development. United Nations, August 4, 1987. Available online. URL: http://

documents-dds-ny.un.org/doc/UNDOC/GEN/N87/184/67/img/N8718467.pdf?Open Element. Accessed April 27, 2007.

[3] G. C. van Kooten and E. H. Bulte. "The Ecological Footprint:Useful Science or Politics?" *Ecological Economics,* Vol. 32, no. 3, pp. 385–389.

[4] Chris Hails, ed. *Living Planet Report 2006.* WWF—World Wide Fund for Nature, 2006, p. 3. Available online. URL: http://www.panda.org/news_facts/publications/living_planet_report/lp_2006/index.cfm. Posted February 12, 2007.

[5] Jared Diamond. *Collapse: How Societies Choose to Fail or Succeed.* New York: Viking, 2004, p. 79.

[6] Diamond, p. 248.

[7] Diamond, p. 162.

[8] Diamond, p. 175.

[9] Diamond, pp. 159–160.

[10] Paul R. Ehrlich. *The Population Bomb.* New York: Ballantine, 1968, p. xi.

[11] Michael Specter. "The Last Drop: Confronting the Possibility of a Global Catastrophe." *New Yorker,* October 23, 2006, p. 62.

[12] M. K. Hubbert. "Nuclear Energy and the Fossil Fuels." Presented before the Spring Meeting of the Southern District, American Petroleum Institute, Plaza Hotel, San Antonio, Texas, March 7–9, 1956.

[13] U.S. Energy Information Administration. "U.S. Crude Oil Field Production." Available online. URL: http://tonto.eia.doe.gov/dnav/pet/hist/mcrfpus1A.htm. Updated March 1, 2007.

[14] Ronald G. Nelson. "'Peak Oil' Is Only a Matter of Time." *Pipeline & Gas Journal,* February 2007, p. 62.

[15] Michael C. Lynch. "The New Pessimism about Petroleum Resources: Debunking the Hubbert Model (and Hubbert Modelers). "Report for Strategic Energy and Economic Research, Inc. Available online. URL: http://www.energyseer.com/NewPessimism.pdf.

[16] Jad Mouawad. "Oil Innovations Pump New Life into Old Wells." *New York Times,* March 5, 2007.

[17] American Association of Petroleum Geologists, Energy Minerals Division. "Oil Shale." Available online. URL: http://emd.aapg.org/technical_areas/oil_shale.cfm. Accessed March 20, 2007.

[18] Alberta Department of Energy. "Oil Sands." Available online. URL: http://www.energy.gov.ab.ca/89.asp. Accessed April 27, 2007.

[19] Christopher Flavin and Nicholas Lenssen. *Power Surge: Guide to the Coming Energy Revolution.* New York: W.W. Norton, 1994, p. 38.

[20] Stewart Brand. "Environmental Heresies." *Technology Review,* May 2005.

[21] John Ritch. "Nuclear Green." *Prospect,* March 1999.

[22] William Rees. "Globalization and Sustainability: Conflict or Convergence?" *Bulletin of Science, Technology and Society.* Vol 22, no. 4, August 2002, pp. 249–268.

[23] Chris Hails, ed. *Living Planet Report 2006.* WWF—World Wide Fund for Nature, 2006, p. 2. Available online. URL: http://www.panda.org/news_facts/publications/living_planet_report/lp_2006/index.cfm. Posted February 12, 2007.

[24] U.S. Department of Energy. "Energy in the Americas." Report, Energy Information Administration. Available online. URL: http://www.eia.doe.gov/emeu/cabs/Archives/theamericas/theamericas.html. Posted July 28, 1999.

[25] Rees, pp. 249–268.

[26] Global Footprint Network, 2006. Available online. URL: www.footprintnetwork.org. Accessed April 27, 2007.

[27] *CIA World Factbook.* "European Union." Washington, D.C.: Central Intelligence Agency, 2007. Available online. URL: http://www.cia.gov/cia/publications/factbook/geos/ee.html. Updated March 15, 2007.

[28] U.S. Census Bureau, Population Division. International Programs Center. "World Population Information." Available online. URL: www.census.gov/ipc/www/world.html. Updated August 24, 2006.

[29] Michael Myser. "Problem No. 4: Dirty Water." *Fortune International.* March 5, 2007, p. B5.

[30] Natalie Hoare. "Severe Water Stress." *Geographical,* August 2006, p. 7.

[31] Jim Yardley. "The Yellow River; China's Path to Modernity Mirrored in a Troubled River." *New York Times,* November 19, 2006.

[32] ———. "The Yellow River; China's Path to Modernity Mirrored in a Troubled River." *New York Times,* November 19, 2006.

[33] Oliver Klaus. "Securing New Resources: German Companies Are Taking on the Desalination Challenge." *Middle East Economic Digest,* August 27, 2004, p. 32.

[34] ———. "Securing New Resources: German Companies Are Taking on the Desalination Challenge." *Middle East Economic Digest,* August 27, 2004, p. 32.

[35] Phil Dickie. "Making Water: Desalination: Option or Distraction for a Thirsty World?" Report of the WWF Global Freshwater Programme, June 2007. Available online. URL: http://assets.panda.org/downloads/desalinationreportjune2007.pdf.

[36] Christian G. Daughton. "PPCPs in the Environment: Future Research—Beginning with the End Always in Mind." *Pharmaceuticals in the Environment, 2nd ed.,* K. Kummerer, ed. New York: Springer, 2004, pp. 463–495.

[37] Thomas Hayden. "A New Angle on Fishing." *U.S. News & World Report,* September 6, 2004, p. 85.

[38] Jean Ziegler. "Report by the Special Rapporteur on the Right to Food." United Nations Economic and Social Council, February 7, 2001, p.5.

[39] Valeria Jefferson. "The Ethical Dilemma of Genetically Modified Food." *Journal of Environmental Health,* July–August 2006, p. 33.

[40] James Clive. "Global Status of Commercialized Biotech/GM Crops: 2006." *ISAAA Brief,* no. 35, 2006.

[41] Alan McHughen. *Pandora's Picnic Basket: The Potential and Hazards of Genetically Modified Foods.* New York: Oxford University Press, 2000, p. 90.

[42] Jeffrey K. McKee. *Nature: The Conflict Between Human Population Growth and Earth's Biodiversity.* Piscataway, N.J.: Rutgers University Press, 2005.

[43] Charlie Furniss. "Too Hot to Trot." *Geographical,* May 2006, p. 51.

[44] Abraham Lustgarten. "Big Oil Dominates, But Old-Economy Companies Aren't the Only Ones Prospering This Year." *Fortune,* July 24, 2006, p. 89.

[45] Sebastian Junger. "Blood Oil." *Vanity Fair,* February 2007, p. 121.

[46] *Intergovernmental Panel on Climate Change Special Report on Carbon Dioxide Capture and Storage,* edited by Bert Metz, et al., New York: Cambridge University Press, 2005.

[47] U.S. Department of Energy, Energy Efficiency and Renewable Energy. "Fuel Cell Vehicles." Available online. URL: http://www.fueleconomy.gov/feg/fuelcell.shtml. Accessed March 19, 2007.

[48] World Wind Energy Association. "Worldwide Installed Capacity and Prediction 1997–2010." Available online. URL: www.wwindea.org. Accessed April 27, 2007.

[49] Amanda Griscom Little. "The Wind and the Willful: RFK Jr. and Other Prominent Enviros Face Off over Cape Cod Wind Farm." *Grist,* January 12, 2006. Available online. URL: http://www.grist.org/news/muck/2006/01/12/capecod.

[50] Joe Truini. "Bill Could Kill Cape Wind Plan; Provision Gives Governors Veto over Offshore Wind Projects." *Waste News,* April 24, 2006, p. 11.

[51] Solarbuzz, LLC. "Fast Solar Energy Facts." Available online. URL: www.solarbuzz.com. Accessed April 27, 2007.

[52] "World's Largest Solar Electric Power Plant." *Space Daily,* June 2, 2005.

[53] World Solar Challenge Web site. URL: http://www.wsc.org.au. Accessed April 27, 2007.

[54] Geothermal Education Office. "Geothermal Energy Facts." Available online. URL: http://geothermal.marin.org/geoenergy.html#using-geo. Updated January 13, 2004.

[55] Alexander H. Roberts. "Geothermal Offers Cheap, Clean Energy." *Westchester County Business Journal,* October 7, 2002, p. FC1.

[56] James M. Grimwood and Barton C. Hacker. "Project Gemini: Technology and Operations—A Chronology: Part 1(B)." Available online. URL: http://history.nasa.gov/SP-4002/p1b.htm. Accessed April 27, 2007.

[57] Lindsay Brooke. "Get Ready for Fuel Cells." *Automotive Industries,* June 1999, p. 36.

[58] Environmental Protection Agency. "E85 and Flex Fuel Vehicles." Available online. URL: www.epa.gov/smartway/growandgo/documents/factsheet-e85.htm. Updated October 2006. Accessed April 20, 2007.

[59] Danielle Murray. "Ethanol: More Than Just Corn." *USA Today Magazine,* November 1, 2005, p. 27.

[60] ———. "Ethanol: More Than Just Corn." *USA Today Magazine,* November 1, 2005, p. 27.

[61] U.S. Department of Energy, Energy Efficiency and Renewable Energy. "Alternative Fuels Data Center." Available online. URL: www.eere.energy.gov. Accessed March 16, 2007.

[62] Bob Knoll. "Greentech: A Civics Lesson with a Multiple-Choice Test." *New York Times,* February 18, 2007.

[63] Natural Gas Vehicles for America Web site. URL: www.ngvc.org. Accessed April 27, 2007.

[64] Jeff Goodell. *Big Coal: The Dirty Secret Behind America's Energy Future.* Boston: Houghton Mifflin, 2006, p. 9.

[65] Gro Harlem Brundtland. "Our Common Future." Report, World Commission on Environment and Development. United Nations, August 4, 1987, p. 51. Available online. URL: http://documents dds-ny.un.org/doc/UNDOC/GEN/N87/184/67/img/N8718467.pdf?OpenElement. Accessed April 27, 2007.

[66] Richard E. Benedick. "The Indispensable Element in the Montreal Ozone Protocol." *Earthmatters,* fall 1999. Available online. URL: www.earthinstitute.columbia.edu/library/earthmatters/sept1999. Accessed March 21, 2007.

[67] United Nations Conference on Environment and Development (UNCED). *Agenda 21: Earth Summit—The United Nations Programme of Action from Rio.* April 1993. Available online. URL: http://www.un.org/esa/sustdev/documents/agenda21/english/agenda21toc.htm. Updated August 11, 2005.

[68] Daniel C. Esty, Marc Levy, Tanja Srebotnjak, and Alexander de Sherbinin. *2005 Environmental Sustainability Index: Benchmarking National Environmental Stewardship.* New Haven, Conn.: Yale Center for Environmental Law and Policy, 2005.

2

Focus on the United States

The United States produces, consumes, and imports more energy than any other country in the world. It is home to only 4 percent of the world's population, but it uses 25 percent of the world's energy supply and 30 percent of the world's electricity.[1] It has the world's largest reserves of coal, the sixth-largest reserves of natural gas, and the 11th-largest reserves of oil. Oil accounts for 40 percent of the country's energy output, coal accounts for 22 percent, and natural gas accounts for 23 percent.[2] Despite this wealth of natural resources, which also includes the largest body of freshwater in the world, the United States faces serious sustainability issues. An oil-based economy and an overall disinclination toward conservation and efficiency have created a culture that encourages overconsumption of resources and prizes economic growth. The country ranked 45th out of 146 countries in the world in the 2005 Sustainability Index published by the Yale Center for Environmental Law and Policy.

HISTORY

The Anasazi

Long before European explorers arrived in North America, Native American tribes exacted their own toll on the land. The Anasazi, an ancient Pueblo civilization of the American Southwest, centered in what are now the states of Arizona, New Mexico, and Colorado, are an example of how unsustainable development resulted in the extinction of a culture. The Anasazi tribes formed around 1200 B.C.E., and, though they were never as numerous as the Central American Maya, they developed an advanced society and a unique architecture. Their multistoried homes remained the tallest man-made buildings in the country up to the middle of the 19th century.

The Anasazi built their homes in canyon walls and fortified them with huge pine logs. The ecosystem of the desert area was delicate. Water was scarce; arable land was negligible; the soil was prone to erosion and deforestation; and a moderate drought could have significant consequences. An extended period of favorable weather from around 900–1130 C.E. may have created a false sense of security and fueled a sharp population increase. In previous centuries, droughts and food shortages would have prompted the Anasazi to migrate to another area and create a new settlement. However, once their population reached a certain level, migration was no longer feasible. In 1130 C.E., a period of prosperity gave way to a 300-year drought.[3] Irrigation practices improved but depleted the groundwater. Scarce resources fueled tribal warfare and fighting. Some archaeological evidence suggests that as the climate deteriorated, the Anasazi burned, dismantled, and abandoned religious structures—possibly to appease the spiritual forces they believed were responsible for their misfortunes. Eventually, all that was left of the once thriving communities were their abandoned homes and other archaeological relics. Survivors splintered into a variety of new tribes that dispersed throughout the West, including the Pueblo and the Hopi.

Adam Smith and the Free Market Economy

While it seems likely that pre-Columbian civilizations blamed their resource and sustainability misfortunes on angry spiritual forces, the European Age of Enlightenment brought new social and political explanations to the fore. Adam Smith (1723–90), the Scottish philosopher and founder of free market economics, wrote of the "diamond-water paradox" in *The Wealth of Nations* (1776): "Nothing is more useful than water; but it will purchase scarce anything; scarce anything can be had in exchange for it. A diamond, on the contrary, has scarce any value in use; but a very great quantity of other goods may frequently be had in exchange for it."[4]

The paradox that water is essential to life yet cheap and diamonds are nonessential yet expensive underscores the problem vexing many countries in regard to their natural resources, especially water. Prices have remained artificially low for decades, spurring economic growth even as resources have become more depleted and polluted. Water is a limited resource, but since it is essential to survival many believe access should be unlimited and relatively inexpensive.

Smith's writing profoundly influenced America's founding fathers. His faith in the law of supply and demand and the idea of the "Invisible Hand"—the market forces that work to keep the economy in balance—became one of the ideas behind the young country's free market economy. When applied to the country's natural resources, the free market economy spurred growth by encouraging individuals to supply the raw materials needed to build a growing nation. Coal mines, logging camps, steel mills, and ultimately oil wells changed the landscape of the country steadily, from east to west, as it was settled during the 18th and 19th centuries.

Population Growth

In the 18th century, immigrants to the American colonies had extremely large families—often 10 children or more. Many founding fathers, particularly Benjamin Franklin (1706–90), welcomed the settlers' high birthrates as virtuous and necessary. The economy was primarily agrarian, and children were considered business assets; they boosted productivity at minimal expense. But with increasing industrialization, this began to change. As early as 1860, particularly on the more-developed East Coast, many couples began to limit their family size and, in doing so, reaped the financial rewards for not having to support so many people. This trend continued almost unabated until the post–World War II baby boom, which peaked in 1957 with 4.3 million births, representing a fertility rate of 3.8 children per woman. After that, birthrates resumed an even steeper decline.[5] This was true for all socioeconomic classes and all ethnic groups, although there have been some minor variations through the years.

Even as fertility rates dropped in the United States, the overall population continued to grow because of immigration. Such growth resulted in increased demands for natural resources. Wood was the dominant source of energy in the United States until 1885, when it was superseded by coal. Soon hydroelectric power became viable and widespread, but coal reigned until after World War II when it was overtaken by petroleum. This shift toward oil represented an enormous sea change. According to the U.S. Energy Information Administration, "annual consumption of petroleum and natural gas exceeded that of coal in 1947 and then quadrupled in a single generation. Neither before nor since has any source of energy become so dominant so quickly."[6]

Energy use continued to grow as family size shrank. The family planning movement brought about a greater use of contraception to aid in limiting family size. Advances in health care reduced infant mortality and raised life expectancy, and thus increased the overall population.

In 1969, Stanford University biology professor Paul R. Ehrlich published his predictions regarding overpopulation in *The Population Bomb*. Ehrlich predicted that millions of people would starve within 20 years as world populations swelled and food supplies fell short of demand. At the time, world population stood at 3 billion, and Ehrlich founded Zero Population Growth, a group that advocated for lower fertility rates around the world. Since then, world population has tripled and yet starvation has been sporadic, thanks to the Green Revolution. Ehrlich continued to advocate for population control and wrote more books on the subject, but scholars with the opposing viewpoint gained prominence as well. Among the most vocal of these was Julian Simon, an economist whose book *The Ultimate Resource* proposed that population growth faced no dire prospects and would in fact contribute to the growth of technology and economic prosperity. He called this idea "free-market environmentalism." Though some natural resources may be limited in a physical sense, he wrote, they were unlimited in an economic sense because they would either be recycled or technology would discover new resources of value. Simon also refuted evidence of environmental pollution and believed that the Earth had enough resources to sustain human civilization for at least 7 billion years.[7] Ehrlich and Simon, both confident in their theories, made a legendary wager in September 1980 regarding the price of five commodities: chromium, copper, nickel, tin, and tungsten. Ehrlich, who believed that rising population and energy consumption would deplete these resources, bet Simon that these commodities would increase in price over the coming decade. Simon, who believed that technology and human ingenuity would prevent these resources from becoming depleted, bet their prices would drop. By September 1990, the wager's end date, the prices for all five commodities had dropped; Simon won the bet. This incident has proven to be an excellent case study for those interested in sustainable development.

Environmental Concerns

By the end of the 1960s, unprecedented industrial growth following World War II also brought about decayed urban landscapes, acid rain, smog, and polluted waterways, which had a negative impact on public health. Economic affluence fueled the nation's car culture and suburban sprawl, leading to steep rises in production and use of coal and oil, with few restraints on industries to control the pollutants they discharged into the air, water, and land. The cold war and the rise of nuclear power made radioactive waste a political issue, and widespread use of pesticides in agriculture began to affect entire ecosystems and reduce biodiversity.

In 1962, a zoologist and marine biologist named Rachel Carson (1907–64) published *Silent Spring*, a book in which she merged her knowledge of science and love of nature in sounding the alarm about overuse of pesticides and fertilizers. *Silent Spring* highlighted how DDT, a widely used insecticide, caused cancer and harmed bird eggs, resulting in a decreased bird population and a "silent" spring. Until 1962, DDT was hailed as a miracle chemical that could wipe out malaria and other diseases in the third world and protect agricultural crops in the United States from disease. But the liberally applied chemical worked its way up the food chain, from insects to birds to trees and fish, with devastating consequences. Along the way, water supplies became polluted, allowing toxicity to build up to dangerous levels in humans. Carson was the first to explain how DDT affected an entire ecosystem.

As a scientist, naturalist, and writer, Carson was influential enough that her book caused outrage among agriculture giants such as Monsanto and those in the pesticide industry, many of whom found reasons to dismiss her. But her reasoning held up to studies and, by 1972, DDT was largely banned in the United States. Carson had become one of the founders of the modern environmental movement.

On April 22, 1970, Wisconsin senator Gaylord Nelson (1916–2005) organized the first national Earth Day. Devised as a onetime, grassroots celebration of the environment, Earth Day was organized in a manner similar to the Vietnam War protests. Major rallies were planned for Washington, D.C., and New York City, and students on college campuses across the country formed peaceful demonstrations to advocate for clean water, clean air, and clean land.

The celebration proved popular and effective. Within three years, the U.S. Environmental Protection Agency (EPA) was established, and two pieces of influential legislation, the Clean Air Act and the Clean Water Act, were signed into law. The laws mandated a transition to unleaded gasoline, required catalytic converters on new automobiles, and established limits for water pollution. The laws are widely held to have been extremely successful in reversing pollution trends.[8] Earth Day continues to be celebrated every April, and over the years it has publicized a growing roster of environmental concerns, including recycling, reduction of waste, organic food, vegetarianism, and alternative energy sources.

On August 7, 1978, President Carter declared a federal emergency in the Niagara Falls, New York, neighborhood of Love Canal. High rates of cancer, birth defects, and chromosome damage afflicted residents whose homes had been built on a former toxic waste dump. Buried chemical waste, including highly poisonous dioxin, was seeping into their basements and evaporating into the household air, resulting in widespread health problems. Persistent grassroots activism by a small group of citizens eventually led the EPA to permanently relocate 800 families, and authorities began to investigate how the situation originated.

Occidental Petroleum had been the last company to dump waste at the site in 1952, though the city of Niagara and the U.S. Army had both previously dumped chemicals in the area. Occidental Petroleum sold the land to the city of Niagara Falls for a dollar after disclosing that the land contained toxins and declaring they would not be liable for any harm caused to future residents. The residents, who had never been alerted to the circumstances surrounding the development of their neighborhood, were left with no legal recourse.

In response to the grassroots groups that had brought the issue to national attention, Congress passed the Comprehensive Environmental Response Compensation and Liability Act (CERCLA) on December 11, 1980. CERCLA, better known as the Superfund Law, was designed to protect citizens by requiring cleanup of abandoned toxic sites and funded through a tax on petrochemical industries—a so-called "polluter pays" strategy. The tax provided an incentive for companies to use fewer toxic substances and provided the funds for the EPA to clean up designated hazardous waste areas. The law also ranked hazardous substances according to priority for cleanup, the top five being arsenic, lead, mercury, vinyl chloride, and polychlorinated biphenyls (PCBs). By 2007, the National Priorities List had approximately 1,300 active Superfund sites.[9] Because of Love Canal, many citizens became aware of the need for government monitoring and corporate responsibility when it comes to protecting land and water from hazardous substances. Ultimately, nearly all the homes in Love Canal were demolished and the land has remained vacant ever since.

Critics point out that in the years since Superfund was enacted, its progress has been slow, costly, and dangerous. In the first 10 years of the program, the government spent roughly $15 billion and completed only 180 cleanups.[10] Even those sometimes endangered nearby residents, as leaking barrels of waste were spilled or otherwise accidentally released into the environment. African Americans in urban areas claim that waste sites near them are ignored in favor of those in wealthier areas, and local government officials complain that the EPA standards for cleanup are so stringent that attracting new industry to former waste sites is nearly impossible.

The OPEC Embargo of 1974

The postwar economic boom was aided by cheap and plentiful oil from domestic and imported sources. The cheap oil allowed rapid industrial expansion and economic growth that trickled down to individuals who could now afford a car and a house in the suburbs. OPEC was formed in 1960 by oil-rich countries who wanted to protect their interests by maintaining a steady oil price on the world market. Over the years, OPEC member nations have fluctuated, but the organization remains headed by Saudi Arabia and dominated by the countries of the Middle East. It has sometimes wielded its power in an effort to influence political matters. This happened most notably on October 17, 1973, when OPEC announced a decrease in oil production and an embargo against countries that supported Israel in the Yom Kippur War; that included the United States. Almost concurrently, OPEC raised the price of oil to record highs in an effort to gain more power on the world stage. The increase in price, from around 38 cents per gallon to 55 cents per gallon, and decline in supply created a U.S. gasoline shortage for the first time since World War II.[11] The embargo lasted until March 1974, but even after the short-term crunch had passed the long-term effects remained. Automakers and consumers traded in large cars for compact cars in order to conserve gasoline, partly in recognition that oil was not as plentiful or as easily obtainable as they had thought. Japanese auto companies gained a foothold in the U.S. market with their already fuel-efficient economy cars. On the advice of President Jimmy Carter (1924–), homeowners conserved heating oil by keeping thermostats lower in the winter. Lawmakers instituted national Daylight Savings Time and lowered the national highway speed limit—both energy-saving measures. Solar power and other forms of renewable energy were briefly in vogue, but, within a few years, energy prices fell and many conservation measures were abandoned or, in the case of the speed limit, overturned.

By the early 1990s, the OPEC oil crisis was a dim memory for most Americans. Low energy prices encouraged many drivers to switch back to larger cars, especially light trucks, minivans, and sport utility vehicles. The information revolution created a market for many new electronic and battery-powered products, including computers, cell phones, DVD players, video games, and plasma televisions. The building industry boomed; new houses grew in size even as the average family size continued to shrink. In 1950, the average new home was 983 square feet, and in 2005 it was 2,434 square feet.[12] Jet travel reached all-time highs, reflecting the unparalleled mobility of the modern world.

Because air and water quality remained high in most areas of the country, many people began to think that environmental problems—at least in the United States—were a thing of the past. Even as scientific proof of global climate change mounted, many individuals concluded that the proof was faulty or simply a scare tactic. As the war on terror took precedence in the national dialogue in 2001, the Bush administration did little to enact laws favoring alternative energy or conservation and instead concentrated on obtaining a steady supply of oil from the Persian Gulf region and other locales. However, on a smaller scale, private companies, state legislatures, educators, scientists, and individuals took up the issues of oil dependency, global warming, sustainable development, and renewable energy and applied them to their own communities. Businesses proved that adoption of green technology was good for the bottom line, and elected officials argued that ending foreign oil dependency was a top priority. The unlikely consequence of this was an alliance between conservatives and environmentalists, since both groups aspired to liberate the United States from dependency on foreign oil.

CURRENT SITUATION IN THE UNITED STATES

A Big Footprint

The ecological footprint of the United States is estimated to be 24 acres per person (or 9.5 global hectares); higher by far than the similarly industrialized but land-poor Japan, which has a footprint of 11.8 acres per person.[13] A sustainable footprint, given the worldwide ratio of people to available land, is reported to be 4.5 acres per person according to the Global Footprint Network. This is the amount of land it takes on average to provide the food and water and absorb the waste of one person. The footprint statistic is intended to promote awareness of each person's effect on the planet. The footprint obviously varies from one individual to the next, depending on the person's lifestyle. A person who lives in a 5,000-square-foot home and drives a luxury SUV on a 50-mile round-trip to work every day and vacations at a second home during the summer has a much larger ecological footprint than someone who lives with a large family in an apartment in New York and does not drive. Nevertheless, the 24-acres-per-person statistic multiplied by a population of 300 million adds up to more acres of land and water—7.2 billion—than the 2.3 billion acres that exist within the country. This means the country is operating in a state of ecological overshoot, the primary symptom of unsustainability.

The size of the U.S. footprint reflects a disproportionate consumption of resources compared to people in other countries. People in the United States generate on average 4.5 pounds of municipal solid waste (MSW) per person per day, up from 2.5 pounds per person per day in 1960. But industry generates by far more waste than consumers; for every ton of garbage produced by individuals (also called *postconsumer waste*), 20 tons of *preconsumer waste* were produced in the initial manufacturing processes for those items.[14] When it comes to MSW, recycling rates have risen since the 1990s, thereby conserving the natural resources used to manufacture paper, tin cans, glass, and plastic containers. Of the 246 million tons of MSW generated in 2005 (nearly 1 ton per person), 54 percent is landfilled, 32 percent is recycled, and 13 percent is incinerated.[15] One of the problems with landfills is that the garbage in them generates methane gas, a greenhouse gas that contributes to global warming. Another major source of methane gas is enteric fermentation, a natural digestive process of livestock, which emits an estimated 15 to 20 percent of the total methane gas in the atmosphere.[16]

However, scientists have found a partial solution to the problem of methane gas emitted from landfills. Landfill gas (LFG) energy projects harness the methane and convert it into electricity. By 2006, 425 LFG projects were operational in the United States, generating 10 billion kilowatt-hours of electricity per year.[17] One such landfill in Ann Arbor, Michigan, for example, generates up to 1 million cubic feet of methane gas per day. In seven years of operation, the LFG operation has generated 43,600 megawatt-hours of electricity and prevented 663,100 tons of carbon dioxide from entering the atmosphere.[18]

OIL

Most of the country's oil reserves are located in Texas, Louisiana, Alaska, and California, but those reserves have been declining steadily. As of 2005, U.S. crude oil production—5.1 million barrels a day—was at a 50-year low, and crude oil imports—10.59 million barrels a day—were at an all-time high. Daily petroleum consumption totaled 20.8 million barrels, of which 44 percent constituted gasoline for trucks and automobiles.[19] A 42-gallon barrel of crude oil can be refined into a 44-gallon barrel of petroleum, which explains how consumption outpaces production.

To guard against oil supply disruptions, the United States maintains the Strategic Petroleum Reserve, a stockpile of 700 million barrels of oil that can be used in extreme circumstances owing to natural disasters or political events. For example, President George W. Bush ordered some reserves to be sold following Hurricane Katrina, when damage to oil production facilities in the Gulf of Mexico caused a spike in gas prices.

According to the U.S. Energy Information Administration, cars and trucks in the United States consumed 9.159 million barrels of gasoline—384.7 million gallons—per day in 2005.[20] Americans drove nearly 3 trillion miles on the nation's highways in 2005, according to the Federal Highway Administration. This represents an all-time high and a 25 percent increase since 1995. More than 241 million registered vehicles are on the road (30 percent of the world's total) for only 199 million registered drivers.[21] Those vehicles emit 45 percent of the world's total automotive carbon dioxide, making the United States the world's largest emitter of automotive carbon dioxide, a greenhouse gas that leads to global warming.

"A coal train that stretches 55,000 miles, long enough to circle the globe twice, carrying 314 million metric tons of carbon—[this is] the amount of CO_2 emitted by U.S. cars and trucks in the year 2004."[22] Yet in 2007 the

United States fell to second place in terms of total CO_2 emissions. China took the top spot for the first time, due mainly to the unprecedented amount of cement needed to sustain the country's building boom. The manufacturing of cement releases large quantities of CO_2 into the atmosphere, and China's lax environmental policies place few, if any, limits on those emissions.[23]

The Dwight D. Eisenhower National System of Interstate and Defense Highways—otherwise known as the freeway—partially accounts for why Americans drive so much. A post–World War II civil engineering project, the interstate system is the most extensive in the world, allowing motorists to drive from one end of the country to the other virtually nonstop. Low Corporate Average Fuel Economy (CAFE) standards also contribute to the amount of oil Americans consume. CAFE standards, which determine how many miles per gallon an automobile must average, were not increased between the mid-1980s and 2007, when the standards were revised to 35 MPG, effective 2020. In fact, since the early 1980s, gas mileage has decreased as Americans turned to larger and heavier vehicles. Many energy analysts believe that even modest fuel efficiency requirements would result in a huge decrease in oil usage and dependence.

Even though Americans consume more energy than anyone else in the world, a statistic called *U.S. energy intensity*—defined as the amount of energy it takes to produce one unit of the gross domestic product (GDP)—actually fell by 44 percent from 1970 to 2000.[24] Yet energy intensity efficiency has been overshadowed by overall growth in GDP. In terms of carbon emissions intensity, the emissions per unit of GDP fell 48 percent over the same time period. These energy savings were due to several factors, including pollution caps mandated by the Clean Air and Clean Water Acts, which resulted in some industries increasing their efficiency to meet tighter emissions regulations; consumer responses to the 1973 OPEC oil embargo that prompted many to switch to more economical vehicles; the increased use of natural gas, which is more efficient than coal and oil; building codes that mandated energy efficiency measures; the switch to an information economy in which service-oriented businesses require less energy than manufacturing plants; more efficient market-driven industrial processes that were less wasteful than older processes; and small increases in the use of renewable resources such as solar, wind, and geothermal power. This reduction in energy intensity resulted in a decline in the annual per capita carbon dioxide emissions in the United States from 20.8 metric tons to 20.2 metric tons from 1980 to 2001, though U.S. carbon emissions remained considerably higher than the average G7 rate, which dropped from 14.2 metric tons to 13.8 metric tons during the same time period.[25]

Even without global warming, the country's dependence on oil could bring about negative consequences due to dwindling supplies. In the 2000s, the George W. Bush administration focused mostly on expanding conventional domestic energy sources, including oil, to meet the country's growing energy needs rather than developing renewable resources. Most experts believe this is short-sighted, while others believe it is sound policy aimed at decreasing the country's dependence on foreign oil. In particular, the Bush administration and many members of Congress would like to open the Arctic National Wildlife Refuge (ANWR) to oil drilling. ANWR is an area of 19 million acres in the Arctic Circle of northeast Alaska, an extremely fragile ecosystem. A 1987 U.S. Department of the Interior geological survey estimated that the area contains between 600 million and 9.2 billion barrels of recoverable oil—a range so wide that it precludes industry experts from making accurate feasibility estimates.[26] Feasibility estimates have been further hindered by prohibitions against exploratory drilling in the region. Conservationists argue that the amount of oil available in ANWR would be depleted quickly, serve only to delay the coming energy crisis, and ruin the fragile arctic ecosystem. Instead, they argue, reasonable conservation efforts, such as increasing automobile fuel efficiency and mileage requirements, could save 10 to 20 times more oil than exists in the ANWR reserves. The Energy Information Administration, an arm of the U.S. Department of Energy, projects that energy needs will rise by 32 percent from 1999 to 2020. Domestic oil production is expected to continue decreasing, with oil imports rising by 60 percent to meet demand.

NATURAL GAS

Natural gas is a fossil fuel often found in conjunction with coal and oil. It is composed primarily of methane—a hydrocarbon—and can also contain helium, propane, butane, and mercury. Natural gas burns cleaner than coal and is more efficient. It is, however, highly flammable and can cause explosions. Because of this, it can be difficult and expensive to transport and makes some consumers uneasy.

The United States has an estimated 192.5 trillion cubic feet of natural gas in known reserves. Most of it is located in the western states of Texas, Oklahoma, and Wyoming. Annual consumption in 2005 was 22.3 trillion cubic feet (Tcf); 4.2 Tcf of that was imported, mainly from Canada. Energy experts expect natural gas demand to increase steadily in the coming decades, primarily due to an increase in the number of natural gas–fired electric power plants.

Most natural gas reaches consumers through pipelines, but the country's existing infrastructure is quickly reaching capacity. Expansion of and improvements to natural gas pipelines and other infrastructure are expected to increase. Over 50 liquified natural gas (LNG) terminals were in the planning stages as of 2006 to handle this increase, but many had been delayed by vocal opposition from local residents concerned about potentially catastrophic explosions from the highly flammable gas.

Natural gas can also be liquefied (LNG) or compressed (CNG) for storage and transported via ship, rail, or road. Methane gas that is not destined for the market (such as that which is captured during oil drilling or which is emitted from landfills) can be captured and pumped back into the ground to prevent emissions from entering the atmosphere in a process called *carbon sequestration.*

Natural gas vehicles (NGV) have gained limited popularity since their introduction in the 1990s. As of 2007, the United States had 150,000 NGVs on the road out of a worldwide total of 5 million. In the United States, they are promoted as a solution to the country's foreign oil dependency and as a clean fuel alternative. Although natural gas is still a fossil fuel, NGVs emit exhaust that is 70 percent lower in carbon monoxide, 20 percent lower in carbon dioxide, and 87 percent lower in nitrogen oxide than gasoline-powered vehicles.[27] Because natural gas fueling stations are not widely available to general consumers, however, makers tout the vehicles for use in municipal and private industry fleets that can install their own fuel-delivery systems. But more options for the private citizen may be on the horizon. As of 2007, California consumers could buy the Honda Civic GX NGV, which was ranked as the cleanest vehicle on the market and was offered with a home fueling system that allowed owners to fill up their cars at home rather than at a hard-to-come-by fueling station.

COAL

The average American consumes 20 pounds of coal each day, mainly in the form of electricity generated by coal-fired power plants.[28] Coal-fired power plants generate the majority of electricity in the United States and burn over 1 billion tons of the fossil fuel per year. Coal's popularity is sustained by the country's abundant reserves—enough to last at least 200 more years—which make it an affordable $1.70 for 1 million British thermal units (BTUs).[29] Coal production in the United States is led by Wyoming, home to the world's largest coal mine. Peabody Energy's Powder River Basin mines hold more potential energy than all the oil fields owned by Exxon Mobil,[30] and the company plans to build two of the largest coal-fired power plants in the world in Illinois and Kentucky.

Of the 1,112 million short tons of coal produced in the United States in 2004, 35 percent came from underground mines in Appalachia, open mines in Wyoming produced 201 million short tons, or 18 percent, and much of the rest came from other western states.

Most coal in the United States is used to generate electricity, and record demand for electricity (4 billion kilowatt hours per year) has pushed coal usage to all-time highs. However, stronger environmental regulations are encouraging many plants to switch to low-sulfur coal, which comes primarily from the western states, from high-sulfur coal, most of which comes from Appalachia.

Although the coal industry remains strong, several factors have affected it in recent years. Transportation problems and weather delays have hindered delivery to customers, and legal problems, particularly in the east and related to environmental concerns, have stalled expansion at some mines. Burning coal is a primary contributor to global warming; mining is an environmentally degrading and hazardous industry; and coal dust and toxins are a major health concern. According to the National Institute for Occupational Safety and Health, fine particle pollution from coal-fired plants results in roughly 900 deaths from pneumoconiosis (black-lung disease) in the country annually.[31] Apart from carbon dioxide emissions, coal-fired plants also emit significant amounts of sulfur dioxide, mercury, and nitrogen oxide—all of which are highly toxic.

NUCLEAR POWER

By the turn of the 21st century, nuclear power generated about 20 percent of the electricity in the United States. A total of 103 reactors nationwide produced 782 billion kilowatt hours of electricity in 2005.[32] Nearly half of that capacity was based in Illinois, Pennsylvania, New York, North Carolina, and South Carolina. Because no nuclear power plants have been built in more than a generation, existing plants have been running near top capacity to meet rising energy demands. After the partial meltdown at Pennsylvania's Three Mile Island in 1979, rising costs, increased safety measures, and public opposition made nuclear power less attractive than it once was. The nation's most recent nuclear reactor, Watts Bar in Tennessee, went online in 1996; many other nuclear reactors have been shut down permanently; and many others are scheduled to do so as well as they become old, inefficient, and expensive to operate.

A resurgence of interest in nuclear power began in 2005, as oil prices began to rise and concerns over climate change gained prominence. Many environmentalists formerly opposed to nuclear power have decided that its dangers are outweighed by the importance of limiting carbon emissions. The Energy Policy Act of 2005 encourages private investment in and offers tax breaks to corporations developing new nuclear reactors.

Complicating the nuclear power picture is the debate over what to do with the long-term, high-level radioactive waste resulting from spent fuel, which totaled 52,000 metric tons by the end of 2005.[33] After a 20-year debate, in 2002 Congress approved Yucca Mountain in Nevada as a long-term nuclear waste depository to which all power plants would ship their waste—waste that has been stored on-site for decades. Many citizens are concerned about the safety issues involved in transporting nuclear waste over public highways or by rail, more so than they are worried about the security of the waste once it reaches Yucca Mountain. Yucca Mountain is scheduled to open as a permanent nuclear waste repository in 2017, though it has been delayed many times in the past and will likely be delayed in the future. Meanwhile, nuclear waste continues to be stored in semipermanent containers throughout the country under various degrees of security.

Infrastructure

The Northeast Blackout of August 14, 2003, in which a large swath of North America from New York through Detroit and Cleveland and most of Quebec lost power simultaneously, highlighted the vulnerability of the U.S. power grid. Forty million people in the United States and 10 million in Canada lost power anywhere from a few hours to several days, making it the largest blackout in North American history. Aging infrastructure combined with a series of small problems led to the shutdown of 256 power plants, including 22 nuclear power plants. Coming on the heels of California's rolling blackouts of 2000 and 2001, which should have been preventable, the situation increased awareness of the magnitude of economic loss due to even short periods without electricity. Financial losses of the 2003 blackout were estimated at $6 billion.[34] Such events underscore how economic sustainability is dependent on sometimes fragile energy networks.

Population

On October 17, 2006, the U.S. Census Bureau declared that the total U.S. population had reached the 300 million mark, making it the third most populous country in the world, well behind China and India but comfortably ahead of fourth-place Indonesia. However, population distribution throughout the country is uneven. High-density areas are clustered in the eastern half of the country and in California, Texas, and Florida. Rural population continues to decline, and more than half the population lives in urban areas. Even though the U.S. fertility rate hovers around replacement levels—2.1 children per woman—the population continues to grow steadily at about 1 million per year, mostly because of immigration. Immigrants often bring large families with them or have many children in the generation after they arrive. Statistics show that as the immigrants' economic status rises and they become acclimated to American culture, their birth rates plummet. U.S. population is forecasted to top 394 million by 2050 before leveling off, though such projections in the past have been of dubious accuracy.[35]

Land, Water, and Biodiversity

The immense biodiversity of the United States is one of the country's greatest assets. More than 200,000 species of plants and animals have been identified within U.S. borders, representing 10 percent of the planet's total.[36] The Tennessee River, for example, is home to more species of fish than exist in all of Europe. This diversity is the result of the country's wide range of ecosystems, from forests to tundra to prairies to desert. Today, however, many species are threatened by loss of habitat as fragile ecosystems are altered, usually by the loss of natural vegetation as development encroaches on previously rural land. An area that is particularly vulnerable to losing several rare species is known as a biodiversity hotspot. In the United States, the most prominent biodiversity hotspot is the California Floristic Province, home of the giant sequoia, the coastal redwood, the giant kangaroo rat, and the California condor.[37]

In 2000, Americans used 408 billion gallons of water every day, most of which was withdrawn for thermoelectric power and agricultural irrigation.[38] Public supply withdrawals totaled 43 billion gallons a day, the majority of which came from surface water supplies rather than groundwater. U.S. lakes and rivers, though not as polluted as they were in the 1970s, remain a source of concern. For example, runoff from America's midwestern farmland deposits 1.5 million metric tons of nitrogen fertilizer into the Mississippi River each year. This upsets the ecosystem of the river and results in the disappearance of species that can no longer be sustained by the altered habitat. Nitrogen levels accumulate in the water as it makes its way to the Mississippi Delta, ultimately resulting in a seasonal *dead zone* in the Gulf of Mexico, hundreds of miles long, in which oxygen levels are too low to sustain life. In a dead zone, larger species of aquatic life are able to leave the area, but smaller species suffocate and die by the millions. Many other dead zones dot the East Coast of the United States, and most of these are caused by excess nitrogen in the watershed and destruction of the wetlands, which can no longer serve their function as a filter that removes pollutants before they reach the ocean.

The Great Lakes, which contain 20 percent of the earth's fresh surface water, have suffered environmental degradation for years due to overfishing, point source pollution, and other factors. The lakes' shores are home to hundreds of factories, power plants, sewage treatment plants, and urban areas.

Polluted waters have made fish toxic, caused some species to become extinct, and intensified the detrimental effects of species invasions. The zebra mussel, for example, was accidentally introduced into Lake Saint Clair in 1988 from an oceangoing vessel that discharged ballast water containing the mussels into the lake. Female zebra mussels produce up to 1 million eggs a year, which form larvae and shells that attach themselves to boats, docks, intake pipes, and even other species of aquatic life. They harm boat motors and eat food that other species depend on for survival. They also alter the chemistry of the water, causing the formation of large, toxic algae blooms that can affect the taste and safety of drinking water. In short, they upset the balance of the ecosystem.

Another Great Lakes' species invasion, that of the sea lamprey, caused a 90 percent drop in the number of trout in Lake Superior from 1952 to 1962. Lamprey attach themselves to fish, either surviving off the fish as a symbiotic parasite or killing the fish outright. The die-off of the trout population allowed its main prey, the alewife, to flourish, causing it to become overpopulated and push out other species of fish from the lakes. The importance of maintaining the biodiversity of the Great Lakes is widely recognized by government officials and private citizens, and attempts to tamper with it have met with vocal opposition. For example, a proposal to withdraw millions of gallons of water from the lakes and ship them to China, which suffers from a shortage of freshwater, was quickly rendered moot by lawmakers when they passed the Water Resources Development Act of 1986, which prohibits withdrawals for any region that does not border the lakes themselves.

While the Great Lakes region enjoys abundant sources of freshwater, the western part of the country suffers from lack of it. Battles over who controls the scarce water resources in California, Arizona, Nevada, New Mexico, and other states in the region have been a part of their political life for generations. In California, the two main sources of water for a population of roughly 36 million people are the Sacramento–San Joaquin Delta, which serves 22 million people, and the Colorado River, which serves everyone else. The Colorado River Compact of 1922 established how much water each of the seven states along the river received; this henceforth became known as "The Law of the River."

The Compact designated Upper Basin and Lower Basin states and allocated water rights for each. For many years, California received adequate water because it benefited from the water allocated to upstream states that went unused. The Law of the River, however, did not foresee the environmental degradation that such massive withdrawals would cause, nor did it take Indian water rights into consideration, nor did it anticipate the huge population growth of California and Nevada in the late 20th and early 21st centuries. The Law of the River was also affected by the dams that were built along the river, notably Glen Canyon Dam in Colorado and Hoover Dam in Nevada, both of which provide significant hydroelectric power to surrounding areas. In 1963, the U.S. Supreme Court reestablished the water rights of Arizona, California, Nevada, and five neighboring Indian reservations. By the year 2000, 90 percent of the Colorado River was diverted for irrigation, to fill massive reservoirs, and for other water withdrawals and no longer consistently reached the Gulf of California.

Alternative Energy Sources

In 2004, renewable energy resources accounted for only 6 percent of the country's energy consumption, and almost half of that came from hydroelectric power. Other renewables, including solar, wind, biomass, and geothermal power, fulfilled just a fraction of the country's energy demands, although experts forecasted a steady, strong growth for the sector in the early 21st century as the United States seeks to limit its dependence on foreign oil. Since the 1980s, development of alternative energy sources has been hampered by high initial investment costs and low fossil fuel prices, although many private companies have managed to make steady improvements in technology, particularly in photovoltaic cells and wind turbines.

COUNTERSTRATEGIES

Conservation Efforts

A 2006 study by the McKinsey Global Institute reported that the growth rate of energy demands worldwide could be cut in half by 2020 through existing technology, conservation, and tighter efficiency standards.[39] Compact fluorescent lightbulbs, solar water heaters, and more efficient insulation on new construction—all readily available products—could save billions in natural resources without necessitating a lifestyle change. The EPA's Energy Star program designated home appliances that exceeded industry efficiency standards, allowing consumers to choose conservation in their durable goods purchases. Despite this, federal mandates to conserve resources or promote renewable energy were not a political priority in the 2000s. Vice President Dick Cheney called conservation a "personal virtue," but excluded such measures from the country's Energy Policy Act of 2005.[40] The Bush Administration believed that raising fuel efficiency standards for automobiles, a conservation measure that had wide support among voters, would hurt small business owners, automakers, and the economy.

The downside of conservation is the tendency of individuals to use more energy as efficiency increases. This idea is known as the Jevons Paradox, after William Stanley Jevons, who first outlined the concept in his 1865 book *The Coal Question*. Jevons noted that following widespread adoption of James Watt's steam engine in England, which was more efficient than the previous Newcomb steam engine, demand for coal went up instead of down. This was because the new steam engines were cheaper to operate since they required less coal than previous engines; thus the number of steam engines increased and the demand for coal increased as well. This concept can be applied to a number of resources. For example, if a family buys an energy-efficient air-conditioning unit, they may decide to run it longer and at lower temperatures than they would a less efficient model. Thus, the gains they made in efficiency are reversed by increased consumption. While the rate of feedback is disputed and depends on the activity in question, common estimates indicate 10 to 40 percent of energy efficiency gains are eventually squandered in accordance with the Jevons Paradox.

The Price of Pollution and Natural Resources

Economists believe that many natural resource problems are the result of industries having never paid a fair price for the pollution they generate or the resources they use (an argument reminiscent of Adam Smith's "diamond-water paradox"). Therefore, they argue, fostering corporate responsibility would engender more favorable environmental practices that would in turn promote sustainable development. That is the idea behind emissions trading, or cap-and-trade practices, in which the government sets a limit ("cap") on the amount of air or water pollution a plant can emit. The plant then receives a license allowing them to emit those pollutants. If the company exceeds those limits, they must pay a fine. If they install pollution control devices and no longer emit all the pollution they are allowed by law, they can sell the unused portion of their pollution license to a company that wishes to exceed the amount for which it is licensed ("trade"). Cap-and-trade programs initiated by the Clean Air Act have had mixed results in reducing sulfur dioxide levels and acid rain. While overall levels of sulfur dioxide and nitrous oxide have decreased, a significant number of plants have increased their emissions, which has not been beneficial for the people who live in those areas.[41] Nevertheless, cap-and-trade programs have proved politically popular; Illinois and New York have both instituted state-based cap-and-trade programs for emissions of volatile organic compounds (VOCs) and carbon dioxide respectively.

Similar international programs to reduce carbon emissions are called for under the Kyoto Protocol. Increasingly, the full spectrum of political and economic entities realizes the advantages of placing a monetary price on pollution, and many business leaders are receptive to cap-and-trade programs because they limit government intervention and work on free market principles. According to Harvard economist Robert N. Stavins, "Setting a real price on carbon emissions is the single most important policy step to take. Pricing is the way you get both the short-term gains through efficiency and the longer-term gains from investments in research and switching to cleaner fuels."[42]

Similarly, conservation of water and land resources could take place through the elimination of subsidies for mining and oil production, logging, fishing, agriculture, livestock, energy companies, and other industries that receive special compensation or exemptions from the government. More radical environmentalists propose vast cost increases for water and energy, and some advocate the elimination of the internal combustion engine altogether.

Environmental Innovation

Even though the federal government has not promoted conservation or renewable energy, Americans have pursued clean-fuel technology and researched ways to lower carbon emissions and preserve natural resources. American universities have created the field of sustainability science, and the cross-pollination between private enterprise and the academic world has resulted in technology that may lead to vast improvements in sustainability in the near future.[43]

HYDROGEN

Hydrogen is the most abundant element in the universe, but it is seldom found by itself in nature, the way coal and oil are. Instead, it is chemically bound to other elements, especially oxygen (a molecule of water is composed of two hydrogen atoms and one oxygen atom). Natural gas is commonly used to release the energy of hydrogen inside a catalytic converter, but this has the disadvantage of emitting carbon dioxide. A more efficient, less polluting (and so far less feasible) way to harness hydrogen's energy is to subject it to electrolysis. Electrolysis is the process by which water is charged with electricity, thereby separating the hydrogen atoms from the oxygen atoms.

Hydrogen was first used as a fuel source in 1794, when the world's first hydrogen generator helped build balloons for reconnaissance missions during the French Revolution.[44] Hydrogen gained prominence in the 1920s and 1930s as the fuel source for dirigibles, until a series of fatal crashes, including the *Hindenburg* disaster on May 6, 1937, in which 36 people died as the zeppelin tried to land in Lakehurst, New Jersey, doomed the nascent industry. Interest in hydrogen next surfaced after the OPEC oil crisis of 1973, when some governments began to fund research into hydrogen fuel use, but that too soon evaporated when gasoline prices returned to lower levels. The third round of interest in hydrogen was instituted in the 1990s as scientific evidence for global warming gained acceptance. Research was sponsored by governments (Japan, Belgium, and Germany led the way with ambitious public works projects devoted to hydrogen), oil companies, automakers, and other private industry players. In 1999, Iceland announced its plan to become the first hydrogen-powered nation in the world.[45] A similar mass effort got under way shortly after that in Hawaii, a state motivated by the fact that all its oil is imported and thus expensive.

Hydrogen fuel cells power the NASA space shuttles, and in recent years automakers have tried to scale down the technology for use in cars. Many industry leaders, including former Ford Motor Company CEO Bill Ford, Jr., believe that such hydrogen fuel cells will replace the gasoline powered internal combustion engine within a generation or two.[46] However, fuel cell technology still has a way to go before it makes a dent in the transportation industry. Fuel cell stacks are heavy, expensive, and require a lot of hydrogen to be stored on board. Generating hydrogen and delivering it to consumers requires a vast, as-yet-unbuilt infrastructure. However, the payoff for developing such a system will be energy independence and an exponential drop in greenhouse gas emissions.

METHANE HYDRATE

Methane hydrate is a frozen mixture of natural gas and water that is found beneath the ocean floor and in the polar permafrost. It looks like ice but burns when lit. Some experts believe that enough methane hydrate exists to power the United States for 2,000 years.[47] The U.S. Geological Survey (USGS) estimates U.S. reserves at 200 trillion cubic feet (Tcf). Significant technological hurdles must be overcome in order to recover the methane hydrate; large-scale efforts to research and develop these systems are in the beginning stages. They may yield fruit as soon as 2020. Japan is leading the way in methane hydrate production, because its energy crunch demands that new sources of energy be found and developed soon.

Detractors believe that methane hydrates do not exist in great enough concentrations to make recovery feasible. Although the total is quite high; it is spread out over a very large area, which makes drilling and extraction difficult. Moreover, methane is still a fossil fuel and will release carbon dioxide when burned.

WIND POWER AND SOLAR POWER

The benefits of wind power and solar power are often hailed in the same sentence, possibly because both resources share several pros and cons. On the pro side, both wind and sunlight are abundant, free, and widely available. On the con side, wind and sunlight can be unpredictable, difficult to transform into sufficient amounts of electricity, and hard to store. After incipient industries failed in the 1970s and 1980s, many people came to believe that wind and solar power would never be feasible on a wide scale and instead favored further development of oil, natural gas, coal, and nuclear energy.

Yet, enough scientists and entrepreneurs continued to work on the issue that wind power grew 26 percent a year in the 1990s; solar power grew 17 percent per year.[48] By 2005, the total wind power capacity in the United States was 6,740 MW, and the American Wind Energy Association expected that to top 15,000 MW by 2009. Most wind power generators are located in the west, with California leading the way, followed by Texas, Iowa, Minnesota, Washington, and Oregon. Solar power has a lower capacity than wind power—a total of 397 MW installed nationwide as of 2005. Again, California dominated the market. In the 1980s, nine solar power plants were constructed in the state, and in 2005 Stirling Energy Systems announced plans to build the two largest solar power plants in the world, at 500 and 300 MW each in the Mojave Desert. In addition, private renewable energy companies fueled a rebound in Silicon Valley, where venture capitalists invested $290 million in the third quarter of 2006 in businesses focused on developing clean technology.[49]

COAL: CARBON SEQUESTRATION

Given the vast coal reserves within the United States, coal will inevitably play a major role in fulfilling the country's energy needs in the coming decades. However, the nearly unanimous consensus is that coal's carbon emissions should be curtailed. One main strategy for curtailing emissions, embraced by government and business entities alike, is carbon sequestration. This is the process by which carbon dioxide is captured and pumped into underground reservoirs. Government incentives for this expensive technology have been limited, and many individuals in the coal industry doubt sequestration's economic practicality. Some believe that vast deposits of carbon dioxide underground could trigger earthquakes. Others fear that if carbon dioxide, which is heavier than air, escapes from underground reservoirs, it might stay close to the ground, block out oxygen, and possibly suffocate people and animals.[50] The Intergovernmental Panel on Climate Change, however, considers such a scenario to be highly unlikely.

To kick-start a national carbon sequestration effort, President George W. Bush announced the FutureGen project in 2003, a plan to build a state-of-the-art coal-fired electricity power plant. The idea is to convert coal to a hydrogen gas, rather than burn it. More than $1 billion will be dedicated to the project, which will involve 10 nations in producing a zero-emissions power plant. Experts hope the project, the goal of which is to capture at least 90 percent of the plant's carbon dioxide emissions, will lead the transformation of the United States from an oil-based to a hydrogen-based economy.[51] As of 2006, carbon sequestration was used by oil companies in off-shore drilling operations as a way to increase oil production. When carbon dioxide is pumped underneath the ocean floor, it boosts the flow of oil into the drills and pipelines.

COGENERATION: COMBINED HEATING AND POWER SYSTEMS

Combined heat and power, sometimes called CHP and sometimes called cogeneration, is a way to obtain both heat and power from a single fuel source. It is a technology, not a new type of system, and it can reduce energy use by up to 70 percent. This efficiency means less fuel is used and fewer greenhouse gases are emitted. Cogeneration can be applied to individual households, businesses, commercial enterprises, schools, large office buildings and hotels, and even manufacturing facilities and municipal power plants.

A CHP system is comprised of several components. The first is a "prime mover"—typically an engine, either a conventional turbine, combustion engine, a boiler, or even a fuel cell. Secondly, the system needs a generator, and, finally, a heat recovery and electrical interconnection. A cogeneration system supplies its own heat, eliminating the need for a separate heat system that would require its own energy supply. According to the United States Combined Heat & Power Association, CHP systems generated 8 percent of the country's electricity in 2005.[52] President Bush's 2001 National Energy Policy included federal tax incentives and streamlined permit processes to spur more cogeneration initiatives.

States Lead the Way in Implementing Solutions

In the absence of national policies addressing specific energy concerns, some states have stepped in to fill the void. Voters in California, for example, passed a statewide program to lessen their contribution to global warming. The state is home to 12.5 percent of the country's population and represents the sixth largest economy in the world. The voter-approved legislation requires all industrial emitters of greenhouse gases to reduce their output by

25 percent by 2020, which will cut carbon emissions by 174 million metric tons.[53]

Portland, Oregon, is a city on the forefront of renewable energy innovation. In 2005, the city of a half-million residents made its goal to purchase 100 percent of its municipal electricity (that which is used to power city offices) from renewable resources. The effort was led by the city's Office of Sustainable Development, which spearheads a number of community programs aimed at fostering energy efficiency and resource conservation. For example, the school lunch program requires cafeterias to serve locally grown produce, the Peak Oil task force is charged with creating an emergency response to an energy crisis, and recycling, composting, and green building programs are extensive. Additionally, Portland was the first city in the United States to mandate a citywide renewable fuels standard, which required a 5 percent blend of biodiesel fuel for all diesel vehicles purchasing fuel within the city limits and a 10 percent ethanol blend for all gasoline.[54]

Minnesota has been active in instituting an energy policy designed to spur private industry to develop wind, solar, and other renewable energy projects and to educate citizens about conservation issues. The Minnesota Ethanol Program generated $1.5 billion and 5,800 jobs for the state in 2005, as farmers grew the corn that was processed as ethanol. These crops generated 550 million gallons of ethanol, which were sold statewide in accordance with the state's 10 percent ethanol requirement for all gasoline vehicles,[55] one of the first such requirements in the country. The state actively promotes wind energy through the Community-Based Energy Development tariff and boasts over 812 MW of installed wind power, making it the fourth largest wind-powered energy provider in the country.

New Urbanism and Green Housing

New urbanism combines urban design, ecology, and sociological factors in promoting sustainable development, ultimately as a way of raising the quality of life in a given area. New urbanists include architects and urban planners who design houses and neighborhoods that discourage energy-intensive urban sprawl and consumer overconsumption and encourage a revitalized community life based on walkable streets, accessible businesses and services, and economic diversity.[56] Inspired by Jane Jacobs, the mid–20th-century sociologist who wrote *The Death and Life of the Great American Cities*, Christopher Alexander, author of *A Pattern Language*, and urban theorist Lewis Mumford, new urbanist architects and planners have developed mixed-use housing where neighborhoods provide a variety of living options, from single-family homes to cottages, flats, condominiums, and apartments that will attract a cross section of the population, from working class families to wealthy singles, from recent college graduates to senior citizens. Communities may be retrofitted into declining urban areas or newly built in existing sprawling suburban areas in an effort to bring a higher population density to an area to promote business and civic-mindedness. To flesh out the feeling of community, new urbanists propose situating conveniences, such as post offices, doctors' offices, corner grocery stores, parks, banks, schools, churches, movie theaters, and community centers within walking distance of residential areas. In such a way, they hope the social fabric of a community will start to mend. Parents will no longer need to drive their children long distances to social events, more errands can be done on foot, and houses that "meet the street" and boast wide porches will encourage neighbors to visit with one another. New urbanism promotes green building, smaller house sizes, mass transportation, reduced consumption—all factors that result in lower energy use and a smaller ecological footprint.

Closely related to new urbanism is the concept of green housing. Green housing means using energy-efficient materials to construct or retrofit a home. It fosters sustainable development by promoting the use of recycled materials, efficient energy design, and taking advantage of the natural environment for heating and cooling (often called passive solar design). Green housing can reduce a family's energy use considerably, saving money in the process.

Two of the first new urbanist communities were Seaside, developed in the 1980s in Walton County, Florida, and Celebration, which began construction in 1994 by the Walt Disney Company in Florida, adjacent to Disney World.[57] Seaside was planned by the founders of the new urbanism movement, Andrés Duany and Elizabeth Plater-Zyberk. Another development is Kentlands in Gaithersburg, Maryland, which has 1,800 homes, cottages, rental units, and condominiums, along with a million square feet of office and commercial space. The development, whose residents call it a neo-traditional urbanist community, was started in 1990 and continues to attract residents who are active in the citizens assembly, which votes on a variety of issues affecting the community.

Opponents of new urbanism call the movement a nostalgic fantasy and say that the developments promote conformity through lack of design options, are isolated, and are attractive to only a small sliver of middle-class professionals. Other critics believe that significant numbers of homeowners will not want to live so closely to those of lower-income levels and that previous efforts to build planned communities (such as Reston, Virginia, in the 1960s) failed to catch on.

CONCLUSION

While the United States has historically had a large appetite for energy consumption, it has also had a great capacity for innovation and change. Government, academic, and private forces recognize the need to implement sustainable development, though exactly what that entails and how it will be brought about are much debated. Grassroots organizations are crucial for raising public awareness of the issues and pressuring legislatures, both state and national, to turn sustainable development into legal policy. The government, through the State Department's Bureau of Oceans and International Environmental Scientific Affairs (OES), interacts with the UN Commission on Sustainable Development and encourages private companies to research and develop innovations that will benefit the environment and the bottom line. Academic institutes attract leading scholars and provide a haven for research that is free from political bias. As with so many other challenges that the United States has faced in the past, the obstacles to curbing energy consumption, preserving natural resources, and implementing sustainable development are enormous. Success depends on long-term education, commitment, and leadership at each level of society.

[1] U.S. Department of Energy. "Energy in the Americas." Report, Energy Information Administration. Available online. URL: http://www.eia.doe.gov/emeu/cabs/Archives/theamericas/theamericas.html. Posted July 28, 1999.

[2] U.S. Department of Energy. "Country Analysis Briefs: United States Profile." Report, Energy Information Administration. Available online. URL: http://www.eia.doe.gov/emeu/cabs/Usa/Profile.html. Posted November 2005.

[3] Jared Diamond. *Collapse: How Societies Choose to Fail or Succeed.* New York: Viking, 2004, p. 152.

[4] Adam Smith. *An Inquiry into the Nature and Causes of the Wealth of Nations.* 5th edition, ed. Edwin Cannan. London: Metheun, 1904, section I.4.13.

[5] Population Reference Bureau. "Total Fertility Rate, 1940–2001." Available online. URL: http://www.prb.org/pdf/USFertilityTrends2.pdf. Accessed April 27, 2007.

[6] U.S. Department of Energy. "Energy in the United States: 1635–2000." Report, Energy Information Administration. Available online. URL: http://www.eia.doe.gov/emeu/aer/eh/intro.html. Accessed April 27, 2007.

[7] Julian L. Simon, ed. *The State of Humanity.* Boston: Blackwell Publishing, 1995, p. 26.

[8] John Flicker. "Audubon View." *Audubon*, January/February 2007, p. 8.

[9] United States Environmental Protection Agency. "National Priorities List." Available online. URL: www.epa.gov/superfund/sites/npl/status.htm. Accessed March 30, 2007.

[10] Keith Schneider. "E.P.A. Superfund at 13: A White Knight Tarnished." *New York Times*, September 6, 1993.

[11] Daniel Yergin. *The Prize: The Epic Quest for Oil, Money, and Power.* New York: Simon & Schuster, 1991.

[12] "New Home Size Reaches All-Time High in 2005." *Nation's Building News,* June 26, 2006.

[13] Miranda A. Schreurs. "Divergent Paths: Environmental Policy in Germany, the United States, and Japan." *Environment,* October 2003, p. 8.

[14] Tufts Recycles! Web site. URL: http://www.tufts.edu/tuftsrecycles/USstats.htm. Accessed April 27, 2007.

[15] Tufts Recycles! Web site. URL: http://www.tufts.edu/tuftsrecycles/USstats.htm. Accessed April 27, 2007.

[16] J. Lerner, E. Matthews, and I. Fung. "Methane Emission from Animals: A Global High-Resolution Database." *Global Biogeochemical Cycles.* Vol. 2, no. 2, pp. 139–156.

[17] Environmental Protection Agency. "Landfill Methane Outreach Program." Available online. URL: http://www.epa.gov/lmop/proj/index.htm.

[18] "Landfill Gas-to-Energy Project." City of Ann Arbor Energy Office. Available online. URL: http://www.a2gov.org/PublicServices/SystemsPlanning/Energy/LandfillEnergy.html. Updated December 2006.

[19] "Basic Petroleum Statistics." Energy Information Administration. Available online. URL: http://www.eia.doe.gov/neic/quickfacts/quickoil.html. Updated July 2007.

[20] "Basic Petroleum Statistics." Energy Information Administration. Available online. URL: http://www.eia.doe.gov/neic/quickfacts/quickoil.html. Updated July 2007.

[21] "U.S. Emits Nearly Half World's Automotive Carbon Dioxide." *Environmental News Service,* June 28, 2006. Available online. URL: http://www.ens-newswire.com/ens/jun2006/2006-06-28-03.asp. Uploaded July 19, 2006.

[22] "U.S. Emits Nearly Half World's Automotive Carbon Dioxide." *Environmental News Service,* June 28, 2006. Available online. URL: http://www.ens-newswire.com/ens/jun2006/2006-06-28-03.asp. Uploaded July 19, 2006.

[23] Netherlands Environmental Assessment Agency. "China Now No. 1 in CO_2 Emissions; USA in Second Position." Available online. URL: http://www.mnp.nl/en/dossiers/Climatechange/moreinfo/Chinanowno1inCO2emissionsUSAinsecondposition.html. Uploaded June 19, 2007.

[24] Howard Geller. *Energy Revolution: Policies for a Sustainable Future.* Washington, D.C.: Island Press, 2003, p. 132.

[25] U.S. Department of Energy. "World Energy Use and Carbon Dioxide Emissions, 1980–2001." Report, Energy Information Administration. Available online. URL: http://www.eia. doe.gov/emeu/cabs/carbonemiss/chapter2.html. Uploaded May 2004.

[26] Geller, p. 132.

[27] Natural Gas Vehicles for America Web site. "Benefits of NGVs." Available online. URL: www.NGVA.org.

[28] Jeff Goodell. *Big Coal: The Dirty Secret Behind America's Energy Future.* Boston, Mass: Houghton Mifflin, 2006, introduction.

[29] Goodell.

[30] Simon Romero. "Two Industry Leaders Bet on Coal but Split on Cleaner Approach." *New York Times*, May 28, 2006.

[31] National Institute for Occupational Safety and Health. "Coal Workers' Pneumoconiosis: Number of Deaths, Crude and Age-Adjusted Death Rates, U.S. Residents Age 15 and Over, 1968–2002," from *The Work-Related Lung Disease Surveillance Report, 2002*, p. 27. Available online. URL: http://www.cdc.gov/niosh/docs/2003-111/2003-111.html. Accessed April 27, 2007.

[32] U.S. Department of Energy. "U.S. Nuclear Generation of Electricity." Report, Energy Information Administration. Available online. URL: http://www.eia.doe.gov/cneaf/nuclear/page/nuc_generation/gensum.html. Accessed March 21, 2007.

[33] Kathy Kiely. "U.S. Nuclear Power Industry Working on Quiet Comeback." *USA Today*, June 19, 2005.

[34] Michael Ha. "Blackout No Mega-cat: Experts." *National Underwriter Property and Casualty*—Risk and Benefits Management, August 25, 2003, p. 5.

[35] Jennifer Cheeseman Day. *Population Projections of the United States by Age, Sex, Race and Hispanic Origin: 1995 to 2050*. U.S. Bureau of the Census, Current Population Reports. Washington, D.C.: U.S. Government Printing Office, 1996, pp. 25–1,130.

[36] Nature Conservancy Web site. Available online. URL: www.nature.org. Accessed April 27, 2007.

[37] Conservation International. "Biodiversity Hotspots." Available online. URL: www.biodiversityhotspots.org. Accessed April 27, 2007.

[38] Susan S. Hutson, et al. "Estimated Use of Water in the United States in 2000." USGS Circular 1268, March 2005, p. 1. Available online. URL: http://pubs.usgs.gov/circ/2004/circ1268. Accessed April 27, 2007.

[39] "Productivity of Growing Global Energy Demand: A Microeconomic Perspective." Report from the McKinsey Global Institute, November 2006, p. 10.

[40] Richard Benedetto. "Cheney's Energy Plan Focuses on Production." *USA Today*, May 1, 2001.

[41] Bruce Geiselman. "Study Criticizes Cap-and-Trade." *Waste News*, January 31, 2005, p. 3.

[42] Steve Lohr. "The Cost of an Overheated Planet." *New York Times*, December 12, 2006.

[43] Schreurs, p. 8.

[44] Jeremy Rifkin. *The Hydrogen Economy: The Creation of the Worldwide Energy Web and the Redistribution of Power on Earth*. New York: Penguin, 2002.

[45] Rifkin, p. 183.

[46] Steve Ford. "Bill Ford Jr. Speaks Out on Sustainability, Hybrids, and a Hydrogen Future." *Green Car Journal Online* 2007. Available online. URL: http://www.greencar.com/index.cfm?content=dialogue6. Accessed April 27, 2007.

[47] Richard Monastersky. "The Ice That Burns!" *Science News*, November 14, 1998, p. 312.

[48] Christopher Flavin. "Energy for a New Century." *World Watch*, March/April 2000, p. 8.

[49] Laurie J. Flynn. "Silicon Valley Rebounds, Led by Green Technology." *New York Times*, January 29, 2007.

[50] Eva Barkeman. "Pssst. Want to Get Rid of CO2? Try Burying It." *Fortune International*, October 30, 2006, p. 18.

[51] FutureGen Alliance Web site. Available online. URL: www.futuregenalliance.org. Accessed April 27, 2007.

[52] United States Combined Heat and Power Association Web site. Available online. URL: http://uschpa.admgt.com/. Accessed April 27, 2007.

[53] John Doerr. "California's Global-Warming Solution." *Time*, September 11, 2006, p. 55.

[54] Office of Sustainable Development, City of Portland, Oregon. "Portland Renewable Fuel Standard." Available online. URL: www.portlandonline.com/osd/index. Accessed April 27, 2007.

[55] Minnesota Department of Agriculture. "The Minnesota Ethanol Program." Available online. URL: http://www.mda.state.mn.us/ethanol/. Accessed April 27, 2007.

[56] Congress for the New Urbanism. *Charter of the New Urbanism*. New York: McGraw-Hill, 1999.

[57] Kelly Easterling and David Mohoney, eds. *Seaside: Making a Town in America*. New York: Princeton Architectural Press, 1996.

3

Global Perspectives

Each country's natural resources provide a unique set of circumstances for its people. A sharp divide exists between developed and underdeveloped countries, with developed countries generally better off in terms of securing the resources they need to grow their economies, albeit not necessarily in a sustainable manner. International organizations, such as the United Nations, try to mediate conflicts between countries with differing priorities. This section highlights several key countries in detail, but snapshots of two other countries—Japan and Nigeria—will help flesh out the larger picture, drawing attention to the wide range of circumstances faced by people in various parts of the world.

JAPAN

Japan has lots of people, comparatively little land, even less arable land, a stalled birthrate, and enormous energy requirements for its technologically advanced economy. Prior to the 20th century, it overharvested old-growth forests, trafficked in endangered wildlife, and hunted whales nearly to extinction. Geographically, the country consists of a series of relatively small islands, one of which is home to Tokyo (the largest metropolitan area in the world), that are vulnerable to earthquakes and tsunamis. These circumstances have created a culture of necessity that prizes efficiency, conservation, and sustainability. Top-down forest management in Japan began as early as the 17th century, and, despite the country's huge, dense population, the land remains 74 percent forested—the highest percentage of any industrialized nation in the world.[1]

Japan enforces strong emissions regulations that make industrial polluters financially responsible for their activities. Industries pay high taxes to support pollution prevention technology and to help pay the medical costs of those affected by pollution, thanks to the Pollution Health Damage Compensation Law of 1973. The result is a sense of responsibility on the part of the private sector for making sure PCBs (polychlorinated biphenyls), arsenic, cadmium, mercury, and smog—all of which have been linked to serious diseases—do not harm the general population. The country's interest in sustainable development increased after the Montreal Protocol of 1987, an international agreement aimed at protecting the ozone layer by limiting CFCs (chlorofluorocarbons) in the atmosphere.[2] By the turn of the 21st century, Japan had become more vocal about air pollution due to the rapid, unregulated industrialization of neighboring China, whose many factories and power plants emitted pollutants that drifted past Japan's borders.

Japan also hosted the UN convention that resulted in the Kyoto Protocol, the treaty to limit worldwide carbon emissions in an effort to curb global warming. Pollution-monitoring sites have been installed throughout Japan, and Japanese regulations are among the strictest in the world. As a result, Japan's ecological footprint in 2003 was estimated to be 4.4 global hectares per person, down from 4.77 global hectares per person in 1999, and less than half the size of the U.S. ecological footprint.[3] Though community and grassroots environmental organizations in Japan are few and far between, the government has become more responsive to issues of sustainable development because of the country's lack of fossil fuels (and corresponding vulnerability to world energy markets) and geographical precariousness.

NIGERIA

Nigeria is the most highly populated country in Africa and the ninth most populous country in the world. The United Nations places Nigeria's total population as of 2004 at 131 million, but high infant mortality rates, high death rates from AIDS, and regional hostility toward census takers make accurate estimates nearly impossible. Everyone agrees that the population is growing and will account for a large percentage of the world's population growth by 2050. Nigerian women have one of the highest fertility rates in the world, averaging 5.3 children each. Although this rate has declined from 7.2 children per woman in 1970, government efforts to lower fertility rates through education and birth control have largely failed. Life in Nigeria is complicated by corrupt military rule, a poor education system, regional conflicts fought by armed warlords, extreme poverty, debilitating pollution, and lack of clean water. Nigeria boasts one of the largest natural gas reserves in the world and the world's 12th largest oil reserves. Corruption exists at the highest levels of government; former president Sani Abacha and his associates, for example, stole at least $2 billion worth of the country's oil revenue, out of a total of $300 to $400 billion oil revenue that has been squandered, misplaced, or stolen since 1960.[4]

Some blame the so-called resource curse for the country's problems. The resource curse refers to the paradox in which countries possessing vast natural resources often suffer economic decline despite the wealth inherent in their resources, often because their resources tend to engender conflict, political corruption, and infighting. The Niger delta along the Atlantic Ocean produces about 800,000 barrels of oil per day. But the nearby megacity of Lagos is home to one of the largest slums on the planet, where millions live and scavenge for food in floating garbage dumps. As a founding member of OPEC, Nigeria is part of the international cartel that controls the price of oil on the world market. But unlike many other OPEC nations, such as Saudi Arabia, Nigeria's economy has never benefited from this unique position. U.S. oil companies have major operations in Nigeria and are sometimes forced to pay millions in bribes in order to prevent warlords from illegally siphoning their oil, sabotaging their pipelines, or kidnapping their executives.[5] This corruption prevents average Nigerians from benefiting from the country's petroleum resources, and the resulting poverty has kept the country's carbon intensity and energy intensity levels the lowest of all the OPEC nations. Because of widespread lack of development, Nigeria's ecological footprint in 2003 was only 1.2 global hectare per person.[6]

Nigeria contains Africa's largest wetlands and rain forest, which are threatened by dams, wildfires, and frequent oil spills (roughly 300 a year). Between 1960 and 1997, oil spills released upward of 100 million barrels of oil into the environment. Many of these spills damaged the country's crucial mangrove ecosystem and made fishing—many people's only livelihood—nearly impossible. Natural gas flaring, a common practice in which excess natural gas is allowed to burn off into the atmosphere, is a by-product of an unregulated oil industry that greatly increases carbon dioxide emissions and acid rain, squanders a potential source of revenue, and produces flames so large and widespread that they can be seen from space.[7] Deforestation is occurring at a rate of 500 square miles per year as rural populations cut trees to burn for fuel. Such dire circumstances preclude the foresight and organization required to implement policies of sustainable development.

In 2006, the Aba Clean Energy Carbon Project announced the building of a new gas-fired power plant to supply electricity to the 1 million residents of Aba, a city in the country's oil-drilling region. The plant will sell its carbon credits to the World Bank, which oversees the Community Development Carbon Fund, a program designed to aid underdeveloped nations. The country has planned a large hydropower electrical plant, and some NGOs are promoting solar energy in rural areas that are beyond the reach of the power grid. Yet widespread political instability threatens these projects.

CHINA

With more than 1.3 billion people as of 2008, the People's Republic of China is the most populous country in the world. Over the past 20 years, what used to be a largely rural population has become increasingly urbanized; more than 100 cities boast populations of more than 1 million people, compared to only nine in the United States.[8] Increasing urbanization and industrialization have led to a huge increase in energy consumption, but China's energy statistics can be tricky to decipher because per capita measurements do not convey the enormity of its total population and because the statistics themselves are often inaccurate or falsified. For instance, China's ecological footprint ranks 70th in the world at 1.6 global hectares per person (well below the world average of 2.2 gha), and carbon emissions per person are .75 metric tons annually.[9] China passed the United States in carbon emissions in 2007,[10] becoming the world leader largely because of its heavy reliance on carbon-intensive coal and its massive cement industry, in which carbon emissions are the most significant by-product of the country's immense building boom. The startling pace of China's industrialization and economic growth can be attributed to its immense human resources and to the transformation of a Soviet-style economy into a market-oriented economy beginning in the 1980s. China continues to be ruled by a single party, the Chinese Communist Party (CCP). Central planning and lack of political opposition have allowed the government to implement solutions to some of its sustainability problems that have taken more time to address elsewhere, including huge public works projects such as the controversial Three Gorges Dam, the equally controversial one-child policy to manage the size of its population, and the recently inaugurated 11th Five-Year Plan, which places top priority on environmental concerns.

History

China is one of the world's oldest civilizations, and for most of its history it has been a rural civilization. From the beginning, it possessed little forested land, making it susceptible to soil erosion and desertification. Following World War II (1939–45) and the Chinese Civil War (1945–49), the Communist Party came to power and established the modern People's Republic of China on the mainland, where the country's vast population and scarce resources influenced the often-harsh governmental policy. When Communist leader Mao Zedong (1893–1976) attempted to reorganize China into agrarian collectives to boost food production during the Great Leap Forward (1958–60), for example, massive crop failures led to the starvation of millions of people.

One of China's enduring cultural beliefs is that nature should be conquered and tamed. This belief underlies several 20th-century engineering megaprojects, which were designed to solve ecological problems by diverting resources on an unprecedented scale. These include the South-to-North Water Diversion Project and the Three Gorges Dam.

MONUMENTAL WATER PROJECTS

From the beginning of his political tenure, Mao realized the country faced a water crisis. Not only did the Yangtze and Yellow (Huang He) Rivers periodically flood and ruin people's livelihoods, but they also flowed mainly through the country's less populated southern half. Regions in the north, where 43 percent of the country's population resided, had access to only 14 percent of the country's water.[11] The north needed what only the south possessed. Thus, in 1952, Mao proposed the South-to-North Water Diversion Project. The 100-year plan called for the construction of three major canal systems to divert water from the sparsely populated, water-rich south to the highly populated, water-poor north. Upon completion of the Central Canal, estimated for 2050, 20 percent of Beijing's water will come from constructed aqueducts. The most ambitious part of the project aims to divert the headwaters of the Yangtze to the Yellow River.[12]

Hydropower is a cornerstone of China's plan to meet its growing energy demands. The Three Gorges Dam on the Yangtze River, scheduled to be completed in 2009, will be the largest such project in the world. Five times the size of the Hoover Dam, the Three Gorges Dam will provide approximately 3 percent of China's electricity (up to 18,200 MW), while 80 percent of the country's electricity will still be derived from coal. However, this 3 percent from the Three Gorges Dam represents a savings of 40 to 50 million tons of coal, 2 million tons of sulfur dioxide, and 100 million tons of carbon dioxide a year.[13] In addition to providing electricity, Chinese officials claim the dam will control the periodically devastating floods that have had such a huge impact on local populations for centuries.

However, the dam has been controversial because of its sheer size. It will have a tremendous impact on the watershed, farmland, and biodiversity of the region. Some scientists believe that microbiotic activity in the dam's vast reservoirs could contribute to greenhouse gas emissions. In terms of the human cost, the project has forced the government to relocate up to 2 million people, whose towns and villages are now under water.[14] Forced relocation of rural villagers to urban areas has caused international concern, and censorship of the government's official statistics reinforces the idea that the sociological costs of the project have been underestimated as much as its financial costs. In the town of Tongshuwan in Hubei Province, for example, where more than 1,000 citizens were resettled, the government stated that 904 of them had moved into new living quarters, planted citrus orchards, and "to the villagers' surprise, their living conditions have improved: their average income was 5.35 times that of 1990's figures."[15] Such a rosy picture is at odds with firsthand accounts from the peasants themselves, who say they never received the compensation they were promised for their land. In October 2007, government officials announced they would relocate 3 to 4 million more people within 10 to 15 years because of unforeseen ecological consequences associated with the dam, such as water pollution and mud slides along the unprotected river banks.[16]

FOOD INDEPENDENCE GIVES WAY TO MARKET-DRIVEN AGRICULTURE

From 1958 to 1961, upward of 30 million peasants died of starvation during Mao's Great Leap Forward, the program designed to shift China's economy from rural and agrarian to urban and industrial. A terrible drought and disastrous agricultural practices resulted in severe food shortages on the collective farms where many workers were forced to live. Millions starved even as Party officials denied that the tragedy was caused by their own policies. It was a textbook case of unsustainable development. In 1959, Mao had to step down as chairman of the People's Republic of China as a result of the failures of the Great Leap Forward. Once the government reversed its policies, China quickly began to produce sufficient food supplies. Widespread starvation was alleviated and farmers were able to feed the country for the next 30 years, with help from the Green Revolution of the 1960s.

In addition to unsustainable farming practices during the Great Leap Forward, the government had begun a push to industrialize the economy. The building boom resulted in more deforestation and pollution from thousands of small-scale, inefficient steel mills and new factories. The Cultural Revolution of 1966 to 1976 represented the next period of great change. Political enemies and perceived enemies of the ruling communists were weeded out in a ruthless reign of terror. Fearing that many factories were vulnerable to its enemies, the government decided to relocate them to rural areas to improve national security. By building new factories in rural areas to replace working factories in urban areas, China duplicated existing manufacturing capacity instead of expanding it, increasing pollution and urbanization in the process, as formerly rural areas became home to the new generation of industrial workers.

The roots of China's current economic growth began following Mao's death in 1976, which brought about the end of the Cultural Revolution and the inauguration of Deng Xiaoping's policy of "Socialism with Chinese characteristics." This policy allowed public and private entities to compete in a capitalist environment, with the goal of attracting foreign investors and boosting economic output. Deng Xiaoping, as leader of the CCP, declared that communism's planned economy and capitalism's market economy were not mutually exclusive. Whereas Mao shunned the educational and social infrastructure that encouraged technological innovation, Deng Xiaoping embraced it. In coopting elements of capitalism to a more fluid idea of a planned economy, he thus created an economic juggernaut of a completely new nature.

By the 1990s, China's concept of food independence had given way to market-driven agriculture. Assuming that China could purchase as much grain on the world market as it needed to survive, farmers were encouraged to switch from low-revenue crops such as rice and wheat to high-revenue crops such as fruits and vegetables, which could be exported for more money than importing their food staples would cost.

Current Situation

CHINA'S POPULATION BOMB

In the 1970s, the Communist government recognized that population growth was more likely to become a hindrance than an asset to the country's economic development. Deng Xiaoping instituted a strict one-child-per-couple policy in 1979 that remains in effect (with some tweaking) today. The policy—the only fertility quota program in the world—applied to ethnic Han Chinese living in urban areas; ethnic minorities were excluded from the policy and rural residents were allowed two children. The policy is usually enforced by means of a "social compensation fee" paid by parents who elect to have a second child. These parents are also responsible for all education and health care costs associated with the second child. Reports of stricter enforcement in rural areas, including forced abortions, have brought allegations of human rights abuses from the international community and prompted President George W. Bush to withhold U.S. funds from the UN Fund for Population Activities, an organization that promotes reproductive health to China and other nations.[17] Despite this, the policy has been successful in reducing fertility rates; by 2006 the fertility rate was 1.73 children per woman, versus 6.0 in 1970.[18]

Even though the one-child policy successfully curtailed the rate of population growth, the total population continued to rise because of population momentum. Population momentum describes the situation in which population increases even though fertility rates have dropped below replacement levels, because the size of the generation that has yet to reach childbearing age is larger than the one before it. China's policy, while having the desired effect in terms of numbers (the fertility rate of 1.7 is well below the 2.1 replacement level), resulted in two unforeseen phenomena. The first was that the gender ratio became unbalanced—as many as 130 boys to 100 girls in some parts of the country—as a result of unreported female births, as well as abortion and female infanticide. When couples desiring a son conceived a daughter instead, the female babies were either aborted or abandoned at state-run orphanages.[19] The gender imbalance gave rise to the idea of China's "missing girls," females that statistically should exist but do not. The flip side of the issue is a surplus of boys who will not be able to find a wife. Many families fear these boys will grow up to be "bare branches," unable to continue the family tree. China faces as many as 30 million men who will become bare branches by 2020,[20] a significant social factor in a country that places supreme importance on marriage and family.

The one-child policy was somewhat relaxed in 2006 to allow city couples to have two children. But concern remains high; China's minister in charge of population has stated the government's target is to keep the country's population below 1.37 billion by 2010.

The second unforeseen phenomenon related to the one-child policy is the "silver tsunami," the term that describes the disproportionate percentage of the population that is retired and no longer contributes to the economy. This places a strain on the remaining workers who must support them. The size of the older generation is indicative of the global aging phenomena seen also in other parts of the world—especially Europe—in which higher levels of education and standards of living have accompanied a drop in fertility rates, resulting in more retirees than workers to support them. In China, this situation is compounded by the fact that the retirees often remain in rural areas while their single child has migrated to an urban area to work in a large factory. The parents are left without a safety net of financial support and health services. By 2020, China will have roughly 265 million people aged 65 and older—more than the total population of Indonesia, the world's fourth most populous country—and only 20 percent of them will have a pension.[21] In addition, though the population may stabilize, the number of households (perhaps a better measure of energy and resource usage) will grow due to smaller family size.

WATER

When it comes to resources, China's biggest problem may be water. It boasts 22 percent of the planet's population, but only 8 percent of its freshwater.[22] Compounding the situation is the disparity in the distribution of water. The northern part of the country has more people but only 14 percent of the water. Nationwide, more than 320 million people do not have access to clean drinking water, a problem exacerbated in the summer of 2006 when China suffered its worst drought in 100 years.[23] The lowest reaches of the Yellow River, the second longest river in China, now run dry more often than not because of upstream irrigation demands. Another problem is the fact that the growing season, when most of the water is needed, does not coincide with the monsoon season, when the river is at its highest levels. The solution, as elsewhere in China, has been to build dams. However, because the Yellow River has an extremely high amount of naturally occurring silt that tends to clog dams, engineers are faced with building dams with limited lifespans.

Even when water is available, pollution often makes it unsuitable for human consumption. Red tides, quickly accumulating floating deposits of phytoplankton that kill nearly all aquatic life in their paths, occur on average 100 times a year in China's seas, and pollution affects 75 percent of its lakes.[24] These red tides, or algal blooms, have various causes, but many scientists attribute them to the nitrate and phosphate runoff that enters the water supply from industry. Apart from this everyday point-source pollution, industrial accidents create emergency situations. In November 2005, for example, a chemical explosion near Harbin, a city of 3.8 million people, killed five people and released a 50-mile slick of cancer-causing benzene in the Songhua River. The city's water supply was cut off for four days while the slick flowed down the river and made its way to Russia. On September 8, 2006, 80,000 residents of Hunan lost access to their water supply when a factory released arsenide into the Xinqiang River. In the year separating those two events, officials tallied 130 other instances of water contamination.[25] In reaction, the government declared it would invest $41 billion to provide clean drinking water for all citizens by 2015.[26]

Another reason for the scarce municipal water supply is the fact that 67 percent of the country's water is used for agriculture, even though agriculture amounts to only 13 percent of the GDP.[27] Many economists feel this unbalanced ratio reflects unsustainable agricultural practices, such as reliance on water-intensive rice crops in areas that suffer from deforestation and soil erosion. Because of these factors, China's water table has been dropping steadily, up to 10 feet per year in some areas—particularly in the north.

DEFORESTATION, DESERTIFICATION, AND THE CHALLENGES OF AGRICULTURE

Only 7 percent of China's land is suitable for farming.[28] Furthermore, soil erosion, deforestation, desertification, destruction of grasslands and wetlands, and urbanization continually decrease the amount of agriculture that arable land can sustain. Unrestricted logging, which since the 1980s has cleared forests in an area four times the size of Hong Kong, is the primary cause of deforestation. The disappearance of vegetation and soil that once absorbed heavy rainfalls causes runoff to drain directly into the rivers, resulting in floods. In 1998, floods caused in part by deforestation killed 4,000 people and caused $24 billion in damage.[29] In reaction, the government instituted the National Ecological Environmental Construction Plan in 1999, which banned logging in forested areas and unsustainable land conversion for industrial purposes.

Arable land in China is scarce, but deserts are abundant and cover more than a quarter of the country. Giant dust storms over the Gobi Desert and other regions, which have darkened skies as far away as North America, have permanently swept away soil necessary for farming. The desert is expanding at a rate of 3,600 square kilometers (1,390 sq. mi.) a year, creating barren vistas where green fields once stood and bringing sand dunes to the outskirts of Beijing.[30] Not all scientists agree on the causes and patterns of desertification, and some even believe the process is reversible. Other scientists believe that desertification has accelerated in the past several decades as the growing population required more food and more land on which to grow it. Farmers turned to land that was marginal at best and exploited its soil and water, eventually exhausting its nutrients and ability to sustain crops. Thus, the land turned into desert, intensifying the cycle. Receding glaciers in Mongolia, the result of global warming, are also contributing to desertification. As meltwater dries up, rivers recede, and more dry land is added to the cycle.

Desertification also reduces biodiversity. Historically, China enjoyed great biodiversity in both plants and animals, being home to the world's only population of Giant Pandas and other rare species. But desertification, deforestation, illegal poaching, industrialization, and shrinking wetlands have endangered many species—up to 25 percent according to some studies.[31] In an effort to stem the decline in biodiversity, the government has declared a total of 13 percent of the country's land as nature preserves. Yet the country still faces a daunting situation. Debilitating sandstorms in urban areas are becoming more common as the deserts expand by roughly 2,236 square miles per year, due in part to population increases in desert areas, clear cutting of vegetation, overgrazing of land, and mismanaged agriculture.[32]

ENERGY RESOURCES AND INTENSITY

China contains 12 percent of the world's coal reserves, and 70 percent of the country's energy was derived from coal in 2006.[33] In 2005, China burned 2 billion more tons of coal than the United States, India, and Russia combined.[34] Even this enormous surge in energy supply has not been enough to keep up with the country's tremendous economic growth. Blackouts due to overburdened power grids are common in rural and urban areas alike, and lack of pollution control requirements in plants running at full capacity has raised sulfur dioxide to lethal levels, killing 355,000 people a year and increasing asthma rates by 40 percent from 2000 to 2005.[35] China has 16 of the world's 20 worst cities for air quality, as well as the city with the worst air quality in the world: Beijing.

China does not have much oil of its own. It has proven reserves of 16 billion barrels (enough for about 14 years), daily production of 3.6 million barrels, and daily consumption of 6.6 million barrels. Thus, China's growing demand for oil, which for generations had been negligible due to its dearth of automobiles, will quickly have an enormous effect on the world market as its citizens' consumption levels increase along with economic growth. Part of China's attempt to gain secure energy resources involves investing in foreign oil operations and establishing long-term agreements with oil-rich countries. By 2006, China was the world's second largest importer of oil and the second highest producer of greenhouse gases, trailing only the United States. In 2005, China's government adopted its first fuel efficiency standards for private automobiles, and many automakers, including Toyota and General Motors, are marketing hybrid gas-electric cars in the country.

Nuclear power is gaining popularity in China. As of 2005, 30 nuclear power plants were in the works as part of the effort to meet the country's surging energy demands. Despite the huge push to increase nuclear capacity, it is forecasted that these plants will eventually account for only 4 percent of the country's electricity.[36]

THE POLLUTION CLOUD

In the city of Wuhai in the tiny province of Ningxia, vast reserves of coal have prompted unprecedented growth along the banks of the Yellow River. In 1998, Wuhai was home to four factories, and by 2006 the total had mushroomed to more than 400. The resulting pollution made the air unfit to breathe and caused so much ash to rain down on surrounding land that nothing would grow. Even hundreds of miles away in Beijing, ash deposited by rain left black spots on cars.[37]

Overall air quality is low in China, as evidenced by the fact that it is home to 16 of the world's 20 most polluted cities and that the air of its 340 largest cities contains unhealthy levels of sulfur dioxide.[38] Sulfur dioxide is emitted from thousands of unregulated coal-fired power plants; it destroys the lungs and causes respiratory problems, prompting many urban residents to wear masks to prevent breathing in dangerous particulates. In terms of the economic costs of air pollution due to lost work time and health care costs, one source estimated the damage at $64 billion in 2004.[39] Adding to the smog are the world's biggest steel-making and cement-making enterprises and a large automobile industry, all of which are part of one of the largest building booms in history. The smog is so thick in some areas that it has resulted in "invisible cities"—those that frequently cannot be seen by orbiting satellites because the air is so opaque.[40]

Significant amounts of this pollution drift beyond China's borders. Japan, South Korea, and even the United States have been visited by the "Asian Brown Cloud," as it is sometimes called. Sunlight-blocking smog originates on the Indian subcontinent and mixes with pollution over China. When the resulting cloud, which can be up to two miles thick, reaches the jet stream over the Pacific Ocean, it is carried thousands of miles to the West Coast of the United States. Some scientists believe the Asian-borne smog is responsible for declining precipitation on both the West Coast and in parts of the Midwest.[41] The cloud is comprised of numerous particulates, including ash from forest fires, carbon dioxide from fossil fuels, sulfur dioxide from coal plants, and aerosols from inefficient cooking methods employed by more than 1 billion people. The cloud brings acid rain, which causes an estimated $13 billion in damage annually to people, agriculture, and ecosystems.[42]

By 2000, China's government was concerned enough about the problem to mandate filters for newly constructed coal-fired power plants and monitoring of air pollution. Leaded fuel for automobiles was banned, and automobiles were required to pass emission tests.

Counterstrategies

CHINA'S AGENDA 21

Sustainable development is China's official policy, but economic growth is its first priority.[43] Nevertheless, the severity of its problems has forced government officials to acknowledge air quality, water quality, and land use issues. Increased awareness of China's predicament has prompted the government to form a number of committees and ministries devoted to working on environmental issues. By the late 20th century, the National People's Congress Environmental and Resources Committee was working in conjunction with local and provincial governments to stem the destruction of the country's resources. China's Agenda 21 is a program designed to address many issues of sustainability that were raised in the 1992 United Nations Conference on Environment and Development. Government officials have enacted a Priority Programme that includes 82 projects covering the following nine priority areas:

1. building for sustainable development
2. sustainable agriculture
3. cleaner production and environmental protection industry
4. clean energy and transportation
5. conservation and sustainable utilization of natural resources
6. environmental pollution control
7. poverty alleviation and regional development
8. population, health, and human settlements
9. global climate change and biodiversity conservation[44]

Many of the government's efforts have been integrated into the country's Five-Year Plans and have the target date of 2010 for completion.

THE GREEN OLYMPICS

In preparation for the 2008 Summer Olympics, which were awarded to Beijing in 2001, China used state-of-the-art green technology to transform the capital city. Beijing boasted a 73-year plan for a 2,800-mile, $6 billion Green Wall of China of newly planted trees around portions of the city to protect it from the sandstorms of the encroaching desert. By 2010, the wall will stretch from outside Beijing to Inner Mongolia, and the entire project will be completed by 2074. Private automobile use was restricted to keep smog levels down, and mass transit was encouraged. The newly constructed Bird's Nest Stadium was solar powered, the Olympic Park was lit by wind power, and 160 geothermal wells heated establishments that hosted foreign guests.[45]

The Olympics prompted other conservation and efficiency projects. Many cities constructed light rail and subway systems, and Shanghai created the world's first commercial bullet train to run on magnetic levitation. Beijing scrapped thousands of high-emissions taxis, converted many vehicles to liquefied natural gas, eliminated lead from the gasoline supply, planned to build five more water treatment plants, and began releasing real-time water quality reports in an effort to attain transparency. The country invited more than 250,000 environmental experts to assist with combating pollution, and they sent 40,000 Chinese nationals abroad to study pollution control issues in other countries.[46] Nonetheless, air pollution continues to be terrible, car use continues to grow, and corruption and poor implementation have plagued environmental plans.

RENEWABLE ENERGY

Douglas Ogden of the China Sustainable Energy Program says that much of China's energy crisis could be alleviated by instituting more stringent efficiency standards for electrical and gas-powered appliances, especially televisions, air conditioners, and refrigerators. The country's 11th Five Year Plan, covering 2006–10, called for a 20 percent improvement in energy efficiency, which would place China at the forefront of global emissions and renewable energy movements.

China's Renewables Law went into effect on January 1, 2006. It aims to provide 10 percent of the country's energy from renewable sources by 2020, up from 1 percent in 2005.[47] The strategy has three major components: 1) introduce regulations that favor generation and marketing of renewable energy sources; 2) make renewable energy financially competitive by providing technology to power producers; and 3) help existing companies implement renewable energy programs on a wide-scale basis and provide the means for private industry to get into the game.

As of 2004, China produced 328 billion kwh of hydroelectric power and by 2006 had consumed 2,604 Mwh of wind power. Since then, officials have announced plans for even more hydroelectric power plants and expanded wind and solar capacity. Wind power and solar power will be generated primarily in rural farming areas that are beyond the reach of the power grid. Given that the Gobi Desert produces huge windstorms, China could conceivably exploit wind power to a much greater extent. However, harvesting power from the far reaches of the desert and transporting it to populated areas are huge technological hurdles, and other sources of energy such as coal are much more cost-efficient. Despite the economic boom of recent decades, millions of China's rural residents still do not have electricity. The government completed the Township Electrification Project in 2005 to provide 29,000 villages with electricity through a vast network of solar power plants linked to a giant solar installation in the Gobi Desert.[48] The Village Electrification Project began in 2005 with the goal of providing electricity to 20,000 additional off-grid towns in remote western regions of the country by 2010. Geothermal power, in which the heat and steam that escape from inside the Earth are harnessed to generate electricity, presents another sustainable and largely unexplored source of power.

China leads the world in solar-powered water heaters. Ten percent of all homes (a total of 30 million) use them, and that percentage will continue to rise in coming years because they are affordable and in compliance with the country's renewable energy laws.[49] Demonstrating its willingness to explore renewable energy, China spent $5 billion on such programs in 2004—more than any other country.[50]

ADDRESSING WATER POLLUTION

The Three Rivers, Three Lakes Project launched by the government in 1995 was the first substantial nationwide effort to deal with water pollution. The program covers the Huai, Liao, and Hai Rivers and the Tai, Chao, and Dianchi Lakes. According to the plan, factories in these areas will need to meet pollution discharge standards or be shut down. Additionally, industrial polluters must clean up their wastewater, and cities of a half-million or more were required to treat 60 percent of wastewater by 2005. To facilitate this, the government planned to build 150 wastewater treatment plants on the Yangtze River by 2009, but progress at many sites has been slow or nonexistent.[51]

Conclusion

China is one of the world's oldest civilizations, with dynastic rule dating back to the 20th century B.C.E. Subsequent dynasties facilitated political unity and international trade via the Silk Road. The country's strength has always been in numbers: By 1000 C.E., the Northern Song Dynasty had a population of more than 100 million. From the highest point on earth—Mount Everest—to the rapidly expanding Gobi Desert, China's geographical characteristics have a major impact on daily life. Vast coal reserves are fueling economic growth and major rivers are being reengineered to bring water to the most densly populated areas. The country's technological ingenuity and political will allow for rapid transitions. Rapid transitions, however, are not always in line with sustainable development. However, pressure from the international community on air pollution and other matters—especially China's attempts to highlight its progressive environmentalism during the Beijing Olympics of 2008—may direct China's extraordinary human and natural resources toward policies of sustainability.

INDIA

Next to China, India is the world's most populous country. In 2006, population stood at 1.1 billion people; one-sixth of all the people on the planet. India's population growth rate is 1.6 percent—double that of China.[52] Lacking population control policies such as those mandated in China, India will become the world's most populous country by 2035 and is poised to reap substantial economic gains through its huge workforce, a phenomenon sometimes called the demographic dividend. Despite enormous educational gains over the last generation, much of India's population continues to suffer from extreme poverty, lack of water, and lack of education; the literacy rate hovers around 60 percent, much lower than China's 91 percent. More than half the working population is in agriculture, though manufacturing and service industries (particularly in the information technology sector) are rapidly expanding. Seventy percent of the population lives in rural areas, but the Mumbai, Delhi, and Kolkata metropolitan areas contain 20 million, 18 million, and 15 million residents respectively, giving them megacity status. About 50 cities in India have metropolitan populations totaling more than 1 million people.

Because it is underdeveloped, India's ecological footprint is a low .80 global hectares per person,[53] and its per capita carbon emissions are only 1.0 metric ton per person.[54] These figures will increase exponentially as India continues to develop and industrialize. Between 1990 and 2001, the country's carbon emissions increased by 61 percent—a rate surpassed only by China. Though India's energy figures may seem low, like China's, it is best to consider them in light of the size of its surging population.

Though they share many issues, India and China differ enormously when it comes to addressing them. India has a parliamentary system of government with a prime minister. Political discourse is open and many parties hold seats in the People's Assembly. This has not necessarily led to a better standard of living for India's citizens, and it tends to politicize issues of water rights and distribution (among other sustainability topics). Controversy over public works projects, such as the Narmada Dam, is high, unlike opposition to China's Three Gorges Dam, which is actively curtailed by the government.

History

Around 2500 B.C.E., the Indus Valley, home of the present-day western states of India and most of Pakistan, became the hub for agricultural trade and commerce. One thousand years later, these architecturally and technologically sophisticated cities were abandoned, possibly because of climate changes in the region, especially drought and cooler weather, which slowly destroyed the region's agriculture.[55]

The Aryan society that moved into the area a few hundred years later was from its earliest days highly stratified into four primary categories: Brahmins (priests), Kshatriya (warriors), Vaishya (traders), and Shudra (laborers). On the very bottom social rung were the untouchables, those who were considered polluted and thus ostracized from society. This social structure had a huge impact on the culture; people undertook occupations based on their caste and were discriminated against or received preferential treatment accordingly. Those in the lower castes were not allowed to receive education and thus wielded no political power. As this system became entrenched, a permanent underclass and persistent poverty evolved.

By the fourth century C.E., Hinduism had taken hold on the subcontinent, leading to India's Golden Age of flourishing culture and government. Beginning in the 10th century, Islam became more popular as Turks and Afghans established themselves in Delhi. Modern India is largely an amalgamation of these Hindu and Muslim traditions. British explorers set up trade outposts in the early 17th century, and by the 18th century they ruled over the subcontinent and proceeded to modernize it to some extent, forming a modern military and boosting education. The British also engaged in aggressive deforestation and the hunting of big game, both of which served to upset the ecological balance of some areas.

Following a peaceful movement spearheaded by Mohandas Gandhi (1869–1948) India gained its independence in 1947 and subsequently became the world's largest democracy. When it opened its markets to foreign investment in the 1990s, it became an attractive choice for Western businesses that were interested in moving their operations overseas to take advantage of a large, educated workforce.

BENGAL FAMINE (1943)

In the 20th century, one of India's greatest humanitarian catastrophes was the 1943 Bengal Famine, in which an estimated 3 million people starved to death.[56] Various environmental and political factors combined to make it the world's worst recorded food disaster up to that time. Amartya Sen, who received the Nobel Prize in Economics in 1998 for his research into the causes of the famine, outlined the contributing factors of the Bengal disaster in his 1981 book, *Poverty and Famines: An Essay on Entitlement and Deprivation.* According to Sen, the cause of the famine was not lack of food per se, but rather a perceived lack of food that led to widespread panic and hoarding among millions in the Bengal region. The British, who ruled India at the time, were too distracted by their involvement in World War II to effectively head off the tragedy. Because the ruling government lacked the resources and will to counteract what was essentially a rumor of a food shortage, people hoarded food and refused to share with neighbors. People died in the shadows of well-stocked stores because the state protected the legal rights of the storeowners to deny food to those who needed it. The poor and the hungry had no legal right to receive food of any kind.[57] Thus, the Bengal Famine can be seen as the result of governmental policies that hindered sustainability despite plentiful resources.

BHOPAL (1984)

Following World War II and India's independence from Great Britain, the country became an attractive location for Western corporations seeking a cheap, never-ending supply of labor and lax laws concerning safety and pollution. The chemical conglomerate Union Carbide, a U.S. company, was one of these corporations, and selected the city of Bhopal in central India as the site of a chemical plant in 1969. The plant, which was operated by a local Union Carbide subsidiary, produced carbaryl, a carcinogenic insecticide composed of highly toxic compounds. On December 3, 1984, 40 tons of deadly methyl isocyanate leaked from a tank at the Union Carbide chemical plant in the heart of the city, resulting in the world's worst industrial disaster. Three thousand people died in the initial incident, and up to 15,000 more died in the following weeks, months, and years. Those who died immediately suffocated from the gas, and many others were trampled to death in the chaos that ensued when residents realized what was happening. Survivors continued to suffer respiratory problems, cancer, birth defects, and a host of other ailments for decades. The facility suffered from poor working conditions and lack of quality control that made a tragedy more likely. Additionally, the location of the plant in a dense, urban area led to a high number of fatalities. The incident highlighted how corporate responsibility—or lack thereof—can affect a local population and led to tighter local emergency response plans in an effort to keep people safe and informed. In terms of sustainability, the incident is notable because those who suffered the most were impoverished and uneducated. Union Carbide built a factory in their midst without alerting them to the dangers it posed. Public awareness of environmental issues grew somewhat in the following years.

NARMADA DAMS (1979)

Like many other countries, two of India's main resource challenges are providing enough electricity to power industrial growth and providing enough water to irrigate the crops necessary to feed its rapidly expanding population. Also like many other countries, India decided to address both issues by building hydroelectric dams. In 1979, the Indian government initiated the Sardar Sarovar Project to build 30 large dams along the Narmada River to produce hydroelectric power, provide irrigation to drought-prone regions, increase the drinking water supply, prevent floods, and stall desertification. Those large dams were to be augmented with a series of 135 medium-sized dams and 3,000 small dams, which combined would flood millions of acres and displace 51,000 families, according to government estimates. But others claimed the number of people affected was closer to 700,000.[58] Moreover, the government's promise of land and/or a cash settlement was fraught with legal red tape that almost invariably left the families with neither land nor money. Despite this, officials continued to let the dams be raised, resulting in even more affected families whose lives were uprooted by the government's poor resettling plans. The project was initially funded by the World

Bank, but the organization backed out in the face of stiff grassroots opposition led by notable public personalities, such as the writer Arundhati Roy, whose book *The Cost of Living* protested the project, and the film *Drowned Out,* which tells the story of a family who drowned after they elected to stay in their home rather than be relocated. Medha Patkar, the leader of the Save Narmada movement, underwent several highly publicized hunger strikes in more than two decades of protests against the project. As late as 2006, the project continued to draw bitter criticism: "With all its issues of federal and state permissions, environmental approvals, and equitable rehabilitation of the inhabitants, [it] could have been a showpiece for foreign investors. Instead, it's a disgrace: a sorry tale of a 20-year delay, cost overruns, state negligence, and bitter local resistance."[59]

Current Situation

POPULATION GROWTH

India's population surge did not begin until well into the 20th century. Until 1920, birthrates and death rates were high, but they were largely in balance. Women had many children, but high infant mortality rates and high mortality rates due to disease, epidemics, and famine kept growth from skyrocketing. After 1920, annual death rates began to fall and birthrates began to rise. Fewer people died from famine and disease, and mass inoculations reduced infant mortality rates. From 1921 to 1931, population increased 10 percent, and after that the discrepancies between birth- and death rates began to accumulate. Between 1961 and 1971, the population increased 24.8 percent, and continued at a similar rate through the end of the century. Taking into consideration the fact that population growth is exponential, a 24.8 percent increase of a population of 500 million people results in 124 million people, but a population increase of 24.8 percent in a country of 1 billion people is 248 million people—almost the entire population of the United States. These numbers translate into a high population density, both in rural and urban areas. This population density, which is the highest in the world for a country of its size, has had a huge impact on rates of poverty, deforestation, soil erosion, air pollution, and water pollution.

In the near term, India's growth is inevitable despite a fertility rate of 2.73 children per woman, which is not too far above the replacement rate of 2.1 children per woman. This rate has already decreased dramatically, from a high of 6 children just a couple generations ago. Contraceptive use remains low and the government continues to promote family planning programs, although forced sterilization, which was common in the 1970s, is no longer a part of these initiatives. Newer strategies tend to be economic in nature and concentrate on increasing education and employment opportunities—especially for women—with the goal of curtailing population growth by promoting later marriages and smaller families.

PROTECTING INDIA'S WILDLIFE

Biodiversity on the subcontinent is wide ranging. From the Himalayan Mountains in the north to the deserts in the south, the climate ranges from tropical to arid, resulting in numerous ecosystems supporting a wide variety of plant and animal species. Efforts to protect India's wildlife began with the formation of a national park system in 1935 and since then have expanded to include numerous biosphere preserves and hundreds of wildlife sanctuaries. The Ministry of Environment and Forests oversees numerous programs to manage sustainability and development issues from protecting wildlife, managing the national parks, and limiting pollution. However, as with the rest of the world, continued development has endangered a significant portion of India's plant and animal species. Following the Earth Summit in 1992, India recognized the importance of protecting its biodiversity, and in 2003 the government passed the Biodiversity Act to fulfill the goals of the UN Convention on Biodiversity. As part of this effort, the National Biodiversity Authority was established to protect natural resources and ensure that commercial activity of a region's genetic material benefits local communities and eliminates what they call "biopiracy," the process by which companies obtain patents and legal rights over a plant's medicinal properties without compensating the indigenous groups that originally developed that medical knowledge.

Tigers and leopards are two of India's most emblematic species, along with the Indian elephant, the Indian rhinoceros, and Asiatic lions—all of which have been endangered for decades. India passed the Wildlife Protection Act in 1972 to promote conservation and protection of all endangered species. Despite government efforts, nearly all of these animals' populations continue to decline, often because development has isolated populations of certain species to a degree that makes reproduction unviable. Corrupt deals between politicians, game wardens, and local packers have also contributed to the decline of endangered species. By 2007, for example, only 1,300 to 1,500 tigers existed in the Indian wild.[60] The National Board for Wildlife has lobbied for extensive measures to protect wildlife from poachers and habitat destruction, including giving soldiers the authority to arrest and/or shoot tiger poachers.

When it comes to aquatic life, attention is focused on the Ganges River, which has been a site of religious purification for thousands of years. The river is holy in the Hindu faith, worshipped as the goddess Ganga, and stretches more than 1,500 miles from its headwaters in the Himalayas to its watershed in Bangladesh. Hindus believe the waters of the Ganges can heal illness and ensure a safe passage to heaven; thus, it is a destination for millions of people who seek to purify themselves by bathing in and drinking it. For much of recorded history, the Ganges was flushed clean each year by the monsoons and by the river's high natural levels of dissolved oxygen, which helped microorganisms break down waste materials. But several centuries ago when India's forests were cleared for agriculture, the loss of the trees' complex root systems intensified soil erosion in the Ganges basin, which in turn lowered agriculture production.

Population increases further upset the balance of the Ganges's ecosystem. The banks of the river are home to one of the highest population densities in the world—1,000 people per square mile—and the plains surrounding the Ganges are home to about 10 percent of the world's population—some 600 million people.[61] Despite being one of the most polluted waterways in the world, the Ganges receives no government protection.

Of the 1.3 billion liters of sewage, both municipal and industrial, that flows into the Ganges daily, almost none is treated.[62] Human corpses, incompletely cremated in religious ceremonies along the banks, mingle with carcasses of livestock and cows. In the town of Varanasi, a holy site where pilgrims gather to cremate the dead and cleanse themselves in the river, coliform bacteria levels are 100,000 per 100 milliliters; the World Health Organization deems only 10 per 100 milliliters an acceptable level.[63] Algae and phytoplankton clog the water and consume oxygen that is desperately needed for the natural breakdown of waste.

Apart from organic waste, industrial waste in the Ganges includes chemicals such as chromium, hydrochloric acid, acetone, lead, PCBs, mercury, dioxins, and DDT. Additionally, the river receives 6 million tons of fertilizers and 9,000 tons of pesticides per year from agricultural runoff.[64] These chemicals accumulate in fish and work their way up the food chain in a process called biomagnification. When these toxins are ingested by people in sufficient amounts over time, they can cause disease. The human cost of this pollution in India is one death every minute from diarrhea, and skyrocketing rates of dysentery, typhoid, cholera, tapeworm, and hepatitis. In Kolkata, 80 percent of the population suffers at least one bout of amoebic dysentery each year.[65]

Pollution along the Ganges has reduced the biodiversity of the region, further intensifying the cycle of environmental damage. Deforestation has ruined the habitats of the elephants, lions, and tigers along the plains and damaged water ecosystems vital to many endangered species, including otters, turtles, and the Ganges dolphin. In the lower reaches of the river, little aquatic life survives at all. In one study, fish introduced downstream from factories in the state of Bihar lived for only five hours before suffocating.[66] Mangrove forests at the delta—the largest in the world—have been decimated and therefore do not provide their cleansing functions and protection against dangerous floods during the monsoons. In Bangladesh, the watershed of the Ganges, the wetlands have been replaced by landfills. The result has been devastating floods that have killed thousands of people.

ENERGY RESOURCES

As in China, the central conundrum of India's energy situation is that a large majority of its people are impoverished and use few resources, yet the country's economy is growing at a rate that requires unprecedented amounts of energy to sustain. According to some estimates, India will require a capacity of 400,000 megawatts of electricity in order to maintain its current rate of economic growth, but as of 2006 it had only 130,000 megawatts.[67] India has large reserves of coal and natural gas, but little petroleum. More than half its energy needs are met by coal, and about 5 percent of its electricity comes from hydropower. It has proven oil reserves of only 5.6 billion barrels, versus daily oil consumption of 2.45 million barrels. Seventy-five percent of its daily oil supply comes from imports.[68] Additional nuclear power plants, coal-fired power plants, and geothermal plants have been proposed to bridge the gap between growing demand and supply. Additionally, some of India's largest cities, most notably New Delhi, are building mass-transit systems to alleviate urban transportation congestion and reduce foreign oil dependency.

RESOURCES AND POVERTY

Approximately 25 percent of India's population (250,000,000 people) lived below India's poverty line in 2006, representing a sharp drop from 36 percent in the early 1990s. (Although by U.S. standards both figures would be much higher.) Unequal distribution of scarce resources has perpetuated an underclass in India, in which many millions of people spend most of their time and money obtaining water and food. According to some government officials, the country's severe water shortage could be solved with simple changes to existing policy, increased rainwater harvesting, and updates to a crumbling infrastructure that squanders 200 million gallons of water each day. The country also needs to regulate its millions of wells in order to curtail the practice of "competitive deepening," in which farmers dig ever-deeper wells to divert water from their neighbors.

Arable land is a healthy 49 percent, but agricultural productivity in India is poor and suffers from damaging monsoons. The Green Revolution of the 1960s, in which high-yield hybrid grains were developed that boosted the available food supply to record levels and staved off famine, was enormously helpful in India and led to its food independence. Although the country's food needs were met for the next 30 years, poor policy implementation often led to water pollution, shortages, and misuse.

By 2006, the growth rate of grain production was just 1 percent, not enough to keep pace with the growing population. Wheat was imported from other countries, and some began to foresee that food independence was waning. The falling food growth rate was due to many issues, including shortages of water due to irrigation mismanagement and overuse of pesticides and fertilizers that depleted the soil.[69] International trade will most likely figure prominently in India's future efforts to feed its population.

WATER INFRASTRUCTURE

India's water crisis threatens the health of millions of people every day. According to a 2005 report by the World Bank, infrastructure constructed in the 1960s and 1970s in the wake of the Green Revolution is in danger of being destroyed through neglect and age.[70] Irrigation systems were not adequately maintained after they were built and must now be scrapped or refurbished at great additional cost. In the absence of enforced regulations, rural and urban residents alike have drilled their own wells to tap underground aquifers, resulting in a steep drop in the water table, increased salination, and arsenic poisoning. Lack of clear water allocation rights means that most people believe they have a right to obtain freshwater but are not responsible for cleaning up polluted water. Thus, increasingly polluted water and lack of adequate waste treatment and sanitation facilities have led to disease and death for millions of citizens.

With few rivers and lakes to depend on, groundwater is the backbone of India's water supply system; 70 percent of the country's irrigation depends on groundwater, as does 80 percent of the domestic supply. But once groundwater is depleted, it takes hundreds of years for those aquifers to be replenished; at current usage rates water needs will outstrip groundwater suppiy by 2020. Another danger is that overdrilling of groundwater can lead to contamination by arsenic and other dangerous substances. Between 35 and 77 million people in West Bengal and neighboring Bangladesh drink water contaminated with arsenic, which can cause lesions, spontaneous abortions, respiratory difficulties, and gastrointestinal problems.[71]

The World Bank's findings have been criticized by some members of India's non-government organizations (NGOs) as a ploy to promote privatization of water sources, something that a majority of citizens oppose (although privately run water systems are common throughout the developed world). A member of India's Research Foundation for Science, Technology and Ecology protested the World Bank report by saying that the country's water is the property of individual communities and should not be run by a central institution.[72] Nevertheless, that has not stopped the World Bank from funding large engineering projects, such as the Narmada Dams, that many fear will create as many new problems as they solve, while doing little to get water into the hands of those who need it most.[73]

The Delhi Jal Board (DJB), the organization that governs Delhi's water, is capable of supplying 650 million gallons of water per day to the city's 16 million residents, but that falls short of demand by as much as 400 million gallons. Much of the water is lost before it reaches the consumer because of leaks in the infrastructure or because it is stolen through illegal connections to the system.[74] A major improvement to the country's water problem would be to harvest more rainwater. According to the World Bank, India's dams can store only 200 cubic meters of water per person, versus 1,000 cubic meters per person for dams in China and Mexico. Harvesting rainwater would be much more cost effective than building expensive dams.

Water shortages are already affecting grain production. In 2006, India imported grain for the first time in six years due to crop shortages caused by drought, water shortages, and bad public policy, reversing a trend of record grain surpluses. Growth in grain production, the shining pride of the Green Revolution, which doubled in India from 1966 to 1990, has started to diminish as the fertilizers, pesticides, and unsustainable levels of irrigation begin to take their toll on the soil.

In 2006, India's Prime Minister Manmohan Singh called for another Green Revolution, but this time, instead of food security, the goal was harvesting lucrative crops for export and importing grain that can be grown more efficiently elsewhere.[75]

SANITATION INFRASTRUCTURE

Apart from an insufficient water infrastructure, India also suffers from a lack of sanitation infrastructure. Less than 5 percent of the country's garbage is landfilled or incinerated properly.[76] Asian companies are seeking to invest in building wastewater treatment plants and landfills to alleviate the problem, but corruption has either halted or hindered many efforts. In 2003, the Indian government adopted the first laws concerning waste treatment when the Supreme Court ruled that cities with populations over 100,000 must provide garbage collection. Yet without the necessary infrastructure, these rules are hard to enforce. Although garbage collection is mandated, disposal is not. The result is a system in which garbage is often removed from the streets and dumped on land adjacent to drinking water supplies.[77]

India's social caste system presents a significant hurdle in solving its garbage problem. Traditionally, only people of the lowest caste have been allowed to pick up garbage, a factor that has greatly complicated the dialogue on how to get the job done efficiently. The French waste management company Veolia has implemented employee policies designed to change that status quo. Beginning in Chennai in 2000, it hired, vaccinated, and gave uniforms to its employees, who were trained in Western business practices of customer service and allowed to profit individually by taking the initiative to sort recyclables from their garbage collection.[78]

Counterstrategies

WATER FOR THE PEOPLE

India's Minister of Water Resources in 2005, Shri Priyaranjan Dasmunsi, advocated rainwater harvesting as a major part of the country's solution to the water crisis. He argued that revitalizing the crumbling infrastructure would be a much more cost-effective strategy than erecting new and costly dams or desalination plants.[79] Also, instituting agricultural practices that use less water and increase productivity would ease the situation. Achieving these goals would require a water-pricing structure that generates revenue to fund improvements. Putting a more accurate price on water would also increase efficiency; people would use only what they needed if they had to pay a fair market price for it. For example, many municipal water systems are heavily subsidized in an effort to bring water to poor people at a low price. But poor people almost never have access to the municipal water system and thus receive none of the water intended for them. Conversely, those who do have access to the water system pay less than 10 percent of what it costs to bring the water into their homes.[80] Additionally, the Ministry of Water Resources recognizes the need to address the three main causes of water pollution: point-source pollution from industrial factories, agricultural runoff, and municipal sewage.

MICROLOANS TO ERASE POVERTY

Microloans are loans of a few hundred dollars, often given to a group of women who intend to use the money to start a business. They may buy an animal or raw materials to make baskets or pottery. In India, microloans create economic opportunities for women, who traditionally have not had such avenues open to them. By giving them the keys to economic freedom, the hope is that they will lift themselves and their families out of poverty, becoming an economic entity in the process. Microfinance lenders require the women to make payments on their loans every week, and a successful track record allows them to borrow more money to expand their enterprise. Microloans are generally given by private banks created for the sole purpose of instituting microcredit; in India one of the largest of these operations is Spandana. Spandana employs 2,000 people and has issued loans to more than 800,000 women.[81]

THE SECOND GREEN REVOLUTION

Following China's lead, in 2006 India's prime minister Manmohan Singh called for a second Green Revolution that would transform the country's agriculture focus from food independence (i.e., harvesting enough grain to feed the entire population) to creating an industry of high-priced fruits and vegetables for export to the world market. The new crops would be exported for a higher price than the cost of importing necessary staples.[82] Singh believes the country has attained permanent food independence and that a return to imports in 2006 was only a temporary glitch caused by artificial price hikes. But some critics believe Singh's plan is doomed by insufficient government subsidies for new technology, equipment, and training for farmers. In addition, the first Green Revolution led to soil contamination, overuse of fertilizers and pesticides, reliance on nonnative and water-intensive crops, and bad irrigation practices that lowered the water table—factors that will continue to have an impact on future agriculture.

MASS TRANSPORTATION

When it comes to air pollution, India followed the lead of other nations in eliminating leaded fuels for automobiles in an effort to reduce air pollution. Lead poisoning from automobile emissions is widely known to lower children's IQs, cause learning disabilities, and impair growth. No amount of lead ingestion is safe; it accumulates in the environment and in the body. While many nations outlawed leaded fuel in favor of unleaded fuel beginning in the 1980s, India mandated such a change only by the year 2000.

In addition, the country began to expand its public transportation system to provide an alternative means of transportation. India has long boasted an extensive railway, one of the world's busiest mass transit systems. Inaugurated by the British in 1853, India's rail system now spans over 39,000 miles and carries 5 billion passengers annually. However, the system has been more useful for long-distance travel than for interurban transport, and it has been plagued in recent years by inefficiency and aging infrastructure. New Delhi, a city of 14 million people, addressed the issue by opening the country's second Mass Rapid Transit System (MRTS) in 2002. Phase one of the Delhi Metro, as it is known, encompasses 40 miles of underground, ground-level, and elevated track on three separate lines. Unlike India's older trains, each metro is air-conditioned and each station is policed by security personnel and cameras. Trains run at 2–3-minute intervals and hold approximately 600 passengers each. Phase two is scheduled to be completed in 2010 and will include 75 additional miles of track and is projected to carry 2.2 million passengers a day. With residents already accustomed to trains and happy to have an alternative to crowded buses, the metro was an instant success. Other cities, including Bangalore and Mumbai, both of which have high populations of technology workers who need reliable transportation to their jobs, are considering building similar systems.

NUCLEAR POWER

India's 16 nuclear power plants are aging, outdated, and lacking sufficient fuel. The government is planning to build seven new nuclear power plants to help mitigate its oil dependency. In 2006, the United States and India Nuclear Cooperation Act paved the way for the development of more nuclear power in India. Under this agreement, the United States will supply the country with technology for nuclear power plants in exchange for implementing safety procedures in their nuclear arms program. The initiative will most likely be spearheaded by multinational U.S.-based companies,[83] but significant issues regarding India's nuclear weapons testing and reprocessing of spent fuel may jeopardize the agreement.

POWER TO ALL BY 2012

About 400 million rural Indians have insufficient electricity or none at all.[84] To solve this problem, the government launched the "Power to All by 2012" initiative, which promoted private, corporate, and government investment in nontraditional energy sources, including biofuels and waste-to-energy technologies. Solar and wind power are especially attractive for rural areas because they do not require sophisticated infrastructure or carbon-emitting fossil fuels. India formed the Ministry of New and Renewable Energy to promote wind and solar power initiatives. Additionally, the Electricity Act of 2003 states that renewable energy sources must provide a certain percentage of a utility's electricity.

GERMANY

Germany was home to 82.4 million people in 2006, making it the second most populous nation in Europe. Its robust industrial economy is the largest in Europe, the sixth largest in the world, and fueled by substantial reserves of coal and natural gas and a highly educated population. Unique to the country was its resilience following devastation in World War II, particularly in West Germany after its division from East Germany in 1949 as the cold war got under way. Following reunification in 1990, Germany faced another difficult economic transition as it absorbed the languishing industrial infrastructure of East Germany and quickly emerged as a leading force in the formation of the European Union.

Because of its high standard of living, Germany has a large ecological footprint, estimated at 4.59 global hectares per person in 2002; roughly equivalent to Japan but less than half the size of the U.S. footprint.[85] Greenhouse gas emissions per capita have been declining in recent years, and in 2004 they stood at 10.5 metric tons of carbon dioxide per person, just a little more than half the U.S. per capita emissions.[86] Germany's advantages include high levels of technology, existing infrastructure, wealth, education, productivity, political activity, and citizen awareness of environmental issues, all of which give the country a unique position when it comes to sustainable development. Unlike in developing nations, population growth has stalled in Germany; instead of having to deal with issues of educating and feeding an ever growing number of citizens, Germany faces the opposite problem of an increasingly elderly population supported by a shrinking workforce.

History

As a sovereign nation, Germany has a short history. The Second German Empire began with unification in 1871 and was replaced by the Weimar Republic following World War I (1914–18). At the end of World War II (1939–45), Germany was divided into the Federal Republic of Germany (West Germany) and the Soviet-controlled German Democratic Republic (East Germany). Following the collapse of the Soviet Union, Germany was reunified in 1990. The country underwent a period of economic adjustment as the vibrant West German economy absorbed the stagnant East German economy and attempted to modernize East Germany's crumbling, inefficient, highly polluted industrial landscape. As many as 1.5 million former East Germans streamed into the western part of the country, and other people left the northern regions of the country for the more prosperous southern regions, a process sometimes called demographic theft.

Power plants in East Germany during the 1970s and 1980s burned lignite coal, which contains a high amount of ash and emits more carbon dioxide than bituminous coal, having a severe impact on the region's air quality and leading to acid rain that defoliated trees and acidified the soil. West Germany, for its part, had a thriving automotive industry that contributed to the region's air pollution. As late as 1996, only 43 percent of the country's forests were considered healthy, and, despite an overall improvement in air quality by 2002, 21 percent of Germany's forests continued to suffer defoliation.[87]

In the early 1980s, a number of issues came to the fore in Germany and around the world that led to the organization of a political party intended to address them. These included acid rain, the Chernobyl nuclear reactor meltdown (1986), the discovery of the hole in the ozone layer (beginning in the mid-1970s), and a growing concern over global climate change. In Germany, it was the Green Party who raised public awareness of these issues through grassroots campaigning and advocacy for environmentally and socially responsible government policy. The Greens, as they are known, spread to many other countries, but gained a foothold in Germany with a platform based on environmental responsibility and liberal views on abortion, immigration, drug use, antimilitarism, and gay rights.

Under Germany's system of government, in which all parties who receive at least 5 percent of the electoral vote gain a proportionate number of seats in parliament, the Greens won their first electoral seats in 1983. They have been a legitimate voice in German politics ever since. The country's constitution was amended in 1994 to mandate sustainable development: "Mindful also of its responsibility toward future generations, the state shall protect the natural bases of life by legislation and, in accordance with law and justice, by executive and judicial action, all within the framework of the constitutional order."[88] By 1998, the Green Party held 47 seats in parliament and ruled in a joint coalition with the Social Democrats. In 2000, the Greens gained even more seats and were instrumental in passing the Nuclear Exit Law, which called for the complete phasing out of nuclear power by 2020. Within the European Union, which itself grew out of the European Coal and Steel Community that was formed in 1951 for the purpose of regulating energy policy, Germany has pushed for a reduction of greenhouse gases and advocated sustainable development. The European Union is a world leader when it comes to research and development of renewable energy sources; EU Commission president José Manuel Barroso has called for a "post-industrial revolution," a transition to a "low-carbon economy," and a stronger treaty to supersede the Kyoto Protocol.[89]

Current Situation

POPULATION DECLINE

Although Germany boasts the largest economy in Europe, the country's demographic window has closed and its large working-age population is a relic of the past. As of 2006, the country's population stood at 82.4 million, with a median age of 42 years (compared to 36.6 in the United States, 33.2 in China, 28.6 in Brazil, and 24.9 in India). Germany was one of the first countries in the modern world to attain negative population growth: -0.03 percent in 2007. Because of plunging fertility rates (1.4 children per woman—among the lowest in the industrialized world), high death rates from an aging population, and an immigration slowdown, the Federal Statistical Office in Germany predicts the population of the country will fall below 74 million by 2050. Of those 74 million, 10 million will be more than 80 years old, making the country one of the first forced to deal with the phenomenon of global aging. Germany's youth ratio will be approximately 33 people under the age of 20 for every 100 people of working age, and the old-age ratio will be 60 retired people for every 100 people of working age. That means every working person will support 1.93 people.[90] The good news is that Germany enjoys the fifth largest economy in the world, widespread affluence, universal literacy, and an excellent education system.

The most visible result of this population decline is an internal migration away from economically stagnant regions. As working-age people move to the southern and western parts of Germany where jobs are plentiful and living standards high, the other parts of the country become increasingly aged and underserved by working people. Cities in the former East Germany in particular have faced a glut of housing, closed schools, and rising municipal fees. In some cases, population decline has been so pervasive that formerly urban areas have become so depopulated that wildlife has returned, including rare species of lynx and wolves.[91]

NATURAL RESOURCES

Germany is one of the world's major consumers of coal, using more than any other country except China, the United States, India, and Russia. More than 50 percent of the country's electricity was generated by coal in 2002. Such a heavy reliance on coal translates into high levels of carbon dioxide emissions. In 2004, Germany emitted 327.44 million metric tons of carbon dioxide from consumption of coal alone, though this figure is substantially less than the 407.26 million metric tons reported in 1991 due to the many inefficient East German factories that were taken off-line after reunification. Including other forms of fuel, Germany emitted a total of 862.2 million metric tons of carbon dioxide in 2004, which makes it the sixth largest carbon polluter in the world.

Germany imports 90 percent of its oil and 75 percent of its natural gas. It is the world's fifth largest consumer of oil, but it consumes only 3.3 percent of the world's annual petroleum supply.[92] When it comes to its fossil fuel resources, Germany has very little oil of its own but significant natural gas reserves and is the world's leading producer of biodiesel. Germany is also the world's leading producer of lignite, or brown coal, and the seventh largest coal producer overall. Despite this, demand outstrips supply and Germany imports 19 percent of its annual coal supply. As of the turn of the 21st century, nuclear power accounted for 30 percent of the country's electricity, but in 2000 the government planned to phase out nuclear power by limiting the operational lifetime of a plant to 32 years, placing the last power plant shutdown around 2020. The move was backed by the Green Party and public opinion, which had come to regard nuclear power as a risky enterprise after the Chernobyl disaster. Despite the agreement, utility companies have continued to lobby to extend plant life to 40 years, and even 60 in some cases, citing the country's increasing energy demands. Concurrently, awareness over greenhouse gas emissions and global warming has caused the public to reconsider nuclear power as a clean and plentiful source of energy.[93] As the debate continues, the first nuclear power plants have been decommissioned.

PHARMACEUTICALS IN THE WATER SUPPLY

In the late 1980s, German scientists found clofibric, a drug used to treat high cholesterol, in the groundwater near a water treatment plant.[94] Further studies turned up many other substances, including phenazone, fenofibrate, ibuprofen, hormones, chemotherapy drugs, and antibiotics. Officials for Germany's Institute for Water Research and Water Technology warned that these substances could accumulate undetected in marine life until the effects are impossible to reverse and are erroneously attributed to evolution or ecological change.[95] This new kind of pollution struck Germany primarily because of its universal health care system and high standard of living. Enough people consume these substances that they have leached into groundwater via excretion. Water treatment plants do not remove them, and thus they enter the water cycle with unknown effects on plants, animals, and people. Similar findings have been discovered in England and the United States. Painkillers, antidepressants, antibiotics, hormones, and personal care products are the major culprits. No major solution has been enacted yet, but many municipalities collect discarded or expired drugs at household hazardous waste collection sites or have established pharmaceutical take-back locations at drug stores and police stations.

Counterstrategies

LEADING THE EUROPEAN UNION IN RENEWABLE ENERGY RESOURCES

Germany's lack of oil reserves has translated into perennially high energy prices, so renewables are widely seen as a cost-effective way to reduce dependency on foreign oil. Farmers have been encouraged to produce rapeseed and maize to convert into biofuels, an initiative that may drive down energy prices. Two million tons of biodiesel fuel were produced in 2005. The German government passed the Renewable Energy Act in 2000, which requires renewable resources to generate twice as much electricity in 2010 as they did in 2000. As of 2006, most of the country's renewable energy came from hydropower, but plans to expand the country's wind power supply with offshore wind farms in the North Sea were in the works. By 2030, as long as technical innovations keep pace, as much as 25 percent of the country's electricity may be provided by wind power,[96] and, by 2050, 50 percent of its total energy may come from renewable resources.

As with other EU countries, Germany has ambitious goals to reduce emissions of greenhouse gases as part of its climate protection program. Between 2008 and 2012, its stated goal is to reduce the six main greenhouse gases (carbon dioxide, methane, nitrous oxide, hydrofluorocarbons, perfluorocarbons, and sulfur hexafluoride) by 21 percent.

SUSTAINABLE AGRICULTURE

Germany has long been cognizant of the need to monitor agriculture to insure its continued success. The EU regulates agriculture within all member countries, including Germany, and the Common Agricultural Policy (CAP) was amended in 2003 to eliminate ecologically unsound practices by limiting subsidies to large farms in favor of promoting smaller farms and organic farms. Germany's Plant Protection Act of 1998 regulates commerce of agricultural products by taking into consideration crop tolerance and the crop's effect on human and animal health, water, and natural balance. The Act includes a pest management component as well. Additionally, the Closed Substance Cycle and Waste Management Act of 1994 provides for the reuse of sewage and other waste products as fertilizer, but also accounts for soil protection by monitoring waste for harmful pollutants.[97]

ENERGY CONSERVATION AND EMISSIONS TECHNOLOGY

Germany is building the world's first zero carbon emissions power plant in a town south of Berlin. The plant is scheduled to go online in 2008, provide up to 30 megawatts of power, and burn coal in a closed environment of pure oxygen instead of air, resulting in cleaner emissions that will be easier to store underground than to emit into the atmosphere. This "oxyfuel" technology is being developed by the Swedish company Vattenfall, which states that strict European Union guidelines make carbon sequestration more affordable than paying carbon dioxide emissions fees mandated under cap-and-trade laws.[98]

WASTE MANAGEMENT

Avoidance, recycling, and environmentally sound disposal is Germany's official credo when it comes to solid waste management. Toward this end, the government passed the Act for Promoting Closed Substance Cycle Waste Management and Ensuring Environmentally Compatible Waste Disposal in 1996. Under this "polluter-pays" system, manufacturers are required to take back packaging for reuse or recycling, with the ultimate goal of recycling 72 percent of glass and aluminum and 64 percent of paper and plastic. These goals have been reached through the "green dot" recovery system, whereby manufacturers pay a licensing fee to Duales System Deutschland (DSD), the company that runs the green dot program, so they can put the green dot on their packaging. When consumers are ready to dispose of green dot packaging, they place it in a designated recycling bin and DSD arranges for pickup and recycling of the items. The program has been so successful that it has been adopted by 21 other EU countries, but some manufacturers criticize it for charging high fees, and even DSD officials make clear that "the green dot trademark is not an environmental symbol, it is a financial symbol. It indicates that payment has been made already for the recycling of the packaging displaying the mark."[99]

Even more ambitious is Germany's 2005 Waste Storage Ordinance, which the government established to fulfill the 1999 EU Landfill Directive. The program bans landfilling of biodegradable waste, supports waste-to-energy systems, and calls for the ultimate closure of all landfills. Even before Germany enacted the program, it had reduced greenhouse gas emissions from landfills from 21 million tons to 11 million tons annually between 1990 and 2003. It is expected to fall to 8 million tons by 2012.[100]

ECO-TAX

In an effort to gain wide compliance with Germany's ambitious energy programs, the government established the Eco-Tax in 1999 to promote conservation, efficiency, and renewable resources. Under the program, taxes were raised on gasoline, natural gas, and electricity, and low-interest loans were given to citizens who installed solar panels on their homes. A host of other energy-saving programs have been enacted, all with an eye toward reducing greenhouse gas emissions and promoting renewable energy resources to an even greater degree than EU or Kyoto Protocol guidelines demand.

HYDROGEN VEHICLES

Germany is home to pioneering automaker BMW, which in 2007 became the first company to build and lease hydrogen-powered vehicles to select consumers. The fleet of 100 7-series sedans looked and performed largely like their conventional counterparts, but they weighed 5,300 pounds and emitted only water vapor. Unlike the fuel-cell vehicles in development in the United States, the hydrogen-powered BMW is based on an internal combustion engine that allows it to reach 100 kph in 9.5 seconds, just a bit slower than BMW's Mini Cooper, and travel 200 kilometers before refueling. The internal combustion engine also allows the vehicle to run on gasoline as a backup, a handy option in a marketplace almost completely devoid of hydrogen refueling stations. Despite the progress made by BMW and the good reviews the hydrogen car received from the automotive sector, BMW CEO Norbert Reithofer echoed other experts when he told reporters that a commercially feasible hydrogen vehicle is still 25 years away.[101]

BRAZIL

With more than 186 million people, Brazil is the fifth most populous nation in the world and the largest country in terms of land size (it is slightly smaller than the United States in land area) and population in South America. Geographically, it encompasses much of the Amazon rain forest—the world's largest—thus making Brazil home to one of the most biologically diverse regions in the world, home to a staggering number of plants and animals found nowhere else on the planet. Many of the rain forest's fragile biospheres are threatened because of widespread deforestation, both legal and illegal, which not only causes the extinction of many plant and animal species but also limits the Earth's ability to absorb carbon dioxide. Slash-and-burn deforestation techniques further emit millions of tons of carbon dioxide into the atmosphere, exacerbating the greenhouse effect and climate change. Pressure from the international community to stem this destruction has met with mixed results.

When it comes to other natural resources, Brazil is a leading producer of gold, platinum, tin, precious gemstones, and uranium, making mining a thriving industry. These mines often produce a significant amount of mercury contamination in surrounding areas and result in environmental degradation from leaching and other processes. Brazil's coastal region contains a significant amount of oil and yet Brazil is a world leader in switching its automobiles from petroleum-based fuel to alcohol- (ethanol-) based fuel.

Two of the world's largest cities—megacities both—are in Brazil. The Greater São Paulo area, with more than 22 million residents, is the world's second largest metropolitan area and boasts a sizable middle class as well as one of the world's largest sprawling slums. Rio de Janeiro is the country's second largest city, with a metropolitan population of around 12 million. Brazil enjoys the ninth largest economy in the world, but also suffers endemic rural poverty in the north, where subsistence farmers illegally clear thousands of acres of rain forest each year to make way for agriculture and cattle grazing. The urban slums create pollution from carbon emissions and lack of infrastructure, and rural poverty aggravates deforestation and dwindling biodiversity. Brazil's ecological footprint in 2003 was 2.2 global hectares per person, down from previous levels, according to the *Living Planet Report 2006.* This statistic reflects the country's use of hydropower and ethanol among urban and wealthy citizens, as well as the low standard of living for many rural residents who lack modern conveniences. Likewise, Brazil's per capita carbon emissions are quite low by world standards; only .56 million metric tons per person per year. Brazil consumes 2.2 percent of the world's total energy, but emits only 1.5 percent of the world's carbon.

History

Brazil is many countries in one. The southern part of the country is the most urban and contains most of the wealth. However, this wealth is highly concentrated among a small class of elites, leaving millions languishing in sprawling slums. For example, the income disparity has led São Paulo's wealthy to segregate themselves into highly fortified neighborhoods, surround themselves with armed guards, and in some instances travel via helicopter in order to escape gridlocked traffic and protect themselves from surging rates of kidnapping and murder—a situation some call "the price of social inequity."[102] The poorest 10 percent of Brazil's population controls just 1 percent of the wealth, whereas the richest 10 percent control 50 percent of the wealth.[103]

In the northern part of the country, where the Amazon Basin is located, the rural poor have higher birth- and mortality rates than their southern counterparts. A depressed economy and lack of industry in these areas have pushed villagers into the rain forest, which they then clear-cut and turn into cattle-grazing land for large international corporations. Brazil is today the world's largest exporter of beef, coffee, orange juice, and sugar, and the second largest exporter of soybeans. Both sugar and soybeans have become a crucial part of the country's economy, and both are harvested primarily in former rain forest areas. The modern-day land grab in Brazil has attracted both speculators from the south and international corporations; individuals can accumulate farms averaging 20,000 to 30,000 acres at prices ranging from \$60 an acre in 1998 to \$700 an acre in 2005—just a fraction of what similar land would cost in the United States.[104] Sweetening the deal is that underpriced land is paired with high profit margins on nearly all crops. With so much revenue at stake, the situation has become violent. Property rights are frequently disputed and attempts to enact land reform have resulted in murder. Unscrupulous farm owners lure impoverished workers to remote regions with the promise of earning \$3 to \$4 per day, but once there they are forced at gunpoint to work seven days a week for no pay, receiving only one meal a day.[105] In 2004, the Brazilian government told UN officials that 25,000 Brazilians work under "conditions analogous to slavery," though other officials place the number closer to 50,000.[106]

Prior to the arrival of European explorers in 1500, the Amazon Basin was home to an estimated 3 to 5 million Indians who had lived in the region for up to 10 millennia. Many of these tribes were destroyed on first contact with the Europeans because their immune systems were not equipped to fight off the explorers' germs. By the end of the 20th century, the native population of the Amazon had declined to about 150,000 to 200,000. When these tribes died out, much of their knowledge of how to live within the rain forest ecosystem died with them. The Portuguese colonized Brazil for the next 300 years, importing African slaves to the area in order to harvest and export brazilwood, sugarcane, coffee, and gold. Brazil gained independence from Portugal in 1822.

In 1839, American inventor Charles Goodyear (1800–60) developed the process of rubber vulcanization, which vastly increased rubber's usefulness in a wide variety of industrial products, most notably tires. Goodyear's discovery led to a rubber boom in the Amazon region, well known for its rubber trees. The area was overrun with entrepreneurs who hired locals to tap the rubber from the trees. The entrepreneurs got rich; the rubber tappers did not. When the British secretly exported rubber seeds to Asia and began to grow a more disease-resistant and higher-yielding variety on its colonial plantations, Brazil's rubber industry went bust in 1910.

Clear-cutting in the rain forest intensified following the construction of the Transamazonian Highway, a 3,000-mile, east-west corridor that made logging and agriculture widely accessible in formerly inaccessible regions. Opened in 1972, the highway was initially planned to run more than 5,000 miles all the way to Peru and Ecuador, making the southern half of the country accessible to rural northerners. But budget difficulties curtailed further expansion and paving after the 1970s. The highway now runs through the states of Pará and Amazonas and is home to thousands of landless peasants who came to the area in the 1970s when the government promised them economic assistance as part of its plan for land reform in the area. Instead, the alternately muddy and dusty highway is mainly a route for loggers, and the region it was meant to open up remains largely inaccessible.

URBAN PLANNING: BRASÍLIA AND CURITIBA

When it comes to Brazil's urban areas, the megacities of São Paulo and Rio de Janiero, with their sprawling slums and rampant growth, are emblematic of the country's vibrant, sometimes chaotic culture. However, Brazil has long been a world leader in urban planning. In 1956, when the government decided to relocate the nation's capital to a more central location, Lúcio Costa was named the principal urban planner of the new city—named Brasília—to be located in southcentral Brazil, and Oscar Niemeyer was named the principal architect. They carved a completely new city out of empty land in the space of 41 months using the 1933 Athens Charter as their guide. The Athens Charter was a landmark document of urban planning authored by the Swiss architect and visionary Le Corbusier, whose notion of "The Functional City" described campuslike green spaces dotted with office buildings and housing, all with an eye toward eliminating the overcrowding and social problem of modern cities. Costa plotted Brasília's streets and buildings in a grid pattern that resembled the shape of an airplane, and Niemeyer designed fluid, white modern buildings that gave the city a coherent look and feel. It officially became the capital of Brazil in 1960 with an inaugural population of 140,000. By 2006, the population had risen to 2.4 million, making it one of Brazil's consistently fastest-growing cities. Much of its original architecture and layout have remained intact, and newer buildings and civil engineering projects (such as the Juscelino Kubitschek Bridge) have attracted world-renowned architects and won major design awards. Brasília is the only modern city named a World Heritage Site by UNESCO, but critics of Le Corbusier have long complained that the campuslike city lacks the density of buildings necessary to create a vibrant social community. They also say that its homogenous architecture renders it sterile—not to mention the fact that its geographical isolation leaves it impervious to the influence and politics of the coastal areas.

Brazil has also shown that urban planning concepts can be used to retrofit existing cities in order to facilitate sustainable development. Curitiba is a city in the southern region of Brazil with a metropolitan area of more than 3 million people. The first attempt to manage the city's growth came in the 1940s when French architect Donat-Alfred Agache submitted the first formal city plan to manage Curitiba's growth at the request of Brazil's governing regime, which wanted to industrialize Brazil quickly. Many of his recommendations proved too expensive to implement, but others were embraced. By 1960, Curitiba's population had risen to 430,000, and new proposals were initiated to help the fast-growing city alleviate congestion and limit air pollution. Stringent development guidelines were drawn up that built on Agache's plan by implementing mass transit improvements, preserving historical areas, and instituting a pedestrian-friendly zone in the central city. This became the new "Curitiba Master Plan," which included provisions to establish a department of urban planning and ordinances relegating industry to the outskirts of the city. By 1992, the population had grown to 1.4 million, and

Curitiba hosted the World Cities Forum to demonstrate its urban planning principles in action, which included a highly efficient bus system that relied on huge buses that could carry up to 270 passengers and high-speed bus stops that facilitated movement through specially designed tube stations. As a result of smart city planning, the population of the area doubled after 1974, automobile use declined by 30 percent, and air quality was much higher than in Brazil's other cities of comparable size.[107]

Current Situation

POPULATION: URBAN AND RURAL

Brazil's population was 186 million in 2006 and growing at a rate of 1.04 percent. It is estimated to reach approximately 246 million by 2035. Yet Brazil has already reached a below-replacement fertility rate of 1.91 children born per woman, representing a huge decrease since 1950 when it was 6.2 children per woman. This decline is due to several factors, including an increase of women in the labor force, higher education levels, and increased urbanization—all factors that correlate with lower fertility rates. However, disparities exist between the rural north and the urban south, with the north still experiencing fertility rates of around 5 children per woman. Ultimately, Brazil will be faced with an aging population, as are Europe and China, as low fertility rates are coupled with increased life expectancy. The rural-to-urban migration is expected to continue, with dire consequences for the rural elderly left behind when their children migrate to the cities.

ENERGY RESOURCES

Like all other countries discussed in this book, Brazil consumes more energy than it produces, making it a net energy importer. It is the 10th largest energy consumer in the world, and both consumption and production of oil, natural gas, and coal are expected to continue rising in the coming years. The country's oil reserves are significant, about 11 billion barrels, most of which are located and recovered offshore. In 2006, it produced 2.1 million barrels per day and consumed slightly more than that. However, as oil production continues to increase, Brazil expects to become a net exporter of oil within several years.

Although Brazil is estimated to have vast natural gas reserves of 11.5 trillion cubic feet, it accounts for only 7 percent of the country's energy consumption. Insufficient infrastructure hinders production and consumption, but new pipelines are in the works that may greatly expand exploration and production.[108] When it comes to coal, Brazil has the largest reserves in Central and South America—around 11.1 billion short tons as of 2003—but its generally high ash and sulfur content make it less suitable for consumption than easily obtained imports. Thus, Brazil imported most of the 23.5 million short tons of coal it consumed in 2004 from the United States and Australia. As part of its efforts to expand its natural resource industries, however, Brazil's goal is to become a net exporter of coal by 2010.[109]

In 2004, Brazil generated 83 percent of its electricity from hydropower.[110] It is also home to the world's largest hydroelectric dam—the Itaipu Power Plant on the Paraná River, operated jointly with neighboring Paraguay—which is capable of generating 12,000 megawatts of electricity. It began operations in 1983 and its final generator went online in 2007; the groundbreaking size and scope of the project garnered it a spot on the American Society of Civil Engineers' list of Seven Wonders of the Modern World.[111] Unlike large hydroelectric projects in other countries, Itaipu has not been the target of widespread protests from local populations or environmental activists abroad. Construction of the dam required relocation of 10,000 families in the region, and as a result some of them became active in Brazil's Landless Worker Movement, and there has been some concern over the massive reservoir's effect on the local climate in terms of added humidity, wind patterns, and fog. The reservoir had a huge impact on local plant and animal species, but these effects were moderated by preventive measures that saved roughly 50 percent of the species that would have otherwise been devastated. Both Brazil and Paraguay have invested considerable sums to promote conservation and sustainable development in the area, including creating wildlife preserves, promoting organic farming, and fish production.[112]

The government's aggressive ethanol fuel program has also been quickly and eagerly adopted by motorists.[113] Brazil is the world's leading producer of ethanol (alcohol-based fuel), generating 282,000 barrels a day in 2005, mainly from sugarcane, which is far more efficient than the corn-based ethanol popular in the United States. Brazil's ethanol is used in over 50 percent of the nation's cars, which as flex-fuel vehicles can operate on any mixture of pure ethanol to pure gasoline. New pipelines are planned to carry ethanol from production facilities to São Paulo, with an eye toward expanding ethanol exports worldwide. In 2005, Brazil exported over 7,000 barrels of ethanol a day to the United States, but further growth was hampered by high tariffs.[114] However, ethanol is still a very small percentage of the overall transport fuel in Brazil. Taking ethanol and hydropower into account, 56 percent of Brazil's energy supply comes from renewable resources.[115] This number reflects a conscious decision on the part of Brazil's lawmakers to free the country from foreign oil dependency and the shortages that could result from a breakdown in that system. For the most part, the country has been successful, but a power shortage in 2001 revealed a flaw in the system—a drought reduced hydropower supplies at a time when new natural gas-powered plants were not yet online. By 2006, however, the power shortage began to wane as the country began increasingly importing oil and relying more on natural gas.

OIL SPILLS

Much of Brazil's oil production is controlled by the state-owned company, Petrobras, and most of the oil is derived from offshore rigs. Lax regulations and lack of oversight have resulted in hundreds of massive oil spills over the years, including a 500,000 gallon spill in the Amazon River after a barge sank, a spill of 340,000 gallons of crude oil in Guanabara Bay in 2000 after the world's largest oil platform sank, and a spill of 323,670 gallons of diesel fuel in the Campos Basin in 2001, both the latter near Rio de Janeiro. Oil spills have damaged many ecosystems, including the mangrove wetlands that act as a buffer against wind and waves and prevent erosion, and have threatened the drinking water of millions of people. These spills represent one of the country's major environmental problems. Destruction of wildlife, marine ecosystems, and the fishing industry have earned Petrobras substantial negative publicity.

THE AMAZON RIVER BASIN

The 1.2 billion-acre Amazon Basin covers portions of Brazil, Colombia, Peru, Venezuela, Ecuador, Bolivia, Guyana, Suriname, and French Guiana and is home to the world's largest rain forest. The rain forest offers more biodiversity than any other region in the world, and 60 percent of this rain forest is within Brazil's borders. The Amazon rain forest contains more than 50 percent of the Earth's remaining rain forest ecosystems and is home to millions of plants and animal species, a vast number of which have not yet been classified. A majority of these species exist nowhere else on Earth, and scientists fear that deforestation may obliterate flora and fauna that hold the keys to medical and scientific advances that could benefit humankind.

Since the 1970s, 20 percent of the rain forest has been destroyed, primarily because of bad management, corruption, poverty, and population increases. The Land Statute of 1964, for example, promoted land-grabbing and clearing by stating that ownership of Amazon land could be claimed by anyone who cultivated it for a year and a day. By 1980, new laws were enacted that allowed those squatting on land for five years to obtain legal ownership of it. Such permissive homesteading laws encouraged land-grabbing, speculation, and cattle grazing. Eighty-five percent of land grabbed under these laws, in fact, led to cattle grazing, which is the most unsustainable use of such land, as it depletes the soil and renders it unusable after 10 years.[116] As of 2006, 220,078 square miles—an area the size of France—had been destroyed despite the fact that most logging in the Amazon Basin has been declared illegal. The law, however, is rarely enforced and deforestation remains common due to population growth, economic necessity, and easy access via new roads that lead into previously treacherous terrain. The felled trees from these endeavors are transformed into lumber that generally remains within the country; most of it is diverted to the cities to meet the needs of the urban building boom. Even in areas that are not cleared by humans, rampant wildfires destroy millions of acres each year. Unintentional forest fires account for half of all burned areas of the basin; slash-and-burn techniques used to clear land for cattle grazing account for the other half. These techniques are as damaging as the deforestation itself. They not only prevent carbon dioxide from being absorbed by the vegetation, but they also introduce carbon dioxide into the atmosphere.

The Amazon's dense canopy of vegetation is a natural defense against greenhouse gases and is therefore crucial to the health of the planet. It functions as the planet's lungs by absorbing huge amounts of carbon dioxide from the air and replacing it with oxygen. This system of natural regulation is damaged by deforestation and represents a significant form of unsustainable development. When trees are destroyed, more carbon dioxide remains in the atmosphere, and less oxygen is introduced. After many years of unregulated clearing, President Lula da Silva signed the Public Forest Management Law in 2006, which allows for limited logging under a plan of sustainable development in an effort to balance the Amazon's environmental integrity against Brazil's economic needs. Deforestation is tracked via satellite photographs, which show ever more acres clear-cut each year. Deforestation peaked in 1995, but between 2001 and 2002 it increased again by 40 percent over the 1995 rate, with 9,840 square miles cleared in 2002 alone.[117] Following the implementation of the 2006 law, annual deforestation dropped to 5,420 square miles.[118]

In 2006, the governor of Pará, a state in the heart of the Amazon, signed a declaration to protect over 63,700 square miles, an area the size of England, which brings the total number of protected square miles up to 42 percent of the Amazon. In addition, authorities are developing better ways to monitor land use on privately owned property to make sure it complies with federal regulations. Poverty is one of the main causes of rain forest destruction, and efforts to ensure sustainable development include providing other economic choices to people in the basin areas who previously have had no means of making a living in the region's nonindustrial, agrarian economy other than engaging in slash-and-burn deforestation.

AIR POLLUTION

In Brazil, air pollution is thought of as a problem in the urban areas, particularly in São Paulo. Rapid population growth has outgrown existing infrastructure, resulting in urban smog composed primarily of automobile exhaust. The situation is compounded by low gas prices, insufficient mass transit systems, and old, inefficient buses. The city's air quality is so bad that in 1999 a new law required drivers to leave their cars home one day a week, thereby eliminating hundreds of tons of carbon dioxide into the atmosphere daily. Smaller, older factories frequently contribute to air pollution in more rural areas because they lack state-of-the-art pollution control devices.

Counterstrategies

TOUGHER REGULATIONS

At the turn of the 21st century, Brazil's Ministry of Environment and Natural Resources enacted stringent penalties for individuals and corporations violating environmental regulations. New developments are subject to government approval and require detailed environmental impact studies before construction can begin. Many of these regulations address oil and mining issues and are aimed at preventing oil spills.

BIOMASS FUEL

Brazil is the world leader in biomass fuels for automobiles. Beginning with the OPEC fuel shortages in the 1970s, Brazil adopted measures to wean itself from its dependence on unpredictable foreign oil by granting industries incentives to develop ethanol-powered cars. Ethanol can be produced from grain crops and paper and wood wastes. Because it is derived from recently grown crops, it does not contribute to carbon dioxide emissions as fossil fuels do. However, farmers had trouble generating enough ethanol to meet demand, and the market for ethanol powered cars declined. With the introduction in 2003 of flex-fuel cars, which can run on any combination of ethanol or gasoline, and a buildup of the infrastructure necessary for delivering ethanol to consumers, the market finally recovered. Cheap and plentiful sugarcane is the crop of choice for the ethanol-filled flex-fuel cars, which now command 70 percent of the automobile market.[119] Sugarcane is highly efficient—many times more so than the corn used as biofuel in the United States—and advances in technology have led to further price drops for ethanol and provided it with a strong foothold in Brazil's economy. However, the harvesting of sugarcane could be more energy efficient. As of 2000, most sugarcane was harvested by first burning the leaves and tops of the plant to make cutting easier. This process eliminates a potential source of biomass material and contributes to air pollution. Forgoing the burning step would increase harvesting efficiency, reduce air pollution, and provide more raw materials for energy use.[120] The downside to this approach is that many harvesters would be put out of work; their manual labor would no longer be required for the slash-and-burn process.

The transition to biofuels has had many benefits. Consumers have saved a total of $120 billion between 1976 and 2005 and benefited from the creation of new jobs and reduced vehicle emissions. Some believe it is stemming the mass internal migration from rural to urban areas.[121] The ethanol industry continued to expand through the 2000s and has contemplated exporting ethanol to countries with limited arable land for producing their own ethanol, primarily those in the European Union and Japan.[122] But as the ethanol industry grows, some foresee negative consequences on the horizon. Foremost is the fact that carbon emissions might not be reduced as much as advertised because of the amount of fertilizer required to grow ethanol crops and the energy required to convert those crops into ethanol.

In 2002, the country adopted a program called Proinfa, which aims to stimulate the development of biomass, wind, and small-scale hydropowers by providing incentives for businesses that use them. Wind power is on the rise in Brazil, even though hydroelectric power provides over 83 percent of the country's electricity.

AMAZON

The Amazon is home to more than half of the world's remaining rain forests. It contains 2.5 million insect species, 40,000 plant species, and 2,000 species of birds and mammals.[123] Worldwide education on the importance of the rain forest has increased international pressure on Brazil and its neighboring countries to protect the basin area. Many nonprofit organizations have taken a vested interest in preserving the Amazon rain forest by promoting sustainable development and fair trade and by opposing deforestation, including the World Wildlife Fund, Greenpeace, the Sierra Club, and the Rainforest Action Network. Former vice president Al Gore spoke extensively of the Amazon's role in cleansing carbon dioxide and other greenhouse gases from the Earth's atmosphere in his Academy Award–winning 2006 film, *An Inconvenient Truth.* Apart from the rain forest's importance to the environment, scientists recognize the role it may play in various medical fields as the curative properties of previously unstudied species are discovered. Despite Brazil's moves to limit destruction of the Amazon, overturning a tradition that favored clear-cutting over preservation will take time. In 2005, President Lula da Silva signed legislation creating an 8.15-million-acre reserve and a 1.1-million-acre national park in the state of Pará, following the assassination of Sister Dorothy Stang, an American-turned-Brazilian activist who worked on behalf of landless workers and the environment.[124] Such actions, however, seem reactionary rather than proactive. Much the same way as plunging fertility rates in China have failed to eliminate population growth, laws that limit the rate of deforestation of the Amazon rain forest have failed to eliminate deforestation altogether.

CONCLUSION

A nation's ecological footprint does not tell the entire story of its sustainability. China, India, and Brazil have smaller ecological footprints than do the United States and Germany, but those smaller footprints are due in part to higher levels of poverty. Poverty in itself is an obstacle to sustainable development because it brings in its wake inefficient use of natural resources (especially water), lack of infrastructure and planning, and insufficient access to education and health care. Conversely, the high standards of living in developed nations correlate with high energy consumption, high greenhouse gas emissions, disproportionate access to natural resources, and a level of consumerism that encourages misuse of land and water resources, mineral resources, and energy resources. When pressed, developed nations have shown an ability to find innovative solutions to these issues, but more often than not the political status quo trumps those who advocate for change. In the 21st century, sustainability issues have become global issues, which cannot be addressed wholly or efficiently through national laws. Organizations such as the United Nations and the World Bank, which are funded by member nations, have taken the lead in collecting data, providing education, and brokering treaties to address sustainability issues such as climate change and population growth on global terms.

---

[1] Jared Diamond. *Collapse: How Societies Choose to Fail or Succeed.* New York: Viking, 2004, p. 365.

[2] Miranda A. Schreurs. "Divergent Paths: Environmental Policy in Germany, the United States, and Japan." *Environment,* October 2003, p. 8.

[3] Chris Hails, ed. *Living Planet Report 2006.* WWF, 2006, p. 30.

[4] Sebastian Junger. "Blood Oil." *Vanity Fair,* February 2007, p. 118.

[5] "Blood and Oil; Nigeria." *Economist* (US), March 17, 2007, p. 52.

[6] Hails, p. 28.

[7] Steve Inskeep. "Oil Money Divides Nigeria: Gas Flaring Continues to Plague Nigeria." Broadcast report, National Public Radio, August 25, 2005. Available online. URL: http://www.npr.org/templates/story/story.php?storyId=4797953. Uploaded August 25, 2005.

[8] Ted C. Fishman. *China Inc.: How the Rise of the Next Superpower Challenges America and the World.* New York: Scribner & Sons, 2005, p. 1.

[9] Hails, p. 30.

[10] "China King of Carbon." *Chemistry and Industry,* July 9, 2007, p. 5.

[11] Lester Brown. "Chinese Water Table Torture." *Grist,* October 26, 2001. Available online. URL: http://www.grist.org/news/maindish/2001/10/26/table/. Uploaded October 26, 2001.

[12] Susan Jakes. "China's Water Woes." *Time International.* October 9, 2006, p. 50.

[13] "Expert: Three Gorges Project Expected to Save 50 Mln Tons of Coal Annually." Chinese Government's Official Web Portal. URL: http://english.gov.cn/2006-05/14/content_280021.htm. Uploaded May 14, 2006.

[14] Fishman, p. 109.

[15] Ministry of Foreign Affairs of the People's Republic of China. "People Are Better Off in Three Gorges Resettlement." Available online. URL: www.china-embassy.org/. Uploaded October 23, 2003.

[16] Howard W. French. "Dam Project to Displace Millions More in China." *New York Times,* October 12, 2007.

[17] Damien McElroy. "China Is Furious as Bush Halts UN 'Abortion' Funds." Telegraph.co.uk, March 2, 2002. Available online. URL: http://www.telegraph.co.uk/news/main.jhtml?xml=/news/2002/02/03/wabor03.xml. Updated March 2, 2002.

[18] *CIA World Factbook.* "China." Washington, D.C.: Central Intelligence Agency, 2007. Available online. URL: http://www.cia.gov/cia/publications/factbook/geos/ch.html. Updated March 15, 2007.

[19] "6.3 Brides for Seven Brothers." *Economist* (US), December 19, 1998, p. 56.

[20] Valerie Hudson and Andrea den Boer. *Bare Branches: The Security Implications of Asia's Surplus Male Population.* Boston: MIT Press, 2005, p. 186.

[21] Peter Engardio. "Global Aging: It's Not Just Europe—China and Other Market Economies Are Aging Fast, Too." *Business Week,* January 21, 2005, p. 40.

[22] Susan Jakes. "China's Water Woes." *Time International.* October 9, 2006, p. 50.

[23] Jakes, p. 50.

[24] Diamond, p. 364.

[25] "Hunan: Arsenic in River Poisons Water for 80,000 People." *Asia News,* September 11, 2006. Available online. URL: http://www.asianews.it.index.php?1=en&art=7173#. Uploaded September 11, 2006.

[26] Jakes, p. 50.

[27] Jakes, p. 50.

[28] Chenggang Wang. "China's Environment in the Balance." *The World & I,* October 1999, p. 176.

[29] Wang, p. 176.

[30] Ben Harder. "China's Deserts Expand with Population Growth." *Science News,* March 4, 2006, p. 142.

[31] Jianguo Liu, et al. "Protecting China's Biodiversity." *Science,* May 23, 2003, p. 1,240.

[32] Ed Ayres. "China's Desertification Is Growing Worse." *World Watch,* July–August 2003, p. 10.

[33] Bay Fang. "China's Renewal." *U.S. News & World Report,* June 12, 2006, p. 37.

[34] Douglas Ogden. "We Don't Need More Power; For Each Dollar of Economic Output, China Wastes 11 Times More Energy than Japan." *Newsweek International,* February 16, 2006, p. 1.

[35] Jeff Goodell. *Big Coal: The Dirty Secret Behind America's Energy Future.* Boston: Houghton Mifflin, 2006.

[36] Brian Bremner and Chester Dawson. "Reactors? We'll Take 30 Please." *Business Week,* October 3, 2005, p. 52.

[37] Jim Yardley. "The Yellow River; China's Path to Modernity, Mirrored in a Troubled River." *New York Times,* November 19, 2006.

[38] Fishman, p. 112.

[39] Bremner and Dawson, p. 52.

[40] Fang, p. 37.

[41] James P. Miller. "Asian Pollution Ill Wind for U.S." *Chicago Tribune,* May 3, 2004.

[42] Wang, p. 176.

[43] Diamond, p. 375.

[44] United Nations Department of Economic and Social Affairs. "China: Country Profile. Implementation of Agenda 21. Review of Progress Made Since the United Nations Conference on Environment and Development, 1992." Available online. URL: http://www.un.org/esa/earthsummit/china-cp.htm. Uploaded November 1, 1997.

[45] Fang, p. 37.

[46] Fang, p. 37.

[47] Fang, p. 37.

[48] Fang, p. 37.

[49] Fang, p. 37.

[50] Fang, p. 37.

[51] Ryan Hodum. "China's Need for Wastewater Treatment, Clean Energy Grows." Worldwatch Institute. Available online. URL: http://www.worldwatch.org/node/4889. Uploaded February 1, 2007.

[52] "It's the People, Stupid." *Economist* (US), March 5, 2005, p. 5.

[53] Hails, p. 30.

[54] U.S. Department of Energy. "Country Analysis Briefs: India." Report, Energy Information Administration. Available online. URL: www.eia.doe.gov/emeu/cabs/India/full.html. Updated January, 2007.

[55] Harvey Weiss and Raymond S. Bradley. "What Drives Societal Collapse?" *Science,* Vol. 291, no. 5504, January 26, 2001, p. 609.

[56] Amartya Sen. *Poverty and Famines: An Essay on Entitlement and Deprivation.* New York: Oxford University Press, 1981, p. 215.

[57] Sen, p. 49.

[58] Dionne Bunsha. "Dam Lies: Indian Government Refuses to Stop Drowning Homes and Villages." *New Internationalist,* June 2006, p. 24.

[59] Manjeet Kripalani. "Dam Debate Dents India's Infrastructure." *Business Week Online,* April 21, 2006.

[60] Nita Balla. "India's Tigers in Crisis, Less than Half Estimated." Reuters, August 3, 2007.

[61] Stephen Brichieri-Colombi and Robert W. Bradnock. "Geopolitics, Water and Development in South Asia: Cooperative Development in the Ganges-Brahmaputra Delta." *Geographical Quarterly,* Vol. 169, no. 1, March 2003, p. 43.

[62] Payal Sampat. "The River Ganges' Long Decline." *World Watch,* July–August 1996, p. 24.

[63] Sampat, p. 24.

[64] Sampat, p. 24.

[65] Sampat, p. 24.

[66] Sampat, p. 24.

[67] Manjeet Kripalani. "India's Nuclear Build-Out; The Country Needs Nuclear Energy to Keep Up Its Rapid Expansion," *BusinessWeek,* August 2, 2006. Available online. URL: http://www.businessweek.com/globalbiz/content/aug2006/gb20060802_030265.htm?chan=search. Uploaded August 3, 2006.

[68] U.S. Department of Energy. Country Analysis Briefs: India. Report, Energy Information Administration. Available online: http://www.eia.doe.gov/emeu/cabs/India/Profile.html. Updated January 2007.

[69] Jason Overdorf. "The Green Devolution: India's Population Is Growing Faster than Farm Output, Threatening One of Its Most Prized Achievements." *Newsweek International,* September 4, 2006.

[70] "World Bank Reports on India's Water Economy Faces Flak." *Financial Express,* October 25, 2006.

[71] "A Nation Poisoned; Contamination in Bangladesh." *Economist,* December 22, 2001.

[72] "World Bank Reports on India's Water Economy Faces Flak." *Financial Express,* October 25, 2006.

[73] Barbara Crossette. "Movement Builds to Fight Harmful Projects in Poor Nations." *New York Times,* June 23, 1992.

[74] "Private Worries; The Water Industry in India." *Economist,* August 13, 2005, p. 53.

[75] "Centre Committed to Second Green Revolution: Manmohan." *Financial Express,* March 7, 2005. Available online. URL: http://www.financialexpress.com/fe_full_story.php?content_id=84613. Uploaded March 8, 2005.

[76] S. Dinaker and Michael Freedman. "Dirty Money." *Forbes,* September 18, 2006, p. 128.

[77] Dinaker and Freedman, p. 128.

[78] Dinaker and Freedman, p. 128.

[79] Michael Specter. "The Last Drop: Confronting the Possibility of Global Catastrophe." *New Yorker,* October 23, 2006, p. 60.

[80] Specter, p. 63.

[81] Tyler Cowan. "Microloans May Work, but There Is Dispute in India over Who Will Make Them." *New York Times,* August 10, 2006.

[82] Jason Overdorf. "The Green Devolution: India's Population Is Growing Faster Than Farm Output, Threatening One of Its Most Prized Achievements." *Newsweek International,* September 4, 2006.

[83] Somini Sengupta. "News Analysis; Interests Drive U.S. to Back a Nuclear India." *New York Times,* December 10, 2006.

[84] "Foundations for the Future: Renewable Energy Technologies Are the Driving Force Behind a Recently Launched Programme to Bring Clean, Affordable Energy Services to People Living in Rural India." *Power Engineering International,* August 2006, p. 61.

[85] Schreurs, p. 8.

[86] U.S. Department of Energy. "Country Analysis Briefs: Germany." Report, Energy Information Administration. Available online. URL: www.eia.doe.gove/emeu/cabs/Germany/Oil.html. Updated December 2006.

[87] U.S. Department of Energy. "Germany: Environmental Issues." Report, Energy Information Administration. Available online. URL: http://www.eia.doe.gov/emeu/cabs/germe.html. Updated September 2003.

[88] Basic Law for the Federal Republic of Germany, Article 20a, p. 23. Amended December 2000. Available online. URL: http://www.bundestag.de/htdocs_e/parliament/function/legal/germanbasiclaw.pdf. Accessed April 27, 2007.

[89] "'Low-Carbon Economy' Proposed for Europe." Associated Press, January 10, 2007. Available online. URL: http://www.msnbc.msn.com/id/16560106/. Accessed October 2007.

[90] "Twice as Many 60-year-olds in 2050 than Newborn Children." Press release, Federal Statistical Office of Germany. Available online. URL: http://www.destatis.de/presse/englisch/pm2006/p4640022.htm. Uploaded November 7, 2006.

[91] "Cradle Snatching; German Demography." *Economist* (US), March 18, 2006, p. 55.

[92] U.S. Department of Energy. "Country Analysis Briefs: Germany." Report, Energy Information Administration. Available online. URL: www.eia.doe.gove/emeu/cabs/Germany/Oil.html. Updated December 2006.

[93] "Nuclear Power in Germany." Nuclear Issues Briefing Paper 46, August 2007, Australian Uranium Association. Available online. URL: http://www.uic.com.au/nip46.htm. Accessed October 2007.

[94] "Pharmaceuticals in Our Water Supplies." *Arizona Water Resources,* July–August 2000. Available online. URL: http://cals.arizona.edu/AZWATER/awr/july00/feature1.htm. Accessed April 27, 2007.

[95] Cornelia Dean. "Drugs Are in the Water. Does It Matter?" *New York Times,* April 3, 2007.

[96] "Germany Aims for 25 Percent Windpower by 2030." Environment News Service, January 29, 2002. Available online. URL: www.ens-newswire.com/ens/jan2002/. Accessed April 27, 2007.

[97] Ludger Giesberts. "Germany Introduces a 'Closed Substance Cycle Waste Management and Waste Disposal Act.'" *International Business Lawyer.* November 1996, p. 494.

[98] Eva Berkeman. "Pssst. Want to Get Rid of CO2? Try Burying It." *Fortune International,* October 30, 2006, p. 18.

[99] "Profit Warning: Why Germany's Green Dot Is Selling Up." Let's Recycle Web site. November 25, 2004. Available online. URL: http://www.letsrecycle.com/features/dsd.jsp. Accessed October 2007.

[100] Susanne Rotter. "The Waste Industry Can Maximize Its Potential for Reducing Greenhouse Gas Emissions by Assuring the Quality of Waste-Derived Fuels and Optimizing WTE Technologies." *Waste Management World,* April 2, 2006. Available online. URL: http://www.waste-management-world.com/display_article/273178/123/ARTCL/none/VFEAT/Comment/. Accessed October 2007.

[101] Luca Ciferri. "Hydrogen Is Still Far from Ready." *Automotive News Europe,* January 8, 2007, p. 10.

[102] Anthony Faiola. "Brazil's Elites Fly Above Their Fears." *Washington Post,* June 1, 2002, p. A1.

[103] Faiola, p. A1.

[104] Richard C. Morais. "The Great Brazilian Land Grab." *Forbes,* July 25, 2005. Available online. URL: http://members.forbes.com/global/2005/0725/052.html. Accessed October 2007.

[105] Kevin G. Hall. "Slavery Exists Out of Sight in Brazil." *Knight-Ridder/Tribune Business News,* September 6, 2004.

[106] Kevin G. Hall. "Slavery Exists Out of Sight in Brazil." *Knight-Ridder/Tribune Business News,* September 6, 2004.

[107] Tim Gnatek. "Brazil: Curitiba's Urban Experiment." *PBS Frontline,* December 2003. Available online. URL: www.pbs.org/frontlineworld/fellows/brazil1203/master-plan.html. Accessed April 27, 2007.

[108] U.S. Department of Energy. "Country Analysis Briefs: Brazil." Report, Energy Information Administration. Available online. URL: http://www.eia.doe.gov/emeu/cabs/Brazil/Background.html. Updated August 2006.

[109] U.S. Department of Energy. "Country Analysis Briefs: Brazil." Report, Energy Information Administration. Available online. URL: http://www.eia.doe.gov/emeu/cabs/Brazil/Background.html. Updated August 2006.

[110] U.S. Department of Energy. "Brazil: Electricity." Report, Energy Information Administration. Available online. URL: http://www.eia.doe.gov/emeu/cabs/Brazil/Electricity.html. Updated August 2006.

[111] American Society of Civil Engineers. "Seven Wonders of the Modern World." Available online. URL: www.asce.org/history/sevenwonders.cfm. Accessed April 27, 2007.

[112] "Brazil: Itaipu's Sustainable Development Program." South American Business Information, September 28, 2004.

[113] Howard Geller. *Energy Revolution: Policies for a Sustainable Future.* Washington, D.C.: Island Press, 2003, p. 166.

[114] U.S. Department of Energy. "Brazil: Oil." Report, Energy Information Administration. Available online. URL: http://www.eia.doe.gov/emeu/cabs/Brazil/Oil.html. Updated August 2006.

[115] Geller, p. 167.

[116] Elizabeth A. Crittenden. "Amazon Deforestation and Brazil Land Problems." Report, Trade and Environment Database, American University. Available online. URL: http://american.edu/TED/ice/brazmigr.htm. Accessed October 2007.

[117] "Amazon Destruction Speeds Up." BBC News, June 27, 2003. Available online. URL: http://news.bbc.co.uk/2/hi/americas/3024636.stm. Accessed April 27, 2007.

[118] "Amazon Deforestation Rates Significantly Down, WWF Urges Tighter Forest Policies." WWF, August 13, 2007. Available online. URL: http://www.panda.org/news_facts/newsroom/index.cfm?uNewsID=111120. Accessed October 2007.

[119] Anna Jagger. "Brazil Drives on Alcohol Use." *ICIS Chemical Business,* January 23, 2006, p. 21.

[120] Geller, p. 180.

[121] Jagger, p. 21.

[122] Jagger, p. 21.

[123] José Maria Cardoso da Silva, et al. "The Fate of the Amazonian Areas of Endemism." *Conservation Biology,* Vol. 19, no. 3, pp. 689–694.

[124] "Brazil Carves Out 2 Vast Preserves in the Amazon Rain Forest." *New York Times,* February 18, 2005, p. A5.

PART II

Primary Sources

4

United States Documents

The documents below are arranged in chronological order and reflect the evolution of thinking in regard to natural resources and sustainable development from the country's colonial days through the advent of the New Urbanism movement. The earliest immigrants were preoccupied with the availability of land in the New World. Only after Manifest Destiny had been achieved and the nation spanned the entire distance from one ocean to the other did conservation of that land enter the equation.

Thomas Jefferson: "Population" from *Notes on the State of Virginia* (1784)

Thomas Jefferson (1743–1826) authored the Declaration of Independence and was the third president of the United States when he sponsored the Lewis and Clark expedition that charted a passage across the continent to the Pacific Northwest. His Notes on the State of Virginia *is his only full-length book and encompasses a multitude of topics relevant to the new nation. He demonstrates keen knowledge of law, politics, education, human nature, geography, science, and history. In the chapter on population reprinted below, Jefferson analyzes the figures available to him regarding the people in his native state of Virginia, including slaves. He further extrapolates future population projections and its effect on the culture of the area, as well as giving insight into the region's marriage rates, life expectancy, and other factors that have an impact on population figures. Noting the difference between Europe and America, he wrote: "In Europe the object is to make the most of their land, labour being abundant: here it is to make the most of our labour, land being abundant."*

The following table shews the number of persons imported for the establishment of our colony in its infant state, and the census of inhabitants at different periods, extracted from our historians and public records, as particularly as I have had opportunities and leisure to examine them. Successive lines in the same year shew successive periods of time in that year. I have stated the census in two different columns, the whole inhabitants having been sometimes numbered, and sometimes the *tythes* only. This term, with us, includes the free males above 16 years of age, and slaves above that age of both sexes. A further examination of our records would render this history of our population much more satisfactory and perfect, by furnishing a greater number of intermediate terms. Those however which are here stated will enable us to calculate, with a considerable degree of precision, the rate at which we have increased. During the infancy of the colony, while numbers were small, wars, importations, and other accidental circumstances render the progression fluctuating and irregular. By the year 1654, however, it becomes tolerably uniform, importations having in a great measure ceased from the dissolution of the company, and the inhabitants become too numerous to be sensibly affected by Indian wars. Beginning at that period, therefore, we find that from thence to the year 1772, our tythes had increased from 7209 to 153,000. The whole term being of 118 years, yields a duplication once in every 27 ¼ years. The intermediate enumerations taken in 1700, 1748, and 1759, furnish proofs of the uniformity of this progression. Should this rate of increase continue, we shall have between six and seven millions of inhabitants within 95 years. If we suppose our country to be bounded, at some future day, by the meridian of the mouth of the Great Kanhaway, (within which it has been before conjectured, are 64,491 square miles) there will then be 100 inhabitants for every square mile, which is nearly the state of population in the British islands.

Here I will beg leave to propose a doubt. The present desire of America is to produce rapid population by as great importations of foreigners as possible. But is this founded in good policy? The advantage proposed is the multiplication of numbers. Now let us suppose (for example only) that, in this state, we could double our numbers in one year by the importation of foreigners; and this is a greater accession than the most sanguine advocate for emigration has a right to expect. Then I say, beginning with a double stock, we shall attain any given degree of population only 27 years and 3 months sooner than if we proceed on our single stock. If we propose four millions and a half as a competent population for this state, we should be 54 ½ years attaining it, could we at once double our numbers; and 81 ¾ years, if we rely on natural propagation, as may be seen by the following table.

In the first column are stated periods of 27 ¼ years; in the second are our numbers, at each period, as they will be if we proceed on our actual stock;

and in the third are what they would be, at the same periods, were we to set out from the double of our present stock.

	PROCEEDING ON OUR PRESENT STOCK.	PROCEEDING ON A DOUBLE STOCK.
1781	567,614	1,135,228
1808 ¼	1,135,228	2,270,456
1835 ½	2,270,456	4,540,912
1862 ¾	4,540,912	

I have taken the term of four millions and a half of inhabitants for example's sake only. Yet I am persuaded it is a greater number than the country spoken of, considering how much inarrable land it contains, can clothe and feed, without a material change in the quality of their diet. But are there no inconveniences to be thrown into the scale against the advantage expected from a multiplication of numbers by the importation of foreigners? It is for the happiness of those united in society to harmonize as much as possible in matters which they must of necessity transact together. Civil government being the sole object of forming societies, its administration must be conducted by common consent. Every species of government has its specific principles. Ours perhaps are more peculiar than those of any other in the universe. It is a composition of the freest principles of the English constitution, with others derived from natural right and natural reason. To these nothing can be more opposed than the maxims of absolute monarchies. Yet, from such, we are to expect the greatest number of emigrants. They will bring with them the principles of the governments they leave, imbibed in their early youth; or, if able to throw them off, it will be in exchange for an unbounded licentiousness, passing, as is usual, from one extreme to another. It would be a miracle were they to stop precisely at the point of temperate liberty. These principles, with their language, they will transmit to their children. In proportion to their numbers, they will share with us the legislation. They will infuse into it their spirit, warp and bias its direction, and render it a heterogeneous, incoherent, distracted mass. I may appeal to experience, during the present contest, for a verification of these conjectures. But, if they be not certain in event, are they not possible, are they not probable? Is it not safer to wait with patience 27 years and three months longer, for the attainment of any degree of population desired, or expected? May not our government be more homogeneous, more peaceable, more durable? Suppose 20 millions of republican Americans thrown all of a sudden into France, what would be the condition of that kingdom?

If it would be more turbulent, less happy, less strong, we may believe that the addition of half a million of foreigners to our present numbers would produce a similar effect here. If they come of themselves, they are entitled to all the rights of citizenship: but I doubt the expediency of inviting them by extraordinary encouragements. I mean not that these doubts should be extended to the importation of useful artificers. The policy of that measure depends on very different considerations. Spare no expence in obtaining them. They will after a while go to the plough and the hoe; but, in the mean time, they will teach us something we do not know. It is not so in agriculture. The indifferent state of that among us does not proceed from a want of knowledge merely; it is from our having such quantities of land to waste as we please. In Europe the object is to make the most of their land, labour being abundant: here it is to make the most of our labour, land being abundant.

It will be proper to explain how the numbers for the year 1782 have been obtained; as it was not from a perfect census of the inhabitants. It will at the same time develope the proportion between the free inhabitants and slaves. The following return of taxable articles for that year was given in.

53,289	free males above 21 years of age.
211,698	slaves of all ages and sexes.
23,766	not distinguished in the returns, but said to be titheable slaves.
195,439	horses.
609,734	cattle.
5,126	wheels of riding-carriages.
191	taverns.

There were no returns from the 8 counties of Lincoln, Jefferson, Fayette, Monongalia, Yohogania, Ohio, Northampton, and York. To find the number of slaves which should have been returned instead of the 23,766 titheables, we must mention that some observations on a former census had given reason to believe that the numbers above and below 16 years of age were equal. The double of this number, therefore, to wit, 47,532 must be added to 211,698, which will give us 259,230 slaves of all ages and sexes. To find the number of free inhabitants, we must repeat the observation, that those above and below 16 are nearly equal. But as the number 53,289 omits the males between 16 and 21, we must supply them from conjecture. On a former experiment it had appeared that about one-third of our militia, that is, of the males between 16 and 50, were unmarried. Knowing how early marriage takes place here, we shall not be far wrong in supposing that the unmarried part of our militia are those between 16 and 21. If there be young men who do not marry till after 21, there are as many who marry before that age. But as the men above 50 were not included in the militia, we will suppose the unmarried, or those between 16 and 21, to be one-fourth of the whole number above 16, then we have the following calculation:

53,289	free males above 21 years of age.
17,763	free males between 16 and 21.
71,052	free males under 16.
142,104	free females of all ages.
284,208	free inhabitants of all ages.
259,230	slaves of all ages.
543,438	inhabitants, exclusive of the 8 counties from which were no returns. In these 8 counties in the years 1779 and 1780 were 3,161 militia.

Say then,

3,161	free males above the age of 16.
3,161	ditto under 16.
6,322	free females.
12,644	free inhabitants in these 8 counties.

To find the number of slaves, say, as 284,208 to 259,230, so is 12,644 to 11,532. Adding the third of these numbers to the first, and the fourth to the second, we have,

296,852	free inhabitants.
270,762	slaves.
567,614	inhabitants of every age, sex, and condition.

But 296,852, the number of free inhabitants, are to 270,762, the number of slaves, nearly as 11 to 10. Under the mild treatment our slaves experience, and their wholesome, though coarse, food, this blot in our country increases as fast, or faster, than the whites. During the regal government, we had at one time obtained a law, which imposed such a duty on the importation of slaves, as amounted nearly to a prohibition, when one inconsiderate assembly, placed under a peculiarity of circumstance, repealed the law. This repeal met a joyful sanction from the then sovereign, and no devices, no expedients, which could ever after be attempted by subsequent assemblies, and they seldom met without attempting them, could succeed in getting the royal assent to a renewal of the duty. In the very first session held under the republican government, the assembly passed a law for the perpetual prohibition of the importation of slaves. This will in some measure stop the increase of this great political and moral evil, while the minds of our citizens may be ripening for a complete emancipation of human nature.

Source: Thomas Jefferson. "Population." *Notes on the State of Virginia,* 1784, Electronic Text Center, University of Virginia Library. Available online. URL: http://etext.virginia.edu/toc/modeng/public/JefVirg.html.

Chief Tecumseh: Address to General William Henry Harrison (c. 1810)

Tecumseh was a chief of the Shawnee tribe; he gave the following address around 1810 in the Indiana Territory to protest the U.S. government's strategy of forcing native tribes to cede millions of acres of land by treaty. Tecumseh's words delineate the differences of opinion regarding land rights between Indian tribes and the nascent U.S. government. The speech includes the famous quote: "Sell a country?! Why not sell the air, the great sea, as well as the Earth? Did not the Great Spirit make them all for the use of his children?"

Houses are built for you to hold councils in. The Indians hold theirs in the open air. I am a Shawnee. My forefathers were warriors. Their son is a warrior. From them I take my only existence. From my tribe I take nothing. I have made myself what I am. And I would that I could make the red people as great as the conceptions of my own mind, when I think of the Great Spirit that rules over us all. I would not then come to Governor Harrison to ask him to tear up the treaty [the 1795 Treaty of Greenville, which gave the United States parts of the Northwest Territory].

But I would say to him, "Brother, you have the liberty to return to your own country." You wish to prevent the Indians from doing as we wish them, to unite and let them consider their lands as a common property of the whole. You take the tribes aside and advise them not to come into this measure. You want by your distinctions of Indian tribes, in allotting to each a particular, to make them war with each other. You never see an Indian endeavor to make the white people do this. You are continually driving the red people, when at last you will drive them into the great lake [Lake Michigan], where they can neither stand nor work.

Since my residence at Tippecanoe, we have endeavored to level all distinctions, to destroy village chiefs, by whom all mischiefs are done. It is they who sell the land to the Americans. Brother, this land that was sold, and the goods that was given for it, was only done by a few. In the future we are prepared to punish those who propose to sell land to the Americans. If you continue to purchase them, it will make war among the different tribes, and, at last I do not know what will be the consequences among the white people.

Brother, I wish you would take pity on the red people and do as I have requested. If you will not give up the land and do cross the boundary of our present settlement, it will be vary hard and produce great trouble between us.

The way, the only way to stop this evil, is for the red people to unite in claiming a common and equal right in the land, as it was at first, and should be now—for it was never divided, but belongs to all.

No tribe has the right to sell, even to each other, much less to strangers.

Sell a country?! Why not sell the air, the great sea, as well as the Earth? Did not the Great Spirit make them all for the use of his children?

How can we have confidence in the white people? We have good and just reasons to believe we have ample grounds to accuse the Americans of injustice, especially when such great acts of injustice have been committed by them upon our race, of which they seem to have no manner of regard, or even to reflect. When Jesus Christ came upon the earth you killed him and nailed him to the cross. You thought he was dead, and you were mistaken. You have the Shakers among you, and you laugh and make light of their worship. Everything I have told you is the truth. The Great Spirit has inspired me.

Source: Chief Tecumseh. "Address to General William Henry Harrison," 1810. Available online. URL: http://www.americanrhetoric.com/speeches/nativeamericans/chieftecumseh.htm.

John Muir: "Wild Wool" (1875) (excerpt)

John Muir (1838–1914) was a preservationist, writer, scientist, and founder and president of the Sierra Club, whose dedication to the Yosemite Valley in California was instrumental in making it the nation's second national park. As a preservationist, he recognized the importance of biodiversity in the fragile ecosystems of California's Sierra Nevada and fought to prevent any form of commercialism in the area. His philosophy stands in contrast to conservationists who believe that development of natural resources can be carefully managed to maintain sustainability. As a preservationist, Muir believed that wild wool obtained from undomesticated sheep was superior to wool harvested from livestock. The following essay, written in 1875 and originally published in the magazine Overland Monthly, *was later collected in the book* Steep Trails. *The essay focuses on the specific properties that make wild wool better and more sustainable than the domesticated version. Muir's evocative writing often lingers on nature's details and exhibits his vast knowledge of botany, geology, geography, and zoology.*

> . . . Wildness charms not my friend, charm it never so wisely: and whatsoever may be the character of his heaven, his earth seems only a chaos of agricultural possibilities calling for grubbing-hoes and manures.
>
> Sometimes I venture to approach him with a plea for wildness, when he good-naturedly shakes a big mellow apple in my face, reiterating his favorite aphorism, "Culture is an orchard apple, Nature is a crab." Not all culture, however, is equally destructive and inappreciative. Azure skies and crystal waters find loving recognition, and few there be who would welcome the axe among mountain pines, or would care to apply any correction to the tones and costumes of mountain waterfalls. Nevertheless, the barbarous notion is almost universally entertained by civilized man, that there is in all the manufactures of Nature something essentially coarse which can and must be eradicated by human culture. I was, therefore, delighted in finding that the wild wool growing upon mountain sheep in the neighborhood of Mount Shasta was much finer than the average grades of cultivated wool. . . .
>
> On leaving the Shasta hunting grounds I selected a few specimen tufts, and brought them away with a view to making more leisurely examinations; but, owing to the imperfectness of the instruments at my command, the results thus far obtained must be regarded only as rough approximations. . . .
>
> The effects of human culture upon wild wool are analogous to those produced upon wild roses. In the one case there is an abnormal development

of petals at the expense of the stamens, in the other an abnormal development of wool at the expense of the hair. Garden roses frequently exhibit stamens in which the transmutation to petals may be observed in various stages of accomplishment, and analogously the fleeces of tame sheep occasionally contain a few wild hairs that are undergoing transmutation to wool. Even wild wool presents here and there a fiber that appears to be in a state of change. In the course of my examinations of the wild fleeces mentioned above, three fibers were found that were wool at one end and hair at the other. This, however, does not necessarily imply imperfection, or any process of change similar to that caused by human culture. Water lilies contain parts variously developed into stamens at one end, petals at the other, as the constant and normal condition. These half wool, half hair fibers may therefore subserve some fixed requirement essential to the perfection of the whole, or they may simply be the fine boundary-lines where and exact balance between the wool and the hair is attained.

I have been offering samples of mountain wool to my friends, demanding in return that the fineness of wildness be fairly recognized and confessed, but the returns are deplorably tame. The first question asked, is, "Now truly, wild sheep, wild sheep, have you any wool?" while they peer curiously down among the hairs through lenses and spectacles. "Yes, wild sheep, you HAVE wool; but Mary's lamb had more. In the name of use, how many wild sheep, think you, would be required to furnish wool sufficient for a pair of socks?" I endeavor to point out the irrelevancy of the latter question, arguing that wild wool was not made for man but for sheep, and that, however deficient as clothing for other animals, it is just the thing for the brave mountain-dweller that wears it. Plain, however, as all this appears, the quantity question rises again and again in all its commonplace tameness. For in my experience it seems well-nigh impossible to obtain a hearing on behalf of Nature from any other standpoint than that of human use. Domestic flocks yield more flannel per sheep than the wild, therefore it is claimed that culture has improved upon wildness; and so it has as far as flannel is concerned, but all to the contrary as far as a sheep's dress is concerned. If every wild sheep inhabiting the Sierra were to put on tame wool, probably only a few would survive the dangers of a single season. With their fine limbs muffled and buried beneath a tangle of hairless wool, they would become short-winded, and fall an easy prey to the strong mountain wolves. In descending precipices they would be thrown out of balance and killed, by their taggy wool catching upon sharp points of rocks. Disease would also be brought on by the dirt which always finds a lodgment in tame wool, and by the draggled and water-soaked condition into which it falls during stormy weather.

No dogma taught by the present civilization seems to form so insuperable an obstacle in the way of a right understanding of the relations which culture sustains to wildness as that which regards the world as made especially for the uses of man. Every animal, plant, and crystal controverts it in the plainest terms. Yet it is taught from century to century as something ever new and precious, and in the resulting darkness the enormous conceit is allowed to go unchallenged.

I have never yet happened upon a trace of evidence that seemed to show that any one animal was ever made for another as much as it was made for itself. Not that Nature manifests any such thing as selfish isolation. In the making of every animal the presence of every other animal has been recognized. Indeed, every atom in creation may be said to be acquainted with and married to every other, but with universal union there is a division sufficient in degree for the purposes of the most intense individuality; no matter, therefore, what may be the note which any creature forms in the song of existence, it is made first for itself, then more and more remotely for all the world and worlds.

Were it not for the exercise of individualizing cares on the part of Nature, the universe would be felted together like a fleece of tame wool. But we are governed more than we know, and most when we are wildest. Plants, animals, and stars are all kept in place, bridled along appointed ways, WITH one another, and THROUGH THE MIDST of one another—killing and being killed, eating and being eaten, in harmonious proportions and quantities. And it is right that we should thus reciprocally make use of one another, rob, cook, and consume, to the utmost of our healthy abilities and desires. Stars attract one another as they are able, and harmony results. Wild lambs eat as many wild flowers as they can find or desire, and men and wolves eat the lambs to just the same extent.

This consumption of one another in its various modifications is a kind of culture varying with the degree of directness with which it is carried out, but we should be careful not to ascribe to such culture any improving qualities upon those on whom it is brought to bear. The water-ousel plucks moss from the riverbank to build its nest, but is does not improve the moss by plucking it. We pluck feathers from birds, and less directly wool from wild sheep, for the manufacture of clothing and cradle-nests, without improving the wool for the sheep, or the feathers for the bird that wore them. When a hawk pounces upon a linnet and proceeds to pull out its feathers, preparatory to making a meal, the hawk may be said to be cultivating the linnet, and he certainly does effect an improvement as far as hawk-food is concerned; but what of the songster? He ceases to be a linnet as soon as he is snatched from the woodland choir; and when, hawklike, we snatch the wild sheep from its native rock, and, instead of eating and wearing it at once, carry it home, and breed the hair out of its wool and the bones out of its body, it ceases to be a sheep. . . .

It is now some thirty-six hundred years since Jacob kissed his mother and set out across the plains of Padan-aram to begin his experiments upon the flocks of his uncle, Laban; and, notwithstanding the high degree of excellence he attained as a wool-grower, and the innumerable painstaking efforts subsequently made by individuals and associations in all kinds of pastures and climates, we still seem to be as far from definite and satisfactory results as we ever were. In one breed the wool is apt to wither and crinkle like hay on a sun-beaten hillside. In another, it is lodged and matted together like the lush tangled grass of a manured meadow. In one the staple is deficient in length, in another in fineness; while in all there is a constant tendency toward disease, rendering various washings and dippings indispensable to prevent its falling out. The problem of the quality and quantity of the carcass seems to be as doubtful and as far removed from a satisfactory solution as that of the wool. Desirable breeds blundered upon by long series of groping experiments are often found to be unstable and subject to disease—bots, foot rot, blind staggers, etc.—causing infinite trouble, both among breeders and manufacturers. Would it not be well, therefore, for some one to go back as far as possible and take a fresh start? . . .

Source: John Muir. "Wild Wool." *Steep Trails,* 1918. Available online. URL: http://www.gutenberg.org/etext/326.

Gifford Pinchot: *The Fight for Conservation* Chapter IV: "Principles of Conservation" (1910) (excerpt)

Gifford Pinchot was the first head of the U.S. Forest Service, which was formed by President Theodore Roosevelt in 1905. As a Republican, Pinchot was later the governor of Pennsylvania. As a pioneer in land use management, Pinchot believed in protecting vast tracts of land from development or destruction and fought for governmental policies that would lead to sustainable use of the country's natural resources, including forests, farmland, and water. He was the architect of many of the policies that shaped the government's approach to resource issues in the early 20th century.

PRINCIPLES OF CONSERVATION

The principles which the word Conservation has come to embody are not many, and they are exceedingly simple. I have had occasion to say a good many times that no other great movement has ever achieved such progress in so short a time, or made itself felt in so many directions with such vigor and effectiveness, as the movement for the conservation of natural resources.

Forestry made good its position in the United States before the conservation movement was born. As a forester I am glad to believe that conservation began with forestry, and that the principles which govern the Forest Service in particular and forestry in general are also the ideas that control conservation.

The first idea of real foresight in connection with natural resources arose in connection with the forest. From it sprang the movement which gathered impetus until it culminated in the great Convention of Governors at Washington in May, 1908. Then came the second official meeting of the National Conservation movement, December, 1908, in Washington. Afterward came the various gatherings of citizens in convention, come together to express their judgment on what ought to be done, and to contribute, as only such meetings can, to the formation of effective public opinion.

The movement so begun and so prosecuted has gathered immense swing and impetus. In 1907 few knew what Conservation meant. Now it has become a household word. While at first Conservation was supposed to apply only to forests, we see now that its sweep extends even beyond the natural resources.

The principles which govern the conservation movement, like all great and effective things, are simple and easily understood. Yet it is often hard to make the simple, easy, and direct facts about a movement of this kind known to the people generally.

The first great fact about conservation is that it stands for development. There has been a fundamental misconception that conservation means nothing but the husbanding of resources for future generations. There could be no more serious mistake. Conservation does mean provision for the future, but it means also and first of all the recognition of the right of the present generation to the fullest necessary use of all the resources with which this country is so abundantly blessed. Conservation demands the welfare of this generation first, and afterward the welfare of the generations to follow.

The first principle of conservation is development, the use of the natural resources now existing on this continent for the benefit of the people who live here now. There may be just as much waste in neglecting the development and use of certain natural resources as there is in their destruction. We have a limited supply of coal, and only a limited supply. Whether it is to last for a hundred or a hundred and fifty or a thousand years, the coal is limited in amount, unless through geological changes which we shall not live to see, there will never be any more of it than there is now. But coal is in a sense the vital essence of our civilization. If it can be preserved, if the life of the mines can be extended, if by preventing waste there can be more coal left in this country after we of this generation have made every needed use of this source of power, then we shall have deserved well of our descendants.

Conservation stands emphatically for the development and use of water-power now, without delay. It stands for the immediate construction of navigable waterways under a broad and comprehensive plan as assistants to the railroads. More coal and more iron are required to move a ton of freight by rail than by water, three to one. In every case and in every direction the conservation movement has development for its first principle, and at the very beginning of its work. The development of our natural resources and the fullest use of them for the present generation is the first duty of this generation. So much for development.

In the second place conservation stands for the prevention of waste. There has come gradually in this country an understanding that waste is not a good thing and that the attack on waste is an industrial necessity. I recall very well indeed how, in the early days of forest fires, they were considered simply and solely as acts of God, against which any opposition was hopeless and any attempt to control them not merely hopeless but childish. It was assumed that they came in the natural order of things, as inevitably as the seasons or the rising and setting of the sun. To-day we understand that forest fires are wholly within the control of men. So we are coming in like manner to understand that the prevention of waste in all other directions is a simple matter of good business. The first duty of the human race is to control the earth it lives upon.

We are in a position more and more completely to say how far the waste and destruction of natural resources are to be allowed to go on and where they are to stop. It is curious that the effort to stop waste, like the effort to stop forest fires, has often been considered as a matter controlled wholly by economic law. I think there could be no greater mistake. Forest fires were allowed to burn long after the people had means to stop them. The idea that men were helpless in the face of them held long after the time had passed when the means of control were fully within our reach. It was the old story that "as a man thinketh, so is he"; we came to see that we could stop forest fires, and we found that the means had long been at hand. When at length we came to see that the control of logging in certain directions was profitable, we found it had long been possible. In all these matters of waste of natural resources, the education of the people to understand that they can stop the leakage comes before the actual stopping and after the means of stopping it have long been ready at our hands.

In addition to the principles of development and preservation of our resources there is a third principle. It is this: The natural resources must be developed and preserved for the benefit of the many, and not merely for the profit of a few. We are coming to understand in this country that public action for public benefit has a very much wider field to cover and a much larger part to play than was the case when there were resources enough for every one, and before certain constitutional provisions had given so tremendously strong a position to vested rights and property in general.

A few years ago President Hadley, of Yale, wrote an article which has not attracted the attention it should. The point of it was that by reason of the XIVth amendment to the Constitution, property rights in the United States occupy a stronger position than in any other country in the civilized world. It becomes then a matter of multiplied importance, since property rights once granted are so strongly entrenched, to see that they shall be so granted that the people shall get their fair share of the benefit which comes from the development of the resources which belong to us all. The time to do that is now. By so doing we shall avoid the difficulties and conflicts which will surely arise if we allow vested rights to accrue outside the possibility of governmental and popular control.

The conservation idea covers a wider range than the field of natural resources alone. Conservation means the greatest good to the greatest number for the longest time. One of its great contributions is just this, that it has added to the worn and well-known phrase, "the greatest good to the greatest number," the additional words "for the longest time," thus recognizing that this nation of ours must be made to endure as the best possible home for all its people.

Conservation advocates the use of foresight, prudence, thrift, and intelligence in dealing with public matters, for the same reasons and in the same way that we each use foresight, prudence, thrift, and intelligence in dealing with our own private affairs. It proclaims the right and duty of the people to act for the benefit of the people. Conservation demands the application of commonsense to the common problems for the common good.

The principles of conservation thus described—development, preservation, the common good—have a general application which is growing rapidly wider. The development of resources and the prevention of waste and loss, the protection of the public interests, by foresight, prudence, and the ordinary business and home-making virtues, all these apply to other things as well as to the natural resources. There is, in fact, no interest of the people to which the principles of conservation do not apply.

The conservation point of view is valuable in the education of our people as well as in forestry; it applies to the body politic as well as to the earth and its minerals. A municipal franchise is as properly within its sphere as a franchise for water-power. The same point of view governs in both. It applies as much to the subject of good roads as to waterways, and the training of our people in citizenship is as germane to it as the productiveness of the earth. The application of common-sense to any problem for the Nation's good will lead directly to national efficiency wherever applied. In other words, and that is the burden of the message, we are coming to see the logical and inevitable outcome that these principles, which arose in forestry and have their bloom in the conservation of natural resources, will have their fruit in the increase and promotion of national efficiency along other lines of national life.

The outgrowth of conservation, the inevitable result, is national efficiency. In the great commercial struggle between nations which is eventually to determine the welfare of all, national efficiency will be the deciding factor.

So from every point of view conservation is a good thing for the American people.

The National Forest Service, one of the chief agencies of the conservation movement, is trying to be useful to the people of this nation. The Service recognizes, and recognizes it more and more strongly all the time, that whatever it has done or is doing has just one object, and that object is the welfare of the plain American citizen. Unless the Forest Service has served the people, and is able to contribute to their welfare it has failed in its work and should be abolished. But just so far as by cooperation, by intelligence, by attention to the work laid upon it, it contributes to the welfare of our citizens, it is a good thing and should be allowed to go on with its work.

The Natural Forests are in the West. Headquarters of the Service have been established throughout the Western country, because its work cannot be done effectively and properly without the closest contact and the most hearty coöperation with the Western people. It is the duty of the Forest Service to see to it that the timber, water-powers, mines, and every other resource of the forests is used for the benefit of the people who live in the neighborhood or who may have a share in the welfare of each locality. It is equally its duty to cooperate with all our people in every section of our land to conserve a fundamental resource, without which this Nation cannot prosper.

Source: Gifford Pinchot. "Principles of Conservation." *The Fight for Conservation,* 1910. Available online. URL: http://www.gutenberg.org/files/11238/11238-h/11238-h.htm.

Theodore Roosevelt: *The Autobiography of Theodore Roosevelt* Chapter XI: "The Natural Resources of the Nation" (1913)

In his autobiography, Roosevelt writes of the political battles involved in passing the Reclamation Act of 1902, which planned for the long-term development of irrigation in the western states. Roosevelt also writes of preserving the nation's natural resources as a whole, including forested lands, soil, and wildlife, in accordance with his deep understanding of and concern for ecology and nature. As president, he was committed to such causes and was outraged when his successor, President Taft, reversed many of his hard-won policies.

While I had lived in the West I had come to realize the vital need of irrigation to the country, and I had been both amused and irritated by the attitude of Eastern men who obtained from Congress grants of National money to develop harbors and yet fought the use of the Nation's power to develop the irrigation work of the West. Major John Wesley Powell, the explorer of the Grand Canyon, and Director of the Geological Survey, was the first man who fought for irrigation, and he lived to see the Reclamation Act passed and construction actually begun. . . .

But Gifford Pinchot is the man to whom the nation owes most for what has been accomplished as regards the preservation of the natural resources of our country. He led, and indeed during its most vital period embodied, the fight for the preservation through use of our forests. He played one of the leading parts in the effort to make the National Government the chief instrument in developing the irrigation of the arid West. He was the foremost leader in the great struggle to coordinate all our social and governmental forces in the effort to secure the adoption of a rational and farseeing policy for securing the conservation of all our national resources. He was already in the Government service as head of the Forestry Bureau when I became President; he continued throughout my term, not only as head of the Forest service, but as the moving and directing spirit in most of the conservation work, and as counsellor and assistant on most of the other work connected with the internal affairs of the country. . . .

The idea that our natural resources were inexhaustible still obtained, and there was as yet no real knowledge of their extent and condition. The relation of the conservation of natural resources to the problems of National welfare and National efficiency had not yet dawned on the public mind. The reclamation of arid public lands in the West was still a matter for private enterprise alone; and our magnificent river system, with its superb possibilities for public usefulness, was dealt with by the National Government not as a unit, but as a disconnected series of pork-barrel problems, whose only real interest was in their effect on the reelection or defeat of a Congressman here and there—a theory which, I regret to say, still obtains.

The place of the farmer in the National economy was still regarded solely as that of a grower of food to be eaten by others, while the human needs and interests of himself and his wife and children still remained wholly outside the recognition of the Government.

All the forests which belonged to the United States were held and administered in one Department, and all the foresters in Government employ were in another Department. Forests and foresters had nothing whatever to do with each other. The National Forests in the West (then called forest reserves) were wholly inadequate in area to meet the purposes for which they were created, while the need for forest protection in the East had not yet begun to enter the public mind.

Such was the condition of things when Newell and Pinchot called on me. I was a warm believer in reclamation and in forestry, and, after listening to my two guests, I asked them to prepare material on the subject for me to use in my first message to Congress, of December 3, 1901. This message laid the foundation for the development of irrigation and forestry during the next seven and one-half years. It set forth the new attitude toward the natural resources in the words: "The Forest and water problems are perhaps the most vital internal problems of the United States." . . .

On June 17, 1902, the Reclamation Act was passed. It set aside the proceeds of the disposal of public lands for the purpose of reclaiming the waste areas of the arid West by irrigating lands otherwise worthless, and thus creating new homes upon the land. The money so appropriated was to be repaid to the Government by the settlers, and to be used again as a revolving fund continuously available for the work. . . .

Although the gross expenditure under the Reclamation Act is not yet as large as that for the Panama Canal, the engineering obstacles to be overcome have been almost as great, and the political impediments many times greater. The Reclamation work had to be carried on at widely separated points, remote from railroads, under the most difficult pioneer conditions. The twenty-eight projects begun in the years 1902 to 1906 contemplated the irrigation of more than three million acres and the watering of more than thirty thousand farms. Many of the dams required for this huge task are higher than any previously built anywhere in the world. They feed mainline canals over seven thousand miles in total length, and involve minor constructions, such as culverts and bridges, tens of thousands in number.

What the Reclamation Act has done for the country is by no means limited to its material accomplishment. This Act and the results flowing from it have helped powerfully to prove to the Nation that it can handle its own resources and exercise direct and business-like control over them. The population which the Reclamation Act has brought into the arid West, while comparatively small when compared with that in the more closely inhabited East, has been a most effective contribution to the National life, for it has gone far to transform the social aspect of the West, making for the stability of the institutions upon which the welfare of the whole country rests: it has substituted actual homemakers, who have settled on the land with their families, for huge, migratory bands of sheep herded by the hired shepherds of absentee owners. . . .

When I became President, the Bureau of Forestry (since 1905 the United States Forest Service) was a small but growing organization, under Gifford Pinchot, occupied mainly with laying the foundation of American forestry by scientific study of the forests, and with the promotion of forestry on private lands. It contained all the trained foresters in the Government service, but had charge of no public timberland whatsoever. The Government forest reserves of that day were in the care of a Division in the General Land Office, under the management of clerks wholly without knowledge of forestry, few if any of whom had ever seen a foot of the timberlands for which they were responsible. Thus the reserves were neither well protected nor well used. There were no foresters among the men who had charge of the National Forests, and no Government forests in charge of the Government foresters.

In my first message to Congress I strongly recommended the consolidation of the forest work in the hands of the trained men of the Bureau of Forestry. This recommendation was repeated in other messages, but Congress did not give effect to it until three years later. In the meantime, by thorough study of the Western public timberlands, the groundwork was laid for the responsibilities which were to fall upon the Bureau of Forestry when the care of the National Forests came to be transferred to it. It was evident that trained American Foresters would be needed in considerable numbers, and a forest school was established at Yale to supply them. . . .

The result of all the work outlined above was to bring together in the Bureau of Forestry, by the end of 1904, the only body of forest experts under the Government, and practically all of the first-hand information about the public forests which was then in existence. In 1905, the obvious foolishness of continuing to separate the foresters and the forests, reenforced by the action of the First National Forest Congress, held in Washington, brought about the Act of February 1, 1905, which transferred the National Forests from the care of the Interior Department to the Department of Agriculture, and resulted in the creation of the present United States Forest Service. . . .

Up to the time the National Forests were put under the charge of the Forest Service, the Interior Department had made no effort to establish public regulation and control of water powers. Upon the transfer, the Service immediately began its fight to handle the power resources of the National Forests so as to prevent speculation and monopoly and to yield a fair return to the Government. On May 1, 1906, an Act was passed granting the use of certain power sites in Southern California to the Edison Electric Power Company, which Act, at the suggestion of the Service, limited the period of the permit to forty years, and required the payment of an annual rental by the company, the same conditions which were thereafter adopted by the Service as the basis for all permits for power development. Then began a vigorous fight against the position of the Service by the water-power interests. The right to charge for water-power development was, however, sustained by the Attorney-General.

In 1907, the area of the National Forests was increased by Presidential proclamation more than forty-three million acres; the plant necessary for the full use of the Forests, such as roads, trails, and telephone lines, began to be provided on a large scale; the interchange of field and office men, so as to prevent the antagonism between them, which is so destructive of efficiency in most great business, was established as a permanent policy; and the really effective management of the enormous area of the National Forests began to be secured. . . .

By 1908, the fire prevention work of the Forest Service had become so successful that eighty-six per cent of the fires that did occur were held down to an area of five acres or less, and the timber sales, which yielded $60,000 in 1905, in 1908 produced $850,000. In the same year, in addition to the work of the National Forests, the responsibility for the proper handling of Indian timberlands was laid upon the Forest Service, where it remained with great benefit to the Indians until it was withdrawn, as a part of the attack on the Conservation policy made after I left office. . . .

In its administration of the National Forests, the Forest Service found that valuable coal lands were in danger of passing into private ownership without adequate money return to the Government and without safeguard against monopoly; and that existing legislation was insufficient to prevent this. When this condition was brought to my attention I withdrew from all forms of entry about sixty-eight million acres of coal land in the United States, including Alaska. The refusal of Congress to act in the public interest was solely responsible for keeping these lands from entry.

The Conservation movement was a direct outgrowth of the forest movement. It was nothing more than the application to our other natural resources of the principles which had been worked out in connection with the forests. Without the basis of public sentiment which had been built up for the protection of the forests, and without the example of public foresight in the protection of this, one of the great natural resources, the Conservation movement would have been impossible. The first formal step was the creation of the Inland Waterways Commission, appointed on March 14, 1907. In my letter appointing the Commission, I called attention to the value of our streams as great natural resources, and to the need for a progressive plan for their development and control, and said: "It is not possible to properly frame so large a plan as this for the control of our rivers without taking account of the orderly development of other natural resources. Therefore I ask that the Inland Waterways Commission shall consider the relations of the streams to the use of all the great permanent natural resources and their conservation for the making and maintenance of prosperous homes." . . .

The most striking incident in the history of the Commission was the trip down the Mississippi River in October, 1907, when, as President of the United States, I was the chief guest. This excursion, with the meetings which were held and the wide public attention it attracted, gave the development of our inland waterways a new standing in public estimation. During the trip a letter was prepared and presented to me asking me to summon a conference on the conservation of natural resources. My intention to call such a conference was publicly announced at a great meeting at Memphis, Tenn.

In the November following I wrote to each of the Governors of the several States and to the Presidents of various important National Societies concerned with natural resources, inviting them to attend the conference, which took place May 13 to 15, 1908, in the East Room of the White House. It is doubtful whether, except in time of war, any new idea of like importance has ever been presented to a Nation and accepted by it with such effectiveness and rapidity, as was the case with this Conservation movement when it was introduced to the American people by the Conference of Governors. The first result was the unanimous declaration of the Governors of all the States and Territories upon the subject of Conservation, a document which ought to be hung in every schoolhouse throughout the land. A further result was the appointment of thirty-six State Conservation Commissions and, on June 8, 1908, of the National Conservation Commission. The task of this Commission was to prepare an inventory, the first ever made for any nation, of all the natural resources which underlay its property. The making of this inventory was made possible by an Executive order which placed the resources of the Government Departments at the command of the Commission, and made possible the organization of subsidiary committees by which the actual facts for the inventory were prepared and digested. Gifford Pinchot was made chairman of the Commission.

The report of the National Conservation Commission was not only the first inventory of our resources, but was unique in the history of Government in the amount and variety of information brought together. It was completed in six months. It laid squarely before the American people the essential facts regarding our natural resources, when facts were greatly needed as the basis for constructive action. This report was presented to the Joint Conservation Congress in December, at which there were present Governors of twenty States, representatives of twenty-two State Conservation Commissions, and representatives of sixty National organizations previously represented at the White House conference. The report was unanimously approved, and transmitted to me, January 11, 1909. On January 22, 1909, I transmitted the report of the National Conservation Commission to Congress with a Special Message, in which it was accurately described as "one of the most fundamentally important documents ever laid before the American people." . . .

Among the most difficult topics considered by the Public Lands Commission was that of the mineral land laws. This subject was referred by the Commission to the American Institute of Mining Engineers, which reported upon it through a Committee. This Committee made the very important recommendation, among others, "that the Government of the United States should retain title to all minerals, including coal and oil, in the lands of unceded territory, and lease the same to individuals or corporations at a fixed rental." The necessity for this action has since come to be very generally recognized. Another recommendation, since partly carried into effect, was for the separation of the surface and the minerals in lands containing coal and oil.

Our land laws have of recent years proved inefficient; yet the land laws themselves have not been so much to blame as the lax, unintelligent, and often corrupt administration of these laws. The appointment on March 4, 1907, of James R. Garfield as Secretary of the Interior led to a new era in the interpretation and enforcement of the laws governing the public lands. His administration of the Interior Department was beyond comparison the best we have ever had. It was based primarily on the conception that it is as much the duty of public land officials to help the honest settler get title to his claim as it is to prevent the looting of the public lands. The essential fact about public land frauds is not merely that public property is stolen, but that every claim fraudulently acquired stands in the way of the making of a home or a livelihood by an honest man.

As the study of the public land laws proceeded and their administration improved, a public land policy was formulated in which the saving of the resources on the public domain for public use became the leading principle. There followed the withdrawal of coal lands as already described, of oil lands and phosphate lands, and finally, just at the end of the Administration, of water-power sites on the public domain. These withdrawals were made by the Executive in order to afford to Congress the necessary opportunity to pass wise laws dealing with their use and disposal; and the great crooked special interests fought them with incredible bitterness. . . .

The things accomplished that have been enumerated above were of immediate consequence to the economic well-being of our people. In addition certain things were done of which the economic bearing was more remote, but which bore directly upon our welfare, because they add to the beauty of living and therefore to the joy of life. Securing a great artist, Saint-Gaudens, to give us the most beautiful coinage since the decay of Hellenistic Greece was one such act. In this case I had power myself to direct the Mint to employ Saint-Gaudens. The first, and most beautiful, of his coins were issued in thousands before Congress assembled or could intervene; and a great and permanent improvement was made in the beauty of the coinage. In the same way, on the advice and suggestion of Frank Millet, we got some really capital medals by sculptors of the first rank. Similarly, the new buildings in Washington were erected and placed in proper relation to one another, on plans provided by the best architects and landscape architects. I also appointed a Fine Arts Council, an unpaid body of the best architects, painters, and sculptors in the country, to advise the Government as to the erection and decoration of all new buildings. The "pork-barrel" Senators and Congressmen felt for this body an instinctive, and perhaps from their standpoint a natural, hostility; and my successor a couple of months after taking office revoked the appointment and disbanded the Council.

Even more important was the taking of steps to preserve from destruction beautiful and wonderful wild creatures whose existence was threatened by greed and wantonness. During the seven and a half years closing on March 4, 1909, more was accomplished for the protection of wild life in the United States than during all the previous years, excepting only the creation of the Yellowstone National Park. The record includes the creation of five National Parks—Crater Lake, Oregon; Wind Cave, South Dakota; Platt, Oklahoma; Sully Hill, North Dakota, and Mesa Verde, Colorado; four big game refuges in Oklahoma, Arizona, Montana, and Washington; fifty-one bird reservations; and the enactment of laws for the protection of wild life in Alaska, the District of Columbia, and on National bird reserves. These measures may be briefly enumerated as follows:

The enactment of the first game laws for the Territory of Alaska in 1902 and 1908, resulting in the regulation of the export of heads and trophies of big game and putting an end to the slaughter of deer for hides along the southern coast of the Territory.

The securing in 1902 of the first appropriation for the preservation of buffalo and the establishment in the Yellowstone National Park of the first and now the largest herd of buffalo belonging to the Government.

The passage of the Act of January 24, 1905, creating the Wichita Game Preserves, the first of the National game preserves. In 1907, 12,000 acres of this preserve were inclosed with a woven wire fence for the reception of the herd of fifteen buffalo donated by the New York Zoological Society.

The passage of the Act of June 29, 1906, providing for the establishment of the Grand Canyon Game Preserve of Arizona, now comprising 1,492,928 acres.

The passage of the National Monuments Act of June 8, 1906, under which a number of objects of scientific interest have been preserved for all time. Among the Monuments created are Muir Woods, Pinnacles National Monument in California, and the Mount Olympus National Monument, Washington, which form important refuges for game.

The passage of the Act of June 30, 1906, regulating shooting in the District of Columbia and making three-fourths of the environs of the National Capital within the District in effect a National Refuge.

The passage of the Act of May 23, 1908, providing for the establishment of the National Bison Range in Montana. This range comprises about 18,000 acres of land formerly in the Flathead Indian Reservation, on which is now established a herd of eighty buffalo, a nucleus of which was donated to the Government by the American Bison Society.

The issue of the Order protecting birds on the Niobrara Military Reservation, Nebraska, in 1908, making this entire reservation in effect a bird reservation.

The establishment by Executive Order between March 14, 1903, and March 4, 1909, of fifty-one National Bird Reservations distributed in seventeen States and Territories from Porto Rico to Hawaii and Alaska. The creation of these reservations at once placed the United States in the front rank in the world work of bird protection. Among these reservations are the celebrated Pelican Island rookery in Indian River, Florida; the Mosquito Inlet Reservation, Florida, the northernmost home of the manatee, the extensive marshes bordering Klamath and Malhuer Lakes in Oregon, formerly the scene of slaughter of ducks for market and ruthless destruction of plume birds for the millinery trade; the Tortugas Key, Florida, where, in connection with the Carnegie Institute, experiments have been made on the homing instinct of birds; and the great bird colonies on Laysan and sister islets in Hawaii, some of the greatest colonies of sea birds in the world.

Source: Theodore Roosevelt. "The Natural Resources of the Nation." In *An Autobiography* (New York: Macmillan, 1913).

Hugh Hammond Bennett: "Erosion and Rural Relief" (1938) (excerpts)

During the Great Depression, the region of the United States that was plagued by huge dust storms—especially Oklahoma—came to be known as the Dust Bowl. The storms were partly the result of drought and unsustainable agricultural practices and they rendered the farmland useless. Devastated families moved west, creating a migration of "Okies" to other regions of the country, especially California. Hugh Hammond Bennett (1881–1960) had been convinced since 1903 that soil erosion was a serious threat to civilization and wrote the influential essay "Soil Erosion: A National Menace" in 1934, which led to the Soil Conservation Act in 1935. Bennett was the founder and head of the Soil Conservation Service, which later became the National

Resources Conservation Service. In the following speech, given on March 9, 1938, to the Special Senate Committee to Investigate Unemployment Relief, Bennett outlines the importance of soil conservation in rural areas, not only for environmental reasons, but also because it will help eliminate rural poverty.

. . . Soil erosion is a serious cause of rural impoverishment. To the nation as a whole, uncontrolled erosion has brought a gradual and continuing reduction of productive agricultural land. Estimates based on a reconnaissance erosion survey of the United States, made in 1935, show that approximately 50 million acres of once productive agricultural land has been virtually ruined for further cultivation. Most of this area has been abandoned, although an occasional farmer hangs on to patches left between gullies. Another 50 million acres is in about as bad condition, but the severely eroded areas are intermingled with patches of better land, so that abandonment has not been so nearly complete. On the latter, considerably more impoverished agriculture is continuing. From a second 100 million acres a large part or all of the topsoil has washed off, and on this many thousands of farmers struggle for a meager living. Erosion is getting actively under way on still another vast area, aggregating something over 100 million acres, and will continue its depredations if agricultural practices are not altered to check the process of land wastage.

To the individual farmer erosion brings increased costs, lowered productivity, and on many farms outright ruin of the land, piece by piece, until frequently, abandonment of entire fields or the whole farm is forced. Erosion is not confined to the poorer and economically submarginal farms, but its incidence is greater and its effect most serious in the economically distressed areas of the country. An examination of the land of the United States classed as economically submarginal shows that most of it is physically poor land, either originally or as the result of erosion. Economic factors, such as low prices, reduced markets, or agricultural surpluses, are perhaps the most serious immediate causes of rural economic distress, but in the long run soil wastage is the most certain cause of permanent agricultural impoverishment. Even in times of great agricultural prosperity, land destroyed by erosion will fail to support a prosperous agriculture. Moreover, a subsistence type of agriculture relatively little affected by the fluctuations of the economic cycle is impossible on land riddled by gullies or stripped to stubborn clay subsoil or to bedrock by continuing sheet erosion. . . .

A demonstration of soil and water conservation was started by the Soil Conservation Service late in 1935 on the watershed of Pecan Creek, near Muskogee, Oklahoma. Cooperative work has been carried out on 203 of the 268 farms in the watershed. Of these, approximately 70 percent were tenants or share-croppers, most of them operating on the basis of one-year arrangements with their landlords. Every year, between cropping seasons, many of the tenants were in the habit of moving to some other farm, for a new start in life. Erosion was very severe on most of the farms, and serious on all of them. Prevailing farm practices were such that the evil was spreading at a progressively increasing rate. Fields and parts of fields were being abandoned to an increasing extent every year. Most of the land was definitely on the way out, insofar as further crop use was concerned.

After two years of cooperative soil and water conservation work, soil washing has been largely controlled with practical farm measures, which at the same time have caused much of the rainfall that formerly ran to waste immediately after every rain of any importance to be stored in the reservoir of the soil for use by crops during dry summer periods.

Better yields are being obtained—more production per acre—as the result of water conservation and stabilization of sloping land, by reason of the introduction of crop rotations, contour cultivation and strip cropping; by the building of protective field terraces and waterways safeguarded with grass; and by closing gullies and retiring highly erodible steep lands to the permanent protection of grass or trees.

. . . many landowners are telling their tenants they can remain where they are so long as they go ahead with these new and helpful practices. A greater love for the land has sprung up in that community, and a consciousness of man's responsibility to defend the soil he tills against the destructive effects of erosion.

Economically, both landlord and tenant have been materially helped, and it is significant that the stability and security given the land of the area have given an increased measure of stability and security to the farm population of the area.

In some parts of the United States the problem of rural distress is more acute. Perhaps there is no extensive area in which the problem is more widespread than in the wind-erosion region of the Great Plains. In that vast area, extending from the Panhandle of Texas to the Canadian border, about 70 percent of the land is affected in some degree by wind or water erosion, and approximately a quarter of the area is affected severely. Social and economic problems of the greatest seriousness exist through the region. Despite the fact that thousands of farm families have left the area in recent years the Federal Government is reported to have spent more than $130,000,000 in various forms of work and drought relief in the Great Plains counties in the three years from April, 1933, to April, 1936. . . .

Erosion may be a result as well as an important cause of rural impoverishment, for farmers may be forced by economic circumstances to disregard the need for soil conservation and to farm their lands exploitatively for as long as they can be made to last under such practice. The impoverished farmer on impoverished land may not have the resources to stop the erosion on his land. He frequently has only a small tract of land and his holding is usually located within some critical erosion area, such as the steeper portion of a watershed. Because the land is poor the farmer is driven to greater efforts to force from it what livelihood he can. This, in turn, further impoverishes what little land is left. Thus, intensive cultivation of sloping land without proper erosion control accentuates both the erosion problem and the relief problem. The poor farmer on poor land frequently is unable, without assistance, to check an impoverishing process which drives both himself and his land from worse to worse. Even in comparatively prosperous communities the occasional poor farmer stands as a special obstacle to adequate soil conservation in the community.

It is on steep land that water erosion usually gets out of control most rapidly, to ruin not only that farm but to damage lower slopes, to cover neighboring valley lands with unproductive sand or clay, and to fill stream channels with the products of wasted land. Where the land is steep, poor, and of complicated topography, the per acre cost of erosion control is far greater than on a comparable downstream area of smoother surface features. Thus, even if all farmers were possessed of equal funds per acre of holdings, the operator on steep land would be at a relative disadvantage in paying for the installation and maintenance of measures and practices necessary for controlling erosion, because of the physical disadvantages of his land. In humid regions, it is on the steeper uplands as a rule that the poorest farmers are concentrated. Where wind erosion is the principal menace, topography is not an important factor, the poorer farmers being located on lands which too generally have been bared of vegetation. Hence, on lands where the need for controlling erosion is most imperative, where the danger to the countryside is greatest, and the cost of control highest, we find poverty preventing a recognition of the need for soil conservation; we see a desperate struggle to wrest a livelihood from eroding hillsides intensifying the danger of downstream damage; and we discover an impoverished citizenry which, irrespective of how keenly it may sense the danger or wish to correct it, is economically unable to do so. . . .

In addition to this large class of "relief" or "submarginal" farmers who find themselves in a position to do little or nothing either for their land or themselves, there is probably a larger group which, due to a combination of erosion, soil exhaustion, and adverse economic factors (as low prices) is progressively approaching this meager subsistence level. An adequate program for this group is important because if nothing is done to arrest their declining economy they, themselves, will soon descend to a relief status, and further costs for relief and rehabilitation, otherwise preventable may have to be assumed.

The connection between rural relief and soil erosion cannot, however, be considered exclusively in terms of individual cases. The problem exists on an area-wide basis. Thus, there is a recognizable degree of correlation between critical erosion areas and areas where the bulk of the farmers are on a marginal or near-subsistence basis. The assumption that farmers of a community are essentially able to control erosion themselves if correctly advised and organized may in some instances overlook the economics of the locality. Where the bulk of a community consists of impoverished farmers on eroding soil, as is true over a large part of such extensive areas as the Appalachian highlands, the middle and upper Rio Grande watershed, and drought and dust stricken portions of the Great Plains, assistance for the correction or arrest of this condition must be sought outside, as well as inside, the community involved. If adequate steps are not taken to better these situations, the passage of time can only witness a progressive intensification of such unfavorable situations, both for the land and for the people on the land. . . .

The Soil Conservation Service was set up by Congress primarily to demonstrate to the farmers of the country how soil erosion could be controlled or prevented. This necessitated the carrying out of an extensive field operations program, and it was in this program that relief workers were found to be so useful. In any extension of conservation operations, as there must be if the Nation's soil is to be conserved, opportunities can be provided for important utilization of rural relief labor. In this connection, it should be pointed out that a number of soil conservation districts have been formed as legal subdivisions of states. Many of these districts will need all possible assistance including labor to establish effective control measures under an applicable, organized plan, and with the technical aid of these agencies equipped for such service.

Source: Hugh Hammond Bennett. "Erosion and Rural Relief," Speech to the Special Senate Committee to Investigate Unemployment Relief, March 9, 1938. Available online. URL: http://www.nrcs.usda.gov/ABOUT/history/speeches/19380309.html.

M. King Hubbert: "Nuclear Energy and the Fossil Fuels" (1956) (excerpt)

M. King Hubbert (1903–89) was the chief geologist for the Shell Oil Company in the 1950s. His influential research concerning the rates of oil production and consumption, which he plotted on a bell curve that came to be known as Hubbert's Curve, warned that known reserves of oil in the United States would reach peak production in 1970. Indeed, his prediction came to pass. In the following influential report, Hubbert gives an overview of the fossil fuels, both in the United States and worldwide, estimating how much is left, where it is, and the feasibility of refining it. He predicts 200+ years of coal remaining, but only 50 or so years of oil. However, he touts nuclear power as a solution to the world's soaring energy needs, believing that it will provide "an order of magnitude" more energy than any other source humans have ever used. Even without the graphs mentioned in Hubbert's text (which have not been reproduced), his observations can be clearly understood.

The fossil fuels, which include coal and lignite, oil shales, and tar and asphalt, as well as petroleum and natural gas, have all had their origin from plants and animals existing upon the earth during the last 500 million years. The energy content of these materials has been derived from that of the contemporary sunshine, a part of which has been synthesized by the plants and stored as chemical energy. Over the period of geological history extending back to the Cambrian, a small fraction of these organisms have become buried in sediments under conditions which have prevented complete deterioration, and so, after various chemical transformations, have been preserved as our present supply of fossil fuels. When we consider that it has taken 500 million years of geological history to accumulate the present supplies of fossil fuels, it should be clear that, although the same geological processes are still operative, the amount of new fossil fuels that is likely to be produced during the next few thousands of years will be inconsequential. Therefore, as an essential part of our analysis, we can assume with complete assurance that the industrial exploitation of the fossil fuels will consist in the progressive exhaustion of an initially fixed supply to which there will be no significant additions during the period of our interest.

Throughout all human history until about the thirteenth century, the human race, in common with all other members of the plant and animal complex, had been solely dependent upon the contemporary solar energy which it had been able to command. This comprised the energy from the food it was able to consume, that of the wood burned for fuel, and a trivial amount of power obtained from beasts of burden, from wind, and from flowing water.

The episode of our present concern began when the inhabitants of northeast England discovered that certain black rocks found along the seashore, and thereafter known as "sea coles," would burn. Thus began the mining of coal and the first systematic exploitation of the earth's supply of fossil fuels. Its greatest significance, however, lay in the fact that for the first time in human history mankind had found a huge supply of concentrated energy by means of which the energy that could be commanded by one person could be greatly increased. The industrialization of the world with its concomitant consequences for the human population has been the direct result of that initial discovery. . . .

Rise of Production of Fossil Fuels

No better record exists of the history of the exploitation of the fossil fuels than the annual statistics of their production. In Figure 1 there has been plotted the world production of coal since 1860 (United Nations, 1955), in Figure 2 the world production of crude oil, and in Figure 3 the combined production of energy from coal and crude oil.

The production of coal in the United States is shown in Figure 4, that of crude oil in Figure 5, and the production of marketed natural gas in Figure 6. The production of crude oil in Texas is shown in Figure 7, and that of marketed natural gas in Figure 8.

Since these curves embody just about all that is essential in our knowledge of the production of energy from the fossil fuels on the world, a national, and a state scale, it is worth our attention to study them briefly. In the first place, it will be noted that there is a strong family resemblance among them. Each curve starts slowly and then rises more steeply until finally an inflection point is reached after which it becomes concave downward. For the world coal production this point was reached about the beginning of

World War I, and for world petroleum production it appears to have been as recently as 1951 or 1952.

For the production of coal in the United States the inflection point also occurred about 1914, and the inflection points for petroleum and natural gas apparently about 1952. The inflection points for the Texas production of oil and gas occur at about the same dates as those for the United States.

A more informative representation of the rate of growth of the production can be obtained by plotting the logarithm of the production rate versus time on semilogarithmic graph paper. This has been done in Figures 9 and 10 for the United States production of coal and crude oil, respectively. It will be noted in each case that the curve approximates a straight line until some definite date and then breaks away sharply downward. In the case of coal this departure from a straight line occurred about 1910, and for crude oil about 1930. All the other production curves shown in the preceding figures behave in a similar manner.

The significance of this is that during the initial stages all of these rates of production tend to increase exponentially with time. Coal production in the United States from 1850 to 1910 increased at a rate of 6.6 percent per year, with the production doubling every 10.5 years. Crude-oil production from 1880 until 1930 increased at the rate of 7.9 percent per year, with the output doubling every 8.7 years.

During the corresponding growth phases, world production of coal increased at the rate of 4.3 percent per year, with production doubling every 16 years, and world production of crude oil increased at a rate of 7 percent per year, with the rate of output doubling every 10 years. . . .

This rapid rate of growth shown by the production curves makes them particularly deceptive with regard to the future length of time for which such production may be sustained. For example, coal has been mined continuously for about 800 years, and by the end of 1955 the cumulative production for all of this time was 95 billion metric tons. It is somewhat surprising, however, to discover that the entire period of coal mining up until 1925 was required to produce the first half, while only the last 30 years has been required for the second half.

Similarly, petroleum has been produced in the United States since 1859, and by the end of 1955 the cumulative production amounted to about 53 billion barrels. The first half of this required from 1859 to 1939, or 80 years, to be produced; whereas, the second half has been produced during the last 16 years. . . .

Reserves of the Fossil Fuels

Coal.—In order to predict the future of the production of the fossil fuels, therefore, it is essential that the best possible estimates of the ultimate reserves be made. In the case of coal world-wide inventories have been made and revised intermittently since 1913. During the last decade an extensive re-examination of the coal reserves of the United States has been in progress by the United States Geological Survey, whose staff has also maintained current information on the reserves of the world. The results of the latest progress report of the Geological Survey (Averitt, Berryhill, and Taylor, 1953), of the recoverable coal reserves of the world, are shown graphically in Figure 14. The total recoverable coal and lignite reserves of the world are now estimated to be about 2,500 billion metric tons, of which the United States has about one-third, the USSR about one-fourth, and China about one-fifth of the total.

The sharp contrast between these figures and earlier estimates of about 6,000 billion metric tons for the whole world requires explanation. The earlier estimates included both thin and deep beds of coal without too much regard for practicable minability. The later estimates have been restricted to beds that are more workable; this has resulted in a reduction from around 6,000 to about 5,000 billion metric tons. More seriously, however, the earlier estimates were of coal in place, whereas the data given in Figure 14 represent recoverable coal assuming a 50-percent loss in mining. This makes the coal reserves directly comparable to the data for petroleum reserves, which also are based upon recoverable oil rather than oil in place.

Crude Oil and Natural Gas.—The comparable data for world crude-oil reserves are presented in Figure 15. Here the distinction must be borne in mind between crude oil or petroleum and total "liquid hydrocarbons" or "petroleum liquids." In the early stages of the petroleum industry, the usable products were crude oil and natural gas, and most petroleum statistics still pertain to those two products. During recent decades, however, due to improved technology there has been an increasing yield of the so-called "natural-gas liquids" obtained as a by-product of natural gas. Statistics on total petroleum liquids, or liquid hydrocarbons, comprise both crude oil and natural-gas liquids.

Since the production curves here considered are of crude oil only, then the pertinent reserve data must also be limited to crude oil. The data in Figure 15 represent the estimated amounts of crude oil initially present which are producible by methods now in use. The cross-hachured part of each column represents the amount which has been consumed already. These estimates of ultimate potential reserves are, with two exceptions, those obtained by L. G. Weeks (1948, 1950a, 1950b, 1952), of the Standard Oil Company of New Jersey, in his detailed studies of the various sedimentary basins of the world. Weeks estimated the ultimate potential reserves of the world to be 610 billion barrels for the land areas, and 400 billion barrels for the continental shelves, or roundly 1,000 billion barrels in total. These estimates included 110 billion barrels for the land area of the United States, and 155 billion barrels for the Middle East, including Egypt.

Subsequently the Middle East has developed into a petroleum province of unprecedented magnitude and Weeks' estimate is now known to be seriously too low. Recently Wallace E. Pratt (1956), in the *Report of the Panel on the Impact of the Peaceful Uses of Atomic Energy*, gave as the proved reserves of liquid hydrocarbons for the Middle East the figure of 230 billion barrels. Since probably not less than 200 billion barrels of this is represented by crude oil, the estimate of the ultimate potential reserves of crude oil in the Middle East has been increased to 375 billion barrels, which can only be regarded as a rough order-of-magnitude figure.

In the case of the United States, Weeks' estimate of 110 billion barrels (based upon production practices of about 1948) was for the land area. . . .

The production record of the past two decades, due in part to improved recovery practices, indicates that Weeks' figure of 110 billion barrels for the land may also be somewhat low. This has accordingly been increased to 130 billion, giving a total ultimate potential reserve of 150 billion barrels of crude oil for both the land and offshore areas of the United States. . . .

The Outlook for the Fossil Fuels

If the world should continue to be dependent upon the fossil fuels as its principal source of industrial energy, then we could expect a culmination in the production of coal within about 200 years. On the basis of the present estimates of the ultimate reserves of petroleum and natural gas, it appears that the culmination of world production of these products should occur within about half a century, while the culmination for petroleum and natural gas in both the United States and the state of Texas should occur within the next few decades.

This does not necessarily imply that the United States or other parts of the industrial world will soon become destitute of liquid and gaseous fuels, because these can be produced from other fossil fuels which occur in much greater abundance. But it does pose as a national problem of primary importance, the necessity, both with regard to requirements for domestic purposes and those for national defense, of gradually having to compensate for an increasing disparity between the nation's demands for these fuels and its ability to produce them from naturally occurring accumulations of petroleum and natural gas.

Finally, there is the possibility of obtaining industrial energy from nuclear sources which we now propose to examine.

Energy from Nuclear Sources

Ever since the explosion of the first nuclear bomb over Hiroshima in 1945, there has been spectacular evidence that the tremendous store of energy contained within the nucleus of certain unstable atoms can at last be released. Gradually during the succeeding years, the veil of secrecy has been lifted until finally, as a result of the United Nations International Conference on the Peaceful Uses of Atomic Energy, held in Geneva during August 1955, virtually complete information on the possible industrial uses of the energy from the fissioning of the uranium has now been made public.

In addition, very active developments in the United States, England, the USSR, and other countries, of large power reactors are under way. Moreover, nuclear-powered submarines are already in successful operation. What, we wonder, is the magnitude of the potential industrial development of energy from these sources? How much uranium or thorium would be required to power an industrial civilization comparable to that now powered by the fossil fuels? And does this quantity exist in a form that is readily obtainable? . . .

Magnitude of Uranium Reserves

What is the magnitude of the supplies? The uranium contents and fuel equivalents of the principal sources of uranium in the United States are shown in Table 6. The ores which are currently being produced, the so-called high-grade ores, are those of the type found principally in the Colorado Plateau. These are said to average about 0.35 percent uranium, or 3500 grams per metric ton, which is equivalent to about 10,500 tons of coal or 45,000 barrels of oil per metric ton of ore. . . .

From these evidences it appears that there exist within minable depths in the United States rocks with uranium contents equivalent to 1,000 barrels or more of oil per metric ton, whose total energy content is probably several hundred times that of all the fossil fuels combined. The same appears to be true of many other parts of the world. Consequently, the world appears to be on the threshold of an era which in terms of energy consumption will be at least an order of magnitude greater than that made possible by the fossil fuels.

As remarked earlier, experimental nuclear-power reactors are already under construction in several parts of the United States, and in the United Kingdom, the USSR, and elsewhere, and nuclear-powered submarines are in successful operation. It will probably require the better part of another 10 or 15 years of research and development before stabilized designs of reactors and auxiliary chemical processing plants are achieved after which we may expect the usual exponential rate of growth of nuclear-power production.

The decline of petroleum production and the concurrent rise in the production of power from nuclear energy for the United States is shown schematically in Figure 29. The rise of nuclear power is there shown at a rate of about 10 percent per year, but there are many indications that it may actually be twice that rate.

Time Perspective

In order to see more clearly what these events may imply, it will be informative to consider them on a somewhat longer time scale than that which we customarily employ. Attention is accordingly invited to Figure 30 which covers the time span from 5,000 years ago—the dawn of recorded history—to 5,000 years in the future. On such a time scale the discovery, exploitation, and exhaustion of the fossil fuels will be seen to be but an ephemeral event in the span of recorded history. There is promise, however, provided mankind can solve its international problems and not destroy itself with nuclear weapons, and provided the world population (which is now expanding at such a rate as to double in less than a century) can somehow be brought under control, that we may at last have found an energy supply adequate for our needs for at least the next few centuries of the "foreseeable future."

Source: M. King Hubbert. "Nuclear Energy and the Fossil Fuels." *Drilling and Production Practice,* American Petroleum Institute, 1956. Reproduced courtesy of the American Petroleum Institute.

President Jimmy Carter: "Energy and the National Goals: Crisis of Confidence" Speech (July 15, 1979)

The following speech was broadcast on live network television on July 15, 1979, in the midst of an energy crisis that saw skyrocketing costs of oil and natural gas and that was at least partially responsible for the country's economic recession. President Carter's approval rating plummeted, and his defeat in the 1980 presidential election was all but assured a few months later when the dismal economic situation was exacerbated by the Iran hostage crisis. In addressing the energy crisis, Carter appeals to Americans' sense of religious and patriotic duty and proposes ambitious programs to develop alternative energy sources in order to reduce U.S. dependence on foreign oil.

We are at a turning point in our history. There are two paths to choose. One is a path I've warned about tonight, the path that leads to fragmentation and self-interest. Down that road lies a mistaken idea of freedom, the right to grasp for ourselves some advantage over others. That path would be one of constant conflict between narrow interests ending in chaos and immobility. It is a certain route to failure.

All the traditions of our past, all the lessons of our heritage, all the promises of our future point to another path, the path of common purpose and the restoration of American values. That path leads to true freedom for our Nation and ourselves. We can take the first steps down that path as we begin to solve our energy problem.

Energy will be the immediate test of our ability to unite this Nation, and it can also be the standard around which we rally. On the battlefield of energy we can win for our Nation a new confidence, and we can seize control again of our common destiny.

In little more than two decades we've gone from a position of energy independence to one in which almost half the oil we use comes from foreign countries, at prices that are going through the roof. Our excessive dependence on OPEC has already taken a tremendous toll on our economy and our people. This is the direct cause of the long lines which have made millions of you spend aggravating hours waiting for gasoline. It's a cause of the increased inflation and unemployment that we now face. This intolerable dependence on foreign oil threatens our economic independence and the very security of our Nation. The energy crisis is real. It is worldwide. It is a clear and present danger to our Nation. These are facts and we simply must face them.

What I have to say to you now about energy is simple and vitally important. Point one: I am tonight setting a clear goal for the energy policy of the United States. Beginning this moment, this Nation will never use more foreign oil than we did in 1977—never. From now on, every new addition to our demand for energy will be met from our own production and our own conservation. The generation-long growth in our dependence on foreign oil will be stopped dead in its tracks right now and then reversed as we move through the 1980's, for I am tonight setting the further goal of cutting our dependence on foreign oil by one-half by the end of the next decade—a saving of over 4 ½ million barrels of imported oil per day. Point two: To ensure that we meet these targets, I will use my Presidential authority to set import quotas. I'm announcing tonight that for 1979 and 1980, I will forbid the entry into this country of one drop of foreign oil more than these goals allow. These quotas will ensure a reduction in imports even below the ambitious levels we set at the recent Tokyo summit.

Point three: To give us energy security, I am asking for the most massive peacetime commitment of funds and resources in our Nation's history to develop America's own alternative sources of fuel—from coal, from oil shale, from plant products for gasohol, from unconventional gas, from the Sun.

I propose the creation of an energy security corporation to lead this effort to replace 2 ½ million barrels of imported oil per day by 1990. The corporation I will issue up to $5 billion in energy bonds, and I especially want them to be in small denominations so that average Americans can invest directly in America's energy security.

Just as a similar synthetic rubber corporation helped us win World War II, so will we mobilize American determination and ability to win the energy war. Moreover, I will soon submit legislation to Congress calling for the creation of this Nation's first solar bank, which will help us achieve the crucial goal of 20 percent of our energy coming from solar power by the year 2000.

These efforts will cost money, a lot of money, and that is why Congress must enact the windfall profits tax without delay. It will be money well spent. Unlike the billions of dollars that we ship to foreign countries to pay for foreign oil, these funds will be paid by Americans to Americans. These funds will go to fight, not to increase, inflation and unemployment.

Point four: I'm asking Congress to mandate, to require as a matter of law, that our Nation's utility companies cut their massive use of oil by 50 percent within the next decade and switch to other fuels, especially coal, our most abundant energy source.

Point five: To make absolutely certain that nothing stands in the way of achieving these goals, I will urge Congress to create an energy mobilization board which, like the War Production Board in World War II, will have the responsibility and authority to cut through the red tape, the delays, and the endless roadblocks to completing key energy projects.

We will protect our environment. But when this Nation critically needs a refinery or a pipeline, we will build it.

Point six: I'm proposing a bold conservation program to involve every State, county, and city and every average American in our energy battle. This effort will permit you to build conservation into your homes and your lives at a cost you can afford.

I ask Congress to give me authority for mandatory conservation and for standby gasoline rationing. To further conserve energy, I'm proposing tonight an extra $10 billion over the next decade to strengthen our public transportation systems. And I'm asking you for your good and for your Nation's security to take no unnecessary trips, to use carpools or public transportation whenever you can, to park your car one extra day per week, to obey the speed limit, and to set your thermostats to save fuel. Every act of energy conservation like this is more than just common sense—I tell you it is an act of patriotism.

Our Nation must be fair to the poorest among us, so we will increase aid to needy Americans to cope with rising energy prices. We often think of conservation only in terms of sacrifice. In fact, it is the most painless and immediate way of rebuilding our Nation's strength. Every gallon of oil each one of us saves is a new form of production. It gives us more freedom, more confidence, that much more control over our own lives.

So, the solution of our energy crisis can also help us to conquer the crisis of the spirit in our country. It can rekindle our sense of unity, our confidence in the future, and give our Nation and all of us individually a new sense of purpose.

You know we can do it. We have the natural resources. We have more oil in our shale alone than several Saudi Arabias. We have more coal than any nation on Earth. We have the world's highest level of technology. We have the most skilled work force, with innovative genius, and I firmly believe that we have the national will to win this war.

I do not promise you that this struggle for freedom will be easy. I do not promise a quick way out of our Nation's problems, when the truth is that the only way out is an all-out effort. What I do promise you is that I will lead our fight, and I will enforce fairness in our struggle, and I will ensure honesty. And above all, I will act. We can manage the short-term shortages more effectively and we will, but there are no short-term solutions to our long-range problems. There is simply no way to avoid sacrifice.

Twelve hours from now I will speak again in Kansas City, to expand and to explain further our energy program. Just as the search for solutions to our energy shortages has now led us to a new awareness of our Nation's deeper problems, so our willingness to work for those solutions in energy can strengthen us to attack those deeper problems.

I will continue to travel this country, to hear the people of America. You can help me to develop a national agenda for the 1980's. I will listen and I will act. We will act together. These were the promises I made 3 years ago, and I intend to keep them.

Little by little we can and we must rebuild our confidence. We can spend until we empty our treasuries, and we may summon all the wonders of science. But we can succeed only if we tap our greatest resources—America's people, America's values, and America's confidence.

I have seen the strength of America in the inexhaustible resources of our people. In the days to come, let us renew that strength in the struggle for an energy secure nation.

In closing, let me say this: I will do my best, but I will not do it alone. Let your voice be heard. Whenever you have a chance, say something good about our country. With God's help and for the sake of our Nation, it is time for us to join hands in America. Let us commit ourselves together to a rebirth of the American spirit Working together with our common faith we cannot fail.

Source: Jimmy Carter. "Crisis of Confidence" Speech, July 15, 1979. Available online. URL: http://www.millercenter.virginia.edu/scripps/digitalarchive/speeches/spe_1979_0715_carter.

Charter of the New Urbanism (1996)

The Congress for the New Urbanism ratified the following charter in 1996. Comprised of architects, urban planners, and developers, the congress promotes sustainable development in the United States through design and planning of dynamic, self-supporting communities that provide the necessities of daily life within designated regions. The goal is to eliminate resource-wasting suburban sprawl and urban blight, which fractures social contracts, renders formerly sustainable development uninhabitable, and promotes further sprawl.

The Congress for the New Urbanism views disinvestment in central cities, the spread of placeless sprawl, increasing separation by race and income, environmental deterioration, loss of agricultural lands and wilderness, and the erosion of society's built heritage as one interrelated community-building challenge.

We stand for the restoration of existing urban centers and towns within coherent metropolitan regions, the reconfiguration of sprawling suburbs into communities of real neighborhoods and diverse districts, the conservation of natural environments, and the preservation of our built legacy.

We recognize that physical solutions by themselves will not solve social and economic problems, but neither can economic vitality, community stability, and environmental health be sustained without a coherent and supportive physical framework.

We advocate the restructuring of public policy and development practices to support the following principles: neighborhoods should be diverse in use and population; communities should be designed for the pedestrian and transit as well as the car; cities and towns should be shaped by physically defined and universally accessible public spaces and community institutions; urban places should be framed by architecture and landscape design that celebrate local history, climate, ecology, and building practice.

We represent a broad-based citizenry, composed of public and private sector leaders, community activists, and multidisciplinary professionals. We are committed to reestablishing the relationship between the art of building and the making of community, through citizen-based participatory planning and design.

We dedicate ourselves to reclaiming our homes, blocks, streets, parks, neighborhoods, districts, towns, cities, regions, and environment.

We assert the following principles to guide public policy, development practice, urban planning, and design:

The region: metropolis, city, and town

1. Metropolitan regions are finite places with geographic boundaries derived from topography, watersheds, coastlines, farmlands, regional parks, and river basins. The metropolis is made of multiple centers that are cities, towns, and villages, each with its own identifiable center and edges.

2. The metropolitan region is a fundamental economic unit of the contemporary world. Governmental cooperation, public policy, physical planning, and economic strategies must reflect this new reality.

3. The metropolis has a necessary and fragile relationship to its agrarian hinterland and natural landscapes. The relationship is environmental, economic, and cultural. Farmland and nature are as important to the metropolis as the garden is to the house.

4. Development patterns should not blur or eradicate the edges of the metropolis. Infill development within existing urban areas conserves environmental resources, economic investment, and social fabric, while reclaiming marginal and abandoned areas. Metropolitan regions should develop strategies to encourage such infill development over peripheral expansion.

5. Where appropriate, new development contiguous to urban boundaries should be organized as neighborhoods and districts, and be integrated with the existing urban pattern. Noncontiguous development should be organized as towns and villages with their own urban edges, and planned for a jobs/housing balance, not as bedroom suburbs.

6. The development and redevelopment of towns and cities should respect historical patterns, precedents, and boundaries.

7. Cities and towns should bring into proximity a broad spectrum of public and private uses to support a regional economy that benefits people of all incomes. Affordable housing should be distributed throughout the region to match job opportunities and to avoid concentrations of poverty.

8. The physical organization of the region should be supported by a framework of transportation alternatives. Transit, pedestrian, and bicycle systems should maximize access and mobility throughout the region while reducing dependence upon the automobile.

9. Revenues and resources can be shared more cooperatively among the municipalities and centers within regions to avoid destructive competition for tax base and to promote rational coordination of transportation, recreation, public services, housing, and community institutions.

The neighborhood, the district, and the corridor

1. The neighborhood, the district, and the corridor are the essential elements of development and redevelopment in the metropolis. They form identifiable areas that encourage citizens to take responsibility for their maintenance and evolution.

2. Neighborhoods should be compact, pedestrian-friendly, and mixed-use. Districts generally emphasize a special single use, and should follow the principles of neighborhood design when possible. Corridors are regional connectors of neighborhoods and districts; they range from boulevards and rail lines to rivers and parkways.

3. Many activities of daily living should occur within walking distance, allowing independence to those who do not drive, especially the elderly and the young. Interconnected networks of streets should be designed to encourage walking, reduce the number and length of automobile trips, and conserve energy.

4. Within neighborhoods, a broad range of housing types and price levels can bring people of diverse ages, races, and incomes into daily interaction, strengthening the personal and civic bonds essential to an authentic community.

5. Transit corridors, when properly planned and coordinated, can help organize metropolitan structure and revitalize urban centers. In contrast, highway corridors should not displace investment from existing centers.

6. Appropriate building densities and land uses should be within walking distance of transit stops, permitting public transit to become a viable alternative to the automobile.

7. Concentrations of civic, institutional, and commercial activity should be embedded in neighborhoods and districts, not isolated in remote, single-use complexes. Schools should be sized and located to enable children to walk or bicycle to them.

8. The economic health and harmonious evolution of neighborhoods, districts, and corridors can be improved through graphic urban design codes that serve as predictable guides for change.

9. A range of parks, from tot-lots and village greens to ballfields and community gardens, should be distributed within neighborhoods.

Conservation areas and open lands should be used to define and connect different neighborhoods and districts.

The block, the street, and the building

1. A primary task of all urban architecture and landscape design is the physical definition of streets and public spaces as places of shared use.

2. Individual architectural projects should be seamlessly linked to their surroundings. This issue transcends style.

3. The revitalization of urban places depends on safety and security. The design of streets and buildings should reinforce safe environments, but not at the expense of accessibility and openness.

4. In the contemporary metropolis, development must adequately accommodate automobiles. It should do so in ways that respect the pedestrian and the form of public space.

5. Streets and squares should be safe, comfortable, and interesting to the pedestrian. Properly configured, they encourage walking and enable neighbors to know each other and protect their communities.

6. Architecture and landscape design should grow from local climate, topography, history, and building practice.

7. Civic buildings and public gathering places require important sites to reinforce community identity and the culture of democracy. They deserve distinctive form, because their role is different from that of other buildings and places that constitute the fabric of the city.

8. All buildings should provide their inhabitants with a clear sense of location, weather and time. Natural methods of heating and cooling can be more resource-efficient than mechanical systems.

9. Preservation and renewal of historic buildings, districts, and landscapes affirm the continuity and evolution of urban society.

Source: Congress for the New Urbanism. "Charter for the New Urbanism," 1996. Available online: http://www.cnu.org/charter. 1997 Congress for the New Urbanism, reprinted by permission.

Richard Cheney: "Remarks by the Vice President to U.S. Energy Association Efficiency Forum." (June 13, 2001)

In his address to the U.S. Energy Association Efficiency Forum, Vice President Dick Cheney outlined the newly inaugurated Bush Administration's energy strategy, which emphasized efficiency as well as increased capacity in generating electricity via coal, gas, and nuclear power. He also briefly addressed President Bush's rejection of the Kyoto Protocol to curb greenhouse gas emissions because the president believed it placed an unfair burden on the United States and did not make China and India accountable for their own carbon emissions and surging energy demands. It is worth noting that Cheney mentioned the rolling blackouts in California, which at the time were attributed to an insufficient and aging infrastructure and recent deregulation, but were later discovered to have been partly caused by illegal market manipulation by employees of Enron. Just six months after this speech, on December 2, 2001, Enron declared the largest bankruptcy in U.S. history.

During the campaign last year, when then-Governor Bush and I were campaigning, we had identified our potential energy problems as one of the possible storm clouds on the horizon of the economy. We looked down the road and tried to identify something that might adversely affect our nation and lead to significant economic difficulties. We thought that the fact that we didn't have a coherent energy policy at that point and there were beginning to be some problems out there was significant.

We were not intending to speak as prophets but, rather, as realists. Since then, of course, we've seen the energy challenges grow significantly into a very serious hardship now for people in California and many places in the West. Across the country, millions of families have had their budgets squeezed by energy costs. From the late '70s to the late '90s, the share of the average family budget devoted to energy had declined, but since 1998, it's actually now on the rise.

Against that background, four days after we were sworn in, the president asked me to sign on as the chairman of a committee of the Cabinet, the National Energy Policy Development Group, to pull together a set of options and some proposals for him that would begin to address what we perceived to be some of the serious problems out there. It was the first comprehensive approach, or attempt to be comprehensive with respect to energy policy for quite some time.

The report we issued last month presented more than 100 recommendations covering virtually the entire range of concerns that face the American people. One of the concerns, obviously, is the aging power grid and the growing problem that we have in getting electricity from the power plant to the light switch. It's clear that we must upgrade and expand the power grid. If we put more connections in place, we'll go a long way towards avoiding future blackouts. Another broad aim is to increase energy supplies from diverse sources; from oil and gas, renewables, coal, hydro and nuclear. This is the kind of balanced approach we think is essential if we're going to meet the country's energy needs down the road and take care of many of our other concerns, especially with respect to the environment.

Good stewardship is a public value in 21st century America. By far, most of us believe in showing due consideration for the air, the water, the land and natural life around us. The president and I believe very deeply that more energy can be acquired while at the same time we provide for a safe, clean environment.

Indeed, an energy shortage is bad for the environment, as we've seen in California, where dirtier plants are now running longer in order to keep the lights on and where competition and efforts to deal with some of the environmental problems have led to a refusal to build plants are now creating demands, for example, for using the water in the dams and reservoirs in the Northwest in a way that may, in fact, damage the salmon population.

It is possible to have more energy and a cleaner environment. Technology allows us to do it, and as we've already seen with the incredible advances in technology that have been employed in locating and producing energy and in using it. This is one of the primary themes of the energy policy we've put forward: to make better use of the latest technology of what we take from the earth. On the production side, it's everything from clean coal technology, which we support, to alternative clean energy sources. It also includes the highly effective new methods that allow much oil production to go forward with minimal impact on the environment. But it's not just a matter of cleaner use. We must become much more efficient in our energy use as well.

For a family or business, energy efficiency can mean lower energy bills. For the country, efficiency helps us make the most of our resources, lowers our reliance on energy imports, and softens the impact of high prices and reduces pollution. Here we seek to continue a path of uninterrupted progress in many fields. Home refrigerators use about one-third of the electricity they used in 1972. Compact fluorescent lights use about 25 percent of the [energy of] incandescent bulbs that they replace. Today's automobiles use roughly 40 percent less fuel per mile driven than they did 30 years ago.

The latest computer screens use a fraction of the power needed on older models. Low power technology has been perfected for many portable and wireless devices.

For the country as a whole our progress in energy efficiency has been nothing short of remarkable. Since the Nixon administration our economy has grown by 126 percent; our use of energy has grown only by 26 percent. Under the president's plan our country will continue to build on this very successful history. We can and we will make even greater strides in energy efficiency going forward.

While such advances cannot alone solve America's energy problems, they can and will continue to play a vitally important role in our energy future. New technologies are proving that we save energy without sacrificing our standard of living, and we're going to encourage these technologies in every way possible.

In pursuing energy efficiency, we must be clear about our purposes. As the president has said, conservation does not mean doing without. Thanks to new technology, it can mean doing better, smarter, cheaper.

With that distinction in mind, we are advancing a number of specific ideas for improving efficiency throughout the economy. First, we'll seek higher federal efficiency standards for appliances wherever this is feasible and economically justified. At present, all refrigerators, freezers, clothes washers, and dishwashers have energy guide levels to let consumers know just how much energy is consumed. The president's also asked the Energy Department to hold other appliances to these standards, wherever it makes sense to do so.

We will also provide better information to consumers by expanding the government's Energy Star program, which identifies the most energy-efficient appliances.

On the consumption of energy, the government is going to lead by example. The federal government is the single largest energy consumer in the United States. Energy use in many federal buildings has already been reduced by 30 percent from 1990 levels, largely by installing energy-efficient technologies. The government has also reduced vehicle and equipment energy use 35 percent.

Our administration will continue this progress under an executive order recently signed by the president which ordered all federal agencies to take extra steps to conserve energy. Military and federal agencies are already exceeding expectations.

Third, we're going to help industry conserve energy by investing in energy-efficient technologies. Everyone here is familiar with combined heating and power, or CHP, systems. For many companies with large needs for both heat and electricity, CHP systems are the way to go. We're asking Congress to give these systems the same depreciation incentives the tax code now gives to power plants.

Fourth, we've directed the secretary of Transportation to review and provide recommendations on establishing CAFE standards with due consideration of the National Academy of Sciences study to be released next month. We don't know yet whether or not any adjustment will be justified, but we're going to eagerly await the secretary's report once the NAS has completed its work. Any new standards should consider efficiency, but also safety, economic concerns and what the impact might be on the automobile industry. We've also called for tax incentives for new kinds of fuel-efficient vehicles, which offer greatly improved fuel economy and sharply reduced emissions.

Fifth, the president has asked the secretary of Energy, Spence Abraham, to conduct a thorough review of energy efficiency R&D programs in light of our national energy policy. It's the nature of things to find that some programs and methods work better than others. We will look for the approaches that hold the most promise for savings in the use of energy. Just yesterday, at the direction of the secretary, meetings were held in Chicago and Atlanta to evaluate performance-based efficiency programs. Five similar meetings are going to be held in different parts of the country in the weeks ahead. When the study is completed, the secretary will then recommend appropriate levels of funding for the most effective of these programs.

As we pursue greater energy efficiency throughout our society as part of a comprehensive energy policy, the gains will be more than economic. Every step we take toward wiser use of energy and more diverse supplies at home will make us that much less dependent on overseas suppliers and less vulnerable to supply shocks imposed on us from abroad.

Then there's the matter of global climate change, which concerns people in every nation. We're the world's largest economy and also the largest producer of man-made greenhouse emissions. Before departing for Europe on Monday, the president called on Congress to fully implement our clean energy technology proposals so that our country can reduce greenhouse gas emissions by significant amounts in coming years.

There's still a great deal to be learned about global climate change. The United States spends more than any other country on climate change research, more than the combined expenditures of Japan and all 15 countries in the EU. And we will continue to lead the scientific effort to find answers.

I have no doubt that we will also be the country that masters the technology to reduce greenhouse gases.

This country has met many great tests over our history. Some have imposed prolonged difficulty and major sacrifice; others have demanded only resolve, ingenuity and clarity of purpose. Such is the case with energy today. We have it within our power to make great strides and to reap great rewards in new jobs, a healthier environment, a stronger economy and a brighter future.

Source: Richard Cheney. "Remarks by the Vice President to U.S. Energy Association Efficiency Forum." Washington, D.C., June 13, 2001. Available online. URL: http://www.whitehouse.gov.

Joseph Romm: "Testimony for the Hearing Reviewing the Hydrogen Fuel and FreedomCAR Initiatives." (March 3, 2004)

Joseph Romm, the author of The Hype about Hydrogen *and the acting assistant secretary of energy under President Clinton, is a proponent of hydrogen energy. In his testimony to the House Science Committee, he cautions that widespread adoption of hydrogen as a fuel source, particularly in automobiles, is many years away and will require huge strides in technology. The stumbling blocks are cheap, safe, and plentiful production of hydrogen, as well as efficient and safe storage of hydrogen, especially for cars, and creation of a state-of-the-art infrastructure to distribute it. Although he acknowledges that a hydrogen economy may eventually become a reality, its pursuit should not be made at the expense of reducing greenhouse gas emissions as much as possible in the immediate future, which is of the utmost importance. Given current technology, producing hydrogen is more energy intensive and polluting than are traditional fossil fuels.*

HYDROGEN and FUEL CELLS

Hydrogen is not a readily accessible energy source like coal or wind. It is bound up tightly in molecules like water and natural gas, so it is expensive and energy-intensive to extract and purify. A hydrogen economy—which describes a time when the economy's primary energy carrier is hydrogen made from sources of energy that have no net emissions of greenhouse gases—rests on two pillars: a pollution-free source for the hydrogen itself and a fuel cell for efficiently converting it into useful energy without generating pollution.

Fuel cells are small, modular, electrochemical devices, similar to batteries, but which can be continuously fueled. For most purposes, you can think of a fuel cell as a "black box" that takes in hydrogen and oxygen and puts out only water plus electricity and heat.

The most promising fuel cell for transportation is the Proton Exchange Membrane (PEM) fuel cell, first developed in the early 1960s by General Electric for the Gemini space program. The price goal for transportation fuel cells is to come close to that of an internal combustion engine, roughly $30 per kilowatt. Current PEM costs are about 100 times greater. It has taken wind power and solar power each about twenty years to see a tenfold decline in prices, after major government and private-sector investments in R&D, and they still each comprise well under 1% of US electricity generation. A major technology breakthrough is needed in transportation fuel cells before they will be practical. . . .

AN UNUSUALLY DANGEROUS FUEL

Hydrogen has some safety advantages over liquid fuels like gasoline. When a gasoline tank leaks or bursts, the gasoline can pool, creating a risk that any spark would start a fire, or it can splatter, posing a great risk of spreading an existing fire. Hydrogen, however, will escape quickly into the atmosphere as a very diffuse gas. Also, hydrogen gas is non-toxic.

AN EXPENSIVE FUEL

A key problem with the hydrogen economy is that pollution-free sources of hydrogen are unlikely to be practical and affordable for decades. Indeed, even the pollution-generating means of making hydrogen are currently too expensive and too inefficient to substitute for oil. . . .

From the perspective of global warming, electrolysis makes little sense for the foreseeable future. Burning a gallon of gasoline releases about 20 pounds of carbon dioxide. Producing 1 kg of hydrogen by electrolysis would generate, on average, 70 pounds of carbon dioxide. Hydrogen could be generated from renewable electricity, but that would be even more expensive and, as we will see, renewable electricity has better uses for the next few decades. . . .

THE CHICKEN-AND-EGG PROBLEM

Bernard Bulkin, Chief Scientist for British Petroleum, discussed BP's experience with its customers at the National Hydrogen Association annual conference in March 2003. He said, "if hydrogen is going to make it in the mass market as a transport fuel, it has to be available in 30 to 50% of the retail network from the day the first mass manufactured cars hit the showrooms." Yet, a 2002 analysis by Argonne National Laboratory found that even with improved technology, "the hydrogen delivery infrastructure to serve 40% of the light duty fleet is likely to cost over $500 billion." Major breakthroughs in both hydrogen production and delivery will be required to reduce that figure significantly.

Another key issue is the chicken-and-egg problem: Who will spend the hundreds of billions of dollars on a wholly new nationwide infrastructure to provide ready access to hydrogen for consumers with fuel-cell vehicles until millions of hydrogen vehicles are on the road? Yet who will manufacture and market such vehicles until the infrastructure is in place to fuel those vehicles? And will car companies and fuel providers be willing to take this chance before knowing whether the public will embrace these cars? I fervently hope to see an economically, environmentally, and politically plausible scenario for how this classic Catch-22 chasm can be bridged; it does not yet exist. . . .

THE GLOBAL WARMING CENTURY

Perhaps the ultimate reason hydrogen cars are a post-2030 technology is the growing threat of global warming. Our energy choices are now inextricably tied to the fate of our global climate. The burning of fossil fuels—oil, gas and coal—emits carbon dioxide (CO_2) into the atmosphere where it builds up, blankets the earth and traps heat, accelerating global warming. We now have greater concentrations of CO_2 in the atmosphere than at any time in the past 420,000 years, and probably anytime in the past 3 million years—leading to rising global temperatures, more extreme weather events (including floods and droughts), sea level rise, the spread of tropical diseases, and the destruction of crucial habitats, such as coral reefs.

Carbon-emitting products and facilities have a very long lifetime: Cars last 13 to 15 years or more, coal plants can last 50 years. Also, carbon dioxide lingers in the atmosphere trapping heat for more than a century. These two facts together create an urgency to avoid constructing another massive and long-lived generation of energy infrastructure that will cause us to miss the window of opportunity for carbon-free energy until the next century. . . .

Two points are clear. First, we cannot wait for hydrogen cars to address global warming. Second, we should not pursue a strategy to reduce greenhouse gas emissions in the transportation sector that would undermine efforts to reduce greenhouse gas emissions in the electric generation sector. Yet that is precisely what a hydrogen-car strategy would do for the next few decades.

HYDROGEN CARS AND GLOBAL WARMING

For near-term deployment, hydrogen would almost certainly be produced from fossil fuels. Yet running a fuel-cell car on such hydrogen in 2020 would offer no significant life-cycle greenhouse gas advantage over the 2004 Prius running on gasoline.

Further, fuel cell vehicles are likely to be much more expensive than other vehicles, and their fuel is likely to be more expensive (and the infrastructure will probably cost hundreds of billions of dollars). While hybrids and clean diesels may cost more than current vehicles, at least when first introduced, their greater efficiency means that, unlike fuel cell vehicles, they will pay for most if not all of that extra upfront cost over the lifetime of the vehicle. A June 2003 analysis in *Science* magazine by David Keith and Alex Farrell put the cost of CO_2 avoided by fuel cells running on zero-carbon hydrogen at more than \$250 per ton even with a very optimistic fuel cell cost. An advanced internal combustion engine could reduce CO_2 for far less and possibly for a net savings because of the reduced fuel bill.

Probably the biggest analytical mistake made in most hydrogen studies—including the recent National Academy report—is failing to consider whether the fuels that might be used to make hydrogen (such as natural gas or renewables) could be better used simply to make electricity. For example, the life-cycle or "well-to-wheels" efficiency of a hydrogen car running on gas-derived hydrogen is likely to be under 30% for the next two decades. The efficiency of gas-fired power plants is already 55% (and likely to be 60% or higher in 2020). Cogeneration of electricity and heat using natural gas is over 80% efficient. And by displacing coal, the natural gas would be displacing a fuel that has much higher carbon emissions per unit energy than gasoline. For these reasons, natural gas is far more cost-effectively used to reduce CO_2 emissions in electric generation than it is in transportation. . . .

CONCLUSION

Hydrogen and fuel-cell vehicles should be viewed as post-2030 technologies. In September 2003, a DOE panel on *Basic Research Needs for the Hydrogen Economy* concluded the gaps between current hydrogen technologies and what is required by the marketplace "cannot be bridged by incremental advances of the present state of the art," but instead require "revolutionary conceptual breakthroughs." In sum, "the only hope of narrowing the gap significantly is a comprehensive, long-range program of innovative, high risk/high payoff basic research." The National Academy came to a similar conclusion.

The DOE should focus its hydrogen R&D budget on exploratory, breakthrough research. Given that there are few potential zero carbon replacements for oil, the DOE is not spending too much on hydrogen R&D. But given our urgent need for reducing greenhouse gas emissions with clean energy, DOE *is* spending far too little on energy efficiency and renewable energy. If DOE's overall clean energy budget is not increased, however, then it would be bad policy to continue shifting money away from efficiency and renewables toward hydrogen. Any incremental money given to DOE should probably be focused on deploying the cost-effective technologies we have today, to buy us more time for some of the breakthrough research to succeed.

The National Academy panel wrote that "it seems likely that, in the next 10 to 30 years, hydrogen produced in distributed rather than centralized facilities will dominate," and so they recommended increased funding for improving small-scale natural gas reformers and water electrolysis systems. Yet any significant shift toward cars running on distributed hydrogen from natural gas or grid electrolysis would undermine efforts to fight global warming. DOE should not devote any R&D to these technologies. In hydrogen production, DOE should be focused solely on finding a low-cost, zero-carbon source, which will almost certainly be centralized. That probably

means we won't begin the hydrogen transition until after 2030 because of the logistical and cost problems associated with a massive hydrogen delivery infrastructure.

But we shouldn't be rushing to deploy hydrogen cars in the next two decades anyway, since not only are several R&D breakthroughs required, we also need a revolution in clean energy that dramatically accelerates the penetration rates of new CO_2-neutral electricity. Hydrogen cars might find limited value replacing diesel engines (for example in buses) in very polluted cities before 2030, but they are unlikely to achieve mass-market commercialization by then. That is why I conclude neither government policy nor business investment should be based on the belief that hydrogen cars will have meaningful commercial success in the near- or medium-term.

The longer we wait to deploy existing clean energy technologies, and the more inefficient, carbon-emitting infrastructure that we lock into place, the more expensive and the more onerous will be the burden on all segments of society when we finally do act. If we fail to act *now* to reduce greenhouse gas emissions—especially if fail to act because we have bought into the hype about hydrogen's near-term prospects—future generations will condemn us because *we* did not act when we had the facts to guide us, and *they* will most likely be living in a world with a much hotter and harsher climate than ours, one that has undergone an irreversible change for the worse.

Source: Joseph Romm. "Testimony for the Hearing Reviewing the Hydrogen Fuel and FreedomCAR Initiatives." Submitted to the House Science Committee, March 3, 2004.

Victoria D. Markham and Nadia Steinzor: "America's Population-Environment Challenge" (2006) (excerpt)

The Center for Environment & Population is a nonprofit organization devoted to public policy and advocacy on issues relating to the human impact on the Earth's environment and seeks to attain sustainable balance between people and their environment. The group's U.S. National Report on Population and the Environment outlines trends in population and their effects on the environment in terms of energy use, land use, water use, pollution, agriculture, biodiversity, and many other issues. In the following excerpt, the authors use U.S. government statistics to demonstrate how energy consumption rates in the United States are outpacing population growth and remain astronomically higher than those of all other nations.

Energy

Today, almost every facet of modern American life is dependent on some form of energy. It is used to beat and cool homes and buildings, power vehicles, and supply electricity. Yet, securing sufficient energy to meet the demands of the country's growing population is a major challenge. As America's per capita energy consumption increases, demands come up against the nation's ability to provide healthy, sustainable energy sources.

Population is linked to energy through the type and amount of energy sources used, and the waste products generated. Two aspects of energy relate to these trends: energy production to keep up with rising demands, and energy consumption. Both have significant environmental impacts on the air, water, and land.

National Overview: U.S. Population and Energy

Energy is generated from non-renewable fossil fuels (such as coal, oil, and natural gas), renewable sources (such as wood, biomass, wind, waves, and the sun), and nuclear power.

The U.S. consumes almost 25% of the world's energy, yet is home to less than 5% of the global population. U.S. energy consumption reached 2.3 billion metric tons oil equivalent, compared to about 10 billion metric tons for the entire world, in 2001. In contrast, Asia, the most populous continent with 3.6 billion people (12 times the U.S. population), consumes just 3 billion metric tons per year. *On a per capita basis, Americans consume nearly 8,000 kilograms of oil equivalent (kgoe), compared to 3,600 by Europeans and 900 by Asians.*

High U.S. consumption levels in comparison to the rest of the world can be attributed to several factors. These include high energy use in homes, offices, stores, and factories, heavy reliance on motor vehicles for personal and commercial purposes, and relatively long distances over which electricity and raw energy have to be transmitted and transported (such as oil and gas from Alaska and Canada to the lower 48 States).

Most (86%) of U.S. energy comes from a combination of oil and natural gas. Nearly one-third of America's overall energy demand is met by imports. About 60% of the oil consumed in the U.S., and 20% of the natural gas supplies, are imported. Coal supplies are extracted domestically and are expected to continue to surpass demand for decades to come.

The U.S. consumes more than 20 million barrels of oil a day, with almost half used to produce gasoline for motor vehicles. About 32% of U.S. energy consumption is used for road transport, compared to 19% in Europe, and 15% in developing countries.

Transportation is the fastest growing energy use sector in the nation, and is expected to continue to grow at an annual rate of increase of about 2% through 2025. In comparison, residential energy consumption (for such purposes as heating, cooling, and electricity) is projected to grow less than 1% per year through 2025, with much of this due to a rise in use of computers, other electronic products, and appliances.

The U.S. population's energy use results in two primary environmental consequences:

Air pollution
Degradation of land, water, plants and wildlife

Air pollution

A rise in airborne pollution is directly linked to growing populations and their energy use—as demand increases, more fossil fuels are extracted, transported, refined, and burned to meet the demand, and more airborne contaminants are produced.

The most common by-product of burning or processing fossil fuels is carbon dioxide (CO_2), the primary greenhouse gas. *The U.S. is the largest CO_2 emitter in the world, accounting for nearly one-quarter of total global emissions.* At current consumption rates, *the U.S. is projected to use 43% more oil and emit 42% more greenhouse gases than current levels by the year 2025.*

Industry and transportation represent the highest energy-use sectors in the country. Passenger vehicles and heavy trucks accounted for 80% of the total amount of energy used in the transportation sector in 2002. Besides carbon emissions, cars and trucks also cause ground level ozone pollution (or "smog"). In addition to decreasing visibility and harming the health of trees and vegetation, smog is associated with heart disease and respiratory ailments in humans.

About 90% of coal is used for electricity generation. Power plants that use coal and other fossil fuels to generate electricity emit about two-thirds of the sulfur dioxide and one-quarter of the nitrogen oxides released into the air nationwide. These two emissions are the primary components of acid rain, a continuing threat to forests and aquatic systems.

About 40% of mercury emissions generated in the nation come from coal-fired power plants. Toxic even in small amounts, mercury causes severe neurological health and other problems in humans, fish, and wildlife and has triggered fish consumption advisories nationwide.

Particulate matter (a product of soot, ash, and smoke) is generated mostly from coal-fired power plants. Negative effects include hampered growth in vegetation and trees and respiratory diseases in humans. More than 240 counties in 22 states were found to be in violation of U.S. air quality standards for particulate matter in 2004, putting the health of more than 100 million people at risk.

Degradation of land, water, plants and wildlife

Much of the nation's energy resources are located in natural environments where land, water, and wildlife can be negatively affected as coal, oil, and natural gas are extracted and transported. The landscape is dotted with more than 500,000 oil wells, nearly 1,400 coal mines, and 300,000 miles of natural gas pipelines. One oil or gas well and its infrastructure requires a minimum of nine acres of land.

Such infrastructure can fragment wildlife habitat and migration paths, while heavy machinery often destroys trees and vegetation and degrades and compacts soil. For example, several studies in Wyoming where oil and methane gas are produced and generated show that every acre disturbed by noise and traffic from drilling causes elk to avoid 100 acres of habitat. Some fragile soils, particularly in desert environments, can take decades or centuries to regenerate. The most common oil exploration technique (the drilling of holes hundreds of feet in the ground) can destroy land surfaces and cause fissures and noise that harm wildlife, vegetation, and water tables.

Both *exploration and extraction processes* use substances such as acids, gelling agents, and diesel fuels that *contaminate soil, as well as aquifers and surface water systems.* Because much fossil fuel extraction occurs in the arid and rapidly growing West, limited water sources come under added pressure. For example, methane and oil drilling draws significant amounts of water, sometimes tens of thousands of gallons per well, to the surface. In some cases, water can comprise up to 98% of the material brought to the surface. Such processed water often becomes saline or tainted with heavy metals and chemicals, and if not treated properly can contaminate water systems and kill vegetation and livestock when it is re-injected into the ground.

Coal mining creates sludge that pollutes streams and rivers and can leave behind a desolate moonscape, polluted with toxic mine wastes. Even when these areas are re-vegetated by coal companies, ecological health and biological diversity are compromised. Evidence of this is particularly clear in parts of the South, where mountaintop removal has become a common coal extraction technique.

The *transport of fossil fuels* poses environmental risks both on land and at sea. An estimated 67 million gallons of petroleum products dripped and leaked from oil and natural gas pipelines nationwide, polluting soil, water, and wildlife habitat during the 1990s. The health and survival of marine life are jeopardized by tanker shipments—nearly 7,600 oil spills (ranging from a few to hundreds of thousands of gallons) occurred in U.S. internal and coastal waters in 2001.

Two other energy sources, *natural gas and nuclear power,* account for an increasing proportion of the nation's power generation. The share of electricity from natural gas nearly doubled (from 9% to 18%) between 1988 and 2002, while nuclear power currently accounts for 20% of electricity generation.

Yet these sources can also have significant negative environmental and human health impacts. The transportation and storage of natural gas requires special care because it is a highly volatile substance, and extraction requires extensive drilling in pristine wilderness areas. Nuclear energy is a double-edged sword—it doesn't emit pollutants when operating soundly, yet accidents in its production and waste storage and transport, along with vulnerability to terrorist threats make it potentially catastrophic for human and ecosystem health or life. The risks of accidents alone are high for millions of Americans who live along vulnerable transport routes for nuclear waste.

Renewable Energy

In light of the environmental problems caused by fossil fuels, nuclear and other conventional forms of energy, "renewable" energy is increasingly seen as an attractive alternative. *Although renewables account for the smallest proportion of all energy sources (6%), they are the fastest growing domestic source, set to increase 1.5% annually through 2020.* An estimated 30 states have the ability to produce all of their electricity from non-hydroelectric renewables and still have power to export. In 2002, biomass (biological matter such as trees, grasses, agricultural crops or other plant material used as fuel or converted for the production of electric power or other fuels) made up about half of all renewable energy (47%), followed by hydroelectric power (45%); geothermal, wind, and solar together made up less than 10% of the renewable energy consumed.

Source: Victoria D. Markham and Nadia Steinzor. "America's Population-Environment Challenges." *U.S. National Report on Population and the Environment.* New Canaan, Conn.: Center for Environment & Population, 2006, p. 43–45. Available online. URL: http://www.cepnt.org/documents/USNaHReptFinal.pdf. Reprinted by permission.

5

International Documents

The first four documents that follow address international sustainable development from an international perspective, focusing on the relatedness of the issues and how solutions must transcend national boundaries. Subsequent documents are devoted to the issues as they are experienced in individual countries in question, both historically and in contemporary political terms.

GLOBAL SUSTAINABILITY

Gro Harlem Brundtland: "Our Common Future" (August 4, 1987) (excerpt)

The Brundtland Report, named for Gro Harlem Brundtland, the former prime minister of Norway and head of the United Nation's World Commission on Environment and Development, defined sustainable development as that which "meets the needs of the present without compromising the ability of future generations to meet their own needs." Formed during the peak years of the African famine, the commission laid the foundation for decades of discussions and programs that aimed to improve the lives of billions of human beings while recognizing that the way to do so is not by depleting resources and devastating the environment. Sustainable development covers many topics, including international economics, population issues, food security, species and ecosystem survival (recognized now as biodiversity, a term that was not popularized until after the report was published), energy issues including renewable and nonrenewable sources, conservation, and efficiency, industrial development, urban growth, water issues, and peace and conflict. The root of unsustainable development, the commission believed, is poverty, which engenders misuse of resources and becomes a destructive, self-perpetuating cycle. Thus, the cornerstone of sustainable development became the elimination of poverty.

FROM ONE EARTH TO ONE WORLD
An Overview by the
World Commission on Environment and Development

1. In the middle of the 20th century, we saw our planet from space for the first time. Historians may eventually find that this vision had a greater impact on thought than did the Copernican revolution of the 16th century, which upset the human self-image by revealing that the Earth is not the centre of the universe. From space, we see a small and fragile ball dominated not by human activity and edifice but by a pattern of clouds, oceans, greenery, and soils. Humanity's inability to fit its activities into that pattern is changing planetary systems, fundamentally. Many such changes are accompanied by life-threatening hazards. This new reality, from which there is no escape, must be recognized—and managed.

2. Fortunately, this new reality coincides with more positive developments new to this century. We can move information and goods faster around the globe than over before; we can produce more food and more goods with less investment of resources; our technology and science give us at least the potential to look deeper into and better understand natural systems. From space, we can see and study the Earth as an organism whose health depends on the health of all its parts. We have the power to reconcile human affairs with natural laws and to thrive in the process. In this our cultural and spiritual heritages can reinforce our economic interests and survival imperatives.

3. This Commission believes that people can build a future that is more prosperous, more just, and more secure. Our report, *Our Common Future,* is not a prediction of ever increasing environmental decay, poverty, and hardship in an ever more polluted world among ever decreasing resources. We see instead the possibility for a new era of economic growth, one that must be based on policies that sustain and expand the environmental resource base. And we believe such growth to be absolutely essential to relieve the great poverty that is deepening in much of the developing world.

4. But the Commission's hope for the future is conditional on decisive political action now to begin managing environmental resources to ensure both sustainable human progress and human survival. We are not forecasting a future; we are serving a notice—an urgent notice based

on the latest and best scientific evidence—that the time has come to take the decisions needed to secure the resources to sustain this and coming generations. We do not offer a detailed blueprint for action, but instead a pathway by which the peoples of the world may enlarge their spheres of cooperation.

THE GLOBAL CHALLENGE

Successes and Failures

5. Those looking for success and signs of hope can find many: infant mortality is falling; human life expectancy is increasing; the proportion of the world's adults who can read and write is climbing; the proportion of children starting school is rising; and global food production increases faster than the population grows.

6. But the same processes that have produced these gains have given rise to trends that the planet and its people cannot long bear. These have traditionally been divided into failures of 'development' and failures in the management of our human environment. On the development side, in terms of absolute numbers there are more hungry people in the world than ever before, and their numbers and increasing. So are the numbers who cannot read or write, the numbers without safe water or safe and sound homes, and the numbers short of wood fuel with which to cook and warm themselves. The gap between rich and poor nations is widening—not shrinking—and there is little prospect, given present trends and institutional arrangements, that this process will be reversed.

7. There are also environmental trends that threaten to radically alter the planet, that threaten the lives of many species upon it, including the human species. Each year another 6 million hectares of productive dryland turns into worthless desert. Over three decades, this would amount to an area roughly as large as Saudi Arabia. More than 11 million hectares of forests are destroyed yearly, and this, over three decades, would equal an area about the size of India. Much of this forest is converted to low-grade farmland unable to support the farmers who settle it. In Europe, acid precipitation kills forests and lakes and damages the artistic and architectural heritage of nations; it may have acidified vast tracts of soil beyond reasonable hope of repair. The burning of fossil fuels puts into the atmosphere carbon dioxide, which is causing gradual global warming. This 'greenhouse effect' may by early next century have increased average global temperature enough to shift agricultural production areas, raise sea levels to flood coastal cities, and disrupt national economics. Other industrial gases threaten to deplete the planet's pro-

tective ozone shield to such an extent that the number of human and animal cancers would rise sharply and the oceans' food chain would be disrupted. Industry and agriculture put toxic substances into the human food chain and into underground water tables beyond reach of cleansing.

8. There has been a growing realization in national governments and multilateral institutions that it is impossible to separate economic development issue from environment issues; many forms of development erode the environmental resources upon which they must be based, and environmental degradation can undermine economic development. Poverty is a major cause and effect of global environmental problems. It is therefore futile to attempt to deal with environmental problems without a broader perspective that encompasses the factors underlying world poverty and international inequality.

9. These concerns were behind the establishment in 1983 of the World Commission on Environment and Development by the UN General Assembly. The Commission is an independent body, linked to but outside the control of governments and the UN system. The Commission's mandate gave it three objectives: to re-examine the critical environment and development issues and to formulate realistic proposals for dealing with them; to propose new forms of international cooperation on these issues that will influence policies and events in the direction of need changes; and to raise the levels of understanding and commitment to action of individuals, voluntary organizations, businesses, institutes, and governments.

10. Through our deliberations and the testimony of people at the public hearings we held on five continents, all the commissioners came to focus on one central theme: many present development trends leave increasing numbers of people poor and vulnerable, while at the same time degrading the environment. How can such development serve next century's world of twice as many people relying on the same environment? This realization broadened our view of development. We came to see it not in its restricted context of economic growth in developing countries. We came to see that a new development path was required, one that sustained human progress not just in a few places for a few years, but for the entire planet into the distant future. Thus 'sustainable development' becomes a goal not just for the 'developing' nations, but for industrial ones as well.

The Interlocking Crises

11. Until recently, the planet was a large world in which human activities and their effects were neatly compartmentalized within nations,

within sectors (energy, agriculture, trade), and within broad areas of concern (environment, economics, social). These compartments have begun to dissolve. This applies in particular to the various global 'crises' that have seized public concern, particularly over the past decade. These are not separate crises: an environmental crisis, a development crisis, an energy crisis. They are all one.

12. The planet is passing through a period of dramatic growth and fundamental change. Our human world of 5 billion must make room in a finite environment for another human world. The population could stabilize at between 8 and 14 billion sometime next century, according to UN projections. More than 90 per cent of the increase will occur in the poorest countries, and 90 per cent of that growth in already bursting cities.

13. Economic activity has multiplied to create a $13 trillion world economy, and this could grow five- or tenfold in the coming half century. Industrial production has grown more than fiftyfold over the past century, four-fifths of this growth since 1950. Such figures reflect and presage profound impacts upon the biosphere, as the world invests in houses, transport, farms, and industries. Much of the economic growth pulls raw material from forests, soils, seas, and waterways.

14. A mainspring of economic growth is new technology, and while this technology offers the potential for slowing the dangerously rapid consumption of finite resources, it also entails high risks, including new forms of pollution and the introduction to the planet of new variations of life forms that could change evolutionary pathways. Meanwhile, the industries most heavily reliant on environmental resources and most heavily polluting are growing most rapidly in the developing world, where there is both more urgency for growth and less capacity to minimize damaging side effects.

15. These related changes have locked the global economy and global ecology together in new ways. We have in the past been concerned about the impacts of economic growth upon the environment. We are now forced to concern ourselves with the impacts of ecological stress—degradation of soils, water regimes, atmosphere, and forests—upon our economic prospects. We have in the more recent past been forced to face up to a sharp increase in economic interdependence among nations. We are now forced to accustom ourselves to an accelerating ecological interdependence among nations. Ecology and economy are becoming ever more interwoven locally, regionally, nationally, and globally into a seamless net of causes and effects.

16. Impoverishing the local resource base can impoverish wider areas: deforestation by highland farmers causes flooding on lowland farms; factory pollution robs local fishermen of their catch. Such grim local cycles now operate nationally and regionally. Dryland degradation sends environmental refugees in their millions across national borders. Deforestation in Latin America and Asia is causing more floods, and more destructive floods, in downhill, downstream nations. Acid precipitation and nuclear fallout have spread across the borders of Europe. Similar phenomena are emerging on a global scale, such as global warming and loss of ozone. Internationally traded hazardous chemicals entering foods are themselves internationally traded. In the next century, the environmental pressure causing population movements may be increased sharply, while barriers to that movement may be even firmer than they are now.

17. Over the past few decades, life-threatening environmental concerns have surfaced in the developing world. Countrysides are coming under pressure from increasing numbers of farmers and the landless. Cities are filling with people, cars, and factories. Yet at the same time these developing countries must operate in a world in which the resources gap between most developing and industrial nations is widening, in which the industrial world dominates in the rule-making of some key international bodies, and in which the industrial world has already used much of the planet's ecological capital. This inequality is the planet's main 'environmental' problem; it is also its main 'development' problem.

18. International economic relationships pose a particular problem for environmental management in many developing countries. Agriculture, forestry, energy production, and mining generate at least half the gross national product of many developing countries and account for even larger shares of livelihoods and employment. Exports of natural resources remain a large factor in their economies, especially for the least developed. Most of these countries face enormous economic pressures, both international and domestic, to overexploit their environmental resource base.

19. The recent crisis in Africa best and most tragically illustrates the ways in which economics and ecology can interact destructively and trip into disaster. Triggered by drought, its real causes lie deeper. They are to be found in part in national policies that gave too little attention, too late, to the needs of smallholder agriculture and to the threats posed by rapidly rising populations. Their roots extend also to a global

economic system that takes more out of a poor continent than it puts in. Debts that they cannot pay force African nations relying on commodity sales to overuse their fragile soils, thus turning good land to desert. Trade barriers in the wealthy nations—and in many developing nations—make it hard for African nations to sell their goods for reasonable returns, putting yet more pressure on ecological systems. Aid from donor nations has not only been inadequate in scale, but too often has reflected the priorities of the nations giving the aid, rather than the needs of the recipients.

20. The production base of other developing world areas suffers similarly from both local failures and from the workings of international economic systems. As a consequence of the 'debt crisis' of Latin America, that continent's natural resources are now being used not for development but to meet financial obligations to creditors abroad. This approach to the debt problem is short-sighted from several standpoints: economic, political, and environmental. It requires relatively poor countries simultaneously to accept growing poverty while exporting growing amounts of scarce resources.

21. A majority of developing countries now have lower per capita incomes than when the decade began. Rising poverty and unemployment have increased pressure on environmental resources as more people have been forced to rely more directly upon them. Many governments have cut back efforts to protect the environment and to bring ecological considerations into development planning.

22. The deepening and widening environmental crisis presents a threat to national security—and even survival—that may be greater than well-armed, ill-disposed neighbours and unfriendly alliances. Already in parts of Latin America. Asia, the Middle East, and Africa, environmental decline is becoming a source of political unrest and international tension. The recent destruction of much of Africa's dryland agricultural production was more severe than if an invading army had pursued a scorched-earth policy. Yet most of the affected governments still spend far more to protect their people from invading armies than from the invading desert.

23. Globally, military expenditures total about $1 trillion a year and continue to grow. In many countries, military spending consumes such a high proportion of GNP that it itself does great damage to these societies' development efforts. Governments tend to base their approaches to 'security' on traditional definitions. This is most obvious in the attempts to achieve security through the development of potentially planet-destroying nuclear weapons systems. Studies suggest that the cold and

dark nuclear winter following even a limited nuclear war could destroy plant and animal ecosystems and leave any human survivors occupying a devastated planet very different from the one they inherited.

24. The arms race—in all parts of the world—pre-empts resources that might be used more productively to diminish the security threats created by environmental conflict and the resentments that are fuelled by widespread poverty.

25. Many present efforts to guard and maintain human progress, to meet human needs, and to realize human ambitions are simply unsustainable—in both the rich and poor nations. They draw too heavily, too quickly, on already overdrawn environmental resource accounts to be affordable far into the future without bankrupting those accounts. They may show profits on the balance sheets of our generation, but our children will inherit the losses. We borrow environmental capital from future generations with no intention or prospect of repaying. They may damn us for our spendthrift ways, but they can never collect on our debt to them. We act as we do because we can get away with it: future generations do not vote; they have no political or financial power; they cannot challenge our decisions.

26. But the results of the present profligacy are rapidly closing the options for future generations. Most of today's decision makers will be dead before the planet feels the heavier effects of acid precipitation, global warming, ozone depletion, or widespread desertification and species loss. Most of the young voters of today will still be alive. In the Commission's hearings it was the young, those who have the most to lose, who were the harshest critics of the planet's present management.

Sustainable Development

27. Humanity has the ability to make development sustainable to ensure that it meets the needs of the present without compromising the ability of future generations to meet their own needs. The concept of sustainable development does imply limits—not absolute limits but limitations imposed by the present state of technology and social organization on environmental resources and by the ability of the biosphere to absorb the effects of human activities. But technology and social organization can be both managed and improved to make way for a new era of economic growth. The Commission believes that widespread poverty is no longer inevitable. Poverty is not only an evil in itself, but sustainable development requires meeting the basic needs of all and extending to all the opportunity to fulfil their aspirations for a better life. A world in

which poverty is endemic will always be prone to ecological and other catastrophes.

28. Meeting essential needs requires not only a new era of economic growth for nations in which the majority are poor, but an assurance that those poor get their fair share of the resources required to sustain that growth. Such equity would be aided by political systems that secure effective citizen participation in decision making and by greater democracy in international decision making.

29. Sustainable global development requires that those who are more affluent adopt life-styles within the planet's ecological means—in their use of energy, for example. Further, rapidly growing populations can increase the pressure on resources and slow any rise in living standards: thus sustainable development can only be pursued if population size and growth are in harmony with the changing productive potential of the ecosystem.

30. Yet in the end, sustainable development is not a fixed state of harmony, but rather a process of change in which the exploitation of resources, the direction of investments, the orientation of technological development, and institutional change are made consistent with future as well as present needs. We do not pretend that the process is easy or straightforward. Painful choices have to be made. Thus, in the final analysis, sustainable development must rest on political will.

Source: Gro Harlem Brundtland. "Our Common Future." *Report of the World Commission on Environment and Development.* New York: United Nations, August 4, 1987. Reprinted by permission.

United Nations: "Rio Declaration on Environment and Development" (June 3–14, 1992)

In 1992, the United Nations Conference on Environment and Development, commonly called the Earth Summit, took place in Rio de Janeiro, Brazil. The conference was attended by an unprecedented number of heads of states, all gathered for the purpose of drafting a treaty to guide global sustainable development. The resulting document was the Rio Declaration on Environment and Development, or simply the Rio Declaration. It is a short document of 27 principles that provides a framework for developing nations, protecting their integrity and indigenous resources and allowing them to attain development equal to industrialized nations. The principles stress the importance of eliminating poverty, understanding that development and the environment are interrelated and require international cooperation.

The United Nations Conference on Environment and Development,

Having met at Rio de Janeiro from 3 to 14 June 1992,

Reaffirming the Declaration of the United Nations Conference on the Human Environment, adopted at Stockholm on 16 June 1972, and seeking to build upon it,

With the goal of establishing a new and equitable global partnership through the creation of new levels of cooperation among States, key sectors of societies and people,

Working towards international agreements which respect the interests of all and protect the integrity of the global environmental and developmental system,

Recognizing the integral and interdependent nature of the Earth, our home,

Proclaims that:

Principle 1

Human beings are at the centre of concerns for sustainable development. They are entitled to a healthy and productive life in harmony with nature.

Principle 2

States have, in accordance with the Charter of the United Nations and the principles of international law, the sovereign right to exploit their own resources pursuant to their own environmental and developmental policies, and the responsibility to ensure that activities within their jurisdiction or control do not cause damage to the environment of other States or of areas beyond the limits of national jurisdiction.

Principle 3

The right to development must be fulfilled so as to equitably meet developmental and environmental needs of present and future generations.

Principle 4

In order to achieve sustainable development, environmental protection shall constitute an integral part of the development process and cannot be considered in isolation from it.

Principle 5

All States and all people shall cooperate in the essential task of eradicating poverty as an indispensable requirement for sustainable development, in order to decrease the disparities in standards of living and better meet the needs of the majority of the people of the world.

Principle 6

The special situation and needs of developing countries, particularly the least developed and those most environmentally vulnerable, shall be given special priority. International actions in the field of environment and development should also address the interests and needs of all countries.

Principle 7

States shall cooperate in a spirit of global partnership to conserve, protect and restore the health and integrity of the Earth's ecosystem. In view of the different contributions to global environmental degradation, States have common but differentiated responsibilities. The developed countries acknowledge the responsibility that they bear in the international pursuit of sustainable development in view of the pressures their societies place on the global environment and of the technologies and financial resources they command.

Principle 8

To achieve sustainable development and a higher quality of life for all people, States should reduce and eliminate unsustainable patterns of production and consumption and promote appropriate demographic policies.

Principle 9

States should cooperate to strengthen endogenous capacity-building for sustainable development by improving scientific understanding through exchanges of scientific and technological knowledge, and by enhancing the development, adaptation, diffusion and transfer of technologies, including new and innovative technologies.

Principle 10

Environmental issues are best handled with the participation of all concerned citizens, at the relevant level. At the national level, each individual shall have appropriate access to information concerning the environment that is held by public authorities, including information on hazardous materials and activities in their communities, and the opportunity to participate in decision-making processes. States shall facilitate and encourage public awareness and participation by making information widely available. Effective access to judicial and administrative proceedings, including redress and remedy, shall be provided.

Principle 11

States shall enact effective environmental legislation. Environmental standards, management objectives and priorities should reflect the environmental and developmental context to which they apply. Standards applied by some countries may be inappropriate and of unwarranted economic and social cost to other countries, in particular developing countries.

Principle 12

States should cooperate to promote a supportive and open international economic system that would lead to economic growth and sustainable development in all countries, to better address the problems of environmental degradation. Trade policy measures for environmental purposes should not constitute a means of arbitrary or unjustifiable discrimination or a disguised restriction on international trade. Unilateral actions to deal with environmental challenges outside the jurisdiction of the importing country should be avoided. Environmental measures addressing transboundary or global environmental problems should, as far as possible, be based on an international consensus.

Principle 13

States shall develop national law regarding liability and compensation for the victims of pollution and other environmental damage. States shall also cooperate in an expeditious and more determined manner to develop further international law regarding liability and compensation for adverse effects of environmental damage caused by activities within their jurisdiction or control to areas beyond their jurisdiction.

Principle 14

States should effectively cooperate to discourage or prevent the relocation and transfer to other States of any activities and substances that cause severe environmental degradation or are found to be harmful to human health.

Principle 15

In order to protect the environment, the precautionary approach shall be widely applied by States according to their capabilities. Where there are threats of serious or irreversible damage, lack of full scientific certainty shall not be used as a reason for postponing cost-effective measures to prevent environmental degradation.

Principle 16

National authorities should endeavour to promote the internalization of environmental costs and the use of economic instruments, taking into account the approach that the polluter should, in principle, bear the cost of pollution, with due regard to the public interest and without distorting international trade and investment.

Principle 17

Environmental impact assessment, as a national instrument, shall be undertaken for proposed activities that are likely to have a significant adverse impact on the environment and are subject to a decision of a competent national authority.

Principle 18

States shall immediately notify other States of any natural disasters or other emergencies that are likely to produce sudden harmful effects on the environment of those States. Every effort shall be made by the international community to help States so afflicted.

Principle 19

States shall provide prior and timely notification and relevant information to potentially affected States on activities that may have a significant adverse transboundary environmental effect and shall consult with those States at an early stage and in good faith.

Principle 20

Women have a vital role in environmental management and development. Their full participation is therefore essential to achieve sustainable development.

Principle 21

The creativity, ideals and courage of the youth of the world should be mobilized to forge a global partnership in order to achieve sustainable development and ensure a better future for all.

Principle 22

Indigenous people and their communities and other local communities have a vital role in environmental management and development because of their knowledge and traditional practices. States should recognize and duly support their identity, culture and interests and enable their effective participation in the achievement of sustainable development.

Principle 23

The environment and natural resources of people under oppression, domination and occupation shall be protected.

Principle 24

Warfare is inherently destructive of sustainable development. States shall therefore respect international law providing protection for the environment in times of armed conflict and cooperate in its further development, as necessary.

Principle 25

Peace, development and environmental protection are interdependent and indivisible.

Principle 26

States shall resolve all their environmental disputes peacefully and by appropriate means in accordance with the Charter of the United Nations.

Principle 27

States and people shall cooperate in good faith and in a spirit of partnership in the fulfilment of the principles embodied in this Declaration and in the further development of international law in the field of sustainable development.

Source: United Nations. "Rio Declaration on Environment and Development," Report of the United Nations Conference on Environment and Development, Rio de Janeiro, Brazil, June 3–14, 1992. Reprinted by permission.

Bjørn Lomborg: *The Skeptical Environmentalist: Measuring the Real State of the World* (2001) (excerpt)

Lomborg's book is an exhaustive analysis of statistics regarding environmental issues, including global warming, food security, poverty, deforestation, biodiversity, fossil fuels, water issues, and pollution. Below is his definition of "The Litany," which he believes is the driving force behind all current efforts to stem damage to the environment and promote sustainable development. The book met with controversy when it was published, with many scientists vociferously objecting to Lomborg's subversion of the status quo, and others hailing his as a voice of reason. Overall, Lomborg does not deny that humanity faces problems or that it will face catastrophe in the future, but he believes that current issues are misrepresented by scientists, the media, and environmentalists who are simply and needlessly alarmist. The truth, he maintains, is that prosperity is rising for a vast majority of people on the planet and will continue to do so for generations.

Part 1: The Litany

> We are all familiar with the Litany: the environment is in poor shape here on Earth. Our resources are running out. The population is ever growing, leaving less and less to eat. The air and water are becoming ever more polluted. The planet's species are becoming extinct in vast numbers—we kill off more than 40,000 each year. The forests are disappearing, fish stocks are collapsing and the coral reefs are dying.
>
> We are defiling our Earth, the fertile topsoil is disappearing, we are paving over nature, destroying the wilderness, decimating the biosphere, and will end up killing ourselves in the process. The world's ecosystem is breaking down. We are fast approaching the absolute limit of viability, and the limits of growth are becoming apparent.
>
> We know the Litany and have heard it so often that yet another repetition is, well, almost reassuring. There is just one problem: it does not seem to be backed up by the available evidence. . . .

Source: Bjørn Lomborg. "Part I: The Litany." *The Skeptical Environmentalist: Measuring the Real State of the World,* translated by Hugh Matthews. New York: Cambridge University Press, 2001, p. 4.

Living Planet Report (2006) (excerpt)

WWF, formerly known as the World Wildlife Fund, is a nonprofit organization that analyzes environmental data and educates people worldwide on global environmental threats. Since 1998 they have released an annual Living Planet Report *in conjunction with the Global Footprint Network. The report illustrates how global sustainability is threatened by ecological overshoot—meaning that humanity consumes resources at a faster rate than the Earth can replenish them. Their recommendations follow the precepts of sustainable development and underscore the lopsidedness of resource use in the United States and other developed countries at the expense of the developing world.*

FOREWORD

WWF began its Living Planet Reports in 1998 to show the state of the natural world and the impact of human activity upon it. Since then we have continuously refined and developed our measures of the state of the Earth.

And it is not good news. The *Living Planet Report 2006* confirms that we are using the planet's resources faster than they can be renewed—the latest data available (for 2003) indicate that humanity's Ecological Footprint, our impact upon the planet, has more than tripled since 1961. Our footprint now exceeds the world's ability to regenerate by about 25 percent.

The consequences of our accelerating pressure on Earth's natural systems are both predictable and dire. The other index in this report, the Living Planet Index, shows a rapid and continuing loss of biodiversity—populations of vertebrate species have declined by about one third since 1970. This confirms previous trends.

The message of these two indices is clear and urgent: we have been exceeding the Earth's ability to support our lifestyles for the past 20 years, and we need to stop. We must balance our consumption with the natural world's capacity to regenerate and absorb our wastes. If we do not, we risk irreversible damage.

We know where to start. The biggest contributor to our footprint is the way in which we generate and use energy. The *Living Planet Report* indicates that our reliance on fossil fuels to meet our energy needs continues to grow and that climate-changing emissions now make up 48 percent—almost half—of our global footprint.

We also know, from this report, that the challenge of reducing our footprint goes to the very heart of our current models for economic development. Comparing the Ecological Footprint with a recognized measure of human development, the United Nations Human Development Index, the report clearly shows that what we currently accept as "high development" is a long way away from the world's stated aim of sustainable development. As countries improve the well-being of their people, they are bypassing the goal of sustainability and going into what we call "overshoot"—using far more resources than the planet can sustain. It is inevitable that this path will limit the abilities of poor countries to develop and of rich countries to maintain prosperity.

It is time to make some vital choices. Change that improves living standards while reducing our impact on the natural world will not be easy. But we must recognize that choices we make now will shape our opportunities far into the future. The cities, power plants, and homes we build today will either lock society into damaging overconsumption beyond our lifetimes, or begin to propel this and future generations towards sustainable living.

The good news is that this can be done. We already have technologies that can lighten our footprint, including many that can significantly reduce climate-threatening carbon dioxide emissions. And some are getting started. WWF is working with leading companies that are taking action to reduce the footprint—cutting carbon emissions, and promoting sustainability in other sectors, from fisheries to forests. We are also working with governments who are striving to stem biodiversity loss by protecting vital habitats on an unprecedented scale.

But we must all do more. The message of the *Living Planet Report 2006* is that we are living beyond our means, and that the choices each of us makes today will shape the possibilities for the generations which follow us.

James P. Leape
Director General, WWF International

INTRODUCTION

This report describes the changing state of global biodiversity and the pressure on the biosphere arising from human consumption of natural resources. It is built around two indicators: the Living Planet Index, which reflects the health of the planet's ecosystems; and the Ecological Footprint, which shows the extent of human demand on these ecosystems. These measures are tracked over several decades to reveal past trends, then three scenarios explore what might lie ahead. The scenarios show how the choices we make might lead to a sustainable society living in harmony with robust ecosystems, or to the collapse of these same ecosystems, resulting in a permanent loss of biodiversity and erosion of the planet's ability to support people.

The Living Planet Index measures trends in the Earth's biological diversity. It tracks populations of 1313 vertebrate species—fish, amphibians, reptiles, birds, mammals—from all around the world. Separate indices are produced for terrestrial, marine, and freshwater species, and the three trends are then averaged to create an aggregated index. Although vertebrates represent only a fraction of known species, it is assumed that trends in their populations are typical of biodiversity overall. By tracking wild species, the Living Planet Index is also monitoring the health of ecosystems. Between

1970 and 2003, the index fell by about 30 per cent. This global trend suggests that we are degrading natural ecosystems at a rate unprecedented in human history.

Biodiversity suffers when the biosphere's productivity cannot keep pace with human consumption and waste generation. The Ecological Footprint tracks this in terms of the area of biologically productive land and water needed to provide ecological resources and services—food, fibre, and timber, land on which to build, and land to absorb carbon dioxide (CO_2) released by burning fossil fuels. The Earth's biocapacity is the amount of biologically productive area—cropland, pasture, forest, and fisheries—that is available to meet humanity's needs. Freshwater consumption is not included in the Ecological Footprint; rather it is addressed in a separate section of the report.

Since the late 1980s, we have been in overshoot—the Ecological Footprint has exceeded the Earth's biocapacity—as of 2003 by about 25 percent. Effectively, the Earth's regenerative capacity can no longer keep up with demand—people are turning resources into waste faster than nature can turn waste back into resources.

Humanity is no longer living off nature's interest, but drawing down its capital. This growing pressure on ecosystems is causing habitat destruction or degradation and permanent loss of productivity, threatening both biodiversity and human well-being.

For how long will this be possible? A moderate business-as-usual scenario, based on United Nations projections showing slow, steady growth of economies and populations, suggests that by mid-century, humanity's demand on nature will be twice the biosphere's productive capacity. At this level of ecological deficit, exhaustion of ecological assets and large-scale ecosystem collapse become increasingly likely.

Two different paths leading to sustainability are also explored. One entails a slow shift from our current route, the other a more rapid transition to sustainability. The Ecological Footprint allows us to estimate the cumulative ecological deficit that will accrue under each of these scenarios: the larger this ecological debt, and the longer it persists, the greater the risk of damage to the planet. This risk must be considered in concert with the economic costs and potential social disruptions associated with each path.

Moving towards sustainability depends on significant action now. Population size changes slowly, and human-made capital—homes, cars, roads, factories, or power plants—can last for many decades. This implies that policy and investment decisions made today will continue to determine our resource demand throughout much of the 21st century.

As the Living Planet Index shows, human pressure is already threatening many of the biosphere's assets. Even moderate "business as usual" is likely to accelerate these negative impacts. And given the slow response of many biological systems, there is likely to be a considerable time lag before ecosystems benefit significantly from people's positive actions.

We share the Earth with 5–10 million species or more. By choosing how much of the planet's biocapacity we appropriate, we determine how much is left for their use. To maintain biodiversity, it is essential that a part of the biosphere's productive capacity is reserved for the survival of other species, and that this share is split between all biogeographic realms and major biomes.

To manage the transition to sustainability, we need measures that demonstrate where we have been, where we are today, and how far we still have to go. The Living Planet Index and the Ecological Footprint help to establish baselines, set targets, and monitor achievements and failures. Such vital information can stimulate the creativity and innovation required to address humanity's biggest challenge: how can we live well while sustaining the planet's other species and living within the capacity of one Earth? . . .

ECOLOGICAL FOOTPRINT: FREQUENTLY ASKED QUESTIONS

How is the Ecological Footprint calculated?

The Ecological Footprint measures the amount of biologically productive land and water area required to produce the resources an individual, population, or activity consumes and to absorb the waste they generate, given prevailing technology and resource management. This area is expressed in global hectares (gha), hectares with world-average biological productivity (1 hectare = 2.47 acres). Footprint calculations use yield factors to take into account national differences in biological productivity (for example, tonnes of wheat per United Kingdom or Argentinian hectare versus world average) and equivalence factors to take into account differences in world average productivity among land types (for example, world average forest versus world average cropland).

Footprint and biocapacity results for nations are calculated annually by Global Footprint Network. The continuing methodological development of these National Footprint Accounts is overseen by a formal review committee (www.footprintstandards.org/committees). A detailed methods paper and copies of sample calculation sheets can be obtained at www.footprintnetwork.org.

What is included in the Ecological Footprint? What is excluded?

To avoid exaggerating human demand on nature, the Ecological Footprint includes only those aspects of resource consumption and waste production for which the Earth has regenerative capacity, and where data exist that allow this demand to be expressed in terms of productive area. For example, freshwater withdrawals are not included in the footprint, although the energy used to pump or treat them is.

Ecological Footprint accounts provide snapshots of past resource demand and availability. They do not predict the future. Thus, while the footprint does not estimate future losses caused by present degradation of ecosystems, if persistent this is likely to be reflected in future accounts as a loss of biocapacity.

Footprint accounts also do not indicate the intensity with which a biologically productive area is being used, nor do they pinpoint specific biodiversity pressures. Finally, the Ecological Footprint, as a biophysical measure, does not evaluate the essential social and economic dimensions of sustainability.

How have the footprint calculations been improved since the last *Living Planet Report*?

A formal process is in place to assure continuous improvement of the National Footprint Accounts methodology. Coordinated by Global Footprint Network, this process has been supported by the European Environment Agency and Global Footprint Network partner organizations, among others.

The most significant change since the *Living Planet Report 2004* has been the incorporation of a new dataset, the United Nations COMTRADE database, to track flows between nations of more than 600 products. This allows more accurate allocation of the footprint embodied in traded goods. Other revisions have improved the accuracy of cropland and forest sections of the calculations.

In previous Living Planet Reports, we reported global hectares specific to each year, as both the total number of bioproductive hectares and world average productivity per hectare change annually. To simplify comparison of footprint and biocapacity results from year to year, in this report all time trends are given in constant 2003 global hectares. Similar to the use of inflation-adjusted dollars in economic statistics, the use of a fixed global hectare shows how absolute levels of consumption and bioproductivity, rather than just the ratio between them, are changing over time. Table 9 shows the conversion of global hectares of selected years into constant 2003 global hectares.

How does the Ecological Footprint account for the use of fossil fuels?
Fossil fuels—coal, oil, and natural gas—are extracted from the Earth's crust rather than produced by ecosystems. When burning this fuel, CO_2 is produced. In order to avoid carbon accumulation in the atmosphere, the goal of the United Nations Framework Convention on Climate Change, two options exist: human technological sequestration, such as deep well injection; or natural sequestration. Natural sequestration corresponds to the biocapacity required to absorb and store the CO_2 not sequestered by humans, less the amount absorbed by the oceans. This is the footprint for CO_2. Although negligible amounts of CO_2 are currently sequestered through human technological processes, these technologies will lower the carbon footprint associated with burning fossil fuels as they are brought online.

The sequestration rate used in Ecological Footprint calculations is based on an estimate of how much carbon the world's forests can remove from the atmosphere and retain. One 2003 global hectare can absorb the CO_2 released by burning approximately 1,450 litres of petrol per year.

The CO_2 footprint does not suggest that carbon sequestration is the key to resolving global warming. Rather the opposite: it shows that the biosphere does not have sufficient capacity to cope with current levels of CO_2 emissions. As forests mature, their CO_2 sequestration rate approaches zero, and they may even become net emitters of carbon.

How does the Ecological Footprint account for nuclear energy?
The demand on biocapacity associated with the use of nuclear power is difficult to quantify, in part because many of its impacts are not addressed by the research question underlying the footprint. For lack of conclusive data, the footprint of nuclear electricity is assumed to be the same as the footprint of the equivalent amount of electricity from fossil fuels. Global Footprint Network and its partners are working to refine this assumption. Currently, the footprint of nuclear electricity represents less than 4 percent of the total global Ecological Footprint.

How is international trade taken into account?

The National Footprint Accounts calculate each country's net consumption by adding its imports to its production and subtracting its exports. This means that the resources used for producing a car that is manufactured in Japan, but sold and used in India, will contribute to the Indian, not the Japanese, consumption footprint.

The resulting national footprints can be distorted, since the resources used and waste generated in making products for export are not fully documented. This affects the footprints of countries whose trade-flows are large relative to their overall economies. These misallocations, however, do not affect the total global Ecological Footprint.

Does the Ecological Footprint take other species into account?

The Ecological Footprint describes human demand on nature. Currently, there are 1.8 global hectares of biocapacity available per person on Earth, less if some of this biological productivity is allocated for consumption by wild species. The value society places on biodiversity will determine how much productivity is reserved as a buffer. Efforts to increase biocapacity, such as monocropping and the application of pesticides, may also increase pressure on biodiversity; this can increase the size of the buffer required to achieve the same conservation results.

Does the Ecological Footprint say what is a "fair" or "equitable" use of resources?

The footprint documents what has happened in the past. It quantifies the ecological resources used by an individual or a population, but it cannot prescribe what they should be using Resource allocation is a policy issue, based on societal beliefs about what is or is not equitable. Thus, while footprint accounting can determine the average biocapacity that is available per person, it cannot stipulate how that biocapacity should be shared between individuals or nations. However, it does provide a context for such discussions.

Does the Ecological Footprint matter if the supply of renewable resources can be increased and advances in technology can slow the depletion of non-renewable resources?

The Ecological Footprint measures the current state of resource use and waste generation. It asks: in a given year, did human demands on ecosystems exceed the ability of ecosystems to meet those demands? Footprint analysis reflects both increases in the productivity of renewable resources (for example, if the productivity of cropland is increased, then the footprint of 1 tonne of wheat will decrease) and technological innovation (for example, if the paper industry doubles the overall efficiency of paper production, the footprint per tonne of paper will be cut by half). Ecological Footprint accounts capture these changes as they occur and can determine the extent to which these innovations have succeeded in bringing human demand within the capacity of the planet's ecosystems. If there is a sufficient increase in ecological supply and reduction in human demand due to technological advances or other factors, footprint accounts will show this as the elimination of global overshoot.

Does the Ecological Footprint ignore the role of population growth as a driver in humanity's increasing consumption?

The total Ecological Footprint of a nation or of humanity as a whole is a function of the number of people consuming, the average amount of goods and services an average person consumes, and the resource intensity of these goods and services. Since footprint accounting is historical, it does not predict how any of these factors will change in the future. However, if population grows or declines (or any of the other factors change), this will be reflected in future footprint accounts.

Footprint accounts can also show how resource consumption is distributed among regions. For example, the total footprint of the Asia-Pacific region, with its large population but low per person footprint, can be directly compared to that of North America, with its much smaller population but much larger per person footprint.

How do I calculate the Ecological Footprint of a city or region?

While the calculations for global and national Ecological Footprints have been standardized within the National Footprint Accounts, there are a variety of ways used to calculate the footprint of a city or region. The family of "process-based" approaches use production recipes and supplementary statistics to allocate the national per capita footprint to consumption categories (such as for food, shelter, mobility, goods, and services). Regional or municipal average per capita footprints are calculated by scaling these national results up or down based on differences between national and local consumption patterns. The family of input-output approaches use monetary, physical, or hybrid input-output tables for allocating overall demand to consumption categories.

There is growing recognition of the need to standardize sub-national footprint application methods in order to increase their comparability across studies and over time. In response to this need, methods and approaches for calculating the footprint of cities and regions are currently being aligned through the global Ecological Footprint Standards initiative. For more information on current footprint standards and ongoing standardization debates, see www.footprintstandards.org.

Source: Chris Hails, ed. "Ecological Footprint." *Living Planet Report 2006.* Gland, Switzerland: WWF, 2006. Available online. URL: www.footprintnetwork.org.

CHINA

White Paper on China's Agenda 21 (March 1994) (excerpt)

China participated in the United Nation's Agenda 21 program that arose from the 1992 Earth Summit in Rio de Janiero, and the following chapter is item number 14 from the Chinese government's agenda. It represents "a strategic alternative for sustainable development with Chinese characteristics." In it, the Administrative Center for China's Agenda 21 outlines a plan to use China's natural resources freely while maintaining China's rapid economic growth, in the hope that economic growth will outpace resource depletion. This strategy is backed by a belief that China is resource-poor in terms of per capita distribution, especially when it comes to water. The government's solution is a market-driven natural resource management system in which the government does not pose restrictions on economic development. However, the government does recognize the need to establish who owns what resources and who has the right to use them, something that was not relevant in previous years under stricter government regimes. Other items on their Agenda 21 include improving sanitation and involving minority groups in instituting change.

"Conservation and Sustainable Use of Natural Resources"

. . . Natural resources are an important material basis for a stable national economy and social development. They can be divided into two categories: the exhaustible, such as minerals, and the inexhaustible, such as forests and grasslands. With industrialization and urbanization, mankind's great demand for natural resources and their large scale exploitation and consumption has resulted in the weakening, deterioration and exhaustion of these resources. One difficult task faced by all countries is to guarantee the lasting utilization of natural resources at the lowest possible environmental cost while still assuring economic and social development. China with its large population and poor economic foundation is engaged in a process of increased urbanization and industrialization. Its natural resources are relatively inadequate and the per capita Gross National Product (GNP) is still lagging behind that of most of the world. The traditional mode of resource consuming development and the current inefficient economy are severely threatening the lasting utilization of natural resources. Therefore, the strategy of choice is to attain economic development at a rate above the world's average while sustaining a continuous increase in growth at relatively low resource and social costs. This is a strategic alternative for sustainable development with Chinese characteristics.

At the present time China is confronted with tough challenges with respect to the sustainable use and conservation of important natural resources. These challenges involve two aspects. Firstly, the per capita resources of China is relatively insignificant. In 1989 the per capita fresh water, cultivated land, forest and grassland of China comprised 28.1%, 32.3%, 14.3% and 32.3% of the world's average, respectively, while the per capita resources figures and ecological quality are still declining or deteriorating. Secondly, the increasing shortage of natural resources, inter alia the shortage of water resources in North China, nationwide shortage of cultivated land and soil degeneration, resulted from the surging population and more-than-adequate dependence of economic development on resources, will become an important constraint to the sustainable, rapid and healthy development of society and economy of China. It is estimated that more than three hundred cities are water-deficient with a total daily water shortage amounting to over 16 million metric tonnes. Shortage of irrigational water has resulted in a yearly reduction of crops output of over 2.5 million tonnes, thus exerting serious impact on industrial production, agriculture and people's daily life. In this respect the sustainable use of water resources is the most pressing problem among those concerning the conservation and sustainable use of all natural resources.

The primary problems pending, with respect to the utilization and protection of natural resources in China are:

(a) Lack of effective mechanisms for the comprehensive management of resources as well as for incorporating the accounting for natural resources into the national economic accounting system, while concurrently, the traditional mode of natural resource management and its legislative system are facing the challenge of the market-oriented economy;

(b) Economic development which is traditionally unduly dependent upon the sole input of resources and energy, and is accompanied by massive extravagance of resources and outflow of pollutants without consideration for the relation between the excessive exploitation and use of resources and deterioration of natural environment;

(c) Distribution of the natural resources by means of administrative intervention which seriously hinders the effective allocation of resources, the establishment of a resource property system and the creation of a resource market;

(d) An irrational resource pricing methodology contributing to severely misrepresenting the market price of resources, which has resulted in devaluing resources, depressing prices of resources and the excessive expansion of the demand for resources;

(e) Lack of an effective mechanism for analyzing the natural resource policy as well as the supporting information for decision making, inter alia a lack of multisectoral analysis of policy and sharing of information which can provoke divergence in policy goals between and among various departments and can lead to a negative impact;

(f) Lack of coordinated and consistent management mechanism and organization has resulted in a decentralized system for resources management.

To ensure that the limited natural resources will satisfy the demand of sustained high speed economic development, China's policies are:

(a) To protect and make economical and appropriate use of resources;

(b) To be engaged in both discovering new resources and in using existing natural resources economically. China must depend on technological progress to tap its resource potential, make full use of the market economy and economic means to achieve effective resources distribution, and insist on efficiency in the utilization of resources and resource intensive economic development;

(c) To implement the development and protection of resources in conjunction with economic construction in order to illustrate the principle of integrating economic and social effects with environmental benefits for the protection and sustainable utilization of natural resources.

This chapter is concerned with five types of natural resources: land, forest, water, minerals and grassland. The general objectives of this chapter are to realize the mode and channel for conservation and sustainable utilization of natural resources, such as to summarize the existing problems in China's exploitation, utilization and protection of the six major natural resources, and to present the project areas for protection and rational use of six major resources. . . .

PROGRAMME AREAS

A. Establishing the Natural Resource Management System Based on the Market Mechanisms and Government Macroeconomic Control

Basis for action

China has formulated and promulgated many laws and regulations aimed at the rational utilization and protection of natural resources. However, very serious problems exist related to the degeneration of natural resources and environmental deterioration. With the continuation of economic reform and the emergence of multitudinous small enterprises and other economic agents which have never existed before, the enforcement of these laws and regulations poses a severe challenge to the market economy. To implement the required sustainable development, the government which is likely to reinforce and amend existing regulations, will take advantage of the economic policy including market incentive means to make the market mechanism play a prominent role in the transformation of ideas and methods for utilization of natural resources.

In China the natural resources predominantly belong to the state. Confusion between the ownership and the rights for the exploitation and handling of resources and lack of clear guidelines defining the economic relations between the central government, the local government and various economic entities have resulted in the irrational allocation of natural resources and low efficiency in the exploitation and utilization of resources. With the deepening of economic reform and development of the market economy, the state has provided private enterprises access to the exploitation of natural resources through a responsibility system or other means. Establishing a natural resource management system based on the market mechanisms in conjunction with the adjustment by the government is being accelerated.

Objectives

The main objective of this programme area is to improve the natural resources management system. The specific objectives are:

(a) To identify the roles to be played by the central government, enterprises and individuals with respect to the ownership, obligations and rights over the use and handling of natural resources;

(b) To introduce a market mechanism for the use and allocation of natural resources which would follow the economic principle "the user pays" to facilitate the effective exploitation of resources in favour of the environment;

(c) To define and improve the role of planning at the national and regional, as well as trans-sectoral levels in the utilization and protection of resources geared to meet the objectives of economic development and current measures of economic reform;

(d) To rectify the existing laws and management system concerning the management and protection of natural resources, following the principle of reinforcing the market economy;

(e) To use economic measures and to a greater extent the market incentives as important supplements to legislation in order to assure the macroeconomic adjustment being undertaken by the government for regulating the market and for rectifying the gyration of pricing policies. . . .

Source: "Conservation and Sustainable Use of Natural Resources." *White Paper on China's Agenda 21.* Beijing: Administrative Center for China's Agenda 21, 1994.

Jiang Zemin's Speech Marking Yangtze-Damming for Three Gorges Project (November 8, 1997) (excerpt)

President Jiang Zemin of China celebrated the damming of the Yangtze River with the following speech on November 8, 1997. The Three Gorges Project was the largest dam in the world at the time and was designed to control flooding and provide hydropower in strategic areas of China. President Zemin claimed that only several hundred thousand people were relocated because of the project (although some believe the real number is well over a million), all of whom are better off now than they were before. The Three Gorges Project was first envisioned by Mao Zedong in the 1950s and had been under construction for decades. Communist leaders of China heralded the project as evidence of the Party's ability "to reshape nature and exploit natural resources." President Zemin also stated that the Three Gorges Dam was proof positive that socialism is the best, most efficient way to build nature-conquering projects.

> ... Today, the world-renowned Three Gorges Water Conservation Project (TGP) has successfully completed the damming of the main course of the Yangtze River. This is a major event in China's efforts to achieve modernization and also a remarkable feat in the history of mankind to reshape the nature and exploit natural resources.
>
> This success will greatly inspire our people of all ethnic groups who are now engaged in reform, opening-up and modernization drive with full confidence....

Seventy years ago, Dr. Sun Yat-Sen, the great forerunner of China's democratic revolution, raised the idea of exploiting the water and hydroelectric resources of the Three Gorges. After the founding of New China, Comrade Mao Zedong, Comrade Deng Xiaoping and other proletarian revolutionaries gave a great deal of their time and thought to the proposed Three Gorges Project. Several generations of Chinese scientists have put in an enormous amount of hard intellectual work. The rapid economic development and markedly increased overall national strength of our country since the initiation of its reform and opening-up have provided adequate conditions for the building of this unprecedented cross-century project. The age-old dream of the Chinese people to develop and utilize the resources of the Three Gorges of the Yangtze River has come closer to becoming true. This proves vividly once again that socialism is superior in being capable of concentrating resources to do big jobs.

Since the twilight of history, the Chinese nation has been engaged in the great feat of conquering, developing and exploiting the nature. The legends of the mythic bird Jingwei determined to fill the sea with small pebbles and the Foolish Old Man resolved to remove the mountains standing in his way and the tale of the Great Yu who harnessed the great floods are just some of the examples of the ancient Chinese people's indomitable spirit in successfully conquering the nature. Such ancient water conservation projects as the Dujiangyan completed over 2,000 years ago and the Grand Canal built in the Sui Dynasty all played an important role in the socio-economic development of their respective time period. The water conservancy and hydro-power project we are building today on the Three Gorges of the Yangtze River, the scale and overall benefits of which have no parallel in the world, will greatly promote the development of our national economy, and prove to be a lasting exploit in the service of the present and future generations. It also embodies the great industrious and dauntless spirit of the Chinese nation and displays the daring vision of the Chinese people for new horizons and better future in the course of their reform and opening-up.

The successful damming of the river marks the completion of the first phase of the TGP and the beginning of its second phase. All participating units in the project must strengthen management in real earnest, ensure good quality of work and continue to do a good job in tackling key scientific problems and conducting experiments so as to ensure power generation by the first group of generators in 2003.

Throughout the construction of the TGP, we should act in accordance with the law governing socialist market economy while giving full play to the socialist spirit of unity and coordination. We should uphold the principle of self-reliance and taking the initiative in our own hands while actively carrying out international cooperation and exchanges. We should bring the initiatives of those foreign-funded enterprises into play and make use of their advantages in capital and technology while fully tapping the advantages and potentials of our own enterprises so that they will make greater contributions to the project and enhance the level of their development up to a new high.

A successful resettlement of the people affected by the TGP is the key to the progress and eventual success of the project. The work, which involves the interests of one million people, is both arduous and meticulous. Party committees and governments at all levels in the TGP-affected areas should summarize the good experience already achieved and constantly do a good job in this regard.

It is imperative to adhere to the policy of development-oriented resettlement of the people, redouble our efforts to afforest the reservoir area and especially the upper reaches of the Yangtze River, take comprehensive measures to constantly improve ecological environment and prevent soil erosion, for it is an important precondition for ensuring lasting peace and political stability as well as a sustainable development of the reservoir area and the entire Yangtze River Valley.

As it is a matter that benefits not only the current generation but our posterity, we should spare no effort year in and year out and allow no negligence or delay at any time.

In short, we should take into consideration the overall situation and a long-term perspective, formulate plans on a scientific basis and adopt practical and effective measures to achieve a coordinated economic, social and ecological development.

The Yangtze River Valley is one of the cradles of the Chinese civilization and the reservoir area is dotted with sites of rich and colorful cultural heritage. We should be very careful to protect the historical relics in this area in accordance with the policy of "focusing on the protection and excavation of key cultural relics."

Leading cadres at all levels involved in the TGP or working in the reservoir area should carry forward the spirit of utter devotion and integrity, lead the masses of people in dauntless struggles and forge ahead so as to turn the TGP into a first-class project of water conservation and power generation in the world while bringing forth a contingent of new talents in this field.

Source: Jiang Zemin. "Jiang Zemin's Speech Marking Yangtze-Damming for Three Gorges Project." November 8, 1997. Available online. URL: http://www.china-embassy.org.

Zhang Weiqing: Speech at the Fifth Asian and Pacific Population Conference (December 16, 2002) (excerpt)

Zhang Weiqing was the minister of the State Family Planning Commission of China. In his speech at the 2002 Asian and Pacific Population Conference, he addressed some of the difficulties China would face in the coming years as the world's most populous country. He also stated that the country's population policy, which included free universal birth control, had been quite successful in alleviating poverty, empowering women, improving education, and producing many other social benefits. Combined with government efforts to improve prenatal care, especially in rural areas, and prevent HIV infections, China believes it has made a significant contribution to the stabilization of world population and has advanced the economic fortunes of all Chinese citizens. He makes no mention of the gender imbalance resulting from China's one-child policy.

. . . Since 1994, the Chinese government has vigorously responded to the call of the ICPD [International Conference on Population and Development] and has fulfilled its commitments to the ICPD with responsibility. We have earnestly implemented the ICPD Program of Action in the Chinese context, and the achievement in this regard has been quite encouraging. Reproductive health and family planning have been integrated with the efforts in poverty alleviation, universal education, women's empowerment, improving social security, public health system, and care for youth, etc. The Chinese government has meanwhile allocated increasing resources in population and family planning programs, particularly in the remote and poverty stricken areas of the country. Family planning and reproductive health services including contraceptives are provided to the people free of charge. China is one of the developing countries that invest substantively in reproductive health care; up to now the service network has extended to all cities and villages throughout the country, and service facilities have been improved, and service capacity upgraded.

The Chinese government has reoriented its family planning and reproductive health program to follow the human centered and quality service approaches that were endorsed by the ICPD Program of Action. As a concrete step, it launched a pilot experiment in quality of care of family planning in 1995. In the pilot areas with the aim to meet the diversified needs and demands of people in family planning and reproductive health, the current system in program management and performance evaluation has been under transformation, informed choice of contraceptives, community-based personalized counseling, and follow-up services were developed, maternal care was enhanced to ensure healthy child-birth, diagnosis and treatment of RTIs [reproductive tract infections] were provided, and information on HIV/AIDS prevention was disseminated. All these measures are integrated with the efforts to assist the people to obtain good and comprehensive reproductive health. The experiment in quality of care has been warmly welcomed by the people and family planning staff and expanded to above 40% areas all around the country. This includes some of the poorest areas in the western region of the country. China's population and family planning program has been moving forward along the direction of the

ICPD in a sound, steady and sustainable manner. The enabling environment created within China's family planning and reproductive health programs has been conducive to China's rapid economic and social development, and the uplifting of the quality of life of Chinese citizens. It has also contributed to the stabilizing of the world population. . . .

Chinese government always attaches great importance to poverty alleviation, and thanks to continuous efforts, the population under the poverty line in rural China has decreased from 250 million in 1978 to 80 million in 1994, and further to 30 million in 2000. The case of China has revealed that population and poverty are very closely related. Poor areas tend to be associated with higher population growth, lower women's status and poorer reproductive health. Poor families tend to have more children with lower education. The experience in China has also demonstrated that it would be helpful to poverty reduction by adhering to family planning approaches, quality services, women's empowerment, women and children's health care promotion, avoiding unwanted pregnancy and abortion, strengthening education on prevention of HIV/AIDS and improving reproductive health. At the same time, it also shows that family planning and reproductive health provisions should be carried out along with the efforts in poverty alleviation, gender equality promotion, increasing women's educational opportunities, income generation for poor people and relieving them from poverty. Chinese experience indicates that concerted development on population economy, resources and environment is a crucial measure for Chinese people to get rid of poverty, and stride towards a well-off society. Providing full-scale quality family planning and reproductive health services are the most effective approach to secure the health of women and children. Protection of legitimate right and interests and encouragement for women to exercise the reproductive rights with voluntariness and responsibility are the preconditions to actualize the primary human rights to survival and development. Chinese government believes further implementation of the Program of Action of the ICPD will improve reproductive health levels, make contributions to poverty alleviation and accelerate all countries achieving the Millennium Development Goals. . . .

China is a developing country with the largest population in the world. By the end of 2001, the population of the Mainland China has reached to 1.27 billion. China is characterized as a country with huge population, lack in arable lands, relatively short in per capita resources and underdeveloped in economy, in particular the considerable unbalance in social economic development between regions within the country. Chinese government consistently attaches great importance to harmonious development between society, economy and population resources and environment and firmly commits itself to family planning programs. Thanks to the enormous efforts of Chinese people, the number of children born to each couple on average has reduced from what used to be around 5 or 6 to 1.8. Then net population increment nevertheless will be expected to remain at 10 million annually in the next ten years or so. The peaks in labor-age population, aging population, and total population will arrive one after another. Population issues still impede sustainable development and are the key factor affecting socio-economic development.

In order to further develop population and family planning programs and promote sustainable development and poverty alleviation, with many years' efforts, the Standing Committee of the National People's Congress of China adopted 'Population and Family Planning Law of the People's Republic of China,' which came in effect September 1, 2002. The Law has documented the successful experiences of China in family planning over the years, drawn lessons from the relevant international experiences, and raised those fundamental policy, regulations and measures in family planning, which are consistent with the principles of democracy and legality to the level of legislation. The adoption and enforcement of the Law will certainly exert significant and profound impact on stabilizing of low fertility, upgrading of family planning performance, safeguarding the legal interests and rights of the peoplel as well as the coordinated development between population and society, economy, resource, environment and sustainable development in China. . . .

Source: Zhang Weiqing. Speech at the 5th Asian and Pacific Population Conference. December 16, 2002, Bangkok, Thailand.

INDIA

Rabindranath Tagore: *Glimpses of Bengal* (1895) (excerpt)

Rabindranath Tagore (1861–1941) was a Bengali poet who received the Nobel Prize for Literature in 1913. His vast body of work spanned many genres, with a concentration on poetry. Born to a wealthy family, he traveled through India extensively and came to identify with the independence movement and support Mahatma Gandhi in the effort to break free from British rule. In the following excerpt from Glimpses of Bengal, Selected from the Letters of Sir

Rabindranath Tagore, 1885–1895, *Tagore writes of his impressions of everyday life in India. He describes a way of life among the masses in India concentrated along the Ganges River and shows the central role the waterway plays in their unindustrialized, agrarian culture. More than 100 years later, everyday life along the Ganges is much the same, except for the vast increase in population that has led to the depletion and pollution of the country's vital waterway.*

February 1891.
We have got past the big rivers and just turned into a little one.

The village women are standing in the water, bathing or washing clothes; and some, in their dripping saris, with veils pulled well over their faces, move homeward with their water vessels filled and clasped against the left flank, the right arm swinging free. Children, covered all over with clay, are sporting boisterously, splashing water on each other, while one of them shouts a song, regardless of the tune.

Over the high banks, the cottage roofs and the tops of the bamboo clumps are visible. The sky has cleared and the sun is shining. Remnants of clouds cling to the horizon like fluffs of cotton wool. The breeze is warmer.

There are not many boats in this little river; only a few dinghies, laden with dry branches and twigs, are moving leisurely along to the tired plash! plash! of their oars. At the river's edge the fishermen's nets are hung out to dry between bamboo poles. And work everywhere seems to be over for the day. . . .

SHAZADPUR.
June 1891.

From the bank to which the boat is tied a kind of scent rises out of the grass, and the heat of the ground, given off in gasps, actually touches my body. I feel that the warm, living Earth is breathing upon me, and that she, also, must feel my breath.

The young shoots of rice are waving in the breeze, and the ducks are in turn thrusting their heads beneath the water and preening their feathers. There is no sound save the faint, mournful creaking of the gangway against the boat, as she imperceptibly swings to and fro in the current.

Not far off there is a ferry. A motley crowd has assembled under the banyan tree awaiting the boat's return; and as soon as it arrives, they eagerly scramble in. I enjoy watching this for hours together. It is market-day in the village on the other bank; that is why the ferry is so busy. Some carry bundles of hay, some baskets, some sacks; some are going to the market, others coming from it. Thus, in this silent noonday, the stream of human activity slowly flows across the river between two villages.

I sat wondering: Why is there always this deep shade of melancholy over the fields arid river banks, the sky and the sunshine of our country? And I came to the conclusion that it is because with us Nature is obviously the more important thing. The sky is free, the fields limitless; and the sun merges them into one blazing whole. In the midst of this, man seems so trivial. He comes and goes, like the ferry-boat, from this shore to the other; the babbling hum of his talk, the fitful echo of his song, is heard; the slight movement of his pursuit of his own petty desires is seen in the world's market-places: but how feeble, how temporary, how tragically meaningless it all seems amidst the immense aloofness of the Universe!

The contrast between the beautiful, broad, unalloyed peace of Nature—calm, passive, silent, unfathomable—and our own everyday worries—paltry, sorrow-laden, strife-tormented, puts me beside myself as I keep staring at the hazy, distant, blue line of trees which fringe the fields across the river.

Where Nature is ever hidden, and cowers under mist and cloud, snow and darkness, there man feels himself master; he regards his desires, his works, as permanent; he wants to perpetuate them, he looks towards posterity, he raises monuments, he writes biographies; he even goes the length of erecting tombstones over the dead. So busy is he that he has not time to consider how many monuments crumble, how often names are forgotten!

Source: Rabindranath Tagore. *Glimpses of Bengal, Selected from the Letters of Sir Rabindranath Tagore, 1885–1895.* Available online. URL: http://www.gutenberg.org/etext/7951.

Jyoti Parikh: "Environmentally Sustainable Development in India." (June 3–5, 2004) (excerpt)

Jyoti Parikh is the executive director of Integrated Research and Action for Development (IRADe). As an academic, she has researched and quantified the living conditions of many Indian citizens, particularly the country's poor, in terms of the pollution that affects them and how economic disempowerment has an impact on their health and makes them vulnerable to environmental degradation. Instituting sustainable development in India, she believes, requires focusing on socioeconomic factors, such as literacy and education, which will in turn have a positive impact on population, land use, and a host of other issues. She is also concerned with the damaging impact of air pollution and insufficient urban infrastructure on public health. Creating sanitation systems, for example, would result in vast improvements in public health, and at a much lower cost than simply addressing health issues while ignoring pollution issues. Poor public health ultimately can derail any other gains by negatively affecting the country's economic growth.

For India, a large country both populated and poor, to develop in an environmentally sustainable [manner] is not an option but a requirement. On one hand, India is faced with environmental degradation from poverty and population pressures, and on the other, from pollution from increased activities due to economic growth and the consequent changing consumption patterns. While the poor depend on the environment for their livelihood, the process of economic development relies on using natural resources to produce goods and services. The waste generated from consuming and producing these goods and services are in turn released back into the environment impacting it. The environment provides security for present and future generations, the health of the environment is closely connected with the health of humans, and it is economically beneficial for countries to prevent environmental degradation. The challenge therefore, in making development compatible with the environment is to restructure the economic system in a way that it will not destroy the environment as economic progress continues. Given our circumstances, how can India develop in an environmentally sustainable manner?

(. . .)

Environmental Quality Management Strategy

Environmentally sustainable development requires a combination of six strategies: economic incentives against polluting, law enforcement, technological interventions such as cleaner technologies, institutional mechanisms, poverty alleviation programs, and people's participation. This section examines how these strategies can be effective.

Law enforcement and other controls

- **Consolidate pollution control laws**—The environment has to be addressed holistically as different media like air, water and soil are interconnected and pollution once generated, can shift in space and time. That is, pollution can be diluted in more water or air or converted into different forms of pollutants viz. burning solid waste and causing air pollution or pollution laws must be consolidated to address this issue.
- **Introduce full liability laws**—Industries and other polluters should be made fully liable for their pollution. After the Bhopal tragedy this should have been obvious, yet the Bhopal victims have not got adequate compensation.
- **Make clean technologies mandatory in new industries**—The current industry growth rates are around 7–8%. In this light, industries being established now will comprise 50% of the market in 9 years (Jayaraman. KS 2001). Cleaner technologies should be made mandatory in such industries so as to reduce pollution in the coming years. Industries are less willing to change their techniques once they are established. Hence, they should be made to take on cleaner technologies right from the start. The technology for small-scale industries can be improved by requiring large-scale capital goods manufacturers to produce less polluting equipment.
- **Make functioning treatment facilities mandatory**—Often, due to mandatory requirements, effluent treatment plants are set up but not operated to save operating costs. Therefore, laws should provide for monitoring operation of these facilities.
- **Require environmental audits for industry**—Environmental impact assessments are often made at the start of the project but prescribed environmental management practices are often forgotten once the project is underway. Regular audits would act as self-monitoring and enhance compliance to standards.
- **Provide effective right to information**—If people have the information about what their neighbouring industry pollutes, they would generate pressures for abatement and treatment. Full liability laws need to be complemented with right to information.

Economic Incentives

- **Appropriate pricing**—Natural resources are often sold at a very low price, leading to their exploitation. For example, the subsidies on irrigation water have led to planting of highly water intensive crops in regions inappropriate for this kind of agriculture. Excessive use of water has also resulted in waterlogging as well as depletion of ground water table making the soil saline. Removing inappropriate subsidies is essential to maintaining natural resources and would encourage development of more environmentally friendly alternatives. Since liberalization this has changed in India. People have also begun to accept appropriate prices for natural resources. Pricing water to reflect its scarcity will encourage users to use it more sparingly.

- **Tax based on pollution load**—Presently, effluent standards are based on best available technology for specific industries. Industries have no incentive to improve standards in such a system. Instead, a pollution tax should be levied so that industries pay taxes in proportion to the pollution they generate. Such a policy will reduce pollution at source and can only work if there is effective monitoring and punishment.
- **Higher credit rating for green industries**—Higher credit rating for green industries will encourage upcoming industries (which are dependent on the market for capital) to be more environmentally conscious. Once right to information and liability laws become effective, rating agencies would take care of this.
- **Reduce subsidies on fertilizers and pesticides**—The current subsidies on fertilizers and pesticides do not ensure that they are used sparingly. Recently, pesticides and fertilizers were found even in bottled soft drinks indicating that the runoff from agriculture is contaminating groundwater at very high levels. Reducing fertilizer subsidies will encourage more controlled use.

Technological interventions

Technological intervention for environmental management does not necessarily imply new inventions. Many environmentally friendly interventions are traditional methods or simple techniques, which have been known but not used.

- **Cleaner technologies**—A great example of how a cleaner technology is a mere modification of an existing one is toilets. Mexico City replaced 350,000 toilets with smaller six-liter flushes and saved enough water to meet the needs of 250,000 more homes (Mexico City's Water Supply: Improving the Outlook for Sustainability, (1995).

In many cases however, active research needs to be conducted in producing cleaner technologies—such as cleaner fuel, more efficient cars etc.

Efficient irrigation—Since 84% of all water in India is used for agriculture, efficient irrigation is the best method to deal with water wastage. For example, applying water to the roots of crops through drip irrigation saves a considerable amount of water, pesticides, and electricity for irrigation. It also prevents soil erosion or water logging (Bhaskar Save, Water-efficient trench irrigation for horticulture).

- **Integrated pest management**—Using integrated pest management (targeting the insects using natural methods) instead of pesticides would reduce pollution greatly.
- **Vermiculture and organic manures**—Vermiculture has been shown to be an effective method to deal with organic solid waste, which is becoming a major problem in urban areas. If the community can be made to sort their garbage (citizen sorting has been effective in many industrialized cities) this can also provide organic manure.

Institutional mechanisms

Central and State pollution control boards need to be strengthened technically by installing modern equipment and training, financially with larger budgets to hire better staff and facilities to monitor the pollution, and politically by keeping them independent and free from political influence. This has to be done at all levels; e.g., at municipalities and gram panchayats levels to control pollution. Suggestions have also been made that industries should be roped into monitor pollution and assist new industries in choosing environmentally friendly technologies. Involving private sector in water supply and sewage treatment in urban areas may prove to be beneficial. Finally, organizing clean technology databanks will aid new industries in making appropriate investment decisions.

People's Participation

It is not possible for the government to monitor pollution and the corresponding acts of all industries and individuals. People must be made stakeholders in the environment through awareness campaigns. Industries are sensitive to public pressure. Experience in the west suggests that firms wish to maintain a green profile when citizens are aware of environmental issues. Through generating awareness, the public could directly affect the environmental practices of industries. As already pointed out right to information and liability laws help a lot in this.

Environmental problems arise because property rights are not well defined. Common property resource management is needed. Often cooperative management with people participation is advocated. However, people's participation is not the magic bullet by itself. When the common property resource is such that user group management can lead to positive sum outcome, then cooperation becomes sustainable. In a zero sum situation the cooperatives often disintegrate once the change agents leave. The problem of free-riding can be dealt through people's participation (when CPR is definable) with an appropriate management structure. For example, the national tree growers cooperative federation has evolved a framework which has been successfully tried in hundreds of cases. The CPR is managed though a collective after defining a community, making members pay a fair price for whatever they take from the CPR and sharing profits equally among all members.

Moving forward technologically:
In addition to environment-specific technologies, mentioned above, India has to move forward technologically in an overall context to avoid pollution at the source. Modern technologies already developed in the developed countries such as better power plants and cleaner vehicles should be considered through technology transfer for pollution measurements.

Technological innovations allow India to develop rapidly in an environmentally sustainable manner by leap-frogging over older technologies. One of the best examples of this in India is the cell phone revolution. The introduction of cell phones in rural areas allows people to bypass the massive project of digging and installing land lines. According to *Telenet,* a telecommunications periodical in India, the growth of mobile services in 2003 has been at 164% while fixed line services are growing at 5.6%. In a country where only there are only 3.68 telephones per hundred people the growth rate of land lines is much too small to make phone services available to all in the near future. A larger focus on developing cleaner technologies is essential. The benefits of increasing communications are enormous. In terms of the environment, they reduce the requirement of transportation as more and more transactions can take place using phones.

Conclusion:
We have seen that India cannot afford to neglect the environment, if sustainable development is desired. The pressures on environment have to be curtailed by reducing population pressures, increasing literacy, environ-

mental awareness drives and poverty alleviation programmes. Poor are victims of environmental degradation but they can also aggravate it if the infrastructure and living conditions do not keep pace with population increase. Rather, the poor have to be turned into agents for environmental restoration by involving them in say forest management, waste management, recycling and so on in manners that create incentives for them to use natural resources in sustainable manner.

Secondly, the economic activities must be conducted using environment conserving and resource saving technologies. Managing environment though better urban designs, improvement in transportation infrastructures and creative use of information technologies needs to be considered seriously.

Thirdly, the strategy for environmental governance should consist of law enforcement, providing economic incentives, people's participation, institutional reforms and support and technological improvements.

The environment is not a luxury for the rich but a necessity for the poor. Therefore, while it is no easy task for India to develop sustainably it is absolutely necessary and requires tremendous cooperation and will. With the determination of the government, private sector, NGOs, and people, India can perhaps achieve sustainable development.

Source: Jyoti Parikh. "Environmentally Sustainable Development in India." Paper given at the 5th annual conference on Indian Economic Policy Reform, June 3–5, 2004, Stanford Center for International Development (SCID). Reprinted by permission.

GERMANY

Petra Kelly: Acceptance Speech of the Right Livelihood Awards (December 9, 1982) (excerpt)

Petra Kelly (1947–1992) was a founder of the German Green Party in 1979 and from 1983 to 1990 she was a member of the Bundestag—the West German Parliament. She worked toward nuclear disarmament, social justice, and women's rights in addition to the idea of ecological preservation upon which the Green Party was founded. In 1982 Kelly was awarded the Right Livelihood Award, often called the Alternative Nobel Peace Prize. The following excerpt from her acceptance speech demonstrates the connections she made between human rights, peace, social justice, and environmental sustainability, which she communicates to the audience with a palpable sense of urgency and outrage.

The Green Party, a nonviolent, ecological and basic-democratic anti-war coalition of parliamentary and outer-parliamentary grass roots oriented forces within the Federal Republic of Germany, is at the moment the only hope I have to change not only the system of structural and personal violence but also to find a way out of the insane policies of atomic deterrence. The Green Party to which I have dedicated my efforts and all my energy in the past 3 years, is committed to basic democracy, to ecology in the broadest sense of the term, to social justice and to non-violence. Military leaders and politicians have in the past aroused partial unity by means of fear, pride, anger, hate, lies. Unity can also be aroused by love and the desire for social justice. When a sufficient number of people, as for example, in my country and also in the Netherlands, the United Kingdom, in the Scandinavian countries, in Japan, in the United States, begin to understand the close relationships between the arms race and international violence, economic ties preservation, social injustice, and ecological instability, then we are on the way to make the right demands for the benefit of humankind, rather than for one nation, one particular class. The global overview of military and social expenditures as presented by the Stockholm Institute for Peace Research (SIPRI) makes a grim reading. It is a dismal reflection of our values as a world community. We have thought it necessary to invest so much more of our wealth in military power than in meeting the needs of society, in meeting the needs of women, children and men.

The Green Party has an underlying thought which states clearly that humankind must not consider the land and what it supports in terms of property a real estate. We are all temporary custodians of the land entrusted to us for passing on unimpaired to future generations. We argue that most urgent and most straight forward disarmament measures required at this juncture from an ecological standpoint are the absolute prohibition of all nuclear weapons, of all atomic, biological, chemical weapons and a complete demilitarization and conversion to protective status of ecologically important regions. Nuclear power states now comprise a large part of the world's population. There is for me only one way out—complete disarmament. The bilateral step by step approaches have failed. Arms control talks and the present hypocritical talks in Geneva and the so-called Zero-option of Mr. Reagan have also failed. We propose unilateral and calculated towards complete disarmament as a solution which we propose not only for the Federal Republic of Germany, but for all European countries, for all countries in the world. Each of our governments must take that first step which it expects the other government to take! And if the governments do not take these first steps, so we shall take these first steps for them! We must work towards a disarmament race. Military balances, the balance of terror, the counting-game, are irrelevant. The greatest criticism that can be made of the nuclear arms race is its total irrelevance to the problems facing us today! World poverty, the diminishing natural resources, overpopulation and pollution—these are the problems we are facing today. The only war we seek should be the war against humankind's ancient enemies—poverty, hunger, illiteracy and preventable disease. . . .

One day the great military alliances must be dissolved by the people in both blocks. And so we must continue to agitate nonviolently for the expulsion of all nuclear of all ABC-weapons and bases from European soil. I am ashamed of the present state of affairs, whereby my country, the Federal Republic of Germany, has become the sixth largest weapons exporter in the world. Over 70% of all West German arms exports go to the developing countries of the Third World. We export weapon components, U-boats and tanks to South American military dictators and to Apartheid regimes. . . .

The anti-war and anti-nuclear movement does not mean negative protest: it is necessarily pro-environment, pro-wood and pro-fields, pro-rivers and oceans, pro-plants and animals, pro-solar energy, pro clean air and above all, pro-people. It is a planetary vision, planetary moral standard, for hungry people, poor people, women, youth the handicapped, the old people, the Amazon tribes, the Aborgines, the inner-city slum dwellers, the oppressed minorities everywhere—we are all in this together . . . We are in fact the realists, we are not only the dreamers of brother- and sisterhood, of nonviolence and of survival. . . .

Our young people don't need the draft, they need jobs, our older people don't heed new weapons of overkill, they need better and more qualitative housing at more affordable prices. Our working people cannot live with inflationary effects of military spending, they need the right to a job, they need the right to work and the right to a qualitative job. Our fly members don't need Cruise Missiles, they need affordable health care. And our children don't need neutron bombs, they need better schools. None of us need the SS 20 or the MX missile, we need an efficient mass transit system. We must bring together on this planet Earth the different groups which have been used to work in an isolation and that means hard work. We must form or grass roots alliance based on shared interests if we are to reach out effectively to a larger audience. We need to develop a nonviolent strategy, not only to stop the deployment of first strike missiles in Europe, but to begin reducing all mass destructive weapons and finally to get rid of them. And I make a last appeal not only to the Peace Movement in Europe, but to the Third World movement everywhere, because especially women and children of the Third World are to perish first. They have already begun to starve. All that is asked of them is to starve quietly. The tragedy of women in the Third World is one that moves me, touches me deeply. There are now about a hundred million children under the age of 5 always hungry. Fifteen million children die every year from infection and malnutrition, and there are about 800 million illiterates in the world, nearly two-thirds of them are women. And while I say this I remember at the same time the multinational company Nestlé that has told women in the Third World to stop breast-feeding and to start feeding lactogen. All this is related directly to our own prosperity and so-called material and economic growth. The developed nations are armed to their teeth and mean not only to hold on to what they have, but to grasp everything they still can. The suffering people of this world must come together to take control of their lives, to wrest political power from their present masters pushing them towards destruction. The Earth has been mistreated and only by restoring a balance, only by living with the Earth, only by employing knowledge and expertise towards soft energies and soft technology, a technology for people and for life, can we overcome the patriarchal ego.

1984 and George Orwell—they are not so far from us, and not so far from us is the police-and-atomic state and the danger of totalitarian regimes—all in the name of making secure the nuclear societies. We must lose our fears and we must speak up and we must demand what is ours and what is our children's. We must begin to rediscover our own nature, we must begin to forge new ways, ways of wholeness, inter-connectedness, balance, preservation and decentralisation.

As Gandhi said, the nonviolence of the weak must become the nonviolence of the brave. I believed that unarmed truth and unconditional love will have the final word in reality.

Source: Petra Kelly. Acceptance Speech at the Right Livelihood Awards, December 9, 1982. Available online. URL: http://www.rightlivelihood.org/kelly_speech.html.

German Council for Sustainable Development: "Landmark Sustainability 2005: Appraisal and Perspectives." (August 10, 2005) (excerpt)

The German Council for Sustainable Development is a government agency that provides detailed analysis of environmental issues for the country. The council's goal is to make Germany a world leader in renewable energy, energy efficiency, and new energy and drive technologies. Disaster prevention—of floods, droughts, and other ecological situations—is another key component of the program. The Council believes that emissions trading throughout the European Union will help the country both ecologically and economically; it also supports an end to subsidies for farmers who overuse the land and an increase in subsidies for environmentally sustainable agricultural policies. It also acknowledges Germany's declining population and the effect it will have on labor issues. To offset a dwindling workforce, the Council advocates providing older workers with job retraining, good working opportunities, and resources to continue their careers past the typical retirement age.

Foreword by former German chancellor Gerhard Schröder

Responsibility for today and tomorrow

Safeguarding prosperity and quality of life for the generations of today and tomorrow is a primary task of sustainable policy.

As no German government before, we have made the principle of sustainable development the guideline for our actions and deeds. This begins by having an ambitious national Sustainability Strategy comprising concrete goals and indicators which we submitted to the World Summit 2002 in Johannesburg. Through this Road Map, we are, for a second time, taking stock of developments to date and, at the same time, indicating the direction that other key political priorities are taking.

To enact a responsible and future-orientated policy, the sole alternative is to gear such a policy to the principle of sustainability. To do so requires an innovative approach which brings all of the different fields of action into line with one another. Sustainability is not about showing environmental policy in a new light but about all of the core themes relevant to our day and age—competitiveness, innovation, education, as well as climate protection, mobility or national social security schemes. In this context, having a responsible policy which truly takes full advantage of the opportunities is more than the sum of all correct individual decisions. Sustainability is both a comprehensive modernisation strategy and our response to the challenge facing us in our day and age—both nationally and internationally.

At present, the key focus in Germany is on attaining sustainable growth—growth that facilitates a high level of employment over a sustainable period, which safeguards the economic foundation of a social welfare state and maintains the natural bases for life. Over and beyond this, demographic change is presenting us with specific challenges. Both are core areas to which we intend to respond in the Road Map for Sustainability.

However, our actions must not be limited to the national stage. Instead, we must pay greater attention to the global threats posed to mankind through poverty, climate change and the shortage of resources and perceive them more as our own existential challenge. Germany is standing up to this responsibility—be it through direct cooperation with other countries or as part of the United Nations.

(. . .)

"Contributions to a Generation Balance Sustainability"—Interim Report submitted by the German Council for Sustainable Development

When grandchildren ask their grandparents whether and in what respects their lives have been worthwhile, this is also fundamentally aimed at an intergenerational balance. By grafting hard to build up the country in the East and the West and making great personal sacrifices along the way, the post-war generation has succeeded in making its work and commitment of importance to the future. In a society with constant but also unequally distributed growth, it appeared only natural that, ultimately, the virtually automatic result of such efforts would be greater opportunities for all and social well-being in the future. Today, this conscientiousness is gradually changing through new knowledge and experience. As a result, the added value of a generation can be endangered by its very own generation: The climate and consumption changes linked to the present-day type of production and consumption can cause long-term damage costs to pile up on society which can call welfare into question and detract from the performance of an entire generation. The same can be said of an uncontrolled, demographic change into the shrinking society. Both would cast a negative light on the intergenerational balance. However, there are also positive developments that make a great difference: The specific use of knowledge held by elderly people to a greater extent than has been the case to date can provide major innovation impetus for society, which establishes future compliance: in education, in social services, in a wholly new concept for mobility services and for Germany's pioneering role in the development of future technologies.

Generations are concerned with more than the chronological offsetting of the national debt, national insurance contributions and shares in estate. Passing down the financial burdens and material affluence of a country from one generation to another in as just a manner as possible is an important goal. Ultimately, however, we are all concerned about leading a good life and how this can be achieved and passed down. As undisputed and proven the general notion of "sustainability" may be at first sight, clearly defining these general considerations continues to provoke discussion and raise issues—although these are perhaps even too few and far between. In the 1980s, the Brundtland Commission drafted the idea of a development "that meets the needs of the present without compromising the ability of future generations to meet their own needs". This concept has since become the subject of UN conferences, government treaties, local Agenda initiatives, research programmes and, to some extent, a part of corporate strategies. National sustainability strategies have emerged in virtually every country on Earth; Germany's Sustainability Strategy includes approaches to taking action on a variety of individual issues. . . .

Central Issues

Demographic Change

The starting points for the intergenerational balance are multiform. Not all of them can or will be processed in detail. However, one issue of particular significance is the impact of demographic change on society and the environment. Even today, far too little is known about how the structure of the population and the inner-German migratory movements affect housing estates, local infrastructures, traffic and consumption, and to what extent society can make a viable contribution. Road construction, for example: Germany's and Europe's traffic and transportation policy calculates that traffic volumes will again grow significantly by up to 16% by 2015. However, it is not clear when exactly from 2015 onwards the baby-boom years reach an age where they will drive less; under certain circumstances, it is even conceivable that the mileage rate will decrease. The example of urban development: As a result of migration, declining tax revenue, vacant houses, an increase in the percentage of elderly people and falling purchase power, shrinking towns and cities are faced with the danger of being caught in a downward spiral—if the signs of the times are not recognised. For this reason, demographic change is a vital issue in the "Generation Balance Sustainability."

Climate Change and Rising Energy Demand

The impact of a changing climate on the economy and society is a further motive for calling for intergenerational justice. Dependence on natural raw materials, such as oil, gas, copper or uranium, continues to rise, and the increasing global competition for resources through the successful industrialisation of large, former developing countries is posing a new challenge for Germany's industry base and for the country's position as a science and education location. Finally, the "self-inflicted" restriction of future decision options caused by fiscal burdens also points to Germany not being safety-tested and this only being developed from the perspective of generation to generation. . . .

"Social Commitment of Companies: Investing in the Future"—Interim Report submitted by the German Council for Sustainable Development

Economic, social and ecological responsibility should form the basis for actions to a greater degree than has been the case to date. This applies to nations, social institutions and companies alike in their respective fields of business. "Corporate Social Responsibility" (CSR), i.e. company acceptance of their responsibility towards society, is one way to implement the concept of sustainable development at the corporate level. Through such a commitment, companies strive to achieve lasting economic success through the credible integration of social and ecological aspects into economic necessities.

At the same time, companies face the challenge of giving consideration to the different and, in part, contradictory interests of their stakeholders such as their customers, investors, employees, suppliers or non-governmental organisations. Through conscious consumers and the increasing interest in "Socially Responsible Investment" (SRI), i.e. a socially ethical investment on the capital market, the need grows to credibly take on board and communicate the calls for sustainability. At the same time, companies need to safeguard the corporate responsibility and competitiveness of the German economy in the face of international comparisons. Companies in Germany have good prerequisites for utilising CSR as an opportunity. The have extensive experience in constructive dialogue with one of their stakeholders, the employee. The tried and tested ways for social partners to enter into dialogue (co-determination being one of them) form a solid framework to achieve this. Added to this, the large majority of companies in Germany consists of small and medium-sized enterprises operating at national or international level where, much like the major companies, their social commitment has often traditionally been exemplary. They assume responsibility, for example, for educating and training young people or become involved in local culture and business development. With a good company management at the helm, economic and social success goes hand in hand.

The German Council for Sustainable Development aims to promote and further develop CSR in Germany. Given the global effort to attain corporate-related sustainability and the findings of the discussion on CSR and European industrial policy initiated by the European Commission, the Council has decided to take up this issue. It is anticipate that the work will be concluded with a recommendation in 2006.

Source: "Landmark Sustainability 2005: Appraisal and Perspectives." Abridged version. German Council for Sustainable Development (RNE), August 10, 2005.

BRAZIL

Maria Graham: *Journal of a Voyage to Brazil, and Residence There, During Part of the Years 1821, 1822, 1823* (1824) (excerpt)

Maria Graham (1786–1844; later Lady Maria Callcott) was a British writer, illustrator, and translator. The daughter of a naval captain (and later the wife of one), she traveled and lived abroad extensively. Her diary charts her association with Brazil's royal family, recently installed following liberation from Portugal, and is evidence of her vast knowledge of botany. Her journal gives a comprehensive picture of Brazil's diverse flora and fauna, as well as its cultivation and economic importance in the era before industrialization.

In 1810 there was an intention of uniting the Guandu with the Itaipu by a short canal; by which means the produce, not only of this district, but of the Ilha Grande, would have been conveyed directly to Rio, without the risk of the navigation outside of the harbour: I know not why the project was abandoned.

Every time I pass through a grove in Brazil, I see new flowers and plants, and a richness of vegetation that seems inexhaustible. To-day I saw passion-flowers of colours I never observed before; green, pink, scarlet, and blue: wild pine apples, of beautiful crimson and purple: wild tea, even more beautiful than the elegant Chinese shrub: marsh-palms, and innumerable aquatic plants, new to me: and in every little pool, wild-ducks, water-hens, and varieties of storks, were wading about in graceful pride. . . .

I walked up to the tea-gardens, which occupy many acres of a rocky hill, such as I suppose may be the favourite habitat of the plant in China. The introduction of the culture of tea into Brazil was a favourite project of the King Joam VI, who brought the plants and cultivators at great expense from China. The tea produced both here and at the botanic gardens is said to be of superior quality; but the quantity is so small, as never yet to have afforded the slightest promise of paying the expense of culture. Yet the plants are so thriving, that I have no doubt they will soon spread of themselves, and probably become as natives. His Majesty built Chinese gates and summer-houses to correspond with the destination of these gardens; and, placed where they are, among the beautiful tea-shrubs, whose dark shining leaves and myrtle-like flowers fit them for a parterre, they have no unpleasing effect. The walks are bordered on either hand with orange trees and roses, and the garden hedge is of a beautiful kind of mimosa; so that the China of Santa Cruz forms really a delightful walk. The Emperor, however, who perceives that it is more advantageous to sell coffee and buy tea, than to grow it at such expense, has discontinued the cultivation. . . .

September 9th—I took two very fine Brazilian boys, who are about to enter the Imperial naval service, to spend the day at the botanical garden, which appears in much better order than when I saw it two years ago. The hedge-rows of the Bencoolen nut (Vernilzia Montana) are prodigiously grown: the Norfolk Island pine has shot up like a young giant, and I was glad to find many of the indigenous trees had been placed here; such as the Andraguoa, the nut of which is the strongest known purge; the Cambucá, whose fruit, as large as a russet apple, has the sub-acid taste of the gooseberry, to which its pulp bears a strong resemblance; the Japatec-caba, whose fruit is scarcely inferior to the damascene; and the Grumachama, whence a liquor, as good as that from cherries, is made: these three last are like laurels, and as beautiful as they are useful. I took my young friends to see the powder-mills, which are not now at work, being under repair; but they learned the manner of making powder, from the first weighing of the ingredients to the filling cartridges: and then we had our table spread in a pleasant part of the garden, under the shade of a jumbu tree, and made the head gardener, a very ingenious Dutchman, partake of our luncheon; which being over, he showed us the cinnamon they have barked here, and the other specimens of spice: the cloves are very fine, and the cinnamon might be so; but the wood they have barked is generally too old, and they have not yet the method of stripping the twigs: this I endeavoured to explain, as I had seen it practised in Ceylon. The camphor tree grows very well here, but I do not know if the gum has ever been collected. The two boys were highly delighted with their jaunt, and I not less so. Poor things! they are entering on a hard service; and God knows whether the two cousins da Costa may not hereafter look back to this day passed with a stranger, as a bright "spot of azure in a stormy sky."

Source: Maria Graham. *Journal of a Voyage to Brazil, and Residence There, During Part of the Years 1821, 1822, 1823.* London: Longman, Hurst, 1824. Available online. URL: http://www.gutenberg.org/etext/21201.

The Brazilian Agenda 21 (2004) (excerpt)

During the Earth Summit in Rio de Janiero in 1992, Agenda 21 was drawn up as a series of declarations to guide individual nations in sustainable development. Many countries devised their own versions of Agenda 21 as a way to tailor the initiative to their specific needs. Brazil was one of these countries, and the following chapter from their 2004 progress report on Objective 16 focuses on many of the environmental issues pertinent to maintaining sustainable development in the country.

Objective 16: Forest Policy, Deforestation Control and Biodiversity Corridors

. . . Brazil is the country of the largest biodiversity in the whole planet and houses the greatest extension of continuous tropical forests. Some figures express Brazil's first position among the mega-biodiversity countries: of the 24,400 species of vertebrates known 3 thousand, or 13% of the total, live in our territory. The number of plants in our country is estimated between 50 and 56 thousand, or 20% of the world total.

If we still do not know the potentiality of the Amazon we will never know what was lost of the Atlantic Forest, which covered around one million square kilometres along the coast, from the South to the Northeast, and which is, today, reduced to less than 7% of its original area. Even so, 1,800 vertebrates are represented in the Atlantic Forest, of which 21% are endemic.

The Amazon, though still our less destructed biome in percentage terms, was deforested between 1978 and 1996 at the unbelievable average of 52 square kilometres a day. Since then, this average has been decreasing little by little. The objective being proposed in this work is to reach the rate of deforestation zero in the next 10 years, in the critical areas of threatened biomes. However, this isn't enough. It is necessary to promote reforestation, the reconstitution of areas which have lost their original vegetation cover.

Brazil has achieved outstanding results in the international scenario of biodiversity policies by adjusting and making operational to the national reality the concept of "biodiversity corridors," which are continuous areas not only of preservation of isolate species but also of preservation of processes of reproduction of interdependant chains of living beings. "Mamirauá" is a remarkable example of a well-succeeded conservation unity, encompassing today 5 million hectares.

It is, therefore, necessary to take measures which guarantee a sustainable exploration of fauna and flora resources without destroying the ecosystems. It is also indispensable that the necessity of the populations living in areas meant to be protected be taken into consideration. All and every initiative should have, as an objective, the improvement of the quality of life of these populations which, legitimately, long for their inclusion into the Brazilian society.

The priority actions for conservation should reflect the actual situation of the biomass. In the Amazon and in the Pantanal, this means the implementation of a system of sizeable conservation unities, compatible with the high biodiversity and the extensive and low impact human occupation character which is meant to be maintained. In more densely populated areas and with significant degradation, like the Atlantic Forest and the caatinga, all that is left should be preserved, and actions to recover and interconnect the existing reservations, in the form of biodiversity corridors, should be undertaken.

The savanna presents a large heterogeneity of antropic occupation and wealth comparable to the Amazon thus justifying the creation and consolidation of "corridors" as much as the conservation of the last big intact areas.

The Atlantic Forest in particular, the objective of deforestation zero and loss of biodiversity zero represent the best hope for survival of the biomes.

The biodiversity corridors allow gathering in the same landscape a set of interconnected protected areas, inserted in a matrix of human occupation contemplating economic activities of all kinds. They are forms of conciliating the human presence and the conservation biodiversity in regional scales in the order of dozens of thousands of square kilometres. In Brazil, five corridors are being implemented in the Amazon, two in the Atlantic Forest, one in the Cerrado and Pantanal, with others still being planning for the transition "savanna-caatinga" and for the "São Francisco" valley.

Actions and Recommendations

Deforestation Control: More Subsidies and Credit Stimulus

- To accomplish the transition from predatory forms to sustainable ones to be put to the use of the Brazilian ecosystems, defining appropriate management instruments for these areas and using indicators to ensure the deforestation Zero targets in the Atlantic Forest. The recovery of the Environmental Protection Areas and the Permanent Protection Areas, giving priority to the biodiversity corridors, is also essential.
- To radically limit the use of burnings as an instrument of soil handling, in view of their highly negative impact on biodiversity, long term soil fertility and human health.
- To stimulate the recovery of deforested and abandoned or underused lands in the form of mosaics of natural biota areas and areas of economic use compatible with the primitive vegetation cover.
- To strategically apply the technological resources available in a way to maintain the integrity of the law protected areas such as the permanent preservation ones, the legal reserves, the conservation units, the ecological corridors, as well as the existing fragments of threatened biomass.
- To limit the concession of credits for the expansion of agricultural borders in areas of environmental fragility, based on information contained in economic ecological mapping and on integrally meeting the current environmental legislation.

- To respect the environmental legislation in its agrarian policies initiatives within Brazil, in both federal and state spheres, aiming at meeting the basic requirements for environmental licensing of undertakings, previously a concession of property titles, thus guaranteeing the demarcation of a legal reserve for the common use of those who have been settled, and the maintenance of the integrity of permanent preservation areas.

Planted Forests: Increase in the Forest Products Offer

- To ensure the control of offer and demand of forest products through the mechanism of concession of sustained exploration of national forests, by means of the elaboration of sustainable forest handling plans, as a means to guarantee the supply of medium and long term forest raw material for both the internal consumer market as well as the timber export market.
- To strengthen the policy of utilisation of forest replacement credits through incentives to the creation of reforestation associations and through the improvement of control as far as meeting the legal provisions is concerned.
- To develop mechanisms of access to credits and subsidies for the recovery of degraded areas, by means of a recomposition of natural biomass in rural properties.
- To support forest research, mainly as to the utilisation of native forest species for reforestation.
- To support measures to improve the economic exploration of standing forests, such as the development of eco-tourism, the extraction of fruit and seeds, as well as the Brazilian participation in the international policy of CO_2 emission by means of the absorption of dividends for carbon sequestration through the maintenance of tropical forests.
- To promote a large campaign of recomposition and averbation of legal reservation areas through the utilisation of compensation mechanisms of one area for the other or through the regeneration of natural explored areas with cattle raising farming activities.
- To stimulate the silvo-cultures (forest planting), in order to guarantee the supply of timber from planted forests.

Protection and Use of Biodiversity

- To expand the public system of conservation unities in a way to ensure the conservation of all the Brazilian biome species, by applying the criteria of geographic, taxonomic and communities and ecosystems representativeness and by prioritising the unities which may give larger contributions to the biodiversity of the system as a whole.

- To enable the maintenance of a biotechnology sector based on the remuneration of biodiversity services, as much in the area of technology and research as in the financing policies, according to competitiveness, regional representativeness and national interests criteria. The areas of pharmacy, natural medicine, perfumes and cosmetics of high aggregated value should also be included, as well as juices and foods, capable of guaranteeing employment and income to the people.
- To support programmes of biodiversity scientific inventory in order to subsidise the conservation decisions and allow the basis for licensing and valorisation of biodiversity products.
- To attribute economic value to biodiversity by inlaying the cost of natural goods depletion, which will enable to evaluate the convenience and possibility of its sustainable exploration.
- To provide resources and capacitate personnel for the biotechnological research, an area in which Brazil has already conquered world recognition, in view of the economic utilisation of fauna and flora products, as well as the utilisation of microbiotics.
- To establish planning mechanisms for sustainable landscapes which may conciliate the formation of protected areas systems with areas of economic use in regional matrices.
- To use indemnisation and environmental compensation resources for the implementation of protected area systems which may preserve the biome on a long term basis, instead of concentrating in emergency mitigating actions.
- To institute norms and create systems of surveillance and control which allow an effective combat to bio pirating.
- To guarantee that detectors of raw materials and/or knowledge, which lead to the economical use of our biodiversity model, be duly remunerated.
- To guarantee the presence of governmental action in determining the legal procedures to a just and equal access, remittance and distribution of the benefits stemming from the use of national genetic resources through the Genetic Property Management Council.
- To revise the "official list of the Brazilian fauna and flora species threatened with extinction" with views to establish protection and plantation development mechanisms as well as breeding areas for their recovery.

Exemplary Actions in Threatened Biomass

- To implement programmes of biodiversity corridors in every biomass with representatives from all the big bio-geographic subdivisions of the regions.
- To educate the local populations making them aware of the importance of preserving the biomass and, at the same time, to offer them options for subsistence and opportunities to improve their quality of life. To encourage the transition from extractable activities to environmental services activities. To stimulate the local communities to be the main beneficiaries of preservation activities.
- To incorporate the Amazon to the national community by preserving its forest and by guaranteeing its sustainable development by stimulating the plantation of forests and agricultural and timber activities in degraded forest areas, with the help of financing from regional banks.
- To speed up the elaboration, in a participative form, of the economic ecological mapping which shall be adopted as a basic instrument for any territorial planning action.
- To effectively integrate the Amazon to the remainder of Brazil by enlarging and strengthening the number of research unities placed in the Amazon, so that the knowledge may be generated and locally applied and traditional knowledge may be absorbed in the process.
- To promote actions of reforestation in order to recover the "caatinga," and of replanting commercial species in order to reduce the pressure over the native vegetation.
- To abolish from the semi-arid area the assistantship in the form of emergency fronts by fostering investments in infrastructure in order to make viable the sustainable development.
- To promote the handling of the "caatinga" in the semi-arid area in order to avoid the formation of desertification nucleuses.
- To capacitate the rural man to make him able to live with the drought by stimulating the use of technologies already proven and divulged by research centres and non-governmental organisations with experience in the handling of natural resources in semi-arid regions.
- To combat the desertification in the North-eastern region by means of a combat to poverty programme together with the valorisation of technology and renewable energy as a substitute alternative to the use of insufficient biomass caused by deforestation.
- To provide means and resources for the use of alternative energy sources in a way to decrease the indiscriminate consumption of the

biomass which aggravates deforestation and accelerates the process of desertification already settled.

- To prioritise the execution of the "Pantanal Programme" and avoid waterways works which alter the cycle of the waters in the region.
- To preserve the savanna by avoiding its deforestation and to substitute the extensive soya culture, an export product of low aggregated value and whose prices have been falling in the international market.
- To guarantee, to the Southeast region, the deforestation zero in the critical zones of the Atlantic Forest, especially in Rio de Janeiro and south of Bahia, including the biodiversity corridors. The objective is to achieve deforestation zero by applying, concomitantly, a native reforestation policy.
- To develop conservation projects of the same conceptual and geographic scale of the big infrastructure projects being propagated by the federal government. To condition the implementation of infrastructure projects to those, which are incorporated in conservation, projects and which may show sustainability in the regional and national biodiversity preservation.

Source: Sustainable Development and National Agenda 21 Policies Commission (CPDS). "Objective 16: Forest Policy, Deforestation Control and Biodiversity Corridors," *The Brazilian Agenda 21: Priority Actions, 2004.*

PART III

Research Tools

6

How to Research Sustainable Development

GETTING STARTED

Research transforms your interests into scholarship and helps you crystallize your beliefs. Whether you want to learn about hydrogen fuel cell vehicles, depletion of fish species in the ocean, encroaching desertification, or worldwide poverty, all you need to start with is an issue that resonates with you.

Sustainable development is a fast-growing field with a fast-growing body of scholarship. Historical data is plentiful and readily available, and new information emerges every week. Your main concern will not be finding information, but rather evaluating the wealth of facts and figures you uncover. Keep an open mind and a discriminating eye while following the tips below.

Select a Topic: Perhaps you live near the ocean and are concerned about frequent storm damage or beach erosion due to shifting weather patterns. Or maybe you live in a desert region where water rights are a major issue in local politics. Possibly you live in a metropolitan area and find yourself spending many hours a week in traffic jams. Each of these issues relates to sustainable development, and each presents a wealth of opportunities to explore local, national, international, and global implications. When you research local water issues, for instance, you will begin to understand how water rights are linked to regional issues of population growth and urban development. Urban development in turn has an impact on land use, agriculture, energy resources, and other factors, all of which cumulatively make up your region's ecological footprint.

Know Your Goal: Formulate a thesis and keep your research focused. Although it is crucial to understand issues related to your topic, make sure you build a case to prove your thesis without wandering too far afield on a tangential issue. For example, with a topic as all-encompassing as sustainable development, it would be easy to begin researching the water crisis in India and end up discussing poverty and lack of education. Make sure you illustrate how poverty and lack of education affect the water crisis, but remember your goal is to highlight water use policies, water pollution, lack of access, and environmental hazards. Similarly, if your goal is to prove that the ecological footprint of the United States is unsustainable, do not get caught up explaining the intricacies of China's ecological footprint or spending too much time outlining the process for distilling ethanol.

Read and Watch the News: Reports about natural resources and sustainable development appear in the media on a daily basis, but they are often not identified as such. It is up to you to realize that a report on rising fuel prices may reflect a supply shortage. Investigate the cause of the shortage; you might find further data related to your topic. Maybe the fuel shortage is related to an oil embargo, a disruption in a major pipeline, or an oil spill in a sensitive ecosystem. Like a good detective, if you connect the dots you may discover a whole new picture. If your town has experienced flooding recently, you may realize it is because a new housing development has encroached on wetlands that used to mitigate the effects of floods. If your state's unemployment rate skyrockets when a major corporation relocates overseas, you may realize the very real local impact of the economic boom in China.

Learn the History of Your Topic: If you choose the population crisis as your topic, begin with Thomas Malthus's *An Essay on the Principle of Overpopulation.* The 200-old document is still relevant, and you will need to be familiar with it in order to understand what the term "modern-day Malthusian" means. Furthermore, understanding Malthus's thesis requires familiarity with the changes wrought by the Industrial Revolution in Great Britain, which in turn necessitates an understanding of sociology, history, scientific advancements, and economics.

Similarly, Paul Ehrlich's 1968 book *The Population Bomb* influenced a generation of researchers, as did Donella Meadows's 1972 book *The Limits of Growth.* Both are seminal works that thrust the authors into the spotlight and fueled a fierce debate over the veracity of their claims. The fact that both books are still in print is a testament to their continued relevance. In reading these primary documents, you will learn how the issues were presented a generation ago. You will also discover firsthand which of the authors' predictions came to pass and which did not. Understanding why an expert's predictions were off the mark will help you appreciate the complexity and unpredictability of the issues and the unforeseen factors that influence them.

For example, in the 1970s and 1980s, many scientists (such as Carl Sagan in *The Nuclear Winter*) were consumed with the possibility of a nuclear winter, and others believed the planet was heading into a new ice age. Many of these same experts now believe the opposite: Global warming is now the greatest crisis we face. What changed their minds? Moreover, if they were wrong about a new ice age, who is to say they are right about global warming? Reading historical documents allows you to realize that dire warnings and statistics have always been around and should be weighed with as much knowledge as possible.

Seek Differing Opinions: Every issue has at least two sides, and you cannot effectively argue in favor of one without addressing the strengths and weaknesses of the opposing viewpoint. In fact, the more exhaustively you analyze (and discredit) the opposing viewpoint, the stronger your case becomes. Perhaps you are researching the destruction of the Amazon rain forest. Your goal is to show how clearing the forest reduces biodiversity, which in turn has a negative impact on sustainable development. You must also consider the experts who believe that development of the rain forest has been beneficial for rural Brazilians because it has created jobs and spurred an ethanol boom that has helped the country reduce its use of fossil fuels. These experts may cite statistics that prove the economic benefits of converting undeveloped land into grazing land for livestock, which ultimately helps to feed the world's growing population. Could there be some truth to this? What motivates the opposition?

Find Points Both Sides Agree On: A crucial but often overlooked tactic in researching an issue is to start with the facts both sides agree on. Determine the point at which the experts' opinions diverge. For instance, almost everyone agrees that fossil fuels are finite resources. How finite is another matter. When it comes to population, almost everyone agrees that world population is growing. Whether this is a good thing or a bad thing is another matter. Everyone agrees that the Amazon rain forest is being cleared. Whether or not this will have an impact beyond the Amazon basin is open for debate. Everyone believes that all people should have access to clean drinking water. So why do a billion humans lack that access? At the point of divergence, concentrate on the statistics each side uses to support its view. Perhaps local governments believe the state should provide clean drinking water; perhaps the state believes it is the duty of the municipalities to provide services for their residents. Use your knowledge of a similar historical situation to postulate a solution. How did a water shortage play out among the Anasazi in the 15th century? Find evidence to suggest whether or not history is likely to repeat itself.

Understand How Issues Are Connected: How does the political process encourage practices that are widely believed to be unsustainable? Why do so many drivers buy SUVs and pickup trucks, knowing they consume more fuel and emit more harmful pollutants into the atmosphere than smaller cars? Why do farmers in the Midwest use so many pesticides and fertilizers when such practices have proven to contribute to the dead zones near the Mississippi Delta? Why do owners of coal-fired power plants in China resist installing pollution control devices, even when the cost is minimal compared to the costs of lost productivity due to the sickness and death caused by air pollution? The answer to all of these questions—as far as there is one—is many-faceted, comprised of economic, social, historical, cultural, and political factors.

Some conservationists advocate transitioning from gasoline-powered internal combustion engines to electric vehicles to reduce carbon emissions and global warming. A thorough understanding of energy issues allows you to realize that most electricity today is generated from coal-fired power plants, which perpetuates a reliance on fossil fuels and simply changes the point of carbon emissions from the vehicle's tailpipe to the smokestack of the power plant. Which is more sustainable? Remember what you learned in science class: For every action, there is an equal and opposite reaction. In other words, sustainable development involves the complex relationships of numerous factors, none of which can be considered in isolation.

Beware of Experts Who Appear to Have All the Answers: The terms *always, never,* and *certain* may indicate a writer's bias. Credible experts welcome attempts to refute their findings, because replication of their data is how science advances and how scientists gain credibility. A scientist proposes a hypothesis and tests it; others are welcomed to duplicate the study or disprove the hypothesis. Likewise, understand that a scientific theory is not simply an opinion that you are free to accept or reject; it is a consistent model of a behavior or phenomenon supported by empirical data. At all points in your research, respect the body of knowledge upon which current beliefs rest, while maintaining enough impartiality to accept new or contrary evidence. Experts who are unwilling to engage in a dialogue with those of differing viewpoints reveal their bias.

On the other hand, how do you track down credible experts? Start with the sources quoted in recent news articles on your topic. An Internet search may turn up more information about that person. Perhaps he or she has written a book, published a study in a peer-reviewed journal, or is a member of a nationally recognized organization. Tracking down this type of information will inevitably lead to uncovering names and links to other organizations. You may soon find you have ferreted out more experts than you know what to do with.

Know Your Own Bias: Bias is not necessarily a bad thing. Acknowledging your bias means knowing what you believe in. Rare is the person who has no opinion about threats to the health of the planet, and acknowledging your beliefs is a crucial step in proving them. For example, if you believe that the Earth has sufficient resources to support a world population of 12 billion, you will gravitate toward research that explores the problem of global aging, and you will find plenty of experts to support your belief. But you should also acknowledge those modern-day Malthusians who believe that such numbers of people will strain the planet's resources beyond capacity.

Understand the Science: If your goal is to prove that transitioning to a hydrogen economy would reduce humanity's global footprint and foster a more sustainable world, you need to know what hydrogen is. You also need to know how fuel cells work. You will benefit from understanding the laws governing energy efficiency and the physics involved in generating that energy. The more comfortable you are with the scientific terminology of your topic, the more compelling your case will be. Switching to fuel cells, which emit only water, seems like the perfect solution to global warming. But if you understand the science, you will acknowledge that many significant hurdles remain before hydrogen can replace petroleum in the world economy. For starters, it is difficult to compress and store; second, PEM fuel cells require platinum, a rare precious metal that might soon become the next depleted natural resource if it became an essential component of all newly manufactured motor vehicles.

Follow Your Hunch: This is where good investigative habits come in handy. For example, one expert believes that Hubbert peak theory is essentially correct and that world oil production will peak within a few years. Another expert believes that new technology will vastly increase the amount of recoverable oil worldwide, effectively shifting peak oil to a couple hundred years in the future. Both experts cite statistics to support their cases, but you have a hunch. You are optimistic about the world oil supply, because you know your history: In the 1970s, experts warned that oil supplies would be depleted by the turn of the century. In fact, the opposite happened. Production soared and world oil prices plummeted. This leads you to suspect that the expert who forecasts oil shortages within the next few years is wrong. How do you turn that hunch into evidence? One way is to investigate the expert's credentials. Is this person a scientist, a government official, a grassroots activist, or the owner of a company that creates photovoltaic cells? Do his or her statistics rely on too many unknown variables? Are the expert's claims full of vivid, unyielding proclamations of disaster? What, then, can you conclude about the person's biases? Keep in mind that it is also your duty to look into the credentials of the experts with whom you agree. If you find out that the expert who claims petroleum will remain plentiful for the next 200 years is a lobbyist for the oil industry, will that change your opinion? Why or why not?

Take Good Notes: Keep a running list of articles you read, Web sites you visit, organizations you research, and statements you quote. Make hard copies of important articles and highlight the quotes you use. Photocopy publication information of the books you read so you can list them properly in your bibliography. A robust bibliography lends credibility to your arguments; it lets readers know you have done your research. It also makes writing your paper easier.

Recognize that research is an ongoing process; new information comes to light all the time and you must be able to integrate it into your writing. Always cite current sources, even if you are reporting on something as ancient as the formation of fossil fuels in the Earth's crust millions of years ago. Scientists are continually learning more about the Earth's geology; if you quote books written 30 years ago (when plate tectonics were disputed, for example), your research may not reflect the current understanding of geologic processes.

Seek Primary Documents: The Internet is invaluable when it comes to tracking down international treaties, government documents, legal briefs, and other primary documents that relate to your topic. Read these documents yourself; do not rely on others' summaries, which could be biased. The presentation of issues, the beliefs that underlie them, and the language used to describe them are factors that cannot be gleaned from secondhand sources.

References to primary documents make your case stronger. For example, the United Nations' Brundtland Report ("Our Sustainable Future") may be dated, having been written in 1987, but it also set the tone for future discussions on sustainable development and defined the terms used in those discussions. It serves as a primary historical document in the field of sustainable development. M. King Hubbert's initial report on peak oil—which turned out to accurately forecast oil production rates in the United States—is an important primary document because it fostered further research and was written by a highly regarded oil industry scientist.

Know the Law: Many of the primary documents you will be able to track down will be legal in nature. Ecolex (www.ecolex.org) is an international index database in which you can search for treaties, national legislation, and court decisions based on keyword, year, country, and issue. The Library of Congress also houses extensive publicly available information on the U.S. legislative process, the Congressional Record, and other official documents at their THOMAS site: http://thomas.loc.gov. Similarly, actions and protocols by the United Nations can be found on its Web site: http://www.un.org/.

Develop an International Perspective: Even if your topic concerns a local or national issue, knowing how the issue is perceived in other parts of the world will give you a broader—and therefore more valid—understanding of it. For instance, maybe your report advocates an international treaty to ban DDT and other pesticides because of the danger they pose to wildlife and human health. Then you read about efforts of the World Health Organization to eradicate malaria in certain African countries by spraying houses with DDT. It sounds like a bad idea. But further research uncovers the fact that millions die of malaria in Africa each year, and a quick, inexpensive, one-time spraying of DDT reduces the number of malaria deaths dramatically. Townspeople who once feared for their lives are elated that malaria is one less problem they have to worry about. Thus, an international viewpoint allows you to see the benefits of DDT in certain situations. In the United States, a prosperous country with many resources and no threat of malaria, a ban on DDT is feasible. But the same standards do not apply across the globe.

USING SOURCES EFFECTIVELY

Online Resources

No doubt about it—the Internet is a lifesaver. You already know not to believe everything you read online. How do you determine whether or not a Web site can be trusted? Most likely, a reputable Web site is run by an individual or group that has a credible offline presence. Credible Web sources do not use pseudonyms; they do provide links to support all claims they make, and exhibit sufficient transparency into who they are, what their goals are, and how they are funded.

That said, there is plenty of solid information accessible to you online that will make your research as top-notch as any professional's. However, some of it is available from subscription-only Web sites or for a fee. The good news is that many of these services are available through your local public or university libraries for free. Call or visit your library and get a librarian to help you.

WIKIPEDIA

This open-source encyclopedia is a great starting point for your research. But do not quote from it and cross-check all facts you find on Wikipedia using independent sources. Because Wikipedia is such a vast database, there is a good chance you can find at least an introduction to the topic you are researching. Often the entry contains footnotes to other Web sites that provide more authoritative information, links to related topics, lists of prominent individuals associated with the topic, and photographs and charts to illustrate the topic. In terms of scientific concepts, Wikipedia entries are often quite detailed and inaccuracies have often been edited out of the entries. However, since it is an open-source encyclopedia anyone can contribute to Wikipedia and thus the quality of the information varies.

GOVERNMENT WEB SITES

Many governments have reputable Web sites that provide a wealth of information. In the United States, Web sites with a *.gov* ending designate legitimate government agencies. You can find detailed statistics from the local to the international level regarding population, growth rates, economic factors, natural resource usage, and energy consumption. For U.S. and world energy information, the Energy Information Administration (www.eia.gov) is useful. Many other organizations cite EIA statistics; so even if they are not perfect, at least you know that they are the basis for much of the policy and research on which other experts rely.

Additionally, most members of the U.S. Congress have Web sites where constituents can keep track of legislation the senator or representative is sponsoring or supporting, and what the elected official is doing with regard to supporting or campaigning against legislation on environmental, developmental, economic, and energy policies that may directly affect you and your community.

FOUNDATIONS AND ACADEMIC INSTITUTIONS

In evaluating an organization, take stock of its Web site. Does it list a street address? How long has it been established? What are its program areas?

Does it have a board of directors? Does it accept members? What is its mission statement? There are no right answers to these questions, only answers that will help you determine the organization's intentions and level of expertise. The membership and purpose of a grassroots organization such as the Sierra Club are much different than the goals of a conservative think tank such as the Heritage Foundation. Both are valid organizations, but the former is geared toward educating the public and the latter is more concerned with influencing government policy.

INTERNATIONAL WEB SITES

The United Nations and the World Bank both have extensive Web portals through which you can find documentation on a myriad of programs. Many international Web sites exist in several languages. The BBC News Web site serves as a major news outlet for English-speakers in Europe and often offers a more international perspective than many U.S. news organizations such as CNN or MSNBC. The *International Tribune Herald* is an English-language daily newspaper that reports news from around the world. Even if you are concerned with a local topic, your research can be informed by data regarding how that topic is approached by other localities. For instance, if legislators propose a new dam to stop flooding in your area, you may find different strategies in place in the Netherlands. The Dutch have been defending themselves against the North Sea for hundreds of years. Their dams are some of the most advanced in the world, and yet they recognize the value in allowing flooding in some areas. In fact, in those areas builders have constructed floating houses that rise and fall with the water level. How might these solutions be applicable in your town?

NONPROFIT ORGANIZATIONS

Nonprofit organizations such as the Sierra Club, the National Geographic Society, and WWF have robust Web sites with articles and links to other sites of interest. When it comes to issues of natural resources, nonprofits frequently are on the side of conservation, not development. Their agenda is usually quite apparent and will be useful in your research in support of one side of the issue.

THINK TANKS AND CONSULTANCY GROUPS

A think tank is an organization that conducts research and formulates policies on specific issues, often for commercial or government clients. Many think tanks make their findings available online, and many think tanks are openly affiliated with a political ideology. This makes them good candidates for exploring the extremes of an issue. In the United States, the American Enterprise Institute and the Heritage Foundation are conservative think tanks that promote policies favorable to corporate and military growth. The Brookings Institution is a centrist organization with a tendency toward liberalism, and the Cato Institute promotes free-market, libertarian views. It is important to remember, however, that many think tanks are funded by industries, such as petroleum companies, automakers, and major military contractors, and may promote policies that favor these corporations.

BLOGS AND CHAT ROOMS

Blogs are useful for gaining a "man on the street" perspective. Keep in mind that a blog written by a college professor may be more valid than one written by a high school student. Some blogs are affiliated with mainstream news organizations, and some exist solely outside the boundaries of traditional media. Following either type can be extremely informative and a great way to become familiar with opposing viewpoints. However, do not quote from blogs (other than in an informal, anecdotal way), do not describe a blogger as an expert unless that person is noted in his or her field beyond the realm of the Internet, and always independently verify claims made by a blogger.

Offline Resources

Offline research is information that was initially broadcast or published in conventional media outlets. This includes books and magazines, documentary films, television news reports, radio reports, etc. Many offline resources have online counterparts or are summarily reprinted or uploaded to the Internet.

NEWSPAPERS

The New York Times, USA Today, Wall Street Journal, Washington Post, Chicago Tribune, Los Angeles Times, and the *Cleveland Plain Dealer* are some of the most respected daily newspapers in the country. Also, news wire services, especially the Associated Press and Reuters, are valuable for breaking news and often serve as the basis for longer reports in the daily newspapers. Most newspapers have online archives that are searchable by date and topic. Articles are often available for a small fee.

GENERAL INTEREST PERIODICALS

Time, Newsweek, U.S. News & World Report, the *New Yorker,* the *Atlantic, Harper's,* the *Economist,* and *National Geographic* are some of the most respected magazines that routinely investigate topics that deal with natural resources and sustainable development. Your library may have back issues from which you can photocopy articles, or you may be able to purchase individual articles from the magazines' online archives. These articles will provide the names of many credible experts and may present a more in-depth look at an issue than available in a daily newspaper.

PEER-REVIEWED JOURNALS

A peer-reviewed journal is one that publishes original studies and research by academics and professionals, but only after the papers have undergone rigorous scrutiny to ensure they adhere to strict scientific standards. This gives the data a degree of validity sometimes absent from less scientific reporting in newspapers and magazines. Articles in peer-reviewed journals are then available to other scientists to quote, use as research, or serve as the basis of further research, with the goal of either replicating the original study's findings or refuting them. In this way, the body of knowledge in a certain field is advanced. Examples of peer-reviewed journals relevant to sustainable development include the *McGill International Journal of Sustainable Development Law;* the *Journal of Engineering for Sustainable Development: Energy, Environment, and Health; Greener Management International: The Journal of Corporate Environmental Strategy and Practice; The International Journal of Sustainable Development; Environment, Development and Sustainability;* and *Urban Ecosystems.*

Articles from peer-reviewed journals are often available through online subscription databases available at larger public libraries and university libraries. You may find articles relevant to your research through abstract and index databases, tools that any librarian can assist you with.

PUBLIC RADIO AND PUBLIC TELEVISION

Both the Public Broadcasting Service (PBS) and National Public Radio (NPR), which receive little corporate funding, broadcast programs that take an in-depth look at various topics. Radio shows are often archived on the NPR Web site (http://www.npr.org/), and PBS (http://www.pbs.org/) shows are frequently available at the library on DVD. Extended interviews with authors and other experts are a hallmark of many long-running PBS and NPR series. Such sources are considered legitimate and can be cited in your writing.

NETWORK AND CABLE TELEVISION

All-news channels, network newscasts, and documentaries on the Discovery Channel or the History Channel sometimes tackle topics regarding natural resources and sustainable development. These shows are frequently repeated and often available on DVD. They may contain interviews with subject experts, but they may not be completely objective in presenting both sides of an issue.

BOOKS

Value the printed page. Read the latest books on your topic to gain detailed insight on new and emerging theories. But as with all media sources, you should be discriminating. Some books are better sources of information than others. Those written by academics, published by major publishers or university presses, and those that provide extensive notes and bibliographies are more likely to be somewhat objective. Ask yourself: What is the author's qualifications for writing such a book?

Consider how the book has been received by the author's peers. Was it reviewed favorably in major newspapers and magazines? Has the book been criticized by other experts? Does the author have a hidden agenda? Perhaps he or she is running for public office or wants to stir up controversy to gain ratings on his or her radio talk show. Finally, reading the book yourself allows you to determine if it has any substance and if it presents new and compelling information.

EVALUATING RELIABILITY AND BALANCE IN SOURCES

How do you know if you can you trust a statistic? One measure of reliability is how often the statistic is quoted by other sources. For instance, the statistic that the United States is home to only 4 percent of the world's population but consumes 25 percent of the world's energy is widely quoted and believed. As long as you cite a major media source in your research, you can consider such a statistic to stand up to scrutiny. Of course, that does not guarantee the statistic is true. If you would like to refute such a statistic, you must cite compelling evidence to the contrary.

Beware of weasel words. Phrases such as "some people say," "experts are convinced," "it is thought to be true," and others that are not followed by specific verifiable claims indicate the author cannot prove nor disprove the statement. Therefore, for your purposes the statement is useless; they serve only to give the author an illusion of credibility. To determine if a source is using weasel words, ask yourself questions such as the following:

- Does the author say who the experts are? What makes them experts?
- Does the author give specifics regarding consensus? For instance, the statement "many experts believe" could mean three experts or thirty. Which is it? Does it matter?
- Is the author relying on the latest data? Where does the author's data come from? If you do not know, consider it suspect.

Interpreting Statistical Information

The better you can analyze statistics, the better you can spot bias and inaccuracies when you come across them. Start by developing a solid understanding of the terms used in the field you are studying. Many systems of measurement are used in the energy industry, and often the numbers are so far removed from a common point of reference that it is hard to grasp the big picture. There is a tremendous difference between a kilowatt and a gigawatt, for example, and knowing the difference will make interpreting information easier.

Systems of measurement differ around the world. The U.S. customary units of miles, gallons, pounds, acres, etc., remains largely in effect despite efforts to convert to the metric system, a transition that many other countries made decades ago. The Standard International units for power, however, are based on metric units and widely used in the United States and abroad.

The Standard International unit of power is the *joule*. One joule represents the amount of energy required to lift 1 kilogram by 10 centimeters on the surface of the earth. One *watt* equals the work done by 1 joule per second. A *kilowatt* is 1,000 watts; a *megawatt* is 1 million watts; and a *gigawatt* is 1 billion watts. Despite these definitions, true understanding of the terms may require comparisons to factors that relate to daily life.

For instance: A computer requires 8 kilowatt hours of energy per year to operate, but what does that mean in terms of fossil fuel usage? One statistic says that a computer requires the equivalent of 967 pounds of coal per year:[1]

- 1 kwh of electricity = 24 hours of television
- 1 kwh of electricity = 1.5 hours of air conditioning
- 1 kwh of electricity = 1.725 pounds of carbon dioxide[2]
- megawatt = 1 million watts (average nuclear power plant = 500–2000 MW)
- gigawatt = 1 billion watts (total wind energy potential in the United States = 10 gigawatts)

Here are some coal statistics:[3]

- 1 lb of coal = 5 pots of coffee
- .5 tons of coal runs an electric stove for one year
- The U.S. has more coal that can be mined than the rest of the world has oil that can be pumped from the ground.

- Electric water heater = 2 tons of coal per year
- Refrigerator = .5 tons of coal per year
- 100-watt lightbulb for 10 hours = 1 lb of coal
- Each person in the United States consumes the energy equivalent of 7,643 pounds of coal per year.
- The amount of solar energy entering the earth's atmosphere each minute is more than the total amount of fossil fuel energy the world uses each year.
- World oil consumption = 1 cubic mile annually.
- World coal consumption = 5,800 million short tons annually, of which 75 percent is used to generate electricity.
- 1 barrel of crude oil = 42 gallons of gasoline.

Beware of similar-sounding measurements. For instance, some people believe that the decrease in the rate of world population growth proves that world population is stabilizing. This is false. What it really means is that population is still growing, but instead of growing at a rate of 5 percent a year it is growing at 4 percent a year.

Keep in mind that statistics change and use the most recent data you can find. While governments often collect data on an annual basis, it sometimes takes a year or more for that information to be collected, analyzed, and published.

Keep It Original

Finally, unless you are quoting a source verbatim and attributing it properly, always paraphrase the information you present or you may be charged with plagiarism. Good note-taking habits include inserting quotation marks around all material you jot down word for word. You must also keep track of source citation information for all quotes. This includes the name of the article, the author, the publication, date of publication, volume, number, month, year, and page number where possible. For a Web site, make sure you have the complete URL as well as the root URL if the data is likely to be moved.

Be aware of fair use copyright laws that restrict how much of a source you can quote. The general rule of thumb is 10 percent, or 100 words, whichever is less. That means in a short article of 100 words, you may quote no more than 10 words total in your paper. For long articles of 1,000 words or more, you should quote no more than 100 words at a time, and the total words quoted should not exceed 10 percent of the entire article. A 2,000-word article, therefore, should have no more than 200 words total included in your paper. Many bloggers quote extensively from copyrighted material and exceed these guidelines; you should not do the same.

Most sources published prior to 1920 are considered in the public domain and are no longer covered under copyright law. You may quote freely from public domain sources, but you must still provide source citations. Examples of public domain material would be excerpts from Malthus's *Essay on the Principle of Population* or Jonathan Swift's *A Modest Proposal.*

Research Until You Are Satisfied

If you find two sources that contradict one another, keep looking until you find a third source—or even more—to nudge the pendulum to one side. Keep an open mind but think critically. Moreover, in the course of writing your paper you may realize you do not have as strong a case as you thought. The solution is to gather more research, perhaps by exploring a different angle of your topic. Sometimes this is as easy as changing the keywords in your searches. For instance, if you are analyzing population trends in Germany, you will also want to search under *East Germany, West Germany,* and *European Union* in order to make sure you have covered all your bases. If you are working on water pollution, you should include in your searches terms such as *groundwater, salinity, water quality, water management,* and *water rights.*

Ultimately, your project will be only as strong as your understanding of your topic. If your research is incomplete or you do not understand the topic fully, you will not be able to present a clear point of view to your readers. Thus, it is better to do too much research and not use some of it than to not do enough in the first place. The good news is that the more research you do up front, the easier it is to buckle down and write your paper when the time comes.

---

[1] How Stuff Works Web site. URL: http://science.howstuffworks.com/question481.htm. Accessed on April 25, 2007.

[2] Watts on Schools Web site. URL: http://www.wattsonschools.com/calculator.htm. Accessed on April 25, 2007.

[3] Colorado Department of Natural Resources. "Colorado Coal." *Rock Talk* 8.2 (Summer 2005): 5.

7

Facts and Figures

POPULATION

1.1 Venn Diagram Representing Sustainability as an Overlap of Social, Environmental, and Economic Factors

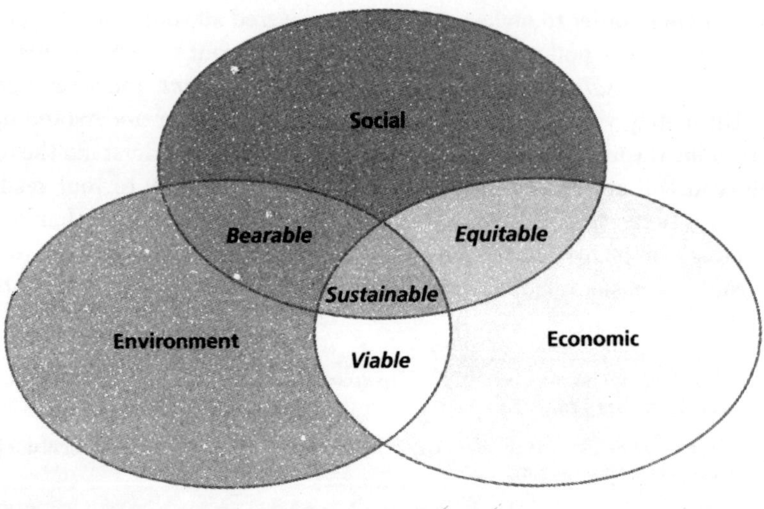

In this definition of sustainability, development must be *viable* for the environment and the economy; it must be *equitable* for the people and the economy; and it must be *bearable* for the people and the environment.

Source: Johann Dréo, March 9, 2006. Creative Commons Attribution ShareAlike 2.0 License.

1.2 Ecological Footprint per Capita for Select Countries, 2002

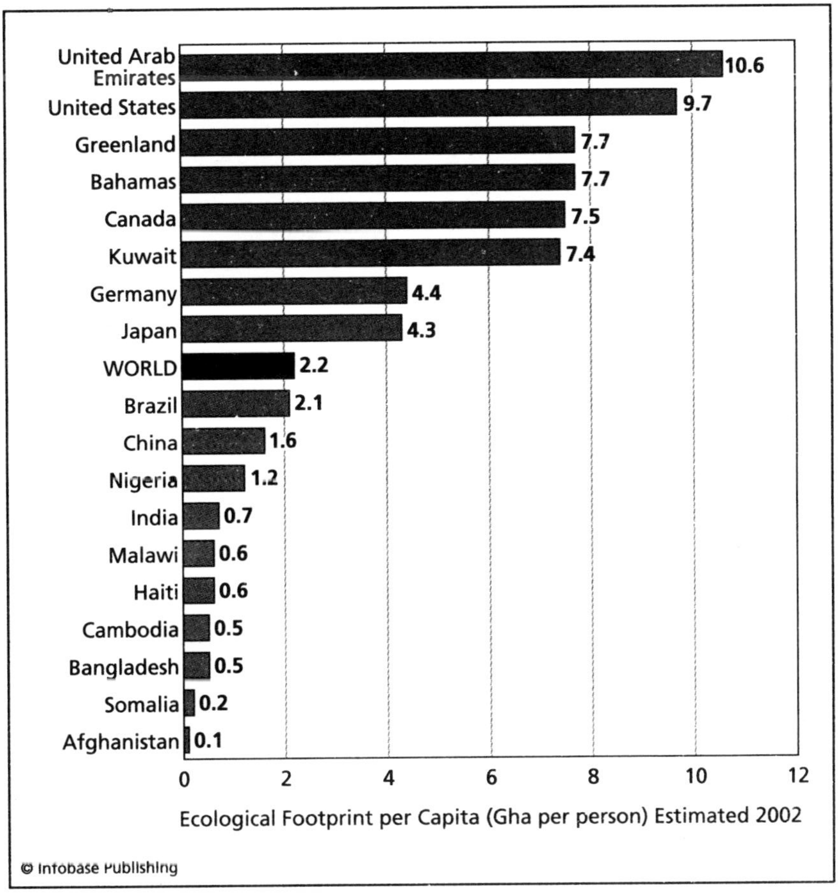

Countries with the largest ecological footprint compared to countries with the smallest ecological footprint, measured in global hectares per person on the basis of 2002 consumption rates.

Source: www.worldmapper.org, 2006 SASI Group and Mark Newman. Data from WWF International and Institute of Zoology, and the Food and Agriculture Organization of the United Nations.

1.3 Population Pyramids of the United States, Brazil, China, Germany, and India for 2008

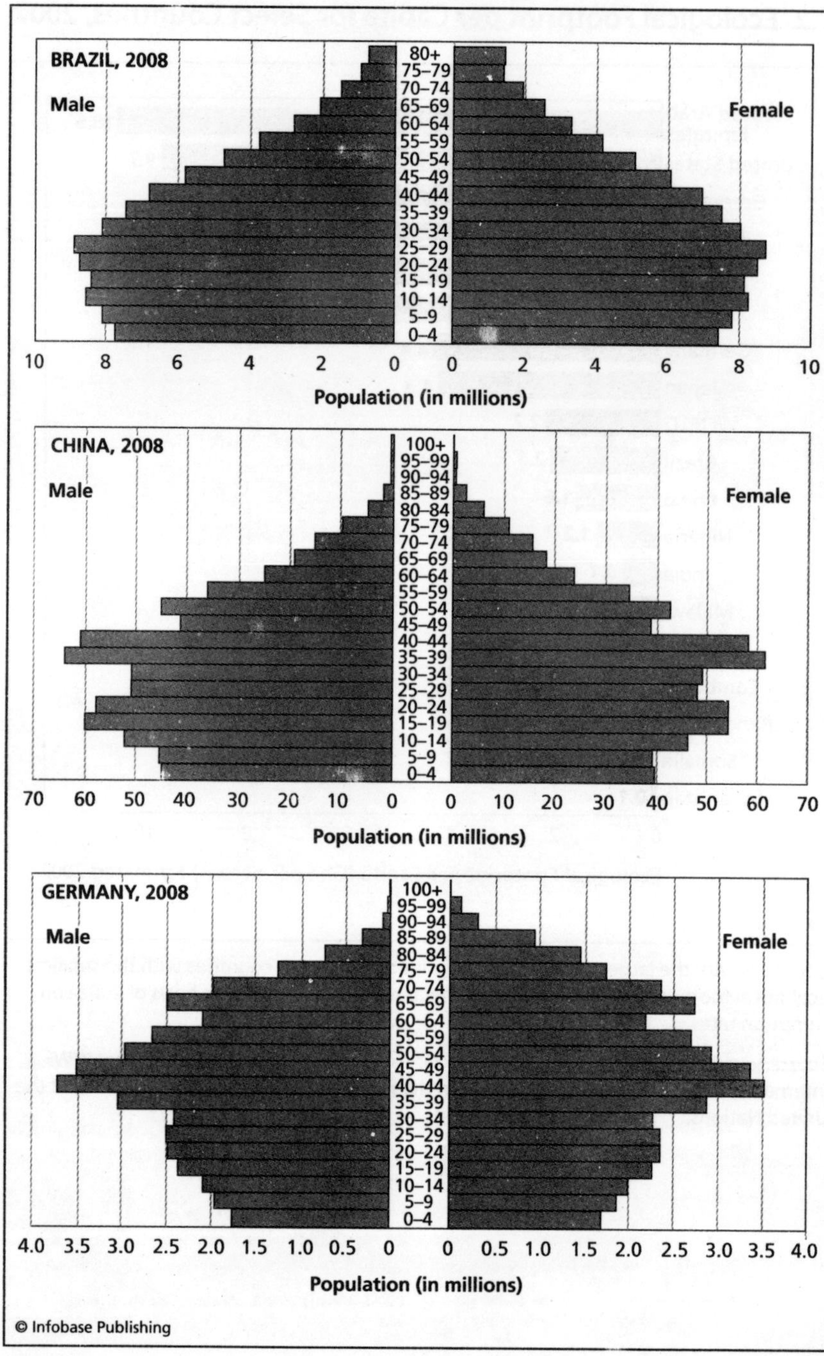

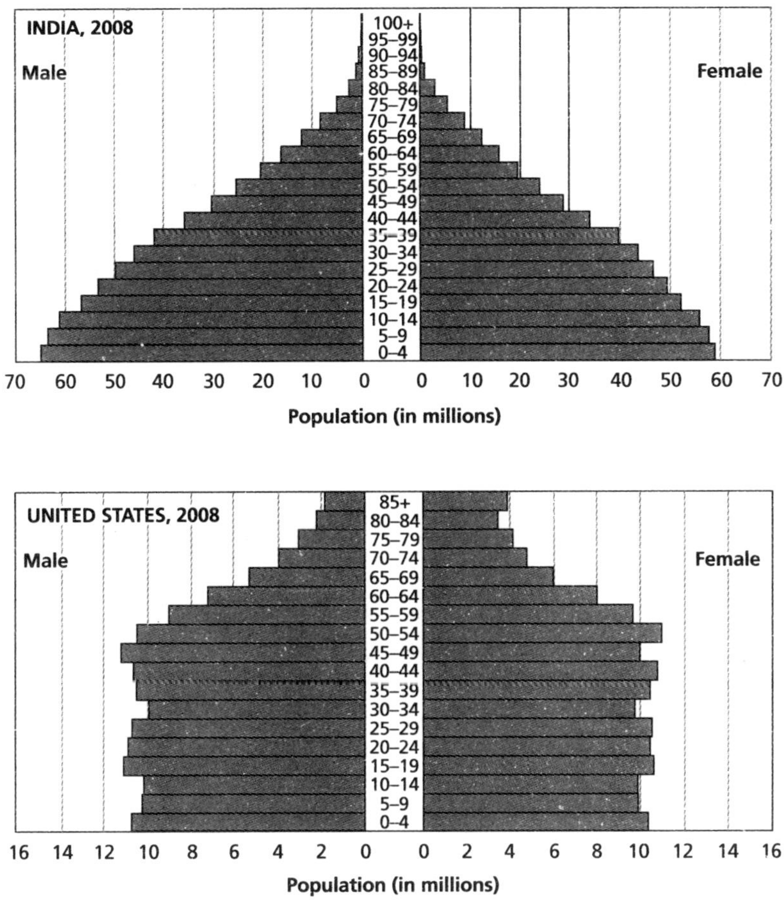

Note that only the population of India still reflects the traditional pyramid shape, which translates into a swelling population in decades to come. By contrast, the United States, Brazil, China, and Germany all have younger generations that are roughly the same size or significantly smaller than previous generations.

Source: U.S. Census Bureau, Population Division.

1.4 Distribution of World Population in 2008

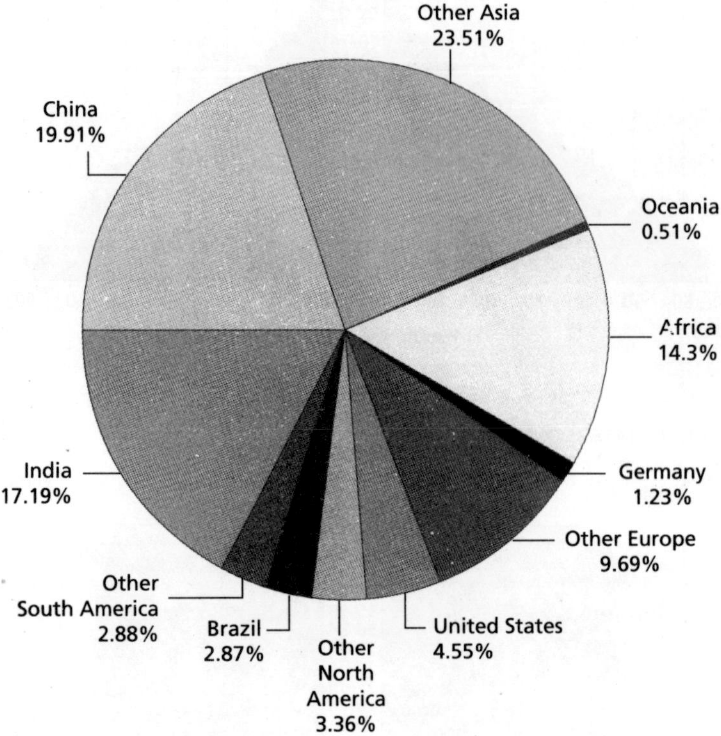

Note that Asia comprises more than 60 percent of the world's population. Developed nations, including the countries in Europe and North America, comprise less than 20 percent of the world's population.

Source: U.S. Census Bureau, International Data Base.

NATURAL RESOURCES AND ENERGY CONSUMPTION

2.1 Energy Consumption in the United States, 1775–1999

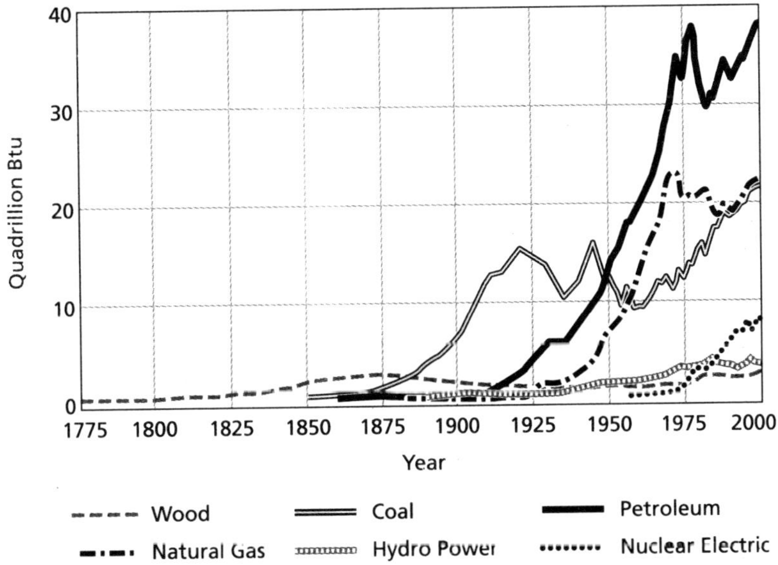

Depicts steady rate of energy consumption in the United States until the 20th century. Note the stability of wood as a fuel source, which today is used roughly in the same proportion as hydropower. Coal, natural gas, and petroleum—all fossil fuels—represent a huge majority of the energy consumed. Also note that coal consumption is continuing to rise.

Source: United States Energy Information Administration. Available online. URL: http://www.eia.doe.gov/kids/history/timelines/index.html.

2.2 Hubbert's Curve Representing Global Peak Oil

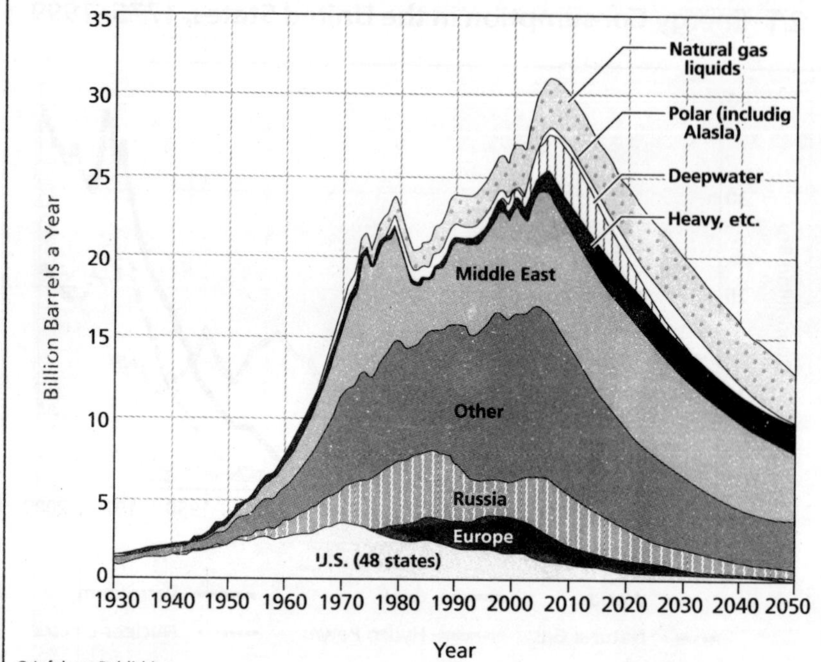

Note that U.S. oil production peaked around 1970, in accordance with M. King Hubbert's theory of peak oil. All other regions are predicted to peak by 2010 and taper off steadily afterward. Produced by ASPO, this chart and its supporting data have many critics, who believe the data is flawed and does not reflect new technology and/or the impact of conservation on statistics. Colin Campbell, the founder of the Association for the Study of Peak Oil & Gas, counters that it is more important to realize a peak is inevitable rather than focus solely on the year it may occur.

Source: Association for the Study of Peak Oil & Gas Newsletter.

2.3 World Coal Production and Consumption, 1996 and 2006

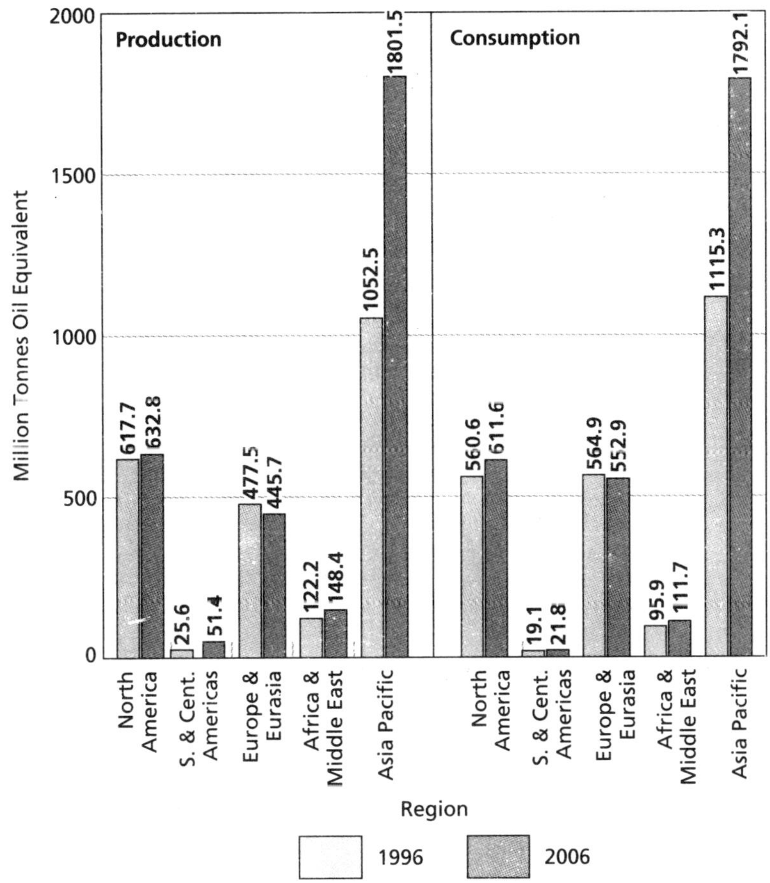

Note the drastic increase in coal production and consumption in Asia, and the low coal consumption in Central and South America.

Source: BP Statistical Review of World Energy, June 2007.

2.4 The Role of Renewable Energy Consumption in the U.S. Energy Supply, 2006

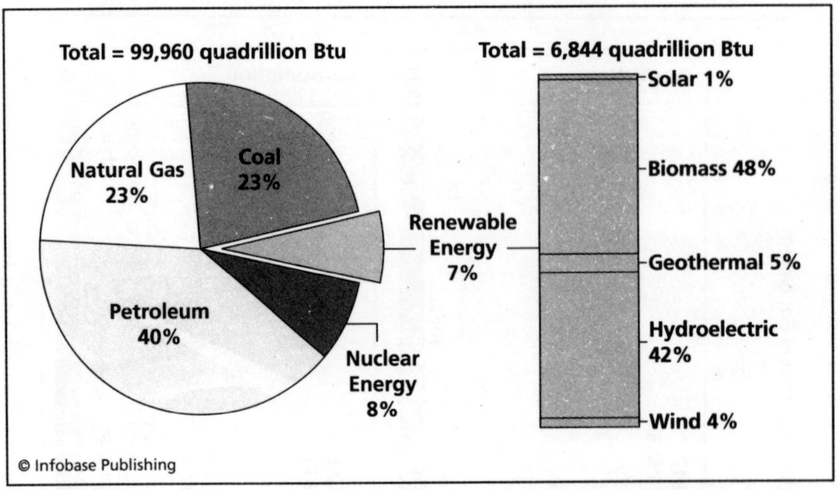

Total renewable energy consumption increased 7 percent between 2005 and 2006 while total U.S. energy consumption declined 1 percent, mainly due to decreased consumption of fossil fuels (including decreased natural gas consumption in the residential sector and decreased coal and petroleum consumption in the electric power sector). Hydroelectric conventional power had the largest absolute year-to-year change at 186 trillion Btu, but this represented only a 7 percent increase, while biofuels consumption increased by 164 trillion Btu or 28 percent, and wind increased by 80 trillion Btu or 45 percent.

Source: U.S. Energy Information Administration, 2006. URL: http://www.eia.doe.gov/cneaf/solar.renewables/page/prelim_trends/rea_prereport.html.

2.5 Regions Facing Severe Water Shortages by 2025

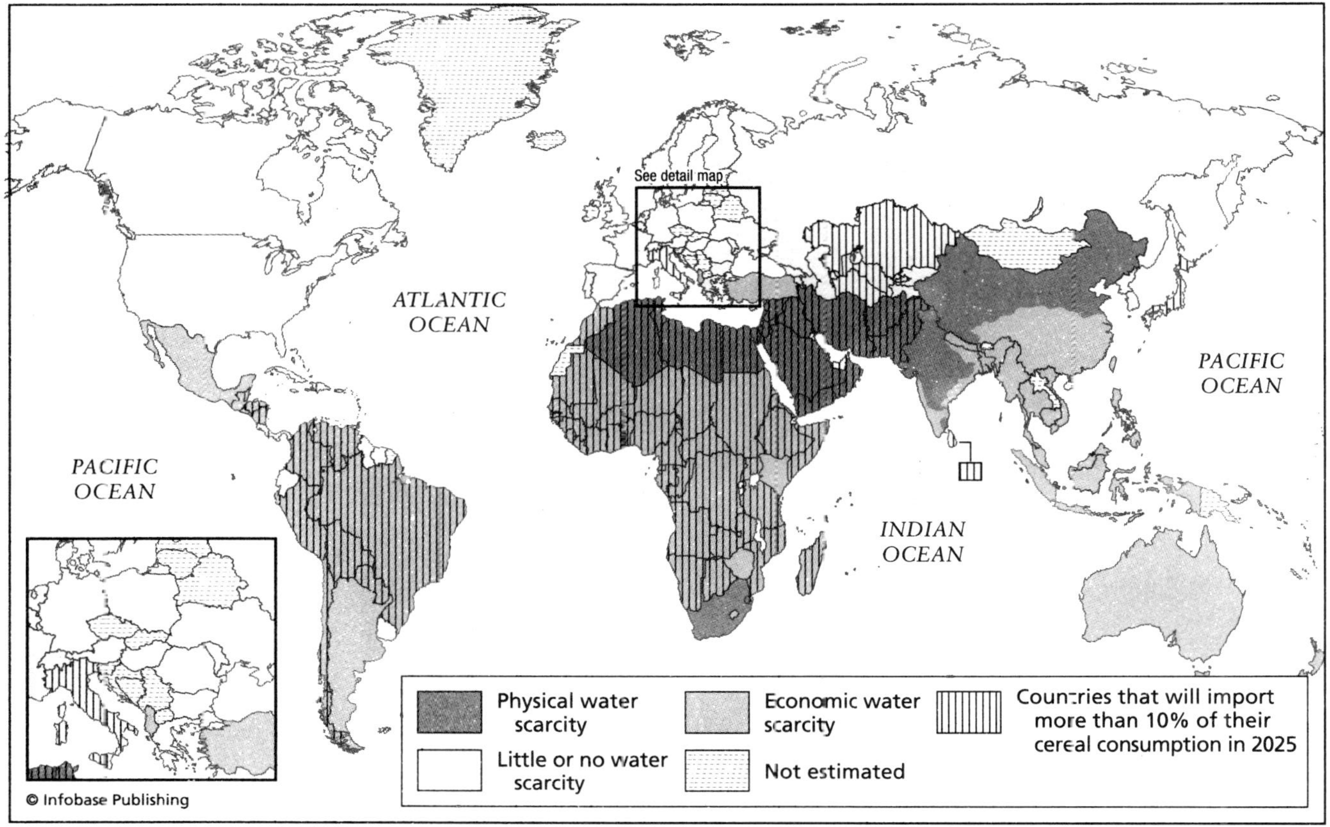

Areas that will suffer the greatest impact are northern China, much of India, the Middle East, Northern Africa, and South Africa. Note that many water-stressed countries will import a significant percentage of grain—an indication of food insecurity.

Source: International Water Management Institute, 2000.

2.6 Percentage of People Without Safe Water and Sanitation Facilities in Brazil, China, Germany, India, and the United States.

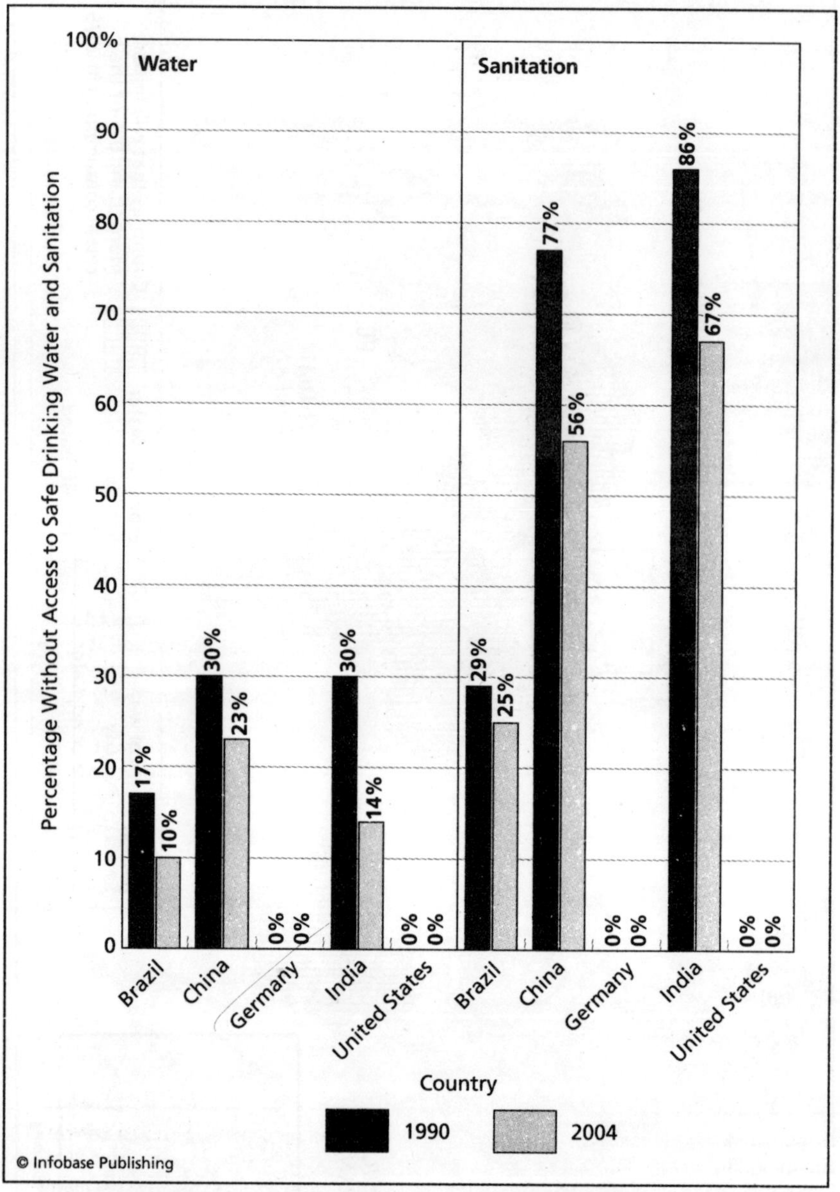

The graphs above document the number of people in each country who lack access to clean, safe drinking water and improved sanitation facilities, respectively.

Source: World Health Organization and UNICEF Joint Monitoring Programme for Water Supply and Sanitation, 2004. http://www.wssinfo.org/en/watquery.html

2.7 Schematic of a Polymer Electrolyte Membrane (PEM) Fuel Cell

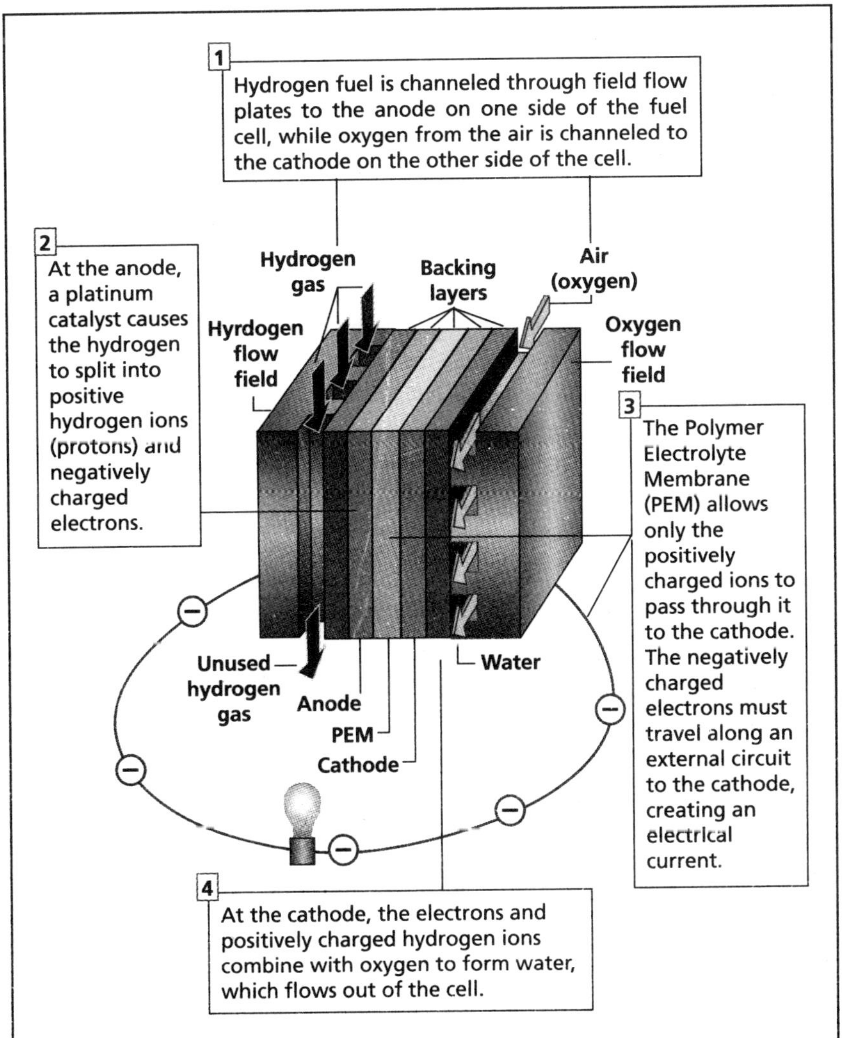

Hydrogen and oxygen react to create an electrical current capable of powering a vehicle, discharging only water. Though it looks simple, generating enough energy through PEM cells to power a vehicle as efficiently as an internal combustion engine still requires many more years of research and development.

Source: U.S. Government.

8

Key Players A to Z

EDWARD ABBEY (1927–1989) environmental activist in the American West and writer. Author of the nonfiction book *Desert Solitaire* (1968) and the novel *The Monkey Wrench Gang* (1975). Abbey was a vocal critic of public land policy and the military-industrial complex and is often considered to have condoned *ecotage,* acts of vandalism, such as burning billboards or disabling construction equipment, in an effort to prevent development.

RICHARD AUTY (1947–) British scholar who proposed the *resource curse* in 1993, the paradox in which countries with vast reserves of natural resources often suffer economic difficulties despite the wealth that comes with the resource.

RONALD BAILEY (1953–) science writer and editor for *Reason* magazine. Author of 1993 book *ECOSCAM: The False Prophets of Ecological Apocalypse,* which is critical of the reports about global warming and the connection between CFCs and the hole in the ozone layer. Bailey believes that false science exaggerates environmental dangers.

GERALD O. BARNEY American physicist and founder of the Virginia-based Millennium Institute, which promotes sustainable development. Directed the Council on Environmental Quality under President Carter and wrote the *Global 2000 Report to the President* in 1981 and *Global 2000 Revisited: What Should We Do?* (1993), which advocates measures to stabilize world population and develop agricultural practices that meet these challenges without destroying arable land in the process.

ALBERT BARTLETT former professor at the University of Colorado at Boulder and a modern-day Malthusian who refers to those supporting the "cornucopian" theory of population growth (such as Julian Simon) as "The New Flat Earth Society." Believes that sustainable growth is an oxymoron and that overpopulation is the greatest danger to civilization. He has given his lecture presentation on the topic, "Arithmetic, Population, and Energy," hundreds of times.

KARL BENZ (1844–1929) German engineer and founder of the Benz Company, credited with inventing the gasoline-powered internal combustion automobile. In 1885, he introduced his Motorwagen, a three-wheeled vehicle that was the first commercially available automobile. Sales were limited by the scarcity of gasoline, which was stocked only in small quantities at pharmacies as a cleaning agent and treatment for head lice.

HENRY BESSEMER (1813–1898) British inventor of the Bessemer process for manufacturing steel, patented in 1855, which greatly lowered production costs and led to an urban building boom in Europe and the United States.

NORMAN BORLAUG (1914–) American agricultural scientist and father of the Green Revolution. Developed high-yield, disease-resistant wheat varieties in the 1960s that were exported to Mexico, Pakistan, and India, which quickly resulted in those countries gaining *food security* and *food independence,* meaning they could now produce enough grain to feed everyone in the country. These advances are estimated by some to have saved up to 1 billion lives and earned Borlaug the Nobel Peace Prize in 1970 for eliminating suffering and possible war over limited resources. In 1986, Borlaug established the World Food Prize, given to those who make substantial advances in science and technology that help agriculturally deficient peoples. His advances have also been shared with Africa and Asia.

STEWART BRAND (1938–) founder and publisher of the *Whole Earth Catalog,* biologist, artist, computer technologist, and futurist. *The Whole Earth Catalog* was first published in 1968 for the purpose of providing readers with useful information to enhance their well-being and sustainability; it actively promoted renewable energy and environmental conservation; and its wide-ranging, informal format is said to have inspired those who later developed the World Wide Web. The 1972 edition sold over a million copies and won the National Book Award. In later years, Brand formed the Global Business Network to foster communication and problem-solving between international corporations with an eye toward sustainability.

RICHARD BRANSON (1950–) British entrepreneur, adventurer, global warming activist, and billionaire. Founded Virgin Records and Virgin Atlantic Airways and instituted the Virgin Earth Challenge, a $25 million prize for the first scientist to develop a way to extract greenhouse gases from the atmosphere.

JERRY BROWN (1938–) American politician, governor of California (1975–83), and candidate for president of the United States, 1980 and 1992. Known for his environmentally progressive beliefs and policies, including his presidential campaign slogan for 1980: "Protect the Earth, serve the people, and explore the universe." Critical of the oil industry and a proponent of solar power.

LESTER R. BROWN (1934–) pioneered the concept of environmentally sustainable development and founded the Worldwatch Institute in 1974, which publishes the State of the World Reports. A MacArthur fellow and founder and president of the Earth Policy Institute, which publishes books and uses the media and the Internet to promote the idea of an *eco-economy* that will ensure prosperity while preserving the Earth.

GRO HARLEM BRUNDTLAND (1939–) Norwegian politician, medical doctor, public health administrator, and leader in sustainable development. Served as prime minister of Norway, 1986–89 and 1990–96, and as the Director General of the World Health Organization in 1998. She was the Chair of the United Nation's World Commission on Environment and Development (WCED), known as the Brundtland Commission, which produced the Brundtland Report and developed the concept of sustainable development.

RACHEL CARSON (1907–1964) American zoologist, biologist, and author. Her book *Silent Spring* (1962) publicized the dangers of pesticides, particularly DDT, due to the way they move up the food chain, ultimately endangering the health of animals and humans. The book was controversial when it was published and was condemned by many chemical companies. The book became a best seller, ignited the modern environmental movement, and ultimately resulted in a ban on DDT. Carson was posthumously awarded the Presidential Medal of Freedom in 1980.

BRANDON CARTER (1942–) Australian theoretical physicist and author of the Doomsday Argument, sometimes called the "Carter catastrophe," which is a probabilistic argument predicting the extinction of the human race based on the estimated number of people born so far. The Doomsday Argument predicts with 95 percent confidence that the human race will become extinct within 9,120 years.

WILLIAM R. CATTON JR. (1926–) professor of sociology and author of the 1980 book *Overshoot: The Ecological Basis of Revolutionary Change*, a modern-day Malthusian tale of the imminent problem resulting from excessive population and scarcity of natural resources.

JOEL E. COHEN (1944–) American mathematician and head of the Laboratory of Populations at Rockefeller and Columbia University in New York City. His research focuses on demography, ecology, epidemiology, and social organization; he is the author of *How Many People Can the Earth Support?* (1995) and a member of the U.S. National Academy of Sciences.

BARRY COMMONER (1917–) American biologist and environmentalist. Commoner founded the Citizens Party and ran for president of the United States on its ticket in 1980. Describes himself as an "eco-socialist" who believes that environmental degradation is caused largely by capitalist technology, not overpopulation.

MARQUIS DE CONDORCET (1743–1794) 18th-century French mathematician, philosopher, Age of Enlightenment rationalist, and contemporary of THOMAS MALTHUS who believed the future would present bountiful harvests enough to feed everyone. This idea of the "perfectibility of society" prompted Malthus's rebuttal, *Essay on the Principle of Population.*

JACQUES-YVES COUSTEAU (1910–1997) French explorer, marine scientist, and filmmaker. Founder of the Cousteau Society in 1973 and host of the popular television show "The Undersea World of Jacques Cousteau." He advocated for oceanic conservation, opposed nuclear dumping at sea, and explored regions of the ocean previously unseen. He received the United Nations Environmental Prize in 1977.

MARIE CURIE (1867–1934) Polish-French physicist and chemist who discovered radioactivity and the elements radium and polonium. Recipient of two Nobel Prizes, one in physics and one in chemistry.

HERMAN DALY (1938–) professor from the University of Maryland's School of Public Affairs who applies economic principles to the goals of sustainable development. Named one of the 100 "visionaries who could change your life" by *Utne Reader.*

JARED DIAMOND (1937–) American biologist, physiologist, and author. In his Pulitzer Prize–winning book *Guns, Germs, and Steel* (1997), he explores the role of ecology in the development of civilizations and argues that civilization is dependent on geography, climate, and access to food and shelter. In *Collapse: How Societies Choose to Fail or Succeed* (2005), he states that mismanagement of natural resources is the primary reason that civilizations have failed in the past. Diamond received the National Medal of Science in 1999.

RUDOLF DIESEL (1858–1913) German inventor who patented the Diesel engine in 1892, a more fuel-efficient design than the 1876 four-stroke cycle

Otto engine that was popular at the time. Diesel believed his engine was superior to others because of its efficiency and its ability to run on vegetable oil and other non-petroleum products.

EDWIN LAURENTINE DRAKE (1819–1880) pioneering petroleum entrepreneur who drilled the first oil well in the United States in Titusville, Pennsylvania, in 1859.

RICHARD C. DUNCAN postulated the Olduvai Theory (1989) that states industrialized society will enjoy a 100-year lifespan, from roughly 1930 to 2030.

THOMAS A. EDISON (1847–1931) American inventor who established the first research laboratory dedicated to continuing innovations in technology. Edison and his employees developed the first commercially feasible incandescent lightbulb and electric distribution system to provide electricity to individual consumers, which was the Pearl Street Station in New York City. It opened in 1882 and provided electricity to 85 local customers via one direct current (DC) generator that was powered by coal.

PAUL R. EHRLICH (1932–) American entomologist and author of *The Population Bomb* (1968), in which he predicted widespread famine and starvation by the 1980s. He has been called a modern-day Malthusian (*see* THOMAS MALTHUS) for his belief that overpopulation will bring about mass starvation. He founded the nonprofit organization Zero Population Growth and is president of the Center for Conservation Biology at Stanford University, where he is the Bing Professor of Population Studies.

FRIEDRICH ENGELS (1820–1895) 19th-century German philosopher and coauthor with Karl Marx of *The Communist Manifesto.* He believed that overpopulation was a myth.

ENRICO FERMI (1901–1954) Italian-American physicist who developed the first nuclear reactor. He produced the first atomic pile, resulting in the first sustained nuclear chain reaction, at the University of Chicago on December 2, 1942. He also worked on the Manhattan Project, but later opposed the development of the hydrogen bomb. He received the Nobel Prize in Physics in 1938.

BILL FORD JR. (1957–) Henry Ford's great-grandson and former president, CEO, and COO of the Ford Motor Company, and the executive chair of Ford's Board of Directors. Ford promotes himself as an environmentalist who plans to make Ford a greener company by manufacturing hybrid vehicles, electric vehicles, flex-fuel vehicles, and fuel cell vehicles. In the early

2000s, he announced plants to increase fuel efficiency by 25 percent in all Ford vehicles, a plan that was later abandoned when the company began losing billions of dollars. His other alternative-fuel vehicle programs were also cancelled following the initiation of the Way Forward program to save the company.

HENRY FORD (1863–1947) American inventor and businessman who revolutionized transportation worldwide through improvements in mass production and the moving assembly line, which enabled him to build an affordable motor vehicle. He founded the Ford Motor Company in 1903 and invented the Model T in 1908, eventually selling over 15 million of them. Having grown up on a farm, Ford initially intended his vehicles to run on grain alcohol (ethanol) that could be easily produced by farmers. He also made advancements in soybean-based plastics and created a plastic vehicle in 1942 that ran on ethanol. In the 1920s, Ford purchased 10,000 square kilometers of the Amazon Basin in Brazil in order to harvest rubber for his cars' tires. Fordlandia, as it was called, was doomed when he tried to impose his rigid industrial organizational structure on Brazilian workers.

JOSEPH FOURIER (1768–1830) 18th-century French mathematician and physicist who first described the greenhouse effect in 1827, recognizing the possibility that global temperatures may rise as a result of solar radiation trapped in the Earth's atmosphere.

BENJAMIN FRANKLIN (1706–1790) American inventor, writer, and statesman. His Franklin stove improved output and efficiency over previous models available in the 18th century and was widely adopted throughout the growing nation, which enjoyed vast reserves of wood to fuel the stove. Franklin also experimented with electricity, came to understand its properties, and invented lightning rods as a way to redirect electricity into the ground so it would not damage buildings.

CHARLES FRITTS American inventor who built the first working solar cell in 1884, using selenium as a semiconductor; the device was only 1 percent efficient.

BUCKMINSTER FULLER (1895–1983) American inventor, architect, author, and visionary. He was concerned with the central question, "Does humanity have a chance to survive lastingly and successfully on planet Earth, and if so, how?" In an effort to answer the question, he invented the geodesic dome and the Dymaxion Car, both of which implemented technologies of efficiency. Fuller created the idea of *spaceship Earth* in his 1963 book *Operating Manual for Spaceship Earth,* which explores the notion that the Earth contains limited resources that should be conserved and preserved. He was concerned with renewable energy—particularly wind and solar power—and critical of fossil fuels. He promoted the idea of sustainability and *ephemeralization* (doing more with less) and founded the Buckminster Fuller Institute in 1983, an interdisciplinary group of scientists and innovators dedicated to improving the quality of life for all people without harming the environment. Members create and implement designs and technology for sustainability.

WILLIAM GODWIN (1756–1836) 18th-century British philosopher and writer whose *Enquiry Concerning Political Justice, and Its Influence on General Virtue and Happiness* (1793) explored the "perfectibility of science," part of which included his *principle of population,* the idea to limit population growth by discouraging sex and encouraging intellectual pursuits. This led THOMAS MALTHUS to respond with his *Essay on the Principle of Population,* in which he claimed that widespread famine and societal decline were imminent if population trends continued. In 1820, Godwin responded to Malthus with *Of Population: An Enquiry Concerning the Power of Increases in the Numbers of Mankind,* in which he called Malthus's theory "a house of cards."

CHARLES GOODYEAR (1800–1860) inventor who discovered how to create vulcanized rubber with sulfur. The discovery was of huge importance to industries who formerly could not rely on uncured rubber because it was unstable and deteriorated quickly. Vulcanized rubber is vastly stronger and longer lasting and has proven indispensable for vehicle tires and a myriad of other industrial applications.

ALBERT GORE JR. (1948–) American politician and environmentalist; recipient of the 2007 Nobel Peace Prize with the Intergovernmental Panel on Climate Change, member of the U.S. House of Representatives, 1977–85; member of U.S. Senate, 1985–93; vice president of the United States, 1993–2001. Author of *Earth in the Balance* (1992), a best-selling book about the dangers of global warming, and *The Assault on Reason* (2007), and the driving force behind the 2006 Academy Award–winning documentary about climate change, *An Inconvenient Truth.* Gore advocates carbon neutrality and hybrid vehicles and is chair of Generation Investment Management, a London-based research firm that promotes social and environmentally responsible investing.

GARRETT HARDIN (1915–2003) American ecologist and microbiologist whose influential 1968 paper "The Tragedy of the Commons," explored Aristotle's theory that states: "That which is common to the greatest number has the least care bestowed upon it." The "tragedy" was that natural resources necessary for the common good are often subject to private interests opposed to the common good. Many of Hardin's writings, especially on population and race, were controversial; he often wrote about overpopulation (advocating forced fertility reduction) and carrying capacity. He wrote *Living within Limits: Ecology, Economics, and Population Taboos* (1993) and *The Ostrich Factor: Our Population Myopia* (1999).

PAUL HAWKEN (1946–) American economist, entrepreneur, and writer. Author with AMORY LOVINS and Hunter Lovins of *Natural Capitalism: Creating the Next Industrial Revolution,* an influential book that outlines how market principles applied to natural resources can lead to a worldwide higher standard of living that is peaceful and beneficial to the environment. Head of the National Capital Institute, which created the World Index for Social and Environmental Responsibility.

M. KING HUBBERT (1903–1989) American geophysicist and researcher for the Shell Oil Company from 1943 to 1964. Hubbert believed that oil production over time could be represented with a bell curve, which came to be known as the Hubbert Curve. He also predicted that U.S. oil production would peak between the late 1960s and early 1970s; in fact, it peaked in 1970. This is called the Hubbert Peak. His research was extrapolated to worldwide petroleum reserves and resulted in the concept of Peak Oil, the point at which world petroleum production will crest; experts place this point anywhere from 2008 to 2050. In his later years, Hubbert advocated greater exploration and adoption of solar power.

JAMES INHOFE (1934–) U.S. senator from Oklahoma who is the ranking minority member of the Senate Committee on Environment and Public Works and a member of the subcommittee on clean air, climate change, and nuclear safety. Inhofe is well-known as a critic of global warming, which he has called "the greatest hoax ever perpetrated on the American people."

JANE JACOBS (1916–2006) 20th-century American-Canadian sociologist, urban theorist, and author concerned with the question, "Do we build cities for people or cars?" Arguing the former, she actively fought the development of expressways and the demolition of entire neighborhoods in New York City in the 1950s and advocated mixed-use, densely populated neighborhoods such as Greenwich Village for establishing a sense of community conducive to a high quality of life. These ideas are explored in *Life and Death of the Great American Cities* (1961) and many of her other writings, all of which inform the theory of New Urbanism. In 2007, the Rockefeller Foundation created the Jane Jacobs Medal for outstanding advances in urban theory and design.

WILLIAM STANLEY JEVONS (1835–1882) 19th-century English economist and political theorist who published *The Coal Question* in 1865, which forecasted a shortage of Britain's coal reserves as a result of increased industrialization. He also originated the concept of the Jevons Paradox, which states that technology that advances the efficiency of a given resource ultimately results in the depletion of that resource because efficiencies encourage overconsumption.

PETRA KELLY (1947–1992) German politician, environmentalist, and peace activist. Founding member of the German Green Party in 1979 and member of the West German Bundestag from 1983 to 1990. Campaigned for human rights, nuclear disarmament, and environmental protection. Awarded the Right Livelihood Award (the alternative Nobel Prize) in 1982. The Petra Kelly Prize for Human Rights, Ecology, and Non-Violence is awarded annually in her honor.

ROBERT F. KENNEDY JR. (1954–) environmental lawyer and activist, son of Robert F. Kennedy. Professor of environmental law for Pace University Law School, senior attorney for the Natural Resources Defense Council, founder of the Waterkeeper Alliance, and active in efforts to fight global warming and control pollution on the Hudson River.

BJØRN LOMBORG (1965–) Danish political scientist, statistician, and author of the controversial *The Skeptical Environmentalist* (2001). In the book, Lomborg refutes claims of global warming, environmental unsustainability, and ecological crises by analyzing scientific data. An outcry from the scientific community led to an investigation by the Danish Committee on Scientific Dishonesty, which ruled that the book misinterpreted scientific data, but Lomborg himself was not guilty due to his lack of expertise over his subject matter. In 2002, Lomborg founded the Copenhagen Consensus, an organization funded by the Danish government that prioritizes global issues according to the principles of welfare economics. The results were published in his 2004 book, *Global Crisis, Global Solutions.*

AMORY LOVINS (1947–) American physicist, energy expert, MacArthur fellow, author, and chair of the Rocky Mountain Institute. Developed the concept of "negawatt power" in 1989 and advocates a "soft-energy path" that diversifies a nation's energy usage and relies on renewable energy sources. Invented the ultra-efficient "hypercar" in 1984 and published *Winning the Oil Endgame* in 2004.

THOMAS MALTHUS (1766–1834) 18th-century British social theorist, whose influential *An Essay on the Principle of Population* (1798) made him one of the first individuals to consider the problem of overpopulation. Malthus understood that population grows exponentially, and he believed that human population would grow unchecked until it reached the *population ceiling,* which would be followed by mass starvation. Malthus estimated the population ceiling would be reached in the middle of the 19th century, and he favored population control as a way to avert the looming crisis.

DONELLA MEADOWS (1941–2001) American environmental scientist and writer. Meadows was a member of the MIT team that developed the World3 computer model for the Club of Rome in 1972 and wrote the book *The Limits of Growth,* which explored global trends in population, the environment, and economics. She was a MacArthur fellow, the founder of the International Network of Resource Information Centers, and the founder of the Sustainability Institute.

JOHN PIERPONT MORGAN (1837–1913) American financier and philanthropist. He formed General Electric and U.S. Steel by merging smaller companies in an effort to achieve economies of scale through consolidation and to make American industry a player on the world stage. He financed NIKOLA TESLA, whose demonstration of the superiority of alternating current (AC) over direct current (DC) led to the widespread adoption of the AC standard for the U.S. power grid. He also owned several mining businesses.

ROBERT MOSES (1888–1981) American urban planner and builder in New York City and Long Island. Moses wielded extraordinary influence over urban planning committees in his day and was largely responsible for the enormous public works projects that shaped New York in the mid-20th century. His huge expressway projects required the demolition of entire neighborhoods and towns, which in turn led to ghettos, blight, and white flight from urban areas. He destroyed houses in order to build public-housing projects and created physical barriers between upscale parts of Manhattan and lower-income areas such as the Bronx and Harlem. He is known for his quotes: "Cities are for traffic" and "If the ends don't justify the means, what does?" Backlash against Moses's wholesale destruction of communities in favor of elevated freeways was spearheaded by JANE JACOBS, who actively opposed Moses' projects and successfully lobbied to save Greenwich Village from being destroyed to make room for a freeway.

JOHN MUIR (1838–1914) Scottish-American naturalist and preservationist who founded the Sierra Club in 1892 and served as its first president. Muir campaigned to preserve Yosemite Valley in California and the Sierra Nevada Mountains from development, logging, and other economic pursuits. He used his knowledge of biology and geology to educate the public on the formation of Yosemite Valley and the dangers it faced from encroaching civilization.

LEWIS MUMFORD (1895–1990) American historian of technology, science, and urban design. Mumford explored urban life from a sociological perspective, ultimately criticizing automobile culture and urban sprawl as pathological developments responsible for many social ills. In *The Myths of the Machine: Technics and Human Development* (1967), he created the idea of *technics*—the relationship between social factors and technology. He coined the term *megamachines* to describe large bureaucracies and industries that coordinate human power for a single purpose, and advocated *biotechnics,* a model for sustainable living based on attaining an optimum level of wholeness and fulfillment. His book *The City in History* (1961) won the National Book Award, and he received the Presidential Medal of Freedom in 1964.

NORMAN MYERS (1934–) British environmentalist and biodiversity expert who created the concept of the *biodiversity hotspot*—an area at high risk for losing a substantial percentage of its plant and animal species, many of which are found only in that location. Myers is an expert on deforestation, mass extinction, and climate refugees and serves as an adviser to the World Bank and the United Nations.

ARNE NAESS (1912–2004) Norwegian philosopher, mountaineer, and founder of the *deep ecology* movement, which stresses self-realization and an understanding of the individual's impact on all living organisms. Naess cited RACHEL CARSON's *Silent Spring* as the inspiration for his environmental beliefs.

THOMAS NEWCOMEN (1663–1729) English ironworker, inventor of the Newcomen steam engine, and father of the Industrial Revolution. Developed a working steam engine around 1710, and by the time of his death dozens of Newcomen steam engines were in use in Britain's mining district, paving the way for exponential industrial growth in the following generations.

RICHARD M. NIXON (1913–1994) American politician and president of the United States from 1969 to 1974. During his presidency, he created the Environmental Protection Agency and initiated conservation measures during the OPEC oil embargo in 1973, including lowering the federal speed limit to 55 miles per hour.

J. ROBERT OPPENHEIMER (1904–1967) American physicist, director of the Manhattan Project, and "father of the atomic bomb." Presided over the first nuclear bomb test (the Trinity test), and after World War II became an adviser to the newly formed U.S. Atomic Energy Commission. Oppenheimer advocated for the control of atomic energy and discouraged the arms race. He was stripped of his government security clearance when he publicly discouraged the nuclear arms race during the cold war. With his colleagues Albert Einstein, Joseph Rotblat, and Bertrand Russell, he formed the Pugwash Conferences on Science and World Affairs in 1957, which seek nuclear détente and resolution to global security threats.

NIKOLAUS OTTO (1832–1891) German inventor of the first four-stroke cycle engine in 1861. In 1876 he improved upon the design with the *Otto Cycle,* an internal combustion engine powered by gasoline.

STANFORD OVSHINSKY (1923–) American inventor, engineer, and founder of Energy Conversion Devices, Inc. (ECD), a company that has developed thousands of semiconductors that have aided the development of solar cells, LCD displays, and batteries for high-tech electronic equipment. He is a proponent of efficient fuel systems and a developer of power systems for hybrid gas-electric vehicles.

GIFFORD PINCHOT (1865–1946) first head of the U.S. Forest Service and originator of the term *conservation* to describe planned use and renewal of land. Pinchot actively sought to preserve forest land in the United States and pushed for the widespread adoption of management based on efficient use of natural resources and elimination of waste.

WILLIAM REES (1943–) Canadian economist and creator of the *ecological footprint* as a quantitative tool for understanding humans' impact on the Earth. He is a founder of the Canadian Society for Ecological Economics and a member of the Global Integrity Project, which monitors governmental corruption worldwide. In *Our Ecological Footprint* (1996), he explores the relationship between the earth's carrying capacity and sustainable development.

JOHN D. ROCKEFELLER (1839–1937) American industrialist, philanthropist, and founder of Cleveland-based Standard Oil. At his height, he was the world's richest man and the first billionaire. The government eventually determined that Standard Oil was an unlawful monopoly and forced it to be broken up into a multitude of smaller companies, among them the companies that became Conoco, Amoco, Chevron, Exxon, and Mobil.

ARUNDHATI ROY (1961–) Indian writer and political activist. She has led protests against India's monumental Narmada Dam project, in which hundreds of thousands of people were relocated, many without adequate compensation. She also opposes globalization, U.S. hegemony,

India's nuclear policy, and ecologically destructive development in India. She has popularized her views through her documentary *DAM/AGE: A Film with Arundhati Roy* (2002), and her essay collection *The Cost of Living* (1999).

JEFFREY SACHS (1954–) influential American economist and director of the Earth Institute at Columbia University. Sachs is also the director of the United Nations Millennium Project, the Quetelet Professor of Sustainable Development at Columbia University, and author of the column "Sustainable Developments" for *Scientific American.* He has published several books, including *The End of Poverty: Economic Possibilities for Our Time* (2005).

CARL SAGAN (1934–1996) American astronomer, astrobiologist, writer, and host of the popular television series *Cosmos: A Personal Voyage* (1980), in which he explored, among many other topics, humans' impact on Earth, the greenhouse effect on Venus, and other issues of sustainability. He was also an anti-nuclear activist and warned of a *nuclear winter,* or global cooling effect, that would result from a limited nuclear exchange.

MARGARET SANGER (1879–1966) American birth control activist who founded the American Birth Control League in 1921. She coined the term *birth control* and believed that women had the right to limit family size, but she also promoted eugenics and racism. She advocated large-scale population control and organized the first World Population Conference in Geneva in 1927. From 1952 to 1959 she was the president of the International Planned Parenthood Federation.

E. F. SCHUMACHER (1911–1977) British economist, environmentalist, and author of *Small Is Beautiful,* a 1973 book that proposed many improvements to use of natural resources that later came to be known as sustainable development.

F. M. SEMENOV drilled first oil well in Baku, Russia, in the 1840s.

AMARTYA SEN (1933–) Indian economist and professor whose work on famine, poverty, and welfare economics earned him the Nobel Prize for Economics in 1998. Among his most notable writings is his 1981 book *Poverty and Famines: An Essay on Entitlement and Deprivation,* in which he determined the cause of the 1943 Bengal famine that killed millions of people (and that he lived through) was not lack of food, but rather inequalities in the system of food distribution that left many people without the means to obtain food. This work influenced the United Nations Development Programme, which aims to prevent famine worldwide. Sen has taught at several universities, including Trinity College, Cambridge, the London School of Economics, and Harvard University.

JULIAN L. SIMON (1932–1998) American free-market libertarian, professor of business administration at the University of Maryland, senior fellow at the Cato Institute, and author of *The Ultimate Resource* (1981). Simon famously refuted PAUL R. EHRLICH (author of *The Population Bomb*) and other modern-day Malthusians by stating that population growth was the solution, not the cause, of many environmental problems, because population leads to innovations in technology that will sustain humankind indefinitely. In *The Resourceful Earth* (1984), he directly refutes the Global 2000 report, released in 1981 by the Council of Environmental Quality, which foresaw widespread environmental degradation and resource shortages.

S. FRED SINGER (1924–) American atmospheric physicist. Singer is the founder and president of the Science and Environmental Policy Project, which disputes global warming, ozone depletion, and other environmental crises he believes have been exaggerated due to political bias or shoddy science. He is the author or coauthor of several books, including *Hot Talk Cold Science: Global Warming's Unfinished Debate* (1998), *Global Climate Change: Human and Natural Influences* (1987) and *Unstoppable Global Warming: Every 1,500 Years* (2007).

ADAM SMITH (1723–1790) 18th-century Scottish philosopher, founder of economics, and author of *The Wealth of Nations* (1776), which advocated ideas that came to be known as free trade, capitalism, and libertarianism. Smith believed that self-interest was advantageous for society and served as the primary mechanism of the *invisible hand* of the market. He was the first to summarize the changes enacted by the Industrial Revolution and outlined the *diamond-water paradox,* which states that although diamonds are not necessary for survival they are considered precious and expensive, but water, which is crucial for survival, is expected by many to be freely available at little or no cost to the consumer.

NIKOLA TESLA (1856–1943) Serbian-American inventor and engineer. Tesla pioneered alternating current (AC) electricity, which led to the *War of Currents* with Thomas Edison, who promoted direct current electricity. Tesla won, and AC power became the standard by which electricity has been distributed to customers around the world. In 1886 he formed Tesla Electric Light and Manufacturing and was a close associate of George Westinghouse, whose company eventually became General Electric. Tesla is credited with inventing the radio, and has been called "the man who invented the 20th century" and "the father of the second Industrial Revolution."

HENRY DAVID THOREAU (1817–1862) American writer, naturalist, and philosopher. He wrote about his solitary two-year hiatus from city life in the book *Walden,* in which he advocates for simple living and communion with nature. Thoreau's writings are widely accepted as a precursor and inspiration for the modern environmental movement.

MATHIS WACKERNAGEL (1962–) co-creator of the ecological footprint concept with WILLIAM REES, professor and lecturer of sustainability issues at many universities, and director of the Global Footprint Network, which publishes the annual *Living Planet Report* in conjunction with WWR International. Co-author of *Our Ecological Footprint: Reducing Human Impact on the Earth.*

JAMES WATT (1736–1819) 18th-century Scottish inventor whose improvements to the Newcomen steam engine vastly accelerated the Industrial Revolution by enabling engines to expand from rural coal mines to urban factories. Watt's steam engine led directly to the locomotive engine, the steamboat, and the *watt*—the International System of Units measurement for electric power.

GEORGE WESTINGHOUSE (1846–1914) American businessman and founder of Westinghouse Electricity and Manufacturing Company in 1896, one of the first companies dedicated to providing electricity on a wide scale to cities and towns. As a friend of NIKOLA TESLA, Westinghouse supported the development of AC (alternating current) transformers, which could distribute electricity over much longer distances than DC (direct current) transformers, which were advocated by Tesla's rival THOMAS EDISON. The battle to establish this standard was known as the *War of the Currents.*

EDWARD O. WILSON (1929–) American naturalist, biologist, environmentalist, sociobiologist, and author. Wilson's books on sociobiology, which is defined as the study of the biological basis of all social behavior, are highly regarded. Two of his books, *On Human Nature* (1979) and *The Ants* (1991), have won the Pulitzer Prize. Wilson has written extensively about the mass extinctions of the 20th century, free will, nature vs. nurture, and was named one of the 25 most influential people in America by *Time* magazine in 1995. He is a member of the National Academy of Sciences, serves as the Pellegrino Research Professor in Entomology at Harvard University, and is a fellow of the Committee for Skeptical Inquiry.

DAVID YERGIN chair of energy consultancy group Cambridge Energy Research Associates (CERA) and author of the Pulitzer Prize–winning book, *The Prize: The Epic Quest for Oil, Money and Power* (1991), which was also filmed as a PBS mini-series. Yergin believes that the Peak Oil theory is flawed and that new technology will increase the amount of oil available worldwide in the coming years.

MUHAMMAD YUNUS (1940–) Bangladeshi banker, economist, originator of microcredit, and founder, in 1976, of the Grameen Bank, which gives loans to poor women in Bangladesh in an effort to give them the economic power necessary to lift themselves and their children out of poverty. Yunus received the World Food Prize in 1994 and the Nobel Peace Prize in 2006 for his work, which he has outlined in his autobiography, *Banker to the Poor* (1999).

9

Organizations and Agencies

Extensive information is available from the following organizations, including statistical data on population, energy use, natural resource reserves; reports, legislation, and international treaties regarding environmental issues, energy consumption, and sustainability; and information from nongovernmental organizations that support philanthropic, educational, and conservation issues worldwide. The list is by no means exhaustive, but simply a representative sampling of organizations that address sustainability on every level from local to international.

Alliance for Global Sustainability
URL: http://globalsustainability.org
Stiftelsen Chalmers Industriteknik
Chalmers Teknikpark
SE 412-88 Göteborg, Sweden

Partnership between the Massachusetts Institute of Technology, University of Tokyo, the Swiss Federal Institute of Technology, and the Chalmers University of Technology in Sweden. Their goal is research and education to bring about a paradigm shift in dealing with sustainability issues, including water, energy, transportation, and the rise of megacities.

American Council for an Energy-Efficient Economy
URL: http://www.aceee.org
1001 Connecticut Avenue NW
Suite 801
Washington, DC 20036
202-429-8873

Nonprofit organization that advocates for energy efficiency for economic security and environmental protection. Conducts assessments, advises policymakers, and organizes conferences. Program areas include energy policy, transportation, and utilities.

American Enterprise Institute
URL: http://www.aei.org
1150 Seventeenth Street NW
Washington, DC 20036
202-862-5800

Conservative, multidisciplinary think tank that refutes global warming and actively researches environmental policy. Promotes free enterprise by seeking limitations of government controls on business and industry.

American Hydrogen Association
URL: http://www.clean-air.org
2350 W. Shangri La
Phoenix, AZ 85028
602-328-4238

Nonprofit organization that promotes the use of hydrogen energy and hydrogen fuel cells for automobiles and seeks to create a U.S. hydrogen energy economy by 2010.

American Petroleum Institute
URL: http://www.api.org
1220 L Street NW
Washington, DC 20005-4070
202-682-8000

National trade association for professionals in the petroleum and natural gas industry. Advocates for the industry in the media, to U.S. Congress, and on the international stage. Collects and maintains data on petroleum, which is presented in the organization's *Weekly Statistical Bulletin.*

American Solar Energy Society
URL: http://www.ases.org
2400 Central Avenue
Suite A
Boulder, CO 80301
303-443-3130

Nonprofit group that promotes all types of renewable energy, including solar, wind, geothermal, hydrogen, and biofuels, and advocates for a sustainable U.S.

energy economy. Publishes *Solar Today* magazine, organizes the National Solar Conference and the National Solar Tour.

Association for the Study of Peak Oil and Gas
URL: http://www.peakoil.net
Box 25182
SE-750 25 Uppsala
Sweden
(46-70) 4250604

Web site maintains links to current news stories regarding oil and gas supplies.

Association of Energy Engineers
URL: http://www.aeecenter.org
4025 Pleasantdale Road
Suite 420
Atlanta, GA 30340
770-447-5083, ext. 210

Professional organization with a wide network of local chapters that promotes energy efficiency through seminars, conferences, and publications. Maintains an active membership, offers certification programs and job lists for energy-related positions. Publishes the peer-reviewed *International Journal of Green Energy.*

Bombay Natural History Society
URL: http://www.bnhs.org
Hornbill House
Shaheed Bhagat Singh Road
Mumbai 400 023, India
(91-22)-22821811

Nature conservation organization founded in Mumbai in 1883 that seeks to preserve biodiversity and promote sustainable development on the Indian subcontinent through scientific research and public education.

Buckminster Fuller Institute
URL: http://www.bfi.org
181 N 11th Street
Suite 402
Brooklyn, NY 11211

Promotes Fuller's work and advocates for continued research into his ideas, particularly those related to design and technology that promote sustainable living.

Carbon Sequestration Leadership Forum
URL: http://www.cslforum.org
CSLF Secretariat
U.S. Department of Energy
FE-27
1000 Independence Avenue SW
Washington, DC 20585
301-903-3820

An international climate change initiative aimed at limiting carbon emissions through sequestration and other technologies. Comprised of 21 countries and the European Commission, with a charter signed in 2003.

Carolina Population Center
URL: http://www.cpc.unc.edu
University of North Carolina at Chapel Hill
CB# 8120, University Square
123 West Franklin Street
Chapel Hill, NC 27516-2524
919-966-2157

Scholarly organization devoted to research and methodology of studying world populations. Web site contains much documentation and many links to worldwide population statistics.

Carrying Capacity Network
URL: http://www.carryingcapacity.org
2000 P Street NW
Suite 310
Washington, DC 20036
202-296-4548

Activist organization that seeks to keep the United States within its carrying capacity through population stabilization, immigration reduction, and resource conservation.

Cato Institute
URL: http://www.cato.org

1000 Massachusetts Avenue NW
Washington, DC 20001-5403
202-842-0200

Conservative think tank established in 1977 that encourages public policy promoting free markets and individual liberty. Program areas include energy, environment, and climate issues.

Center for Strategic and International Studies
URL: http://www.csis.org
1800 K Street NW
Washington, DC 20006
202-887-0200

Bipartisan nonprofit organization promoting global security and prosperity. Has launched many programs dealing with demography and population, energy, and global aging.

Center for the Environment and Population
URL: http://www.cepnet.org
161 Cherry Street
New Canaan, CT 06840
203-966-3425

Nonprofit organization that sponsors research, policy, and outreach regarding population, resources, consumption, and the environment. Publishes the *U.S. National Report on Population and the Environment.* Also publishes some state reports.

Centre for Alternative Technology
URL: http://www.cat.org.uk
Machynlleth
Powys SY20 9AZ UK
(44-1654) 705950

Promotes renewable energy and green building for individual consumers with an extensive online "green shop" of building supplies, including photovoltaic cells. Offers courses in green building and many how-to publications.

China Population Development and Research Center
URL: http://www.cpirc.org.cn
PO Box 2444
Beijing 100081

People's Republic of China
(86-10) 62173519

English-language Web site presents a clearinghouse of information on population issues in China, including reproductive health, urban migration, and aging.

China Sustainable Energy Program; The Energy Foundation
URL: http://www.efchina.org
1012 Torney Avenue, #1
San Francisco, CA 94129
415-561-6700

Forms alliances with China's government agencies to promote energy efficiency and renewable energy in China through policy decisions made at the national and regional levels.

Clean Air World
URL: http://www.cleanairworld.org
STAPPA/ALAPO
444 North Capitol Street NW
Suite 307
Washington, DC 20001
202-624-7864

Coordinated effort of the State Territorial Air Pollution Program Administrators and Association of Local Air Pollution Control Officers (merged as the National Association of Clean Air Agencies) to reduce air pollution both globally and within the United States. Concerned both with greenhouse gases that cause global warming and other pollutants, such as lead and mercury.

Club of Rome
URL: http://www.clubofrome.org
Steckelhoern 9
D-20457 Hamburg
Germany
(49-40) 819607-14

A global think tank comprised of business executives, economists, scientists, and government officials confronting the *world problematique,* the Club's term for the "set of the crucial problems—political, social, economic, technological, environmental, psychological and cultural—facing humanity."

Conservation International
URL: http://www.conservation.org
2011 Crystal Drive
Suite 500
Arlington, VA 22202
703-341-2400

Nonprofit organization concerned with protecting earth's living heritage and preserving biodiversity. Stresses harmonious coexistence between humans and other species, especially within biodiversity hotspots across the globe.

Convention on Biological Diversity
URL: http://www.cbd.int
413 Saint Jacques Street
Suite 800
Montreal QC H2Y 1NY
Canada
514-288-2220

Signed by 150 nations at the 1992 Earth Summit, the Convention on Biological Diversity promotes sustainable development and is governed by a secretariat under the United Nations Environmental Programmes.

The Earth Institute at Columbia University
URL: http://www.earthinstitute.columbia.edu
405 Low Library, MC 4335
535 West 116th Street
New York, NY 10027
845-365-8565

Conducts research projects in many disciplines, including earth sciences, biology, engineering, health, and the social sciences, regarding key initiatives, which include climate, poverty, water, energy, urbanization, and ecosystems. Brings together the world's leading scientists to adapt existing knowledge and technology to help the poor and alleviate suffering, all while protecting the Earth.

Earth Policy Institute
URL: http://www.earth-policy.org
1350 Connecticut Avenue NW
Washington, DC 20036
202-496-9290

A small nonprofit founded by Lester R. Brown that advocates for a sustainable *eco-economy* through its publications, the media, and the Internet. Promotes the idea of sustainable development and provides insight on how governments, businesses, and individuals can make the transition.

Energy Information Administration
URL: http://www.eia.doe.gov
1000 Independence Avenue SW
Washington, DC 20585
202-586-8800

An agency of the U.S. Department of Energy that provides in-depth statistics, analyses, and forecasts for the United States and many countries of the world, in terms of natural resource reserves and usage. Provides links to experts on many topics and a telephone hotline to obtain statistics and data. Promotes sound policy and market efficiencies.

German Council for Sustainable Development
URL: http://www.nachhaltigkeitsrat.de/english.html
Wissenschaftszentrum Berlin für
Sozialforschung gGmbH
Reichpietschufer 50,
D-10785 Berlin, Germany
(49-30) 25491-780

Agency established by the German government in 2001 for the purpose of advising government policy regarding sustainable development. Provided a National Strategy on Development that was presented to the UN World Summit on Sustainable Development in 2002; promotes social dialogue.

German Energy Agency
URL: http://www.dena.de
Deutsche Energie-Agentur GmbH (dena)
Chausseestrasse 128a
10115 Berlin, Germany
(49-30) 72 61 65 – 600

Web site available in English; the Berlin-based organization promotes energy conservation and renewable energy within Germany via public private partnerships.

Global Environmental Institute
URL: http://www.geichina.org
Suite 1-401, Building No. 5
New World Villa
Chongwen District
Beijing 100062, China
(86-10) 6708-3192

Beijing-based nonprofit, nongovernmental environmental organization that works toward sustainable development across China and the world, originated in 2003. Seeks to integrate sustainable economic practices and sound development in rural areas that preserves biodiversity while allowing for economic empowerment.

Global Footprint Network
URL: http://www.footprintnetwork.org
1050 Warfield Avenue
Oakland, CA 94610
510-839-8879

Compiles National Footprint Accounts using public data from all countries; engages in research and policy. Promotes the global footprint concept through community outreach and through the development of standards by which sustainability can be measured.

Global Wind Energy Council
URL: http://www.gwec.net
Renewable Energy House
Rue d'Arlon 63-65
1040 Brussels
Belgium
(32-2) 400 1029

Established in 2005 to serve as an international forum for wind energy. Works to influence policy and educate the international community to promote wind energy as a leading energy source of the 21st century.

International Atomic Energy Agency
URL: http://www.iaea.org
1 United Nations Plaza
Room DC-1-1155

New York, NY 10017
212-963-6010 or 6011

Created in 1957 following President Eisenhower's "Atoms for Peace" speech at the UN, with a mission to foster nuclear verification and security, safety and technology transfer. In recent years the organization has worked to prevent nuclear terrorism.

International Energy Agency
URL: http://www.iea.org
9, rue de la Fédération
75015 Paris
(33-1) 40 57 65 00/01

Formed during the 1973 oil crisis, the organization advises its member countries on energy that will be reliable, clean, and affordable for its citizens. Member countries include the United States, Canada, the United Kingdom, Germany, France, and Australia.

International Institute for Environment and Development
URL: http://www.iied.org
3 Endsleigh Street
London, England
WC1H 0DD
(44-20) 7388-2117

NGO founded in 1971 that partners with individuals and groups in the developing world to pursue projects in both rural and urban settings. "IIED acts as a catalyst, broker and facilitator and helps vulnerable groups find their voice and ensure their interests are heard in decision-making. Environmental sustainability is a core concern but not at the expense of people's livelihoods."

International Institute for Sustainable Development
URL: http://www.iisd.org
161 Portage Avenue East
6th Floor
Winnipeg, Manitoba, Canada
R3B 0Y4
204-958-7700

Canadian-based nonprofit group that works on an international basis with business leaders, government leaders, and NGOs to limit climate change, loss of biodiversity, and environmental degradation and to promote sustainable development through establishment of networks, foreign investment, and economic understanding.

International Union for the Scientific Study of Population
URL: http://www.iussp.org
3–5 rue Nicolas
F-75980
Paris cedex 20, France
(33 1) 56 06 21 73

Founded in 1927 at the first World Population Conference, which was organized by Margaret Sanger. Continues to organize conferences, publish papers, and reports by various scientific groups researching population issues.

Megacity Task Force of the International Geographical Union
URL: http://www.megacities.uni-koeln.de
Department of Geography, University of Cologne
Albertus-Magnus-Platz
D-50923 Köln, Germany
(49 221) 470 7050 and 470 7055

German-based organization that seeks to solve the problems of megacities on a global scale through international dialogue, research, and development of best practices. Program areas include population issues and risk assessment. Maintains data on all world megacities.

Millennium Institute
URL: http://www.millennium-institute.org
2200 Wilson Boulevard
Suite 650
Arlington, VA 22201
703-841-0048

Works toward establishing a global community and a peaceful, sustainable future. Promotes application of systems literacy and modeling tools in public policy and the private sector. Has programs in Africa, the Balkans, Southeast Asia, Latin America, and the United States that concentrate on energy, population, and environmental issues.

National Coal Council
URL: http://www.nationalcoalcouncil.org

1730 M Street NW
Suite 907
Washington, DC 20036
202-223-1191

Advisory committee to the U.S. Secretary of Energy; also reviews federal policies in accordance with the Office of Coal Research Act. Membership comprised of scientists, government officials, NGO leaders, and corporate officers.

National Council for Science and the Environment
URL: http://www.ncseonline.org
1707 H Street NW
Suite 200
Washington, DC 20006-3918
202-530-5810

Nonprofit organization dedicated to strengthening the scientific basis by which environmental policy is made. Nonpartisan and focused on maintaining scientific accuracy in such issues as forest management and wildlife habitats. Serves as home to the *earth portal,* which sponsors the academic-written Encyclopedia of Earth.

National Environmental Trust
URL: http://www.net.org
1200 18th Street NW
Fifth Floor
Washington, DC 20036

Nonprofit organization dedicated to public awareness of health and quality of life issues as they relate to the environment. Serves as a link between citizens and the scientific community and promotes citizen-participation in policymaking.

National Geographic Society
URL: http://www.nationalgeographic.com
1145 17th Street NW
Washington, DC 20036-4688
800-647-5463

Founded in 1888, a nonprofit organization dedicated to inspiring people to care about the world. Extensive program areas in wildlife, marine life, astronomy, conservation, ecology, and sustainability. Publishes many periodicals, including *National Geographic* magazine, and coordinates many educational outreach programs for school-age children.

National Resources Defense Council
URL: http://www.nrdc.org
40 West 20th Street
New York, NY 10011
212-727-2700

A million-plus-member nonprofit organization that seeks to safeguard the Earth through applications of law and science. Promotes stewardship and sustainability in many program areas, notably wildlife and habitat protection, clean air and energy, global warming, water and oceans, and green living.

National Science Foundation
URL: http://www.nsf.gov
4201 Wilson Boulevard
Arlington, Virginia 22230
703-292-5111

Federal agency created in 1950 to promote scientific progress and to secure the national defense. Funds university research with federal monies and maintains communication with major research initiatives in all scientific disciplines, including those related to energy.

Natural Gas Vehicles for America
URL: http://www.ngvc.org
400 N. Capitol St. NW
Washington, DC 20001
202-824-7366

National trade organization that promotes NGV as safe, clean, and fuel-efficient. Also promotes hydrogen-powered vehicles and promotes the interests of companies dedicated to expanding these markets to corporate and individual consumers.

Natural Resources Conservation Service
URL: http://www.nrcs.usda.gov
USDA, NRCS, Office of the Chief
1400 Independence Avenue SW
Room 5105-A
Washington, DC 20250
202-720-7246

Established in 1935 to help private landowners conserve soil and water. Program areas include public outreach in all 50 states, advising on international affairs, and extensive programs focusing on maintaining the environmental quality of agricultural land, wetlands, grasslands, grazing lands, and water.

New Urbanism.org
URL: http://www.newurbanism.org
824 King Street
Suite 103
Alexandria, VA 22314

Urban planning organization dedicated to developing communities that address environmental issues such as Peak Oil, global warming, smart transportation, sustainable development, and quality of life. Promotes communities that are walkable, diversified, and integrated.

Optimum Population Trust
URL: http://www.optimumpopulation.org
12 Meadowgate, Urmston
Manchester M41 9LB UK
(07976) 370 221

U.K.-based nonprofit think tank that seeks population stabilization as a step toward sustainability. Advocates for population reduction through technology and awareness. Conducts research that measures the effects of population on energy use, natural resources, aging, and economic issues. Maintains live world population clock on Web site.

Organisation for Economic Cooperation and Development
URL: http://www.oecd.org
2, rue André Pascal
F-75775 Paris Cedex 16
France
33 1.45.24.82.00

Organization of member countries that works to address world economic issues; the International Energy Administration is a subgroup. Web site maintains a wealth of statistics regarding energy, the environment, economics, and other issues.

Population Connection
URL: http://www.populationconnection.org
2120 L Street NW
Suite 500

Washington, DC 20037
202-332-2200 or 1-800-767-1956

Founded by Paul Ehrlich as Zero Population Growth in the 1960s, a nonprofit that seeks to stabilize world population in an effort to attain sustainability and long-term well-being. Focuses on educational programs for children, research, advocacy, and international dialogue. Publishes *The Reporter*, a quarterly magazine.

Population Reference Bureau
URL: http://www.prb.org
1875 Connecticut Avenue NW
Suite 520
Washington, DC 20009-5728
800-877-9881 or 202-483-1100

Informs and empowers individuals worldwide on the links between population, health, and the environment. Works with policymakers in developing countries to enact initiatives regarding fertility and birth control; children and family issues; population aging, inequality, gender imbalance, and poverty; migration and urbanization.

Population Resource Center
URL: http://www.prcdc.org
1725 K Street NW
Suite 1102
Washington, DC 20006
202-467-5030

Promotes accurate use of population statistics and data in public policymaking.

Population Studies Center
URL: http://www.psc.isr.umich.edu
University of Michigan
426 Thompson Street
Ann Arbor, MI 48106-1248
734-763-1543

An interdisciplinary academic community comprised of experts in the fields of anthropology, economics, natural resources, geography, political science, psychology, public health, and statistics. Promotes independent research of domestic and international population issues.

Rainforest Alliance
URL: http://rainforest-alliance.org
665 Broadway
Suite 500
New York, NY 10012
212-677-1900

Founded in 1987, the Rainforest Alliance works to conserve the biodiversity of the world's rain forests by advocating for land-use and business practices in forestry and agriculture that promote the economic growth of a region without damaging the environment. Works to bring sustainable coffee, chocolate, bananas, wood, and other products to consumers.

Redefining Progress
URL: http://www.rprogress.org
1904 Franklin Street
6th floor
Oakland, CA 94612
510-444-3041

Organization "works with a broad array of partners to shift the economy and public policy towards sustainability." Program areas include environmental justice, ecological footprints of individual municipalities, and climate change.

Renewable Energy Policy Project (REPP)
URL: http://www.repp.org
1612 K Street NW
Suite 202
Washington, DC 20006

Promotes aggressive adoption of renewable energy sources, including hydropower, bioenergy, geothermal, wind, solar, and hydrogen power, as well as efficiency increases, through policy analysis and research.

Renewable Fuels Association
URL: http://www.ethanolrfa.org
1 Massachusetts Avenue NW
Suite 820
Washington, DC 20001
202-289-3835

Trade association for the U.S. ethanol industry that promotes research, policy, and advocacy to expand the domestic ethanol market. Works at the federal, state, and local levels and with government officials, industry leaders, and citizens.

Rocky Mountain Institute
URL: http://www.rmi.org
1739 Snowmass Creek Road
Snowmass, CO 81654-9199
970-927-3851

Colorado-based NGO founded by Amory Lovins and L. Hunter Sheldon in 1982. Conducts research and consults on issues of sustainability, especially those associated with energy and resources, and promotes the adoption of the "soft-energy path."

Securing America's Future Energy (SAFE)
URL: http://www.secureenergy.org
1055 Thomas Jefferson Street NW
3rd Floor
Washington, DC 20007
202-609-9891

Nonpartisan advocacy and public policy organization dedicated to reducing America's dependence on oil. Stresses that transitioning away from oil is an issue of national security and forms alliances between businesses and government officials to promote policies that will reduce oil consumption.

Sierra Club
URL: http://www.sierraclub.org
85 Second Street
2nd Floor
San Francisco, CA 94105
415-977-5500

The largest and oldest grassroots environmental organization in the United States, founded by John Muir in 1892. Lobbies for the preservation of natural areas and ecosystems and for responsible use of the earth's resources. Publishes books, magazines, and lobbies for environmentally sustainable legislation.

Society of Petroleum Engineers
URL: http://www.spe.org
PO Box 833836

Richardson, TX 75083-3836
972-952-9393

Professional organization promoting research and technology for those involved in the petroleum industries. Also encourages public education in issues relating to petroleum and related energy issues. Maintains a library of online papers and research materials available by subscription.

Stockholm Environment Institute
URL: http://www.sei.se
Kräftriket 2B
SE-106 91 Stockholm
Sweden

Nonprofit think tank and research organization that works on international, national, and local levels to promote sustainable development. Its scientists are concerned with the issues of climate change, acid rain, renewable energy, and clean water, and build alliances with other worldwide organizations to impact public policy.

Sustainability Institute
URL: http://www.sustainer.org
3 Linden Road
Hartland, VT 05048
802-436-1277

Founded by Donella Meadows, the organization studies the root causes of unsustainability in order to restructure systems that will result in a sustainable world using Meadows's 12-step system dynamics.

United Nations Division for Sustainable Development
URL: http://www.un.org/esa/sustdev
Department of Economic and Social Affairs
2 United Nations Plaza
Room DC2-2220
New York, NY 10017
212-963-8102

Agency responsible for carrying out Agenda 21 through partnerships with other UN agencies, consensus-building with UN member countries, and facilitating inter-organizational cooperation. Works to implement social, economic, and environmental policies on national, regional, and international levels that will result in sustainable development.

United Nations Environment Programme
URL: http://www.unep.org
United Nations Avenue, Gigiri
PO Box 30552, 00100
Nairobi, Kenya
(254-20) 7621234

African-based UN agency that advocates for sustainable development and environmental protections. Works with other UN agencies, international organizations, national governments, NGOs, and other groups to assess environmental concerns and promote change based on knowledge and technology.

United Nations Population Division
URL: http://www.un.org/esa/population/unpop.htm
2 United Nations Plaza
Room DC2-1950
New York, NY 10017
212-963-3179

Prepares documentation, analysis, policies, and builds consensus among member nations regarding global trends of population and development. Organizes many programs, including those regarding migration; infant, child, and maternal mortality rates; the AIDS crisis; and fertility levels and contraceptive use in developing countries.

U.S. Agency for International Development (USAID)
URL: http://www.usaid.gov
Ronald Reagan Building
Washington, DC 20523-1000
202-712-4320

Government agency providing economic and humanitarian assistance to developing nations. Fosters economic growth, agriculture and trade, global health, democracy, conflict prevention, and humanitarian assistance. Main areas of assistance are sub-Saharan Africa, Asia and the Near East, Latin America and the Caribbean, Europe, and Eurasia. Environmental program areas include biodiversity, climate change, energy, land management, pollution, and water resources.

United States Census Bureau
URL: http://www.census.gov

4700 Silver Hill Road
Washington, DC 20233

U.S. government agency since 1902. Conducts census of the population and many other annual surveys to gauge the business, activities, and economic interests of the citizenry. Web site provides a world population clock and access to the latest population data on all towns and states in the country, and extensive collection of data, including population pyramids, poverty and genealogy statistics, and economic indicators.

U.S. Department of Energy
URL: http://www.energy.gov
1000 Independence Avenue SW
Washington, DC 20585
1-800-dial-DOE

Government department charged with maintaining energy security in the United States, along with nuclear security, scientific discovery and innovation, and environmental responsibility. Web site offers vast amount of data pertaining to fossil fuels, carbon sequestration, hydrogen, energy efficiency, and major policy initiatives.

U.S. Department of Transportation
URL: http://www.dot.gov
400 7th Street SW
Washington, DC 20590
202-366-4000

Federal agency responsible for the nation's transportation system, created in 1966 by President Johnson. Includes the Federal Aviation Administration, the Federal Highway Administration, the Federal Railroad Administration, and other agencies that cover waterways and safety issues. Sets CAFE standards with the EPA, under the National Highway Traffic Safety Administration.

U.S. Department of the Interior
URL: http://www.doi.gov
1849 C Street NW
Washington, DC 20240
202-208-3100

Government agency responsible for protecting and managing U.S. natural resources. Manages public lands, including the national parks, promotes responsible and sustainable use. Governs many other agencies, including the

Bureau of Reclamation, the Bureau of Indian Affairs, U.S. Geological Survey, U.S. Fish and Wildlife Service, National Parks Service, Bureau of Land Management, and the Office of Surface Mining.

U.S. Environmental Protection Agency (EPA)
URL: http://www.epa.gov
Ariel Rios Building
1200 Pennsylvania Avenue NW
Washington, DC 20460

Created in 1970 with the mission to protect human health and the environment within the United States. Employs scientists, engineers, and policy analysts. Develops and enforces regulations mandated by congressional law.

U.S. PIRG
URL: http://uspirg.org
44 Winter Street
4th Floor
Boston, MA 02108
617-292-4800

Federation of state Public Interest Research Groups. Conducts research and advocates for public policy to protect health and well-being. In terms of environmentalism, program areas include energy issues (especially promoting renewable energy sources), combating global warming, food safety, water safety, ocean protection, and land conservation.

Woods Hole Research Center
URL: http://www.whrc.org
149 Woods Hole Road
Falmouth, MA 02540-1644
508-540-9900

Scientific and advocacy organization dedicated to protecting the integrity of the Earth's environment. Conducts research, provides education, and analyzes policies, especially those pertaining to land use in various hotspots, such as the Amazon Basin, the Congo, Eurasia, and North America. Works locally and regionally to assist communities with resource management.

World Bank
URL: http://www.worldbank.org

1818 H Street NW
Washington, DC 20433
202-473-1000

A consortium of 185 member countries that provide credit, low-interest loans, and grants to developing nations in order to reduce poverty and raise living standards. Monies support health, education, and infrastructure initiatives, in hopes of achieving the UN's Millennium Development Goals for sustainable living.

World Business Council for Sustainable Development
URL: http://www.wbcsd.org
1744 R Street NW
Washington, DC 20009
202-420-7745

International association of 190 companies whose primary business is sustainable development. Advocates for sustainability, demonstrates compatibility of business interests and sustainability, especially as it relates to energy issues and global climate change.

World Energy Council
URL: http://www.worldenergy.org
5th Floor Regency House
1-4 Warwick Street
London W1B 5LT UK
(44 20) 7734 5996

Established in 1923, the World Energy Council is a nongovernmental, nonprofit organization with member committees in over 90 countries that works "to promote the sustainable supply and use of energy for the greatest benefit of all people." Programs focus on coal, petroleum, natural gas, hydropower, and renewable energy sources.

World Future Society
URL: http://www.wfs.org
7910 Woodmont Avenue
Suite 450
Bethesda, MD 20814
301-656-8274

Nonprofit organization focusing on research and advocacy regarding the social and technological issues that are affecting society. Acts as a clearinghouse of ideas and publishes *The Futurist,* a bimonthly magazine. Publishes forecasts based on current trends. Forecasts include a steady migration of younger citizens from the U.S. to abroad in the coming generation, water scarcity in China that will have global impact, India prevailing over China economically in the long run, and global warming impacting world economies.

World Health Organization
URL: http://www.who.int/en
Avenue Appia 20
1211 Geneva 27
Switzerland
(41 22) 791 21 11

UN agency established in 1948 to work toward the health and well-being of all people by reducing poverty and creating sustainable health care systems, and meeting the UN Millennium Development Goals.

World Resources Institute
URL: http://www.wri.org
10 G Street NE
Suite 800
Washington, DC 20002
202-729-7600

Environmental think tank focusing on transitioning society into sustainable living conditions. Core program components include combating global climate change, protecting ecosystems, and using market forces to provide economically feasible ways of protecting the environment.

Worldwatch Institute
URL: http://www.worldwatch.org
1776 Massachusetts Avenue NW
Washington, DC 20036-1904
202-452-1999

Publishes information aimed to transition to an environmentally sustainable and socially just society, most notably its annual *State of the World* report and the bimonthly *World Watch* magazine.

10

Annotated Bibliography

The following annotated bibliography focuses on natural resource and sustainable development issues in the United States and in China, India, Germany, and Brazil, the countries examined in chapter 3. Entries are grouped in the following six categories:

Energy: Fossil Fuels and Nuclear Power

Energy: Renewable Resources

Water Issues

Sustainable Development

Environmentalism

Population Issues

Each category is subdivided into four sections: *Books, Articles and Papers, Web Documents,* and *Films.*

ENERGY: FOSSIL FUELS AND NUCLEAR POWER

Books

Black, Brian. *Petrolia: The Landscape of America's 1st Oil Boom.* Baltimore, Md.: Johns Hopkins University Press, 2003. A history of the Oil Creek Valley in Pennsylvania's Allegheny Mountains from 1859 to 1873, where the first widescale pit drilling took place without regard for the economic and environmental concerns of the region. Within a few years, the region was ruined, both ecologically and socially.

Campbell, C. J. *The Coming Oil Crisis.* Essex, England: Multi-Science Publishing Inc., 2004. Written by an oil industry insider, the book examines the scientific evidence for dwindling oil supplies and outlines the problems in store for countries who do not prepare for a transition to other energy sources.

Chambers, Ann, Barry Schnoor, and Stephanie Hamilton. *Distributed Generation: A Nontechnical Guide.* Tulsa, Okla.: Pennwell Books, 2001. Distributed Generation (DG) is the process by which large corporations can diversify the types of energy they create and how they deliver it to customers. Intended for the nonexpert, the book explains how existing energy companies might employ diesel engines, fuel cells, microturbines, and photovoltaic cells in their businesses.

Clarke, Duncan. *The Battle for Barrels: Peak Oil Myths and World Oil Futures.* London: Profile Books, 2007. Author believes Peak Oil is not commensurate with the "end of oil" and the "end of civilization," as some often claim. As an economist and the chair and C.E.O. of a private consulting firm that advises governments and oil companies, Clarke disputes the underlying premise of Peak Oil and believes it does not take today's reality into consideration.

Deffeyes, Kenneth S. *Beyond Oil: The View from Hubbert's Peak.* New York: Hill & Wang, 2005. Envisions a world without fossil fuels, which the author believes may come sooner rather than later. Focuses on geology, geophysics, and the social implications of a declining oil supply, which may include famine, war, and political upheavals.

Goodell, Jeff. *Big Coal: The Dirty Secret Behind America's Energy Future.* Boston, Mass.: Houghton Mifflin, 2006. Exposé on the coal mining industry in the United States, focusing on how and why coal will continue to be a primary energy source well into the 21st century, despite the dangers and health problems it causes. Goodell states that the effects of global warming can be mitigated through carbon trading and sequestration.

Goodstein, David. *Out of Gas: The End of the Age of Oil.* New York: W. W. Norton, 2005. Caltech professor Goodstein believes that oil reserves will be depleted by 2100 and that governments and businesses should plan for the postpetroleum world now, in order to create technology that will enable society to peacefully transition to the age of hydrogen and nuclear fusion.

Heinberg, Richard. *The Party's Over: Oil War and the Fate of Industrial Societies.* Gabriola Island, British Columbia: New Society Publishers, 2003. Declares that the world will enter a new era within a few years as oil production peaks, forcing industrialized nations to transition to a different energy source in order to remain economically stable.

Huber, Peter W., and Mark P. Mills. *The Bottomless Well: The Twilight of Fuel, the Virtue of Waste, and Why We Will Never Run Out of Energy.* New York: Basic Books, 2005. Discusses the world's growing need for energy and how that need will fuel economic development and spur increased activity in current resources, especially coal and nuclear power. The authors propose the concept of "virtuous waste," the idea that waste produced through energy inefficiency is a good thing because that waste allows users to put the energy to good use.

Humphreys, Macartan, Jeffrey Sachs, and Joseph E. Stiglitz. *Escaping the Resource Curse. Initiative for Policy Dialogue at Columbia.* New York: Columbia University Press, 2007. Includes papers addressing the resource curse by various experts, particularly that presented by oil. Includes information on the role of the state in negotiating oil contracts, how to auction oil rights, and how to handle the economic ramifications of oil.

Jaccard, Mark. *Sustainable Fossil Fuels: The Unusual Suspect in the Quest for Clean and Enduring Energy.* New York: Cambridge University Press, 2006. Author believes that fossil fuels can be used responsibly and sustainably while new technologies are created that will transition us permanently to renewable energy sources. Fossil fuels represent the cheapest, cleanest source of energy to bridge the gap to the future.

Klare, Michael T. *Blood and Oil: The Dangers and Consequences of America's Growing Dependency on Imported Petroleum.* New York: Metropolitan Books, 2004. Klare negatively assesses the Bush Administration's energy policy, especially the 2001 National Energy Policy, which states that U.S. oil supplies need to be diversified across many countries. He states that a more sound policy would be to wean the United States off foreign oil completely.

Lederman, Daniel, and William F. Maloney, eds. *Natural Resources, Neither Curse Nor Destiny.* New York: World Bank Publications, 2006. Compiled by economists with the World Bank, the book presents economic analyses and historical data on countries with abundant natural resources, especially those in Latin America. States that the "curse" can be avoided with applied knowledge, infrastructure, and good government.

Phillips, Kevin. *American Theocracy: The Peril and Politics of Radical Religion, Oil, and Borrowed Money in the 21st Century.* New York: Viking, 2006. Phillips, author of the 1969 classic *The Emerging Republican Majority,* believes that oil, religion, and debt are the three main issues that threaten the security of the United States. His insights on oil—its history in particular—provide compelling evidence that nations who cannot foresee their own energy needs have been doomed to second-tier status throughout history.

Roberts, Paul. *The End of Oil: On the Edge of a Perilous New World.* Boston, Mass.: Houghton Mifflin, 2004. Looks at the modern energy economy and the rough transition it faces as the issues of global warming and the development of India and China compound the problem of declining oil production. Focuses on how the government and American citizens need to act in concert to develop hydrogen fuel cells and other solutions.

Simmons, Matthew R. *Twilight in the Desert: The Coming Saudi Oil Shock and the World Economy.* Hoboken, N.J.: Wiley, 2005. Sheds light on the secretive Saudi government and uses information from the Society of Petroleum Engineers to speculate on the actual oil reserves present in Saudi Arabia. Examines the relationship between the United States and Saudi Arabia.

Simon, Julian Lincoln. *The Ultimate Resource 2.* Princeton, N.J.: Princeton University Press, 1996. A revised edition of the 1981 book that disputes any crisis of natural resources because economics favors human innovation, in which resource scarcity leads to rising prices and incentives to conserve resources or find new ones. Simon often focuses on resources such as copper, tin, oil and zinc, which are valuable in industry and have fallen in price over the years, lending credibility to his hypothesis—natural resources are infinite.

Tamminen, Terry. *Lives Per Gallon: The True Cost of Our Oil Addiction.* Washington, D.C.: Island Press, 2006. Written by the former Secretary of the California Environmental Protection Agency, the book concentrates on the health effects of petroleum addiction, from birth defects to asthma and emphysema, caused by carbon emissions and other pollution. Argues that companies do not provide sufficient safeguards to protect public health and advocates legal action to enact industry reform.

Yergin, David. *The Prize: The Epic Quest for Oil, Money, and Power.* New York: Vintage, 1991. Pulitzer Prize–winning, best-selling book from an energy expert that outlines the geopolitical rise of the oil industry and its modern-day consequences. The book became a PBS mini-series seen by over 20 million people.

Articles and Papers

Altman, Daniel. "What to Do When the Oil (Or the Innovation) Is Gone?" *New York Times,* May 28, 2006, p. B5. Article about possible shortages of oil, platinum, and copper, relating the scenario to shortages of whale oil in the 19th century. Some experts believe that technology can overcome these shortages, and that the shortage of greatest concern is labor.

Ansfield, Jonathan. "The Coal Trap; Beijing Battles for Control of a Runaway Industry That Both Powers China, and Threatens Its Future." *Newsweek International,* January 15, 2007. Expose of the unregulated coal industry in China, which will soon be responsible for the country surpassing the United States as the largest carbon emitter in the world. Government officials recognize reform and efficiency are necessary, but will take years to achieve.

Bailey, Ronald. "Peak Oil Panic: Is the Planet Running Out of Gas? If It Is, What Should the Bush Administration Do About It?" *Reason* 38.1 (2006): 22–29. Believes the problem is not Peak Oil per se, but hostile regimes that will manipulate the world market. The most important problem is the fact that costly, necessary infrastructure is owned by governments, which may not be able to update it to keep pace with demand.

Barkeman, Eva. "Pssst. Want to Get Rid of CO_2? Try Burying It." *Fortune International,* October 30, 2006, p. 18. Article on the Vattenfall project in Germany that will be the world's first zero-carbon emissions power plant. The plant will rely on carbon sequestration technology.

Bartlett, Albert A. "An Analysis of U.S. and World Oil Production Patterns Using Hubbert-Style Curves." *Mathematical Geology* 32.1 (2000): 1. According to his calculations, the author believes that three-quarters of U.S. oil reserves had been produced through 1995 and that world oil production would peak in 2004.

Bremner, Brian, and Chester Dawson. "Reactors? We'll Take Thirty, Please." *Business Week,* October 3, 2005, p. 52. Examines U.S. corporate investment in China's growing nuclear power industry, which will be funded partially by France's Areva Group, U.S.'s Westinghouse Electric, Japan's Mitsubishi Heavy Industries, and Russia's AtomStroyExport.

Chapman, Rob. "How Hybrids Fit into the Energy Puzzle." *Automotive News* 81.6230 (November 20, 2006): 16D. Written by an automotive expert, the article gives details on how hybrid vehicles work, how their efficiency surpasses traditional vehicles, and how they may transform the automotive industry.

Forney, Matthew. "China's Quest for Oil." *Time,* October 18, 2004. Outlines China's vast energy needs and its efforts to secure oil to continue its economic boom. China is forming partnerships with other countries, notably Russia, in order to reduce their reliance on Middle East oil. Some countries, however, are pulling out of partnerships with China because of low profit potential.

Gavin, James. "Demanding Times for South Asia's Giant." *Petroleum Economist* 72.10 (October 2005): 26. Detailed report on India's growing oil and gas industries, with corresponding statistics broken down by industry sectors.

Hill, Patrice. "Energy Crisis Rekindles Interest in Nuclear Power." *Insight on the News,* April 23, 2001. Article that quotes nuclear industry insiders on the safety, reliability, and plentiful supply of nuclear power, making it the best candidate to alleviate the country's dependence on foreign oil.

Hoffman, Carl. "The Oil Rush." *Popular Mechanics* 184.3 (March 2007): 70. Report on the current mining operations of oil sands in Alberta, Canada, at the Muskeg River Mine, 275 miles north of Edmonton. The mine has built a 300-mile pipeline that delivers a slurry of oil, sand, and mud to processing plants. With the price of oil rising, business is booming.

Junger, Sebastian. "Blood Oil." *Vanity Fair,* February 2007, pp. 112–122. Investigative report by award-winning journalist into the violent corruption surrounding Nigeria's oil industry, which includes kidnapping, torture, and murder of Nigerians and international workers alike. Government corruption at all levels, to the tune of billions of dollars, has made the country's oil supply extremely vulnerable to theft and terrorism and has left citizens among the poorest in the world, without even basic necessities such as water, electricity, and roads.

Kiely, Kathy. "U.S. Nuclear Power Industry Working on Quiet Comeback." *USA Today,* June 19, 2005. Outlines several governmental developments that may reawaken the dormant nuclear power industry, including support from U.S. senators formerly opposed to expansion of nuclear power and environmentalists, such as Stewart Brand, who believe that nuclear power will be part of the solution to global warming.

Kolbert, Elizabeth. "Unconventional Crude." *New Yorker,* November 12, 2007, p. 46. Investigative report about the boomtown of Fort McMurray, Alberta, due to the surging demand for oil derived from its tar sands, and the impact on the environment of extracting what is estimated as 1.7 trillion barrels of oil from the area.

Kripalani, Manjeet. "India's Nuclear Build-Out; The Country Needs Nuclear Energy to Keep Up Its Rapid Expansion, and Bush Wants to Help Provide It." *Business*

Week Online, August 3, 2006. Article about the United States and India Nuclear Cooperation Act of 2006.

Laherrere, J. H. "Learn Strengths, Weaknesses to Understand Hubbert Curve." *Oil and Gas Journal* 98.16 (April 17, 2000): 63. A detailed, technical article that applies Hubbert modeling to resources in various geographical locations, including the United States, Alaska, and Russia. Warns that Hubbert modeling is useful only if strict data standards are met and also considers the effect of world population on model outcomes.

Lohr, Steve. "Energy Use Can Be Cut by Efficiency, Survey Says." *New York Times,* November 29, 2006. Report of a McKinsey Global Institute survey stating that the growth rate of energy consumption could be cut in half within 15 years if strict efficiency measures are practiced, such as using fluorescent lightbulbs, solar water heaters, and more efficient appliances.

Lustgarten, Abrahm. "The Dark Magic of Oil Sands—Canada Has Oil Reserves Second Only to Saudi Arabia's, and a Black-Gold Rush Is On." *Fortune* 152.7 (2005): 136. A lengthy article about the boomtown of Fort McMurray, Alberta, which is home to a large mining operation that turns the oil sands into refined petroleum for the world market. Once thought too expensive to be worth the investment, because obtaining refined petroleum from the sands costs up to seven times more than conventional mining operations (it takes two tons of sand to make one barrel of oil), the oil sands are now the focus of intense business capital and investment as they become increasingly important on the world stage.

Lynch, Michael C. "The New Pessimism about Petroleum Resources: Debunking the Hubbert Model (and Hubbert Modelers)." *Minerals and Energy—Raw Materials Report* 18.1 (2003): 21–32. Believes that Hubbert modelers are wrong in their predictions of Peak Oil, because they are inconsistent in their arguments and they publish data selectively, ignoring that which does not conform to their views.

Maxwell, Charles T. "Investing on the Hubbert Curve." *Oil and Gas Investor* 22 (January 2002): 67–69. Written by an energy analyst who has worked in the oil industry since 1957. He believes Peak Oil is coming, but it will bring new opportunities for investors as economies shift into new technologies and solutions. Optimistic about the ability of business and government to deal with change.

Mouawad, Jad. "Oil Innovations Pump New Life into Old Wells." *New York Times,* March 5, 2007. Article about efforts to extract more oil from developed oil fields using new technology. Cites energy experts who refute the idea of Peak Oil, stating that new technologies will vastly increase available reserves in the coming years.

Nelson, Ronald. "A Crude Awakening: 'Peak Oil' Is Only a Matter of Time." *Pipeline and Gas Journal* 234 (2007): 62. Despite flat prices, the author believes Peak Oil is coming soon—possibly in 2007—and may halt worldwide economic growth. However, the Peak will be obvious only in hindsight, and may be accompanied by war and shrinking world population.

Ritch, John. "Nuclear Green." *Prospect,* March, 1999. Article that explores the future possibilities of nuclear power, which is still hampered by public mistrust and the inability of politicians to speak openly about it.

Romero, Simon. "2 Industry Leaders Bet on Coal but Split on Cleaner Approach." *New York Times,* May 28, 2006. Profiles opinions and efforts of Peabody Energy's CEO Gregory H. Boyce and American Electric Power's CEO Michael G. Morris to reduce carbon dioxide emissions from their plants. Morris favors government regulations of new technology that would result in fewer emissions, but Boyce claims that regulation should be left to the market, not the government, because the technology is so far unproven and cost prohibitive.

Sengupta, Somini. "News Analysis; Interests Drive U.S. to Back a Nuclear India." *New York Times,* December 10, 2006. Report on cooperation between the U.S. and India, from the highest levels of government to the commercial sector.

Spaulding, Christopher. "It's a Natural Gas." *Contractor* 44.10 (October 1997): 43. Article outlining the benefits of switching to natural gas–powered vehicles for company fleets.

Web Documents

Carbon Sequestration Leadership Forum. "An Energy Summary of Brazil." February 1, 2007. Available online. URL: http://www.cslforum.org/brazil.htm. Summarizes the country's energy statistics from 1993 through 2003 in regard to petroleum, natural gas, coal, electricity, and carbon emissions. Uses data from the Energy Information Administration.

Carbon Sequestration Leadership Forum. "An Energy Summary of China." February 1, 2007. Available online. URL: http://www.cslforum.org/china.htm. Summarizes the country's energy statistics from 1993 through 2003 in regard to petroleum, natural gas, coal, electricity, and carbon emissions. Uses data from the Energy Information Administration.

Carbon Sequestration Leadership Forum. "An Energy Summary of Germany." February 1, 2007. Available online. URL: http://www.cslforum.org/germany.htm. Summarizes the country's energy statistics from 1993 through 2003 in regard to petroleum, natural gas, coal, electricity, and carbon emissions. Uses data from the Energy Information Administration.

Carbon Sequestration Leadership Forum. "An Energy Summary of India." February 1, 2007. Available online. URL: http://www.cslforum.org/india.htm. Summarizes the country's energy statistics from 1993 through 2003 in regard to petroleum, natural gas, coal, electricity, and carbon emissions. Uses data from the Energy Information Administration.

Carbon Sequestration Leadership Forum. "An Energy Summary of Japan." February 1, 2007. Available online. URL: http://www.cslforum.org/japan.htm. Summarizes the country's energy statistics from 1993 through 2003 in regard to petroleum, natural gas, coal, electricity, and carbon emissions. Uses data from the Energy Information Administration.

Carbon Sequestration Leadership Forum. "An Energy Summary of the United States of America." February 1, 2007. Available online. URL: http://www.cslforum.org/usa.htm. Summarizes the country's energy statistics from 1993 through 2003 in regard to petroleum, natural gas, coal, electricity, and carbon emissions. Uses data from the Energy Information Administration.

Energy Information Administration (EIA). *International Energy Outlook 2006.* Report, Office of Integrated Analysis and Forecasting. Washington, D.C.: U.S. Department of Energy. Available online. URL: http://www.eia.doe.gov/oiaf/ieo/pdf/0484(2006).pdf. A graphics-intense report charting world energy use according to type (oil, natural gas, coal, electricity, and carbon emissions) and end-use sector (residential, commercial, transportation, etc.), with current usage statistics and forecasts through 2030.

Follath, Erich. "The Coming Conflict: Natural Resources Are Fueling a New Cold War." *Spiegel Online,* August 18, 2006. Available online. URL: http://www.spiegel.de/international/spiegel/0,1518,429968,00.html. Lengthy article about the end of cheap oil and the political struggles that will ensue as nations struggle to obtain adequate supplies.

Inskeep, Steve. "Oil Money Divides Nigeria: Gas Flaring Continues to Plague Nigeria." Report, National Public Radio (August 25, 2005). Available online. URL: www.npr.org/templates/story/story.php?storyID=4797953. Outlines Nigeria's efforts to end the polluting, wasteful practice of natural gas flaring. Increasingly, the gas is liquefied and shipped to markets around the world, but Shell Oil admits that it will continue to employ flaring after the 2008 deadline.

National Energy Policy Development Group. *National Energy Policy.* (May 2001). Available online. URL: http://www.gcrio.org/OnLnDoc/pdf/nep.pdf. Comprehensive energy policy created by a committee chaired by Vice President Dick Cheney that relies heavily on increasing fossil fuel exploration, advocates for expansion of nuclear power, acknowledges the coming energy crisis, and promotes clean and efficient energy.

Films

Charcoal People, DVD. Directed by Nigel Noble, Buena Park, Calif: Vanguard Cinema, 2002. A 1999 documentary about charcoal makers in the rain forest of Brazil, a generation of impoverished workers who burn wood to make charcoal that is combined with iron in the production of steel. The workers feel they have no choice but to clear-cut the rain forest for wood, making them pawns in international corporations that produce the raw materials for first-world countries.

Empires of Industry—Black Gold: The Story of Oil, DVD. New York: A&E Home Video, 2005. A History Channel documentary on the history of the oil industry, particularly in the United States. Charts the rise of Exxon, Mobil, Standard Oil, and the other major companies, and discusses the impact of OPEC beginning in the 1970s.

The End of Suburbia: Oil Depletion and the Collapse of the American Dream, DVD. Directed by Gregory Greene. Paris, Ontario, Canada: Electric Wallpaper, 2004. Documentary about how the rise of the suburb in post–World War II America will impact Peak Oil, especially when gas prices skyrocket and many people find themselves unable to afford the lifestyle to which they have become accustomed.

Harlan County, U.S.A., DVD. Directed by Barbara Kopple. Criterion, 2006. Award-winning 1976 documentary about the violent, deadly 1973 strike at a Kentucky coal mine. When workers decided to unionize, the company sent scabs in to replace the workers and hired thugs to break the strike through violence and intimidation. Apart from the labor dispute, the film documents how coal miners in late 20th-century America continued to be impoverished and ill-treated.

An Inconvenient Truth, DVD. Directed by Davis Guggenheim. Los Angeles, Calif.: Paramount, 2006. Academy Award–winning documentary of Al Gore's slide show on global climate change, which he believes is caused by carbon emissions and other greenhouse gases—primarily the result of burning fossil fuels.

Oil on Ice, DVD. Directed by Bo Boudart and Dale Djerassi. Lightyear Video. Documentary about U.S. energy policy as it relates to the Arctic National Wildlife Refuge, which contains significant oil reserves but which is protected from drilling by law.

60 Minutes—Coal Cowboy, DVD. Directed by Arthur Bloom. New York: CBS. Segment of the popular television show that aired on February 26, 2006. Leslie Stahl interviews Montana governor Brian Schweitzer, who believes the state's coal reserves can be transformed into synthetic fuel.

60 Minutes—The Oil Sands, DVD. New York: CBS. Segment of the popular television show from January 22, 2006, that explores the oil sands of Alberta, Canada, which some believe holds billions of barrels of petroleum that could be crucial on the world market in the coming years. Others believe the oil sands present technological hurdles that will prevent them from becoming a miracle solution to the coming oil shortage.

60 Minutes—Vive Les Nukes, DVD. New York: CBS. Segment of the popular television show that aired on April 8, 2007, in which Steve Kroft visits France, which derives most of its electricity from nuclear power, making it less dependent on foreign oil and giving it a relatively small carbon footprint. Kroft examines the U.S. nuclear energy industry, which seems poised for a comeback in light of global climate change.

ENERGY: RENEWABLE RESOURCES

Books

Berger, John J. *Charging Ahead: The Business of Renewable Energy and What It Means for America.* Revised ed. New York: Henry Holt, 1999. Concentrates on outlining the plan to switch industrialized nations to cleaner, renewable resources and leave fossil fuels behind. Optimistically, the author maintains that fossil fuels and nuclear power are on the way out, and photovoltaic (solar) power, wind power, biomass power, and geothermal power are the wave of the future.

Bradford, Travis. *Solar Revolution: The Economic Transformation of the Global Energy Industry.* Cambridge, Mass.: MIT Press, 2006. Bradford, a former investment fund manager, believes solar power is the wave of the future because advances in technology will make it cheap and practical, and it has the advantage of being able to bypass the fragile electrical grid. Explores growing use of PV cells in Japan, Germany, and the American West.

Flavin, Christopher, and Nicholas Lenssen. *Power Surge: Guide to the Coming Energy Revolution.* New York: W. W. Norton, 1994. Published by the Worldwatch Institute, the book describes how developed economies will shift away from oil and coal in the coming years and toward more sustainable forms of energy, including wind and solar, which are cleaner and decentralized. This radical shift will have far-ranging ramifications for the structure of the economy.

Geller, Howard. *Energy Revolution: Policies for a Sustainable Future.* Washington, D.C.: Island Press, 2003. Detailed examination of the economic and political factors involved in transforming various countries' energy supply to renewables. Pays special attention to the behavior of energy markets, capitalization, building and infrastructure concerns, and public perception. Enumerates various success stories around the globe, including wind power in Denmark and more efficient cookstoves in China.

Hoffmann, Peter. *Tomorrow's Energy: Hydrogen, Fuel Cells, and the Prospects for a Cleaner Planet.* Cambridge, Mass.: MIT Press, 2001. Presents a history of hydrogen as an energy source, from Jules Verne to Buckminster Fuller, and how hydrogen can be created and used in homes, vehicles, and businesses both safely and efficiently.

Romm, Joseph J. *The Hype about Hydrogen.* Washington, D.C.: Island Press, 2004. Romm headed fuel cell technology programs for the Department of Energy under President Clinton. Though he is a proponent of hydrogen power, the hydrogen economy, and automotive fuel cells, he believes the technology and costs have not and will not reach reasonable levels in the foreseeable future. To deal with the impending energy crisis, he advocates intense research and development efforts in many areas including hydrogen power.

Articles and Papers

Birger, Jon. "The Great Corn Gold Rush." *Fortune* 155.7 (April 16, 2007): 74. Report on the skyrocketing price of corn, which has become a valuable commodity for the production of ethanol. The ethanol plant building boom is changing the way farmers do business in the American Midwest; their profits are soaring, but so are their costs for equipment, rent, and supplies, leading some experts to believe that a crash is not far behind.

Bradsher, Keith. "Paying in Pollution for Energy Hunger." *New York Times,* January 9, 2007. Part of the *Times* series "The Energy Challenge," which looks at the popularity of polluting diesel generators in areas of India and China that do not have access to the electrical power grid. Explores attempts in India to transition these generators from diesel fuel and kerosene to biomass fuel made from the locally grown dhaincha. Also covers the popularity of solar water heaters in China.

"Brazil: The New Electricity Model Has Been Approved and 2005 Will See the Dawn of a New Era That Should Guarantee Supply for Years to Come." *Power Engineering International,* March 2005. Focus on Brazil's energy plan, highlighting hydropower, coal, natural gas, and geothermal power.

Brooke, Lindsay. "Green Technology; Prequel to a Hydrogen Future: Driving G.M.'s Fuel Cell Prototype." *New York Times,* September 24, 2006. Favorable review of the Sequel, a hydrogen fuel cell vehicle. The same technology will be used in G.M.'s Project Driveway in 2007, a test program of 100 fuel-cell vehicles that will have a 300-mile range and weigh more than two tons.

Carter, Adrienne, and Adam Aston. "Harvesting Green Power; Farmers Are Sowing the Seeds of an Alternative Energy Future." *Business Week,* November 13, 2006, p. 60. Article about Midwestern farmers converting to corn crops for ethanol and the financial ramifications—both good and bad—they face; states limiting carbon emissions to a significant degree may require too much farmland. Also mentions the growth of wind energy in the rural sector.

Fang, Bay. "China's Renewal." *U.S. News & World Report* 140.22 (June 12, 2006): p. 37–38, 40. Examines successes in China's early efforts to adopt renewable energy sources, into which $5.5 billion was invested in 2004. Solar energy, biofuels, and wind energy projects will be visible in time for the 2008 Summer Olympics.

Flavin, Christopher. "Energy for a New Century." *World Watch* 13.2 (March 2000): 8. Proposes that an energy revolution is necessary even before oil supplies start to dwindle and calls for a technological transition on par with the digital revolution of the late 20th century.

"Foundation for the Future: Renewable Energy Technologies Are the Driving Force Behind a Recently Launched Programme to Bring Clean, Affordable Energy Services to People Living in Rural India." *Power Engineering International* 14.7 (August 2006): 61. Article about General Electric's Rural Electrification Program for India, which promises "Power to All by 2012."

Hewitt, Ben. "Power Pioneers: At the End of a Yearlong Quest, Our Man Off-the-Grid Taps into the Wind, Ramps Up His Solar Array, and Surveys the Future of Energy Production." *Popular Mechanics* 184.1 (January 2007): 82. Explores the promise of decentralized energy and the technology available to citizens who wish to reduce their carbon footprint. Article includes a look at an anaerobic digester that transformed 38,000 gallons of cow manure into 9.8 kw of electricity that a farmer sold back to the power company for $124,000.

Jagger, Anna. "Brazil Drives on Alcohol Use." *ICIS Chemical Business,* January 23, 2006, p. 21. Profile of Brazil's fledgling ethanol industry and bright prospects for its expansion.

Moran, Tim. "Fuel for the Future: Iceland Has Vast Resources to Produce Hydrogen." *Automotive News* 81.6230 (November 20, 2006): 32. Story about General Motors executives who traveled to Iceland to observe the country's geothermal energy infrastructure, which makes Iceland a world leader in sustainable energy. Automotive designers hope to incorporate geothermal energy technology into the hydrogen production process for automobiles, although all recognize the logistic problems of storing and transporting hydrogen.

Osse, Sergio. "Brazil Moving Ahead with Biofuel Initiatives." *Southwest Farm Press*, December 14, 2005. Outlines the government's National Agroenergy Plan, which attempts to regulate production of sugarcane ethanol.

Rather, John. "Is the Answer Blowing in the Wind?" *New York Times*, November 5, 2006. Profile of the wind energy sector in the United States, which is led by Texas and California, with many East Coast wind farms in the planning stages. Public reaction against huge wind turbines is growing, however, and many remain unconvinced that they can provide enough energy to meet needs in a cost-effective manner.

Raymond, Mark. "New Law Gives Renewables Big Boost: China's Renewables Law Comes into Effect on 1 January 2006." *Modern Power Systems* 25.0 (October 2005): 30. Focuses on China's Renewables Law, which promotes hydropower, solar, wind, geothermal, and biomass energy, and which is being partially funded by the World Bank.

Richtel, Matt. "Start-up Fervor Shifts to Energy in Silicon Valley." *New York Times*, March 14, 2007. Highlights the strong growth of "clean-tech" companies in northern California, an area with considerable venture capital money and brain power, which may prove to be similar to the dot-com boom of the 1990s. Most of the clean-tech start-ups seek to develop and market innovations related to solar power, ethanol, carbon sequestration, and other green-energy technology.

Shnayerson, Michael. "Quiet Thunder." *Vanity Fair*, May 2007, pp. 266–271. A look at the new generation of electric and hydrogen-powered vehicles, many of which are being spearheaded not by the big automakers, but by Silicon Valley entrepreneurs.

Timmons, Heather. "Energy From the Restless Sea; A Renewable Source, and Clean, But Not Without Its Critics." *New York Times*, August 3, 2006, p. C1. Article about advances in wave power generators, which are being tested in Hawaii, New Jersey, Scotland, England, and Australia, and which might some day lead to "wave farms" able to supply consistent energy to the grid.

Williams, Dede. "Germany and Biorenewables." *Chemistry and Industry*, April 3, 2006, p. 12. Report on Germany's Degussa BioRenewables Day, a conference of international industry energy experts that presented ways to expand biofuel sources, such as rapseed, biodiesel, flax, and hemp.

Wilson, Kevin A. "High-End Hydrogen: BMW Puts Its Duel-Fuel V12 on the Road." *AutoWeek* 56.50 (December 4, 2006): 36. Review of BMW's 7 Series hydrogen-powered flex-fuel sedan, stating that its performanceis comparable to gasoline-only vehicles, but acknowledging that mass-produced hydrogen vehicles are still 20 years away.

Web Documents

Energy Information Administration. *Renewable Energy Annual 2004*. Report from the EIA Office of Coal, Nuclear, Electric and Alternate Fuels. Washington, D.C.:

U.S. Department of Energy, June 2006. Available online. URL: http://www.eia.doe.gov/cneaf/solar.renewables/page/rea_data/rea.pdf. Comprehensive data regarding renewable energy trends, solar thermal and photovoltaic collector manufacturing, geothermal heat pumps, and green pricing programs in each state. Includes many charts and graphs.

Geothermal Education Office. "Geothermal Energy Facts." Available online. URL: http://geothermal.marin.org. Student-oriented Web site that explains the science of geothermal energy, along with where and how it is being used today.

International Energy Agency. *Renewables in Global Energy Supply: An IEA Fact Sheet.* Paris, France: IEA, January, 2007. Available online. URL: http://www.iea.org/textbase/papers/2006/renewable_factsheet.pdf. Provides detailed data by country and region regarding current usage of renewable energy sources and forecasts the supply and transition through 2030 and advancement of technology through 2050. Optimistic about biofuels and hydrogen.

U.S. Clean Coal Technology Demonstration Program. *Environmental Benefits of Clean Coal Technologies. Topical report, no. 18.* Washington, D.C.: U.S. Department of Energy, 2001. Available online. URL: http://www.fossil.energy.gov/programs/powersystems/publications/Clean_Coal_Topical_Reports/Enviromental_ Benefits.pdf. Accessed on April 24, 2007. A highly technical report that presents detailed analysis of how to reduce carbon and sulfur emissions from coal-fired power plants, through such techniques as wet scrubbing and dry sorbent injection.

Films

60 Minutes—The Ethanol Solution, DVD. New York: CBS. Segment of the popular television show that aired on May 7, 2006, in which Dan Rather looks at the success of the ethanol industry in Brazil and explores whether the same situation is possible in the United States.

Who Killed the Electric Car?, DVD. Directed by Chris Pain. Los Angeles, Calif.: Sony Pictures. Documentary about the popular EV-1 electric car, produced by General Motors in the 1990s. Despite the success of the program and happy customers who wanted to keep their cars, the automaker destroyed all the vehicles. Though electric cars still depend on electricity generated by fossil fuels, they do not rely on gasoline and thus emit no carbon dioxide themselves.

WATER ISSUES

Books

Blackbourn, David. *The Conquest of Nature: Water, Landscape and the Making of Modern Germany.* New York: W. W. Norton, 2006. A history of Germans' relationship with nature, particularly the Rhine River, the country's main waterway. As with rivers in all other industrialized areas, the Rhine lost much volume to industrialization in the 20th century. Engineers successfully regulated the river to make it do what they wanted, enabling it to become a major economic thoroughfare that transported goods.

Briscoe, John, and R. P. S. Malik. *India's Water Economy: Bracing for a Turbulent Future.* New York: Oxford University Press, 2006. Report of a World Bank study, which brought protests from some in India's government, who claimed the World Bank has an agenda to privatize the nation's water supply.

Clover, Charles. *The End of the Line: How Overfishing Is Changing the World and What We Eat.* New York: New Press, 2006. Explores the damage done to the ocean's fisheries through changing eating habits and rising demand for many species, which impacts the entire ecosystem of an area.

Economy, Elizabeth C. *The River Runs Black: The Environmental Challenge to China's Future.* Ithaca, N.Y.: Cornell University Press, 2005. Author is the director of Asia studies at the Council on Foreign Relations and writes about the economic and political causes of China's environmental crises, which include rampant pollution, water shortages, desertification, and other forms of environmental degradation.

Pearce, Fred. *When the Rivers Run Dry: Water—The Defining Crisis of the Twenty-First Century.* Boston, Mass.: Beacon Press, 2006. Illustrates how the world's major rivers are dwindling because of water mismanagement and how water rights will become a major political and economic issue in the near future. Also covers the environmental effects of mismanagement, which range from desertification to drained aquifers.

Reiser, Marc. *Cadillac Desert: The American West and Its Disappearing Water.* Revised ed. New York: Penguin, 1993. A book-length work of journalism that traces water policy in the West, its effect on the land, the Native Americans who once lived there, and the development of California, Las Vegas, and other large cities in a region that could not support such large populations without significant engineering feats, most notably Hoover Dam.

Roy, Arundhati. *The Cost of Living.* New York: Modern Library, 1999. Comprised of two previously published essays by the award-winning novelist. "The Greater Common Good" focuses on the social costs of India's Narmada Dam, which Roy says will displace nearly 40 million people, many of them illiterate, stripping them of their homes, villages, and livelihoods. Roy criticizes the World Bank and the government of India, among other institutions, for not having the best interests of the Indian people in mind.

Shiva, Vandana. *Water Wars: Privatization, Pollution and Profit.* Cambridge, Mass.: South End Press, 2002. Shiva, a physicist, environmental activist, and leader of the International Forum on Globalization, looks at how increasing privatization of water diverts necessary resources from the poor to benefit the elite and believes that conflict over water in the 21st century may overshadow the conflict over oil. Offers an action plan to preserve water for all.

Simon, Paul. *Tapped Out: The Coming World Crisis in Water and What We Can Do About It.* New York: Welcome Rain, 2002. The former U.S. senator from Illinois wrote this volume about the vast numbers of people who live and die without adequate drinking water each day. He calls for meaningful price controls, pollution control, and better management, both in the United States and around the world, especially in India and the Middle East.

de Villiers, Marq. *Water: The Fate of Our Most Precious Resource.* New York: Mariner Books, 2001. Investigation into impending worldwide water shortages; the author travels widely—to the Sea of Galilee, Victoria Falls, the Volga River, and the American West—examining political and scientific aspects of water issues at each location, finding most of them suffering from overpopulation, pollution, and desertification.

Ward, Diane Raines. *Water Wars: Drought, Flood, Folly and the Politics of Thirst.* New York: Riverhead, 2003. Ward heads a nonprofit conservation organization in India and has firsthand experience with water mismanagement. The book includes chapters on oceans, giant public works projects, river basins, the greening of the desert, floodplains, and case studies of the Netherlands and the Florida Everglades.

Articles and Papers

Archibold, Randal C., and Kirk Johnson. "No Longer Waiting for Rain, an Arid West Takes Action." *New York Times,* April 4, 2007. Report on the water crisis in the American West, which is the result of a sustained drought since 1999 and which has drastically reduced the amount of water available from the Colorado River and lowered the level of Lake Powell by 80 feet. Much of the reduction is due to shrinking snowpack in the Rocky Mountains caused by global warming. Several states, including Montana, Wyoming, Nevada, and Utah, are seeking solutions that involve pipelines and litigation.

Blackburn, Peter. "Amazon Dam Project Draws Heated Opposition in Brazil." Report for Reuters Limited, December 7, 2006. Environmentalists and local populations join together to protest a hydropower plant that would flood the Madeira River, one of the Amazon's main tributaries.

Bunsha, Dionne. "Dam Lies: Indian Government Refuses to Stop Drowning Homes and Villages." *New Internationalist* 390 (June 2006): 24. Article about the Narmada Dam project, which will require resettlement of over 50,000 families. Tracks progress of government resettlement plans and finds them inadequate. In most cases, families did not receive enough money to buy even a fraction of the land to which they were entitled, and almost 90 percent of the cash compensation given to affected families was deducted for taxes. No infrastructure has been built in the resettlement areas and even more families will be displaced as the government decides to raise the height of the dam more than previously allowed.

Fair, C. Christine. "The Indus Water Fight." *Atlantic Monthly* 292.1 (July–August 2003): 90. Article about the political tensions between Pakistan and India created by the water shortage in the region bordered by the two countries.

Graff, James. "A Thirst for Growth. Your Water Supply May Be Controlled by a French Company—Even If You Live in China." *Time,* March 26, 2007, p. A8. Article about the French company Veolia and others who are stepping into the business of water filtration, which has traditionally been a municipal concern. Also mentions the dangers of the aging U.S. water infrastructure, which private companies are not required to replace.

Guterl, Fred, Kristin Kovner, and Emily Flynn. "Troubled Seas." *Newsweek International,* July 14, 2003, p. 46. Explores the effect of overfishing in marine environments, which has removed nine out of 10 large predator species of fish, upsetting the ecosystem in ways not yet understood. Though many species remain undiscovered, some believe that up to 90 percent of the world's fish have been harvested beyond sustainability.

Jackson, J. B., et al. "Historical Overfishing and the Recent Collapse of Coastal Ecosystems." *Science* 293.5530 (2001): 629–637. The authors investigate historical incidents of damage to coastal ecologies and determine that overfishing causes a huge upset in the balance of an ecosystem that often takes many decades to become evident. They argue that ocean management needs to be proactive and not wait for changes to become manifest.

Jakes, Susan. "China's Water Woes." *Time International* 168.15 (October 9, 2006): 50. Profile of the water crisis in China, focusing on pollution and the massive South-to-North Water Diversion project.

Jia, Shaofeng, et al. "Industrial Water Use Kuznets Curve: Evidence from Industrialized Countries and Implications for Developing Countries." *Journal of Water Resources Planning and Management* 132.3 (2006): 183. Study provides evidence that the Kuznets Curve explains variances in industrial water pollution; areas benefiting from higher incomes generally correspond to lower levels of pollution. This is true especially in the Western countries that belong to the Organization for Economic Cooperation and Development, although income thresholds vary.

Klaus, Oliver. "Securing New Resources: German Companies Are Taking on the Desalination Challenge." *Middle East Economic Digest* 48.35 (August 27, 2004): 32. Article that explores the growing feasibility of desalination as a solution to lack of potable water worldwide.

Mann, Charles C. "The Rise of Big Water." *Vanity Fair,* May 2007, p. 122. Article about the privatization of water in the United States and around the world, especially in China. The author argues that French companies such as Veolia will inevitably fail due to corruption, mismanagement, and idiosyncracies of the market.

Monastersky, Richard. "The Ice That Burns." *Science News* 154 (November 14, 1998): 312. Article about the energy possibilities of methane hydrates.

"A Nation Poisoned; Contamination in Bangladesh." *Economist,* December, 22, 2001. Report on wells contaminated with arsenic, which serve between 35 and 77 million people, which the World Health Organization calls "the largest mass poisoning of a population in history."

"Private Worries; The Water Industry in India." *Economist* (US), August 13, 2005, p. 53. Story about water issues in Delhi, which is governed by the Delhi Jal Board. Complicating the agency's job is a surging population, low water revenues, and the difficulties in monitoring water usage. Efforts to regulate the system have brought complaints of water privatization, which India is strongly against.

Sampat, Payal. "The River Ganges' Long Decline." *World Watch* 9.4 (July–August 1996): 24. Profile of pollution in the Ganges, highlighting hot spots from the headwaters to the watershed.

Sengupta, Somini. "Thirsty Giant: In Teeming India, Water Crisis Means Dry Pipes and Foul Sludge." *New York Times,* September 29, 2006. Report on the water crisis in India, which in New Delhi is so bad that municipal taps provide water for only a few hours each day. The crisis is made worse by lack of a sewage system and water filtration plants. The Yamuna River in New Delhi provides the city's drinking water and serves as its main sewer. Efforts to clean it up have failed.

Specter, Michael. "The Last Drop: Confronting the Possibility of Global Catastrophe." *New Yorker,* October 23, 2006, p. 60–71. Report from India on the country's infrastructure and water policy problems, which exacerbate the shortage problem. Author interviews Priya Ranjan Dasmunshi, India's Minister of Water Resources, about the seemingly insurmountable task he faces in securing water for an expanding population.

"World Bank Report on India's Water Economy Faces Flak." *Financial Express,* October 25, 2006. Reports Indian officials' reaction to the World Bank Report stating that India needs stronger national control of its water resources. Officials took offense at the report, stating that water rights should be controlled at the local, not national level, and that the World Bank is now criticizing practices that it put in place within the country.

Yardley, Jim. "China Chemical Spills Spur Plan to Guard Water Supply." *New York Times,* January 12, 2006. Report of diesel fuel spill on the Yellow River and a cadmium spill along the Yangtze River in China, which came on the heels of a benzene spill on the Songhua River that disrupted the water supply for 3.8 million people.

———. "The Yellow River; China's Path to Modernity, Mirrored in a Troubled River." *New York Times,* November 19, 2006. Investigative piece in which Yardley travels the 3,000 miles of the Yellow River, exploring problems at the headwaters (depletion of the aquifers and glaciers that feed the river) to rapid, uncontrolled development in the inner provinces of factories that pollute and stress the river, to the delta, which is a privately owned oil field. Concentrates on the huge push toward urbanization and industrialization that has resulted in water pollution, shortages, and other ecological disasters related to the river basin.

Web Documents

"China Says Water Pollution So Severe That Cities Could Lack Safe Supplies." *China Daily,* June 7, 2005. Available online. URL: http://www.chinadaily.com.con/english/doc/2005-06/07/content_449451.htm. News article in which Chinese officials acknowledge that severe water pollution and shortages are urgent problems that need to be addressed.

Embassy of the People's Republic of China in the United States. "People Are Better Off in Three Gorges Resettlement," December 18, 2006. Available online. URL: www.china-embassy.org. Press release that presents evidence that those resettled from areas flooded by the dam are more economically secure than they were previously, enjoying their new homes, and making more money than they had as farmers.

———. "Three Gorges Dam Will Improve Climate, Citrus Production," December 18, 2006. Available online. URL: www.china-embassy.org. Press release outlining that one of the unintended favorable consequences of the dam, due to its large reservoirs and flood-control properties, is an agricultural climate that will be favorable to orange trees and other citrus products, leading to a new source of revenue for the agricultural sector.

The Global Water Crisis: Evaluating U.S. Strategies to Enhance Access to Safe Water and Sanitation: Briefing and Hearing Before the Committee on International Relations, House of Representatives, One Hundred Ninth Congress, First Session, June 29, 2005. Washington, D.C.: U.S.G.P.O., 2006. Available online. URL: http:// commdocs.house.gov/committees/intlrel/hfa22262.000/hfa22262_0f.htm. Accessed on April 24, 2007. Focuses on the Water for the Poor Act of 2005 and states that the coming water crisis should be treated with the same sense of urgency as the HIV/AIDS epidemic. Committee believes that lack of water could become a threat to national security and to prepare it will spend $1.5 billion to secure resources and help meet the United Nations Millennium Development Goals.

"Pharmaceuticals in Our Water Supplies." *Arizona Water Resource* 9.1 (July–August 2000). Available online. URL: http://cals.arizona.edu/AZWATER/awr/july00/feature1.htm. Article about the presence of drugs in U.S. water supplies and in Germany, including over-the-counter substances, antibiotics from livestock runoff, and prescription medications such as birth control pills and antidepressants. Water filtration plants cannot eradicate such substances from the supply, leading experts to speculate on the long-term consequences.

Talberth, John, et al. "The Ecological Fishprint of Nations: Measuring Humanity's Impact on Marine Ecosystems." Oakland, Calif.: Redefining Progress, 2006. Available online. URL: http://www.rprogress.org/newpubs/2006/FishprintofNations2006.pdf. Accessed on April 24, 2007. Report of the nonprofit organization Redefining Progress that outlines the destruction of commercial fish stocks, due to overfishing and other practices that began in the 1970s. Repeats warnings that at current rates, all major commercial fish species will collapse by 2048.

United Nations Environment Programme (UNEP). "Challenges to International Waters: Regional Assessments in a Global Perspective." Nairobi, Kenya: UNEP, 2006. Available online. URL: http://www.giwa.net/publications/finalreport/. Accessed on April 24, 2007. Report of water quality worldwide, especially in the rivers and seas of developing countries. Concludes that "human activity has weakened the ability of aquatic ecosystems to perform essential functions, which is compromising human well-being and sustainable development."

World Bank. "India's Water Economy: Bracing for a Turbulent Water Future." October 5, 2005. Available online. URL: http://www.worldbank.org.in/WBSITE/EXTERNAL/. Summarizes the report on water issues in India and provides links to the report and other World Bank water resource Web pages.

Films

The Blue Planet: Seas of Life, DVD. Directed by Alastair Fothergill. London: BBC Video, 2002. A four-disc series that explores the impact humans have had on the oceans.

Drowned Out, DVD, Directed by Franny Armstrong. Oley, Penn.: Bullfrog Films, 2002. Documentary about the people of Jalsindhi, India, a village that will be submerged by the Narmada Dam. Armstrong documents how residents make the choice to move to the slums, move to a resettlement village, or stay in their homes and drown.

Ganges: River to Heaven, DVD. Directed by Gayle Ferraro. Berkeley, Calif.: Berkeley Media, 2005. Award-winning documentary that follows four families as they prepare to release the bodies of their loved ones into the Ganges River in the ancient city of Varanasi. The film explores how the ancient religious Hindu rituals exist alongside modern-day pollution and desecration of the holiest of rivers.

Jacques Cousteau: Odyssey, DVD. Los Angeles, Calif.: Warner Home Video, 2005. A multidisc set that includes all 12 episodes of the 1978 series, in which Cousteau sails throughout the world, examining ocean, lake, and river ecosystems, and how people have lived in harmony—or not—with them over the centuries. In particular, he sails down the Nile in an effort to explain how the ancient Egyptians dealt with the unique ecosystem of the region and how it has changed through massive irrigation projects in the 20th century. He also visits Easter Island and other inhospitable, isolated regions in which civilization has succumbed to the harsh landscape.

Panihari: The Water Women of India, DVD. Directed by Abi Devan and Sudhi Rajagopal. Beverly Hills, Calif.: Choices, Inc., 2006. Documentary on the Panihari ("women who fetch water") in the desert of Rajasthan, India. As much about the water crisis of India as it is about the plight of women in developing regions decimated by poverty.

SUSTAINABLE DEVELOPMENT

Books

Bigg, Tom, ed. *Survival for a Small Planet: The Sustainable Development Agenda*. London: Earthscan, 2004. Anthology from leading experts edited by the senior researcher at the International Institute for Environment and Development. Published by Earthscan, which focuses solely on books about sustainable development, energy, and natural resources.

Catton, William R. *Overshoot: The Ecological Basis of Revolutionary Change*. Champaign: University of Illinois Press, 1980. Landmark book that introduced the concept of *carrying capacity* and how it will be reached soon as the Age of Exuberance (which began in 1492) results in too many people fighting for too few resources.

Comstock, Gary. *Vexing Nature: On the Ethical Case against Agricultural Biotechnology.* Norwell, Mass.: Kluwer Academic Publishers, 1995. Discusses the problems of genetically modified food (GMF), dividing the issue into intrinsic and extrinsic components. He states that germ plasm is altered through GMF, which could have devastating, irreversible results that outweigh the benefits and the harm of pesticides used in traditional agriculture. New genes in new plants may also result in genetic pollution.

Daly, Herman E. *Beyond Growth: The Economics of Sustainable Development.* Boston: Beacon Press, 1997. Author has worked on sustainable development issues for the World Bank and has declared the idea an oxymoron. Concerned with the ethical aspects of modern life and questions whether countries should pursue economic development at all. Believes globalization is antithetical to sustainable development.

Diamond, Jared. *Collapse: How Societies Choose to Fail or Succeed.* New York: Viking, 2004. Presents evidence of how many past civilizations, from the Vikings to the Anasazi to the inhabitants of Easter Island, have doomed themselves to extinction by ignoring their effect on the environment through unsustainable resource use (cutting down all the trees, or engaging in agricultural practices that promote drought) and overpopulation. Draws the link between these past, sometimes glorious and thriving cultures to contemporary societies.

Federoff, Nina, and Nancy Marie Brown. *Mendel in the Kitchen: A Scientist's View of Genetically Modified Foods.* Washington, D.C.: Joseph Henry, 2004. A generally favorable view of GMF from a member of the National Academy of Sciences, stating that the benefits of improved harvests and disease resistance most likely outweigh negatives. Golden rice enriched with vitamins may save many lives, thus it is not the "frankenfood" that GMF opponents purport it to be.

Fishman, Ted C. *China Inc.: How the Rise of the Next Superpower Challenges America and the World.* New York: Scribner, 2005. Concentrates on how China's development will impact its own economy and those of other nations as it positions itself as the manufacturing juggernaut of the world, often without policies regarding fair trade, product quality, workers' rights, and other factors common in other industrialized nations.

Fox, Michael. *Beyond Evolution.* New York: Lyons Press, 1999. Discusses "genetic pollution" due to GMF and believes it will lead to diminished biodiversity and irreversible changes to all ecosystems. He also looks at whether or not the industry could be successfully regulated and how corporations would address problems.

Hawken, Paul, Amory Lovins, and Hunter Lovins. *Natural Capitalism: Creating the Next Industrial Revolution.* Boston: Little, Brown, 1999. The authors envision a clean, sustainable world of high living standards in which business proves to be beneficial to the environment. The solution is to apply market principles to natural resources.

Annotated Bibliography

Horn, Greg. *Living Green: A Practical Guide to Simple Sustainability.* Topanga, Calif.: 2006. A handbook for individuals that covers trends in sustainable health, home, and living. Includes a resource and product guide to personal care products, building materials, and energy systems.

Jacobs, Jane. *The Death and Life of Great American Cities.* New York: Vintage, 1992. A reprint of Jacobs's landmark 1961 work in which she analyzes the problems with modern urban planning, which have resulted in land misuse, slums, poverty, fractured social networks, and sprawl. With an emphasis on New York, she uses her academic expertise to understand what makes an urban culture thrive and how planners and builders can capitalize on those factors and thus ensure the sustainability of cities in the future.

Leman-Stefanovic, Ingrid. *Safeguarding Our Common Future: Rethinking Sustainable Development.* Albany, N.Y.: State University of New York Press, 2000. Author takes a philosophical view of sustainability based on Martin Heidegger's theory of phenomenology. Focuses on how sustainability requires wide-scale changes in thinking.

McHughen, Alan. *Pandora's Picnic Basket: The Potential and Hazards of Genetically Modified Foods.* New York: Oxford University Press, 2000. A primer on genetically modified foods, concentrating on the science involved in order to explain their possible benefits and detriments. While acknowledging that increased yields will be advantageous to developing nations, he also believes that chemical manipulation of biologically nondiverse crops has no precedent in nature and therefore long term consequences are unknown.

McKibben, Bill. *Deep Economy: The Wealth of Communities and the Durable Future.* New York: Times Books, 2007. "More is not better," says McKibben, who favors new economic models based on local economies and local resources in order to maintain a sustainable future.

———. *Hope, Human and Wild: True Stories of Living Lightly on the Earth.* Minneapolis, Minn.: Milkweed Editions, 2007. A reprint of the 1998 book in which the author examines cities such as Curitiba, Brazil, and Kerala, India, that have implemented reforms and planning that facilitates a high standard of living and sustainability.

Meadows, Donella. *The Limits of Growth.* New York: Signet, 1972. Bestselling book by the Club of Rome, a group of MIT scientists who formulated the World3 computer model that forecast possible outcomes if humanity overshoots the carrying capacity of the earth. One of the earliest works on sustainable development.

———, Jorgen Randers, and Dennis L. Meadows. *Limits to Growth: The 30-Year Update.* White River Junction, Vt.: Chelsea Green Publishing, 2004. The Club of Rome updates their original work and discusses how their original model came close to mirroring the environmental situation of the past several decades. They continue to warn against overshooting the planet's carrying capacity, state that humanity is close to collapse, and offer ideas for better use of resources and the likely outcomes of various scenarios.

Monte, Mike. *Cut and Run: Loggin' Off the Big Woods.* Atglen, Pa.: Schiffer Publishing, 2002. A history of the logging industry in the upper Great Lakes region from the 1880s to the 1940s, during which logging towns boomed and the industry flourished, until the ecology was decimated and the loggers moved on, abandoning towns and leaving the local economy in ruins.

Rogers, Peter, Kazi F. Jalal, and John A. Boyd. *An Introduction to Sustainable Development.* Cambridge, Mass.: Harvard Division of Continuing Education, 2006. Textbook on sustainability issues, covering the environment, economy, social implications, domestic and international concerns, water, energy, forests, and industry.

Schumacher, E. F. *Small Is Beautiful: Economics As If People Mattered,* 25th Anniversary Edition. Vancouver, British Columbia, Canada: Hartley and Marks, 2000. Update of the 1973 publication in which Schumacher, an economist and former president of the U.K.'s National Coal Board, explores the ramifications of infinite growth in a finite environment. Argues for better land use, more education, and sustainable policies, in the modern world and the third world, to achieve prosperity for all.

Sen, Amartya. *Poverty and Famines: An Essay on Entitlement and Deprivation.* New York: Oxford University Press, 1981. Sen is an economist, Nobel laureate, famine survivor, and the world's leading thinker on the relationship between poverty and famine, which he demonstrates is more often than not caused by political and economic policies of disenfranchisement and unfair resource distribution that entrenches the underclass.

Smith, Philip B., and Eric Thurman. *A Billion Bootstraps: Microcredit, Barefoot Banking, and the Business Solution for Ending Poverty.* New York: McGraw-Hill, 2007. Smith, a self-made millionaire, believes that microcredit will become a major tool in solving many of the most stubborn cases of poverty in the 21st century and that it presents an opportunity for individual charitable donations that is an improvement over traditional nonprofit organizations.

Yunus, Muhammad. *Banker to the Poor: Micro-Lending and the Battle Against World Poverty.* New York: PublicAffairs, 2003. Autobiography of the Nobel Prize–winning Yunus, who founded the Grameen Bank in Bangladesh in the 1970s and established micro-lending with a loan of $27.

Articles and Papers

Alcott, Blake. "Jevons' Paradox." *Ecological Economics: The Journal of the International Society for Ecological Economics* 54.1 (2005): 9. Author believes that the Jevons' Paradox (the idea that increases in efficiency of an energy source leads to more of the resource—not less—being consumed) deserves priority with economists, because so many policy recommendations make the false assumption that efficiency gains will yield energy savings.

Ayres, Ed. "China's Desertification Is Growing Worse." *World Watch,* 16.4 (July–August 2003): 10. Article on how unsustainable agricultural practices are increasing China's rate of desertification.

Bruck, Connie. "Millions for Millions." *New Yorker,* October 30, 2006, pp. 62–73. Investigation into how different systems of microcredit are used in various countries. Profiles Muhammad Yunus, who received the Nobel Peace Prize for his work with the Grameen Bank, and Pierre Omidyar, founder of eBay, who has given $100 million to Tufts University to create a microcredit program based on free-market principles. Includes firsthand look at Pro Mujer microcredit clients in Mexico.

Cowan, Tyler. "Microloans May Work, but There Is Dispute in India Over Who Will Make Them." *New York Times,* August 10, 2006. Cowen visits the Poverty Action Lab at MIT, interviews economic professors who specialize in microfinance, and discovers flaws in the system that may limit its effectiveness.

Gore, Al. "The Energy Electranet." *Newsweek,* December 18, 2006. Gore, a leading voice of the environmental movement, describes how the electranet will transform the power grid, allowing consumers to sell surplus energy back to the utilities while generating that energy more efficiently. States that with good leadership in government and the private sector, huge gains in energy technology are within reach and could mitigate the effects of global warming.

Miller, Claire Cain. "Easy Money." *Forbes* 17.11 (November 27, 2006): 134. Profile of the booming microcredit industry in India, demonstrating how microloans have become less successful as they have gained popularity.

Monastersky, Richard. "A New Science Breaks Down Boundaries." *Chronicle of Higher Education* 53.9 (October 20, 2006). Article about the rise of sustainability science as an academic discipline, which has been recognized by the National Academy of Sciences as such, and its roots in the academic research that gave rise to the Green Revolution in the 1960s.

Overdorf, Jason. "The Green Devolution; India's Population Is Growing Faster Than Farm Output, Threatening One of Its Most Prized Achievements." *Newsweek International,* September 4, 2006. Investigates threats to India's food independence as supply gains dwindle and the prime minister calls for a second Green Revolution to be fueled by technology and reliance on the world market. Critics warn that switching to a new strategy while some areas of the country remain agriculturally inefficient and unsustainable is bad policy.

Pachauri, R. K. "The Future of India's Economic Growth: The Natural Resources and Energy Dimension." *Futures* 36.6–7 (August–September 2004): 703. Detailed overview of factors that affect India's sustainable development, including population, water shortages, soil erosion, waste disposal, air pollution, economic concerns, and energy security.

Packer, George. "The Megacity: Lagos Becomes an Urban Test Case." *New Yorker,* November 13, 2006, pp. 62–75. Report from Lagos, Nigeria, one of the most poverty-stricken and unsustainable megacities in the world, which suffers from extreme water and air pollution, lack of sanitation, insufficient infrastructure, and social problems due to lack of basic services and security.

Ryan, Alison. "City of Portland's Search for Renewable Energy Sources Are Ongoing." *Daily Journal of Commerce* (Portland, Oreg.), December 12, 2006. Report about the city's plan to buy its municipal electricity from providers who use renewable energy sources, a project spearheaded by the city's Office of Sustainable Development. The process has been hampered by price issues.

Shoumatoff, Alex. "An Eco-System of One's Own." *Vanity Fair,* May 2007, pp. 203–209. A breakdown of a typical American's daily impact on the environment, in terms of the resources used (and pollution generated by) consumption of electricity, the environmental damage caused by petroleum-based plastic products, excessive use of water and paper resources, the rare metals used in cell phones derived from mines in Africa that are destroying gorilla habitats, consumption of hormone-infused meat and dairy products, and greenhouse gas emissions from automobiles.

———. "The Gasping Forest." *Vanity Fair,* May 2007, pp. 272–287. Lengthy report about the destruction of the Amazon rain forest, which is being destroyed at a rate of 7,500 square miles per year, threatening millions of species of plants and animals and impacting global warming.

Web Documents

Duncan, Richard C. "The Olduvai Theory: Energy, Population, and Industrial Civilization." *The Social Contract,* winter 2005–06. Available online. URL: http://www.thesocialcontract.com/pdf/sixteen-two/xvi-2-93.pdf. Duncan's original paper theorizing that industrialized society has a roughly 100-year lifespan, from 1930 to 2030.

Hails, Chris, ed. *Living Planet Report 2006.* WWF, 2006. Available online. URL: http://assets.panda.org/downloads/living_planet_report.pdf. The complete report of humanity's ecological footprint from a global perspective and broken down by country. Contains many graphics and charts on footprint measurements, including analysis of water resources and usage.

"Humans Will Need Two Earths, Report Claims." Report, MSNBC.com, October 25, 2006. Available online. URL: http://www.msnbc.msn.com/id/15398149. News report about the publication of the *Living Planet Report 2006,* which calculates the size of each country's ecological footprint. The report states that the Earth is currently in "ecological overshoot" because humans demand 25 percent more natural resources than the planet is able to provide annually.

Union of Concerned Scientists. "World Scientists' Warning to Humanity," November 1992. Available online. URL: http://www.ucsusa.org/ucs/about/1992-world-scientists-warning-to-humanity.html. A document that reads like a manifesto, formulated by 1700 of the world's leading scientists, including many Nobel laureates. The warning points out in particular the dangers of global warming, overpopulation, misuse of water resources, and industrial pollution, and advocates diverting economic resources away from destructive endeavors (such as war) and putting them toward addressing these issues.

"UN Millennium Development Goals." www.un.org/millenniumgoals/ (February 1, 2007). Online summary of the goals outlined at the Millennium Summit in

2000, the largest gathering of world leaders in history. Target date for completion is 2015; the goals range from eliminating poverty to providing education to preserving natural resources.

Wackernagel, Mathis, et al. "Tracking the Ecological Overshoot of the Human Economy." *PNAS: Proceedings of the National Academy of Sciences of the United States of America,* June 27, 2002. Available online. URL: http://www.pnas.org/cgi/content/full/99/14/9266. Scientific research article peer-reviewed by Edward O. Wilson that analyzes existing data from 1961 to 1999 and determines that humanity may have reached ecological overshoot in the 1980s.

Films

Cane Toads: An Unnatural History, DVD. Directed by Mark Lewis. New York: First Run Features, 2001. Documentary released in 1987 about the introduction of the Hawaiian sugarcane toad into Queensland, Australia. Though the species introduction was designed to eliminate insect pests from crops, they themselves became pests, multiplying to infestation levels and creating an upset in the local ecology.

China from the Inside, DVD. Alexandria, Va.: PBS Home Video, 2007. A four-episode series that highlights various aspects of contemporary China. Episode 2, "Women of the Country," focuses on population issues, the gender disparity, and the economic disenfranchisement of women. Episode 3, "Shifting Nature," explores land, air, and water pollution from expanding industry and huge water diversion projects.

City Life, DVD. Produced by Luke Gawin. Oley, Pa.: Bullfrog Films, 2002. A 22-part series on urban issues worldwide, from the slums of Sao Paulo, Brazil, to water pollution in Chengdu, China, to urban planning successes in Barcelona, Spain.

The Ecological Footprint: Accounting for a Small Planet, DVD. Directed by Patsy Morthcutt. Oley, Pa.: Bullfrog Films, 2005. A 30-minute film written and hosted by Mathis Wackernagel, the cocreator of the ecological footprint concept.

The Future of Food, DVD. Directed by Deborah Koons Garcia. Canoga Park, Calif.: Cinema Libre, 2004. Documentary about genetically modified food, its unknown effects, and the secrecy of multinational agribusinesses who have developed and marketed GMF to a relatively unsuspecting public.

Koyaanisqatsi: Life Out of Balance, DVD. Directed by Godfrey Reggio. Los Angeles, Calif.: MGM, 2002. Artistic, narratorless film from 1984 that explores the beauty of the natural world with the havoc created by humans upon it. Dramatic filmmaking and an original score by Philip Glass have made the film and its companion, *Powaqqatsi* (1988), legendary.

Life 4, DVD. Produced by Luke Gawin and Dick Bower. Oley, Pa.: Bullfrog Films, 2005. A 27–part, 676-minute series on the United Nations Millennium Development Goals.

ENVIRONMENTALISM

Books

Avery, Dennis T., and S. Fred Singer. *Unstoppable Global Warming: Every 1,500 Years.* Lanham, Md.: Rowman & Littlefield, 2007. Written by two of the leading skeptics of global warming, the book purports that global warming is cyclical and natural and current trends are not a threat.

Bailey, Ronald. *Eco-Scam: The False Prophets of Ecological Apocalypse.* New York: St. Martin's Press, 1993. Described as a polemic by some critics, the book refutes evidence of global warming, world hunger, water and air pollution, and other environmental ills. Bailey singles out the work of population theorist Paul Ehrlich and environmentalist Lester Brown for encouraging unfounded doomsday scenarios.

Belasco, Warren. *A History of Food.* Berkeley, Calif.: University of California Press, 2006. Examines the interconnectedness of industry, agricultural practices, resources, economics, and the environment as it relates to what ultimately ends up on the dinner table. Belasco takes a historical approach in relating what previous experts thought would happen to our food supply, from Thomas Malthus and William Godwin through the futurists of the 1970s who envisioned millions subsisting on algae.

Gelbspan, Ross. 2004. *Boiling Point: How Politicians, Big Oil and Coal, Journalists and Activists Are Fueling the Climate Crisis—And What We Can Do to Avert Disaster.* New York: Basic Books, 2004. Gelbspan is a Pulitzer Prize–winning journalist who blames industrialists and politicians for what he sees as a global environmental crisis. Gelbspan proposes alternative energy as a solution to some problems and emphasizes the need to transition away from fossil fuels completely and quickly.

Gore, Al. *Earth in the Balance: Ecology and the Human Spirit.* New York: Houghton Mifflin, 1992. Written before Gore became vice president of the United States, the book looks at environmental issues such as climate change and how individuals' relationships with nature need to be reevaluated if catastrophe is to be avoided. Includes a detailed "Global Marshall Plan" of changes that could be implemented by concerned countries who demonstrate the will to address the issues.

Jayne, Mark. *Cities and Consumption. Routledge Critical Introductions to Urbanism and the City.* London: Routledge, 2006. Examines how urban life changes consumption habits and how those consumption habits in turn impact the city, becoming a self-reinforcing cycle.

Kahn, Matthew E. *Green Cities: Urban Growth and the Environment.* Washington, D.C.: Brookings Institution Press, 2006. Focuses on economic implications of urban growth and how sprawl and environmental destruction can be curtailed through market principles. Discusses the environmental Kuznets Curve, which is an inverted-U relationship between pollution and income.

Annotated Bibliography

Kennedy, Donald, ed. *Science Magazine's State of the Planet 2006–2007.* Washington, D.C.: Island Press, 2006. Features 18 chapters written by leading experts on population, water, fisheries, climate change, energy, and other topics.

Kolbert, Elizabeth. *Field Notes from a Catastrophe.* New York: Bloomsbury, 2006. Investigative journalism by a *New Yorker* correspondent into the causes and effects of global climate change that takes the author from the Arctic Circle to the rain forests and beyond. Kolbert interviews many scientists all over the world and reports their dire warnings about what has already happened and what is going to happen.

Lappe, Frances Moore. *Diet for a Small Planet.* New York: Ballantine, 1971. Landmark book in which Lappe draws a connection between people's diets and their effect on natural resources, and the impact of agribusiness on land issues. Advocates vegetarianism and pays special attention to amino acids and protein as the foundation for a sustainable diet that conserves agricultural resources.

Lomborg, Bjørn. *The Skeptical Environmentalist: Measuring the Real State of the World.* New York: Cambridge University Press, 1998. Controversial book by a Danish academic and statistician who claims that a closer look at the data behind environmental problems often reveals evidence that things are not nearly as bad as many other scientists and activists claim.

Michaels, Patrick J. *Meltdown: The Predictable Distortion of Global Warming by Scientists, Politicians, and the Media.* Washington, D.C.: Cato Institute 2004. Written by a climatologist who does not dispute evidence of global warming, but who believes its effects will be mild and easy for humanity to adapt to.

Perkins, John H. *Geopolitics and the Green Revolution: Wheat, Genes, and the Cold War.* New York: Oxford University Press, 2003. Perkins, a biologist, relates the history of the Green Revolution throughout the 20th century, focusing on the period between 1950 to 1970, in which the United States took the lead in solving food shortages. Also contains chapters on postimperial Britain and the Rockefeller Foundation's work in Mexico during World War II.

Shapiro, Judith. *Mao's War Against Nature: Politics and the Environment in Revolutionary China.* New York: Cambridge University Press, 2004. Illustrates how Mao Zedong's policies carried out his belief that nature should be subservient to the revolution. Toward that end, he cleared forests and reversed rivers in the name of agriculture, power, and industry, ultimately leading to massive deforestation, water and air pollution, and famine.

Simon, Julian L. *The State of Humanity.* Boston, Mass.: Blackwell Publishing, 1995. A collection of essays by 50 scholars on topics ranging from deforestation, air pollution, natural resources, destruction of the ozone layer, food production, and poverty. Also covers social issues such as homelessness and crime and discusses the media's role in how these issues are viewed by the public.

Sitarz, Dan. *AGENDA 21: The Earth Summit Strategy to Save Our Planet.* Boulder, Colo.: EarthPress, 1993. Sitarz, an environmental attorney, abridged the original 900-page United Nations report into a more comprehensible 300-page digested version.

Wackernagel, M., and W. Rees. *Our Ecological Footprint: Reducing Human Impact on the Earth.* Gabriola Island, British Columbia, Canada: New Society Publishers, 1996. First espoused the concept of the ecological footprint, which gained wide popularity quickly and led to the annual *Living Planet Report* by the WWF, which tracks ecological footprint by country.

Walker, Brian, and David Salt. *Resilience Thinking: Sustaining Ecosystems and People in a Changing World.* Washington, D.C.: Island Press, 2006. Authors are pioneers in the concept of resilience thinking, which is a theory about how to manage natural systems for sustainability. Topics include wetlands, water issues, coral reefs, and land issues, with case studies involving the Everglades, the Goulburn-Broken Catchment in Australia, the Kristianstads Vattenrike in Sweden, and the Lake District in Wisconsin.

Articles and Papers

Brand, Stewart. "Environmental Heresies." *Technology Review,* May 2005. Brand, the founder of the *Whole Earth Catalog,* foresees environmentalists changing their tune when it comes to nuclear power, population control, urbanization, and genetically modified foods. He believes nuclear power will be central to solving global warming, that urbanization naturally reduces population growth and eliminates poverty, and that genetically modified foods use fewer pesticides and yield bigger harvests.

Deacon, Robert, and Catherine Norman. "Does the Environmental Kuznets Curve Describe How Individual Countries Behave?" University of California at Santa Barbara, Departmental Working Papers, April 5, 2004. Available online. URL: http://repositories.cdlib.org/ucsbecon/dwp/05-04/. Accessed on April 25, 2007. Authors argue that the Environmental Kuznets Curve, a graphical depiction of pollution as a function of income, can be explained by other factors and therefore does not exist.

Dinakar, S., and Michael Freedman. "Dirty Money." *Forbes* 178.5 (September 18, 2006): 128. Article about private waste management initiatives in China and India.

Doerr, John. "California's Global-Warming Solution." *Time* 168.11 (September 11, 2006): 55. Column about California's legislation to reduce greenhouse gases, which requires industrial polluters to reduce carbon emissions by 25 percent by 2020.

Furniss, Charlie. "Too Hot to Trot." *Geographical* 78.5 (May 2006): 51. Lengthy article about the devastation wrought by global warming in biodiversity hotspots. Examples given are the polar bears in the Arctic, who are drowning at high rates due to the melted icepack that makes their hunting ground too far away, penguins in the Antarctic, birds in the North Sea region, coral reefs worldwide, and many species native to island and tropical habitats.

Jefferson, Valeria. "The Ethical Dilemma of Genetically Modified Food." *Journal of Environmental Health* 69.1 (July–August 2006), p. 33. Presents the pros and cons of GMF, and urges researchers to proceed with caution. While GMF may be able to prevent hunger in some parts of the world, long-term and adverse consequences are still unknown.

Liu, Jianguo, et al. "Protecting China's Biodiversity." *Science* 300.5623 (May 23, 2003): 1,240. Authors advocate for the expansion of conservation efforts in China and suggest they should be created at the national level rather than the local level. Existing sanctuaries are too small to protect endangered ecosystems and are regarded by local communities as barriers to economic development. Calls for increased conservation education.

Lohr, Steve. "The Cost of an Overheated Planet." *New York Times,* December 12, 2006. Part of the *Times* series "The Energy Challenge," which highlights efforts to impose carbon trading on the coal industry to limit greenhouse gas emissions.

Margolis, Mac. "Under Construction; Brazil Has Tried for Decades to Keep Developers Out of the Amazon. What's Needed Is a Realistic Plan to Help Them." *Newsweek International,* April 11, 2005, p. 38. Profile about competing interests in the Amazon between environmentalists and developers, highlighting how poverty creates incentives for rural people to engage in illegal development.

Marshall, Jessica. "Environmental Health: Megacity, Mega Mess." *Nature* 437.7057 (2005): 312–314. Examines urban air pollution in Jakarta, Indonesia, and surmises that such pollution in other megacities will continue to play a major role in the disease burden of developing countries.

Miller, James P. "Asian Pollution Ill Wind for U.S.," *Chicago Tribune,* May 3, 2004. Article about how the Asian brown cloud travels on the jet stream to the West Coast of the United States, ultimately impacting the weather patterns over the Midwest.

Ogden, Douglas. "We Don't Need More Power; For Each Dollar of Economic Output, China Wastes 11 Times More Energy than Japan." *Newsweek International,* February 6, 2006, p. 1. Focuses on the inefficiencies of China's coal industry and consumer sector.

Romero, Simon. "Two Industry Leaders Bet on Coal but Split on Cleaner Approach." *New York Times,* May 28, 2006. Part of the *Times* series "The Energy Challenge," the article profiles coal industry executives from Wyoming and Ohio on their differing strategies for limiting coal's impact on climate change, including the prospects for carbon sequestration.

Schreurs, Miranda A. "Divergent Paths: Environmental Policy in Germany, the United States, and Japan." *Environment* 45.8 (October 2003): 8. Profile of energy policies in the world's three largest economies, contrasting the large U.S. ecological footprint with Germany's aggressive government policies (courtesy of the Green Party) and Japan's turnaround on environmental issues since the 1980s, which now make it a world leader in limiting emissions and pollution.

Wang, Chenggang. "China's Environment in the Balance." *The World & I* 14.10 (October 1999): 176. Profile of China's environmental problems, including water pollution, air pollution, water shortages, deforestation, soil erosion, desertification, solid waste pollution, and acid rain. Examines various government policies recently enacted to reverse pollution trends, as well as the billions spent in policies created in the 1970s and afterward, all of which predated much of the current pollution.

Wilson, E. O. "Problems Without Borders." *Vanity Fair,* May 2007, p. 164–166. A short article that accompanies the results of the Worldmapper project between the University of Michigan and the University of Sheffield. Includes 6 world maps that illustrate the disproportionate distribution of fuel imports, extinction of plant species, deforestation, wood and paper imports, municipal waste, and recycling.

Web Documents

Bremner, Brian. "What's It Going to Cost to Clean Up China?" *Business Week Online,* September 28, 2006. Available online. URL: http://www.businessweek.com/globalbiz/content/sep2006/gb20060927_774622.htm?chan=top+news_top+news+index_global+business. States that the economic cost of pollution in China was $64 billion in 2004 and that efforts to reverse this trend will initially cost $135 billion and negatively impact the country's economic growth.

Embassy of the People's Republic of China in the United States. "Three Gorges Environmental Protection Program Launched." Press release. Available online. URL: http://www.china-embassy.org/eng/zt/sxgc/t36503.htm. Accessed on February 1, 2007. Announces plans to improve water quality on the Yangtze River by closing paper mills, building waste water treatments plants, reducing soil erosion, and protecting biodiversity.

———. "People Are Better Off in Three Gorges Resettlement." Press release. Available online. URL: http://www.china-embassy.org/eng/zt/sxgc/t36504.htm. Accessed on February 1, 2007. Government claims include that most of the 10,400 resettled in areas affected by the dam project have new homes, government pensions, and good jobs. Overall their standard of living is much higher than it was before resettlement.

Encyclopedia of Earth. Available online. URL: http://www.eoearth.org/. Accessed February 16, 2007. An open-source encyclopedia with articles written by experts from numerous countries on issues pertaining to science, geography, and natural resources.

Energy Information Administration. "Country Analysis Briefs: Brazil." Available online. URL: http://www.eia.doe.gov/emeu/cabs/brazilenv.html. Uploaded September 2003. U.S. government profile of environmental issues in Brazil, including deforestation, carbon sequestration, air pollution, oil spills, energy consumption and intensity, ethanol and biofuels, and other renewable energy sources.

Energy Information Administration. "Country Analysis Briefs: Germany." Available online. URL: http://www.eia.doe.gov/emeu/cabs/germe.html. Uploaded September 2003. U.S. government profile of environmental issues in Germany, which includes statistics on air pollution, energy use, carbon emissions, government policies, per capita energy consumptions, and energy intensity.

Energy Information Administration. "Country Analysis Briefs: India." Available online. URL: http://www.eia.doe.gov/emeu/cabs/indiaenv.html. Profile of environmental issues in India, including air pollution, lack of pollution policy enforcement, energy consumption, carbon emissions, carbon intensity, and renewable energy sources.

Energy Information Administration. "Country Analysis Briefs: Nigeria." Available online. URL: http://www.eia.doe.gov/emeu/cabs/nigenv.html. Uploaded September 2003. U.S. government profile of environmental issues in Nigeria, including water pollution and violence in the Niger Delta, air pollution due to natural gas flaring, oil spills, energy consumption, and carbon emissions.

Energy Information Administration. "Country Analysis Briefs: United States." Available online. URL:http://www.eia.doe.gov/emeu/cabs/Usa/Full.html. Uploaded September 2003. U.S. government statistics regarding energy use, capacity, growth, and intensity in the United States, including all sectors of the oil industry from exploration to refinement. Details on natural gas supplies, demands, and pipelines, production rates for coal and electricity, nuclear power, hydroelectric power, and renewables.

"Kyoto Protocol to the United Nations Framework Convention on Climate Change." Kyoto, Japan, December 11, 1998. Available online. URL: http://unfccc.int/resource/docs/convkp/kpeng.html. An international agreement comprising 28 articles that outlines a strategy to reduce greenhouse gas emissions worldwide. It was notably adopted by a majority of the nations involved, but not the United States, who refused to ratify it on the grounds that it unfairly targeted U.S. industries and would harm the economy and, furthermore, that it did not address the issue of natural resource use in developing countries, notably India and China.

Otten, Edward J. "The Effect of Human Population on Biodiversity." Ecology.org Web site. Available online. URL: http://www.ecology.org/biod/habitat/human_popl.html. Accessed February 1, 2007. Proposes that overpopulation by humans is responsible for reduction in biodiversity through five processes: overharvesting, alien species introduction, pollution, habitat fragmentation, and habit destruction.

Pope John Paul II. "The Ecological Crisis a Common Responsibility." January 1, 1990. Rome: The Holy See. Available online. URL: http://www.vatican.va/holy_father/john_paul_ii/messages/peace/documents/hf_jp-ii_mes_19891208_xxiii-world-day-for-peace_en.html. A message from the Pope on the World Day of Peace in which he stresses that stewardship of the Earth is God's will for people and is explicitly stated in the Bible.

Shen, Junyi. "A Simultaneous Estimation of Environmental Kuznets Curve: Evidence from China." *China Economic Review* 17.4(2006): 383. Available online. URL: http://ideas.repec.org/p/osk/wpaper/0409.html. Author analyzes existing pollution data from China to see if it fits the EKC hypothesis in which environmental degradation is assumed to have an inverse-U relationship with per capita income. Finds that five pollutants do support the EKC hypothesis, but two others do not.

Srinivasan, J., and Sulochana Gadgil. "Asian Brown Cloud—Fact and Fantasy." *Current Science* 83.5 (2002): 586. Available online. URL: http://www.ias.ac.in/currsci/sep102002/586.pdf. Accesssed April 24, 2007. A response to the UNEP report *The Asian Brown Cloud: Climate and Other Environmental Impacts,* stating that it was sensationalistic and not scientific. States that the haze is generated in conjunction with the monsoon season and that it has no appreciable impact on crop yields worldwide.

United Nations Environment Programme. *The Asian Brown Cloud: Climate and Other Environmental Impacts.* Report prepared by the Center for Clouds, Chemistry, and Climate (C^4), 2002. Available online. URL: http://www.cleanairnet.org/caiasia/1412/articles-37081_resource_4.pdf. Accessed April 24, 2007. Initial report commissioned by the UNEP and written by C^4; charted the development and progress of the Asian Brown Cloud (also sometimes called the Atmospheric Brown Cloud), which develops annually from December through April and can travel halfway around the world in two days. The report states that its findings are based on limited climate models, but they do present evidence that the cloud is man-made and may reduce solar radiation on the Earth's surface by as much as 15 percent, thereby having a significant effect on rainfall patterns worldwide.

U.S. Department of Energy Office of Public Affairs. "Abraham Announces Pollution-Free Power Plant of the Future." Press release. February 27, 2003. Available online. URL: http://www.fossil.energy.gov/news/techlines/2003/tl_futuregen1.html. Announcement of the FutureGen power plant initiative, which will be "the prototype power plant [that] will serve as the test bed for demonstrating the best technologies the world has to offer," including carbon sequestration.

Films

Hurricane on the Bayou, DVD. Directed by Greg MacGillivray. Chatsworth, Calif.: Image Entertainment, 2007. Documentary about the destruction of the wetlands on the Mississippi Delta, and how the removal of that natural environmental barrier left New Orleans and surrounding areas much more vulnerable to the impact of Hurricane Katrina than they would have been otherwise.

National Geographic: Strange Days on Planet Earth, DVD. Directed by Mark Shelley. Washington, D.C.: National Geographic Video, 2005. Two-disc set in which various phenomena are discovered to be related, such as windstorms in Africa and a rise in childhood asthma half a world away. Explores topics from climate change to water pollution to pesticides, to biodiversity, and the surprising influences they have on seemingly disparate events.

Nobelity, DVD. Directed by Turk Pipkin. Thousand Oaks, Calif.: Monterey Video, 2006. Documentary in which nine Nobel Prize laureates are interviewed about their ideas on solving the world's problems, from poverty to environmental degradation.

Planet Earth, DVD. Silver Spring, Md.: Discovery Communications, 2007. An 11-episode series that presents footage from all areas of the globe—land and water—and explores the biodiversity of the planet. The five-DVD set includes a bonus three-part documentary, "The Future," that is dedicated to "revealing the vulnerability of the natural history of the earth."

POPULATION ISSUES

Books

Brown, Lester R., et al. *Beyond Malthus: Nineteen Dimensions of the Population Problem.* New York: W. W. Norton, 1999. Brown advocates for intense family planning and education worldwide to solve the population problem, which he believes is the underlying cause of many social ills, including water shortages, food dependence, collapse of the ocean's fisheries, deforestation, energy shortages, waste, and poverty.

Cohen, Joel E. *How Many People Can the Earth Support?* New York: W. W. Norton, 1995. Cohen is a population expert at Rockefeller University in New York, and his book does not answer its own question, but rather concentrates on explaining how quality of life and technology will impact the planet's maximum carrying capacity.

Davis, Mike. *Planet of Slums.* New York: Verso, 2006. Davis analyzes research regarding megacities and highlights the problems of the urban destitute. He recognizes that they are the fastest growing demographic on the planet, and yet bad or nonexistent social policy nearly ensures they will continue to suffer. As a constituency, no one speaks for them, and the informal social systems that have arisen in their settlements are far from a picture of anarchic utopia.

Ehrlich, Paul R. *The Population Bomb.* New York: Ballantine, 1968. Landmark book that brought the topic of overpopulation to the masses. While the widespread famine that Ehrlich forecasted did not come to pass, the book remains a controversial tome that continues to spark debate over whether or not the earth's population is nearing its limit.

Entwisle, Barbara, and Paul C. Stern, eds. *Population, Land Use, and Environment: Research Directions.* Washington, D.C.: National Academies Press, 2005. A textbook that collects many research studies on population issues in the United States and other regions, including the Amazon, Thailand, China, Vietnam, Mexico, and Egypt. Many papers focus on how increasing population affects land use in urban areas.

Evans, Karin. *The Lost Daughters of China.* Los Angeles, Calif.: Tarcher, 2001. Personal account of an American woman who travels to China to adopt a baby girl who was abandoned shortly after birth by her mother. Provides an outsider's perspective on China's reproductive policies, especially as they affect women and the many infant girls who are abandoned each year.

Firor, John, and Judith Jacobsen. *The Crowded Greenhouse: Population, Climate Change, and Creating a Sustainable World.* New Haven, Conn.: Yale University Press, 2002. The authors believe that reaching sustainability requires two revolutions: a social revolution that will improve education and equity of all peoples, especially that of women in developing countries, and a technical revolution that will address energy and pollution issues.

Grant, Lindsey. *Juggernaut: Growth on a Finite Planet.* Santa Ana, Calif.: Seven Locks Press, 1996. Considers population as it affects emerging countries, consumption in the developed world, food production, energy issues, pollution, climate change, and issues that pertain to the social well-being of nations.

———. *The Case for Fewer People: The NPG Forum Papers.* Santa Ana, Calif.: Seven Locks Press, 2006. Addresses global aging, weighing economic, immigration, and natural resource issues and finds that population control is necessary in the United States and around the world. Outlines a plan for "optimum population," both in rural and urban areas.

Hudson, Valerie M., and Andrea M. den Boer. *Bare Branches: The Security Implications of Asia's Surplus Male Population.* New ed. Boston: MIT Press, 2005. Examines the possible social fallout in China and India from high levels of female infanticide. Argues that the growing gender imbalance may result in a bachelor subculture in which underemployment, violence, crime, and lowered status of women lead to war and more global implications.

Longman, Phillip. *The Empty Cradle: How Falling Birthrates Threaten World Prosperity and What to Do About It.* New York: New American Press, 2004. Purports that falling birthrates are more problematic than overpopulation and should be considered an issue of national importance. Incentives should be given to young couples to have large families and to head off the coming disaster to the workforce and the economy.

McKee, Jeffrey K. *Sparing Nature: The Conflict Between Human Population Growth and Earth's Biodiversity.* Piscataway, N.J.: Rutgers University Press, 2005. Argues that as human population surges other species of plants and animals get pushed out of the way. Looks at examples from the previous 2 million years, such as the extinction of the woolly mammoth and the giant ground sloth.

Moffett, George D. *Critical Masses: The Global Population Challenge.* New York: Viking, 1994. Outlines the problems that rapid population growth may cause, including mass migration, desertification, megacities without basic infrastructure to support millions, and disproportionate poverty in underdeveloped countries, particularly in Africa.

Neuwirth, Robert. *Shadow Cities: A Billion Squatters, A New Urban World.* New York: Routledge, 2004. A sociological exploration of the vast slums of many modern countries, including Brazil, India, Kenya, and Turkey. Illustrates how squatters have formed their own neighborhoods and culture on the fringes of society, without basic necessities such as water and electricity, which are prone to gang warfare and drugs. Discusses the role of the United Nations in helping alleviate the strain of squatter cities and gives a historical overview of how 19th century squatters in London and New York became integrated into the mainstream fabric of city life.

Stein, Bruce A., Lynn S. Kutner, and Jonathan S. Adams, eds. *Precious Heritage: The Status of Biodiversity in the United States.* New York: Oxford University Press, 2000. Heavily illustrated guide to the 200,000 species of plants and animals in the United States, their history, migration patterns, and threats to their existence. Highlights current and future biodiversity hotspots as development and other ecosystem-altering phenomena encroach on their territory.

Wattenberg, Benjamin J. *The Birth Dearth: What Happens When People in Free Countries Don't Have Enough Children.* New York: Ballantine, 1987. Leading neoconservative thinker Wattenberg was one of the first to propose that one of America's problems in the future would be too few people, not too many. Problems will range from the economic difficulties of too few workers to support the multitudes of elderly and retired, to loneliness suffered by those who have no children, grandchildren, or extended family members to share their lives with.

Articles and Papers

"Cradle Snatching; German Demography." *Economist* (US), March 18, 2006, p. 55. Explores the concept of "demographic theft" in Germany as the plunging birthrates and internal migration affect the economy.

"Decline and Fall? After Years of Frightening Headlines about the Runaway Growth of the World's Population, Does the 'Birth Dearth' Mean We Face a Population Implosion?" *Geographical* 77.3 (March 2005): 54. Examines the "birth dearth" of industrialized countries and suggests that economic decline can be offset by increasing immigration and delaying retirement. Also acknowledges that population growth continues to be a problem in developing countries.

Dietz, Thomas, Elinor Ostrom, and Paul C. Stern. "The Struggle to Govern the Commons." *Science* 302.5652 (December 12, 2003): 1,907. A long article that looks back to Garrett Hardin's 1968 essay "The Tragedy of the Commons" and evaluates the situation at the turn of the 21st century. The authors find that local institutions are better at preserving limited resources, but that the modern world is increasingly eliminating most such institutions. Thus, overpopulation continues to endanger world resources.

Eberstadt, Nicholas. "Demographic Clouds on China's Horizon." *American Enterprise* 9.4 (July–August 1998): 54. Article about the problems of an aging population, as the smaller one-child generation is outnumbered by the larger population of retirees and older people.

Engardio, Peter. "Global Aging: It's Not Just Europe—China and Other Emerging-Market Economies Are Aging Fast, Too." *Business Week*, January 21, 2005, p. 40. Focuses on the aging workforce in Europe, where pensions will not be enough to support people after retirement. Even more significant problems are likely to develop from an aging population in China and other less developed countries. Worldwide, people will need to work past current retirement ages, and economies will need to accommodate older workers.

Fehrenbach, Pete. "Too Many People, and More on the Way; Environmental Problems Caused by Population Growth May Get Worse Before They Get Better." *Waste News* 10.26 (March 28, 2005): 10. Explores the relationship between population growth and environmental devastation, which often involves overconsumption, and suggests making water a market commodity in order to address distribution, pollution, and sanitation issues.

"The Fertile Century." *Geographical* 77.3 (March 2005): 50. Explains how the 20th century can be considered the century of population. It began with relative population stability, because most countries experienced high birthrates and high death rates. However, economic and social developments led to a "demographic transition," which will ultimately result in population stability once more from a balance of low birthrates and low death rates. But during the 1900s, the transition was incomplete, resulting in a huge population surge mostly because birthrates continued to climb and death rates plummeted.

French, Howard W. "China Scrambles for Stability as Its Workers Age." *New York Times,* March 22, 2007. Profile of China's aging population, focusing on a retiree who must find a new job after she reaches the age of 50, because her pension and her one child are not enough to support her. Even though pensions in China are meager, more than 500 million rural peasants will receive none.

Gribbin, August. "Overpopulated Megacities Face Frightening Future." *Insight on the News,* August 21, 2000, p. 30. Article about the rise of megacities as the rural populations of developing countries migrate to urban areas. Megacities present significant challenges when it comes to security, sanitation, energy, education, water, and health issues. Most megacities are not equipped to deal with these huge populations, and several organizations, including USAID and the Los Alamos National Laboratory, have launched programs that send experts to megacities to help local officials grapple with urban expansion.

Harder, Ben. "China's Deserts Expand with Population Growth." *Science News* 169.9 (March 4, 2006): 142. Brief article stating that China's deserts grew at a rate of 3,600 kilometers per year in the 1990s as human development destroyed grasslands, and agriculture, livestock grazing, and deforestation depleted other land.

"It's the People, Stupid." *Economist* (US), March 5, 2005, p. 5. Article about population in China and India, focusing on China's aging population and India's population growth, which the country views as an asset. Also mentions unbalanced sex ratios in favor of boys in both countries.

Johnson, Paul. "Let's Have More Babies!" *Forbes* 177.8 (April 17, 2006). Historian Johnson laments falling fertility rates in developed countries, which he believes are spurred by the decline of marriage as an institution and the economic costs of raising children in an urban, industrialized environment.

Mandel, Michael. "Productivity Trumps Demographics; That's Why Repeated Warnings that Population Growth—Or Lack Thereof—Would Destroy Economies Have Always Turned Out False." *Business Week Online,* September 13, 2004. Author asserts that overpopulation is not an issue; economic growth can negate any problems that demographics create.

Ramos, Luiz R. "Ageing in Brazil." *Ageing International,* Spring 2000, p. 58. Detailed analysis of demographic trends in Brazil, focusing on disparities between the north and the south.

Web Documents

Day, Jennifer Cheeseman. "National Population Projections." Report of the U.S. Census Bureau. Available online. URL: http://www.census.gov/population/www/pop-profile/natproj.html. Uploaded January 18, 2001. Examines trends in U.S. population growth based on government data. Steady immigration, longer life expectancies, and stalled fertility rates will result in a steady population increase to around 392 million by 2050, with the population becoming increasingly older.

Federal Statistical Office Germany. "Population Development in Germany until 2050." Available online. URL: http://www.destatis.de.presse/englisch/pm2006/p4640022.htm. Uploaded November 7, 2006. Highlights Germany's aging population.

Hardin, Garrett. "The Tragedy of the Commons." *Science* 162 (1968): 1,243–1,248. Available online. URL: http://dieoff.org/page95/htm. A landmark essay in which Hardin relates current resource problems to overpopulation and the idea of the "Tragedy of the Commons," first mentioned by William Lloyd in his 1833 book on overpopulation. Hardin believes people "must relinquish the freedom to breed" in order to solve the world's problems.

Ogawa, Naohiro. "Changing Age Structures of Population in Asia and Their Implications for Development." Presented at the panel discussion "Challenges of World Population in the 21st Century: The Changing Age Structure of Population and Its Consequences for Development," New York, October 12, 2006. Available online. URL: http://www.un.org/esa/population/publications/2006Changing_Age/Ogawa.pdf. Compendium of population pyramids and other statistical data regarding population growth in China, Japan, and other Southeast Asian countries.

Population Division of the United Nations Department of Economic and Social Affairs. "World Urbanization Prospects: The 2005 Revision." New York: United Nations, 2006. Available online. URL: http://www.un.org/esa/population/publications/WUP2005/2005WUPHighlights_Final_Report.pdf. Detailed report of the official population estimates of all capitals and urban areas worldwide in 2005. Contains numerous charts and graphs comparing population changes over the past 50 years.

Films

NOVA: World in the Balance—The Population Paradox. Boston, Mass.: WGBH, 2004. Explores the population issue in its current incarnations: overpopulation in the developing world and global aging in the developed world.

The Open Road: America Looks at Aging, DVD. Directed by Nina Gilden Seavey. New York: First Run Features, 2005. A documentary that first aired on PBS, which explores the economic, social, and cultural issues related to the aging of the Baby Boomers in the United States during the coming years.

Chronology

8000 B.C.E.

- World population is approximately 5 million.

3000 B.C.E.

- Coal is burned for funeral pyres in Britain, but humankind's main source of energy is wood. Mesopotamians use petroleum in building, roadmaking, and medicine. The Chinese refine oil and use it for heat and light.

600 B.C.E.

- Static electricity is observed and documented by the Greeks.

200 B.C.E.

- The Chinese use natural gas to make salt.

1 C.E.

- World population is approximately 300 million.

200–400

- Coal trade begins in Britain.

c. 900

- The Classic Period of Maya civilization in modern-day Mexico ends, possibly because of environmental problems caused by the worst drought in 7,000 years. Resources for the densely populated city-states became scarce, leading to their collapse.

984

- Norse people arrive in Greenland and form the Eastern and Western Settlements, ultimately reaching a population of perhaps 5,000 during the Medieval Warm Period, when coastal areas are suitable for farming.

1000

- World population is approximately 310 million.

1150

- A 300-year drought commences in the western region of the United States, decimating the Anasazi tribes, who have built densely populated pueblos and developed a culture that cannot withstand the deforestation and water shortages they face.

c. 1400

- The Eastern and Western Norse settlements in Greenland die out. Evidence points to malnutrition and a sudden end among the last survivors. Some experts believe the extinction was prompted by the Little Ice Age, a climate change that made agriculture in the region nearly impossible.

1524

- Spanish conquistador Hernan Cortez discovers the Maya in modern-day Mexico, its civilization comprised of just a few thousand people who know little about the once vast empire and its nearby ruins in the jungle.

1701

- Coal is discovered near Richmond, Virginia.

1722

- Dutch explorer Jacob Roggeveen discovers Easter Island on Easter Sunday in a remote area of the South Pacific. The island is inhabited by 2,000 to 3,000 people, who are suffering from scarce resources and deforestation. At its height, the island is believed to have been home to 10,000 to 15,000 people before its decline started around 1200.

1729

- Jonathan Swift writes *A Modest Proposal: For Preventing the Children of Poor People in Ireland from Being a Burden to Their Parents or Country, and for Making Them Beneficial to the Publick,* a satirical pamphlet in which he advocates eating children as a solution for overpopulation.

Chronology

1748

- The first commercial U.S. coal mining operation opens in Richmond, Virginia.

1752

- Benjamin Franklin flies a kite with a key attached during a storm, proving that static electricity and lightning are the same thing.

1765

- Scottish inventor James Watt engineers improvements to the steam engine, providing the technological foundation for the Industrial Revolution.

1790

- First U.S. census is conducted under Secretary of State Thomas Jefferson and returns a count of 3.9 million people. The country's largest city is Philadelphia, with 42,000 residents.

1798

- Thomas Malthus writes his landmark *Essay on the Principle of Population* and creates the concept of the "population ceiling." Malthus believes that human population will grow unchecked until humanity faces mass starvation, which he predicts by the middle of the 19th century. He is among the first to understand that population grows exponentially and to argue for population control.

1800

- Italian physicist Alessandro Volta invents the electric battery. The volt is named after him.

1804

- World population reaches 1 billion.

c. 1815

- The U.S. Army Corps of Engineers engages in a massive project to fortify New Orleans from floodwaters.

1821

- British chemist and physicist Michael Faraday invents the electric motor.

1827

- French physicist Joseph Fourier discovers the greenhouse effect as it refers to solar radiation trapped in the Earth's atmosphere, resulting in a rise in global temperatures.

c. 1833

- Commercial oil production begins in the Chechen Republic.

1833

- Oxford professor William Forster Lloyd publishes *The Tragedy of the Commons,* a book about population that refutes Adam Smith's idea of the "invisible hand" of the free market. A common pastureland, Lloyd states, is available to all, but cattle-owners have only a short-term interest in increasing the size of their herd and no long-term interest in preserving the common. The result is that cattle-owners will bring too many cattle to the pasture, causing the land to exceed its carrying capacity and become overgrazed, thereby resulting in the permanent depletion of grazing land.

1838

- German scientist Christian Friedrich Schönbein develops the concept of the fuel cell and publishes his findings in the January 1839 edition of *Philosophical Magazine.*

1839

- The photovoltaic effect is first observed by Alexandre-Edmond Becquerel.

1843

- Welsh scientist William Robert Grove develops the first fuel cell, using the blueprint outlined by Schönbein in 1838. The fuel cell uses hydrogen and oxygen to produce electricity.

1844

- Samuel Morse invents the electric telegraph, allowing messages to be relayed quickly across great distances.

1845

- New Bedford, Massachusetts, is the U.S. capital of whaling, home to 300 whaling ships that produce nearly a half-million barrels of whale oil a year, which is the highest quality used in oil lamps. Whaling goes into decline in 1859, after the first oil well is established in Pennsylvania.

1846

- The first oil well is drilled in Baku, Russia, by engineer F. M. Semenov. The city first began trading its oil around 300, and by the late 1600s it contained around 500 hand-dug wells that produced refined oil used for lighting and ointments throughout Persia and Russia.

Chronology

1859

- ***August 27:*** Edwin L. Drake drills the first oil well in the United States in Titusville, Pennsylvania.

1865

- English economist William Stanley Jevons publishes *The Coal Question,* which forecasts a decline in British coal reserves as a function of increased usage due to rising industrialization. His Theory of Utility will prove similar to Hubbert's Peak Oil predictions in the 1950s.

1872

- ***March 1:*** President Ulysses S. Grant signs a congressional bill establishing Yellowstone National Park, the nation's first such designation, which preserves the land for the enjoyment of the people. The 3,468-square-mile park covers parts of Wyoming, Montana, and Idaho and is home to hundreds of unique geothermal features and animal species.
- Robert Angus Smith, a scientist in Manchester, England, one of Britain's leading industrial towns, observes acid rain for the first time and coins the term. It is not studied more closely until the 1960s.

1876

- German engineer Nikolaus Otto invents the first internal combustion engine, which combusts fuel in an enclosed piston chamber. It becomes known as the Otto cycle.

1878

- English inventor Joseph Swan invents the incandescent lightbulb, but it does not burn long enough to make it practical.
- Thomas Edison forms the Edison Electric Light Company in New York City with financing from industrialist J. P. Morgan and others. He devises improvements to the lightbulb that enable it to last for 40 hours—a vast improvement over the competition.

1879

- ***December 31:*** Edison demonstrates his improved incandescent lightbulb in his Menlo Park, New Jersey, laboratory and files a patent for it a month later.

1882

- ***January:*** Edison inaugurates the first electric power station at Holborn Viaduct in London, England, which uses steam power to generate direct current (DC) electricity for a limited number of customers in the area.

- ***September 4:*** Edison brings the Pearl Street generating station online in New York, providing DC power to 59 customers in lower Manhattan. The power is generated by coal-fired generators and lights up 5,000 bulbs.
- The first hydroelectric power plant opens in Wisconsin.

1883

- American inventor Charles Fritts builds the first solar cell, which uses selenium as a semiconductor. The device has only 1 percent efficiency.
- The Niagara Falls Power Company is formed to build a hydroelectric power plant on the U.S. side of the falls. The company hires George Westinghouse to design the system.

1892

- ***May 28:*** The Sierra Club is founded in San Francisco by preservationist John Muir, who becomes its first president. The club promotes the natural beauty of the Sierra Nevada mountains and educates people about the importance of maintaining its undeveloped state.
- Rudolf Diesel invents the Diesel engine, which originally runs on vegetable oil.

1893

- Inventor Nikola Tesla and the Westinghouse Electric Company unveil an AC (alternating current) power system at the World Columbian Exposition in Chicago. It is capable of distributing electricity across longer distances than Edison's DC system and ultimately becomes the standard by which electricity is delivered to consumers across the country.

1896

- The world's first large-scale hydroelectric plant begins operating in Niagara Falls, New York, with generators producing up to 75 megawatts of power that are carried to Buffalo, 20 miles away.

1902

- Congress establishes the Bureau of Reclamation to build dams and aqueducts in the American West.
- Willis Carrier invents the first electric air conditioner, which is used in industrial factories.

1904

- The world's first geothermal power plant goes online in Larderello, Italy.

Chronology

1905

- German physicist Albert Einstein develops the equation for mass-energy equivalence: $E = mc^2$, which later makes nuclear energy possible.

1908

- ***September 27:*** The first Model T rolls off the assembly line of the Ford Motor Company's plant in Detroit, Michigan.

1916

- President Wilson creates the National Park Service.

1927

- ***August 29–September 3:*** The first World Population Conference is held in Geneva, Switzerland, and is organized by birth-control activist Margaret Sanger. The conference concentrates on the influence of population on social, economic, and political situations and results in the formation of the International Union for the Scientific Study of Population, which is based in Paris.

1931

- Construction begins on Boulder Dam on the Arizona/Nevada border, later renamed Hoover Dam. Construction is completed in 1936.

1938

- German scientists Otto Hahn, Lise Meitner, and Fritz Strassmann produce the world's first successful experiment in nuclear fission.

1942

- ***December 2:*** Enrico Fermi produced the first successful nuclear chain reaction at the University of Chicago. The experiment results in the plutonium used for the atomic bomb dropped on Nagasaki.

1943

- The Bengal Famine kills an estimated 5 million people in British-ruled India, when hoarding and panic by individuals and low governmental priority leads to severe food shortages during World War II. It is the world's worst recorded food disaster.

1947

- The Doomsday Clock makes its first appearance on the cover of the *Bulletin of the Atomic Scientists.* The clock is a visual representation of the likelihood of nuclear war, with midnight representing an attack. The clock shows seven minutes to midnight; in the following years the clock is periodically changed. In 1953 it reaches two minutes to midnight, its closest time ever.

1951

- ***December 20:*** The EBR-1 nuclear reactor in Arco, Idaho, is the first to generate electricity.

1952

- China's South-to-North Water Diversion Project is initiated under Mao Zedong. In three phases, the program will divert water resources from the sparsely populated southern portion of the country to the more populated and water-needy northern portion. The project is scheduled to be completed in 2050.

1954

- ***June 27:*** The first nuclear power plant designed to generate electricity for a power grid goes online in Obninsk, USSR.

1955

- The World Health Organization begins a program to get rid of malaria worldwide using DDT.

1956

- Shell Oil geophysicist M. King Hubbert publishes his forecast of U.S. oil production, which he states will peak in the early 1970s.

1957

- First commercial nuclear power plant, the Beaver Valley Nuclear Generating Station, goes online in Shippingport, Pennsylvania.

1958

- Mao Zedong's "Great Leap Forward" is enacted in the People's Republic of China. In the push to transition from an agrarian to an industrialized nation, agricultural reforms cause the starvation deaths of millions of people through 1962, when the reforms are abandoned.

1959

- British inventor Francis Thomas Bacon develops a feasible fuel cell, which is installed in a tractor that is exhibited across the United States.

Chronology

1960

- Construction begins on the Aswan High Dam on the Nile in Egypt. The reservoir begins filling in 1964.
- The Geysers, the world's largest geothermal power plant, opens in California and provides 1360 MW, enough electricity for a city of 1 million.
- The Organization of Petroleum Exporting Countries (OPEC) is established.

1962

- A fire ignites in an underground coal mine in Centralia, Pennsylvania. Efforts to extinguish the fire fail, and it continues to burn indefinitely—well past 2007. Experts estimate that the coal seam will provide enough fuel for the fire to burn at least 250 years. In 1984, Congress allocated funds to relocate the town's residents, after which only 12 people remained, making it a modern-day ghost town.

1963

- U.S. Congress passes the Clean Air Act.

1966

- Beginning of China's Cultural Revolution under Mao Zedong, in which a massive transition to an urban economy results in migrations from rural to urban areas along with rapid industrialization.
- U.S. Congress passes the Clean Air Act Amendment.
- A wave power plant on the River Rance in France goes online.

1968

- ***April:*** The Club of Rome, an organization dedicated to exploring the connection between resource consumption and economic growth is founded by Aurelio Peccei and Alexander King.
- Garrett Hardin publishes "The Tragedy of the Commons" in the journal *Science,* arguing that when it comes to resources, what is important to all is governed by none.
- Paul R. Ehrlich publishes *The Population Bomb.*
- USAID director William Gaud dubs recent improvements in worldwide grain yields the "Green Revolution." The drought-resistant, high-yield strains are exported to countries suffering from food shortages and high population growth, thereby avoiding famine.
- Stewart Brand publishes the first *Whole Earth Catalog,* a guide to environmentally friendly products that encourages a generation of young people to contemplate their impact on the natural world.

1969

- ***June 22:*** The Cuyahoga River in Cleveland, Ohio, catches fire. It is not the first time that debris and foreign substances in the river have sparked a fire. The first one was in 1936, but this fire comes at a time when the general public is increasingly concerned about water pollution.

1970

- ***January 19:*** Two oil tankers collide underneath the Golden Gate Bridge, causing an 800,000-gallon oil spill in the San Francisco Bay. The event resulted in changes to the Coast Guard traffic system that were later adopted as part of the Clean Water Act.
- ***December 2:*** The Environmental Protection Agency is formed by President Richard Nixon.
- U.S. Congress passes the Clean Air Act Extension.
- The First Earth Day is celebrated in San Francisco.
- U.S. oil production peaks, as M. King Hubbert predicted in 1956.
- The Club of Rome creates the World3 computer model at MIT, which analyzes 120 variables and predicts that the world will run out of oil within 20 years.

1971

- Frances Moore Lappe publishes *Diet for a Small Planet.*

1972

- Federal Water Pollution Control Act of 1972 goes into effect. The Clean Water Act gives authority for administering wetlands to the U.S. Army Corps of Engineers.
- *The Whole Earth Catalog* wins the National Book Award.
- *The Limits to Growth* is published by Donella Meadows and the MIT-based Club of Rome.
- The TransAmazonian Highway opens in Brazil's Amazon Basin. The highway is 4,800 kilometers long and provides easy access for loggers to clear-cut the rain forest.

1973

- ***October 16:*** Following the Yom Kippur War, OPEC announces it will embargo oil destined for countries that supported Israel during the war. The embargo results in widespread shortages of gasoline and soaring prices in the United States and many other Western countries.

- The Pollution Health Damage Compensation Law goes into effect in Japan.
- The Endangered Species Act became U.S. law in an effort to protect animal and plant species from extinction due to "the consequences of economic growth and development untempered by adequate concern and conservation."
- British economist E. F. Schumacher publishes the landmark book *Small Is Beautiful,* in which he writes that society is unsustainable due to its misuse of natural resources.
- John and Alice Tyler establish the Tyler Prize for Environmental Achievement, an annual $200,000 prize awarded at the University of Southern California for individuals whose work in science, energy, medicine, and related fields significantly benefits humanity.

1974

- Lester R. Brown founds the Worldwatch Institute, which works to promote social justice and sustainable development throughout the world and publishes the annual State of the World reports on the status of various resources, such as water and farmland, and how they are impacted by human development.

1976

- The Grameen Bank Project is founded in Bangladesh by Muhammad Yunus as a tool for helping women rise out of poverty. The Bank is the first large-scale microcredit project.
- The Resource Conservation and Recovery Act (RCRA) becomes a federal law in the United States. The law provides the EPA with mandates to protect the public from the dangers of waste disposal; encourage the three R's—reduce, reuse, recycle; and clean up hazardous waste.

1977

- ***August 4:*** The U.S. Department of Energy, a cabinet-level department, is organized.
- U.S. Congress passes a Clean Air Act extension.
- Amendments to the Water Pollution Control Act passed and the act became known as the Clean Air Act.

1978

- ***August 7:*** President Carter declares a federal emergency in Love Canal, a neighborhood in Niagara Falls, New York, and residents whose houses were built on a toxic waste dump are forcibly relocated.

1979

- ***March 28:*** The Three Mile Island Nuclear Power Plant in Harrisburg, Pennsylvania, suffers a partial meltdown. No injuries are reported, but public sentiment turns against nuclear power.

1980

- ***June 30:*** President Carter signs the Energy Security Act into law. It is comprised of six major acts: U.S. Synthetic Fuels Corporation Act, Biomass Energy and Alcohol Fuels Act, Renewable Energy Resources Act, Solar Energy and Energy Conservation Act, Geothermal Energy Act, and the Ocean Thermal Energy Conversion Act.
- ***December 11:*** Congress enacts the Superfund Law (the Comprehensive Environmental Response, Compensation, and Liability Act—CERCLA) to facilitate the cleanup of toxic waste sites no longer owned or maintained by specific corporate entities.

1981

- The Council on Environmental Quality, commissioned by President Carter in 1997, releases its Global 2000 Report to the President, which predicts that by the year 2000, the world will be overpopulated and suffering crises related to the scarcity of resources and degradation of the environment.
- Julian Simon publishes *The Ultimate Resource,* a landmark book that refutes the notion that humanity is running out of natural resources, because scarcity of a resource results in higher prices and spurs ingenuity to discover other resources. The "ultimate resource" is the ability of human beings to adapt to their environment.

1982

- ***December 5:*** The Merrimac River in Times Beach, Missouri, floods, and 95 percent of the population is evacuated. On December 23, the EPA announces dangerous levels of dioxin in the area, and residents are permanently relocated.

1983

- The Green Party wins its first seats in West Germany's Parliament.
- The Itaipu Power Plant on the Paraná River goes online. Run jointly by Brazil and Paraguay, it is the world's largest power plant.
- Australian astrophysicist Brandon Carter develops the Doomsday argument of human extinction, based on the mathematical statistics of the number of people who have been born throughout history. The Doomsday argument

states that there is a 95 percent chance that humans will become extinct within 9120 years. This is also known as the Carter catastrophe.

1984

- ***December 2:*** Over 3,000 people die suddenly when 40 tons of methyl isocyanate are released from a Union Carbide pesticide plant in Bhopal, India. Up to 20,000 more people die in the months following the accident, and tens of thousands more are permanently disabled. It is considered the worst industrial disaster in history.

1986

- ***April 26:*** A reactor explosion at the Chernobyl Nuclear Power Plant near Kiev, Ukraine, in the USSR causes a nuclear meltdown that is considered to be the worst nuclear accident in history. Roughly 50 deaths are attributed to direct radiation exposure following the explosion, and the incident forces the permanent resettlement of 336,000 nearby residents.
- Norman Borlaug, the scientist largely responsible for the Green Revolution of the 1960s, establishes the World Food Prize, an annual award given to an individual who makes a substantial advance in science and technology that helps agriculturally deficient peoples.

1987

- ***September 16:*** The Montreal Protocol is opened for signature in an effort to limit the manufacture and use of CFCs to help reduce holes in the ozone layers over Antarctica and the Arctic Circle.
- U.S. Congress passes amendments to the Clean Water Act.
- The Brundtland Report, titled "Our Common Future," is published by the UN World Commission on Environment and Development (WCED). It outlines guiding principles for sustainable development as it is generally understood today.
- The first World Solar Challenge is raced in Australia by 11 teams driving from Darwin to Adelaide (over 1,800 miles) in solar-powered vehicles. General Motors's Sunraycer wins, with an average speed of 67 miles per hour.

1988

- The Intergovernmental Panel on Climate Change is established by the United Nations World Meteorological Organization (WMO) and the UN Environment Programme (UNEP) to evaluate global climate change.
- Entomologist E. O. Wilson popularizes the concept of biodiversity in his book of the same name, which summarizes the conference proceedings of the 1995 National Forum on Biological Diversity.

- The Multiple Use Strategy Conference is held in Reno, Nevada, which results in the "wise use" movement, comprised of industries and individuals who make their living from the mining and refining of natural resources and who lobby against government controls on land use and advocate unrestricted development on private land.

1989

- ***March 24:*** The *Exxon Valdez* oil tanker runs into a reef in Alaska's Prince William Sound, spilling between 11 and 30 million gallons of crude oil into the water. Although it is not the largest oil spill in U.S. waters, it takes place in an environmentally fragile ecosystem at great cost to the area's wildlife.
- Richard C. Duncan proposes the Olduvai Theory, which states that industrial civilization will last approximately 100 years, from 1930 to 2030. The theory takes into account the idea of Peak Oil, population growth, economic growth, and ecological overshoot. The theory supports the idea of a modern Malthusian catastrophe.
- Physicist Amory Lovins creates the concept of negawatt power and proposes the "soft energy path," both of which advocate for increased energy efficiency, conservation, and expansion of renewable energy sources.

1990

- U.S. Congress passes a Clean Air Act amendment.

1991

- ***January 23:*** The largest oil spill in history is caused by Iraqi forces attempting to foil a landing by U.S. Marines during the Gulf War by opening a valve at the Sea Island offshore terminal in Kuwait and by dumping oil from several tankers located in the Gulf. The spill is estimated to be approximately 100 miles long, 40 miles wide, and 4 inches thick, and is thought to be anywhere from 5 to 27 times larger than the *Exxon Valdez* oil spill.
- **September 26:** Eight scientists enter the Biosphere 2 in Oracle, Arizona. They will remain in the completely enclosed biome for two years, in the first extended experiment to create a self-contained habitable environment.
- ***November 6:*** Oil well fires in Kuwait are extinguished. The retreating Iraqi army set fire to 800 oil wells in Kuwait, which burned for 8 months, consumed 6 million barrels of oil a day, and produced black rain in Iran.

1992

- ***June 3–June 14:*** The Earth Summit takes place in Rio de Janeiro, Brazil. It is sponsored by the United Nations Conference on Environment and Development (UNCED) and results in the United Nations Framework Convention on

Climate Change (UNFCCC) and Agenda 21, signed by 178 governments, of local and international practices to be adopted in minimizing human impact on the environment.

- Canadian ecologist William Rees originates his concept of the *ecological footprint,* a diagnostic tool used to illustrate the extent of human impact on the planet.

1993

- ***September 26:*** The Biosphere 2 experiment ends in controversy, when the scientists emerge from the artificial biome. The experiment was compromised when oxygen was pumped in from the outside after carbon dioxide levels became dangerously high. Additionally, the subjects suffered continual hunger that was on occasion alleviated by the introduction of outside food.

1994

- Construction begins on the Three Gorges Dam in China, which will be the largest hydroelectric dam in the world when it is completed. Structural work is largely finished in 2006.

1996

- William Rees and M. Wackernagel publish *Our Ecological Footprint: Reducing Human Impact on the Earth,* which popularizes the concept of the ecological footprint and raises awareness of ecological overshoot.

1997

- ***December 11:*** The Kyoto Protocol to the United Nations Framework Convention on Climate Change is negotiated in Japan. Countries that ratify the Kyoto Protocol agree to reduce carbon emissions and other greenhouse gas emissions, and engage in emissions trading in an effort to curb global warming. India and China, however, are not required to reduce their emissions.
- The Toyota Prius is introduced as the world's first commercially available gasoline/electric hybrid vehicle and is named Car of the Year in Japan. The Prius is available worldwide by 2001.

1998

- ***June–July:*** Floods in China exacerbated by deforestation kill roughly 4,000 people and leave 14 million homeless. Twenty-five million hectares of farmland are flooded.

1999

- ***October 12:*** The earth's population reaches 6 billion people, according to the United Nations Population Fund.

- Germany establishes the Eco-Tax to promote renewable energy by taxing fossil fuels.

2000

- ***June:*** California is beset by rolling blackouts caused by energy speculators.
- ***September:*** The Millennium Summit in New York, which is the largest gathering of world leaders in history, results in the UN Millennium Declaration.
- Germany passes the Renewable Energy Act and the Nuclear Exit Law, which will phase out nuclear power in the country by 2020.

2002

- **August 26–September 4:** The World Summit on Sustainable Development is held in Johannesburg, South Africa, and results in the adoption of the Johannesburg Declaration of Sustainable Development.
- The Global Climate Coalition, an organization designed to block adoption of the Kyoto Protocol in the United States is disbanded. The organization counted among its members Exxon, Ford, Royal Dutch/Shell, Texaco, British Petroleum, General Motors, and DaimlerChrysler.
- Brazil adopts the Proinfa program, which provides incentives to foster the development of biomass, wind power, and small-scale hydropower energy sources.

2003

- ***May:*** The European Union adopts the Biofuels Directive, which mandates that 5.75 percent of its energy must come from biofuels by 2010.
- ***August 14:*** The North American Blackout in the northeastern United States and parts of Canada affects 50 million people. It is caused by a catastrophic shutdown of the power grid starting near Cleveland that cascades within seconds to other major plants in the Great Lakes and Eastern seaboard regions. The event highlights the frailty of the nation's power infrastructure, which could not accommodate the demands of a hot summer day.
- ***August:*** A heat wave in Europe, in which temperatures top 100°F for several weeks, results in over 14,000 deaths in France and thousands more in Germany, Italy, Spain, and the United Kingdom. Total casualty estimates range from 35,000 to 50,000. The heat wave is widely attributed to global warming and its human costs to insufficient emergency response plans.
- ***September 27–28:*** A power failure cuts service to more than 56 million people in Italy. To date, it is the largest power failure in world history.
- The U.S. Clear Skies Act of 2003 places limits on sulfur dioxide, nitrous oxide, and mercury emissions.

2004

- ***May 17:*** The Stockholm Convention on Persistent Organic Pollutants is entered into force after being ratified by 128 parties. Persistent organic pollutants (POPs) are substances that are harmful to human health and that bioaccumulate when they are introduced into the environment. The Stockholm Convention calls for the elimination of nine of the "dirty dozen" chemicals (aldrin, chlordane, dieldrin, endrin, heptachlor, hexachlorobenzene, mirex, toxaphene, and polychlorinated biphenyls [PCBs]), restricts DDT use to malaria control, and limits the production of dioxins and furans.

2005

- ***February 16:*** The Kyoto Protocol is entered into force after being ratified by Russia, thereby attaining the 55 percent rule, which states that the Protocol will become effective when 55 percent of worldwide greenhouse gas emissions come under control of the treaty. By 2007, the Kyoto Protocol is ratified by 169 countries, with the United States and Australia the only major nations abstaining.
- ***August 29:*** Hurricane Katrina makes landfall near the Louisiana-Mississippi border. The Category 5 storm decimates many towns along the coast, and more than 1,800 people die when the levees that hold back Lake Pontchartrain break and flood the below-sea-level areas of New Orleans. Hundreds of thousands are displaced. Causing more than $81.2 billion in damage, the storm is the costliest natural disaster in U.S. history.
- ***September 24:*** Hurricane Rita, the fourth most intense hurricane ever recorded, makes landfall on the Texas-Louisiana border, causing $11.3 billion in damage.
- ***October 25:*** Hurricane Wilma, the most intense hurricane ever recorded, makes landfall on the Florida coast, causing $28.8 billion in damage.
- The Swedish government forms the Commission on Oil Independence and announces its intention to phase out oil and other fossil fuels by 2020. The oil phaseout calls for increased energy efficiency, conservation, and a switch to renewable energy where possible. The country aims to be a world leader in reducing carbon emissions and promoting sustainable development. Within a year, however, the Commission's status is in doubt after the Social Democratic Party loses the general election.

2006

- ***January 1:*** China's Renewables Law goes into effect, which stipulates that 10 percent of the country's energy must be provided by renewable resources by 2020.

- ***May 24:*** *An Inconvenient Truth,* a documentary film on global warming directed by Davis Guggenheim and starring former U.S. vice president Al Gore, is released by Paramount Classics. A companion book reaches number 1 on the *New York Times* Best-seller List on August 13, 2006. The film wins the Academy Award for Documentary Feature Film in February 2007.
- ***December 18:*** President George W. Bush signs the United States–India Peaceful Atomic Energy Cooperation Act, stating that it is an important step in addressing the energy and security needs of the world's two largest democracies in the 21st century.
- India's Prime Minister Singh calls for a second Green Revolution to transform the focus of the country's agricultural industry from food security to free market enterprise.
- Seventy percent of all new vehicles purchased in Brazil are flex-fuel vehicles that run on ethanol.
- World population reaches 6.5 billion.

2007

- ***February 2:*** The IPCC releases its fourth assessment, stating that global warming is unequivocal, is almost certainly caused by emissions of greenhouse gases into the atmosphere by humans, will continue for centuries, and will have a significant impact on weather, temperature, and rising sea levels.
- ***February 9:*** Sir Richard Branson announces the Virgin Earth Challenge, a $25 million prize for the first person to devise a way to remove 1 billion metric tons of carbon gases from the atmosphere each year for ten years.
- ***March 22:*** The United Nations designates the day World Water Day and plans events around the globe to highlight the severity of water issues in many countries. More than 1 billion people worldwide lack access to clean drinking water, resulting in the deaths of approximately 3,900 children each day from diarrhea.
- ***December 19:*** The Clean Energy Act of 2007 is signed into law. Among its provisions are an increase in CAFE standards to 35 MPG for all cars and light trucks by 2020, an increase in production of biofuel accelerated research and development of alternative energy, and a phaseout of incandescent lightbulbs by 2014.

2008

- The Summer Olympics in Beijing is billed as the "Green Olympics," and many facilities are built to promote energy conservation and renewable energy resources.

- The world's first zero-carbon emissions power plant is scheduled to go online south of Berlin.
- ***January 10:*** Tata Motors of India unveils its new Tata Nano, the least expensive production car in the world, priced at, $2500. "The People's Car," as it is dubbed, appeals to India's new, surging middle class.

2012

- ***October 18:*** The world's population will reach 7 billion people, according to estimates by the U.S. Census Bureau.
- Target completion date for India's Power to All by 2012 initiative.

2015

- Target completion date for the United Nations' Millennium Development Goals, which aim to halve poverty worldwide, combat HIV/AIDS, ensure universal education, gender equality, and environmental sustainability.

2050

- World population estimated to be 8,918,724,000.
- Target completion date for China's South-to-North Water Diversion Project, begun in 1952.

Glossary

acid rain Precipitation with a pH of less than 5.0, usually caused by emissions of sulfur and nitrogen into the atmosphere, which can negatively impact forests, freshwater habitats, and buildings.

Agenda 21 The United Nations–sponsored program to facilitate sustainable development on an international scale in the 21st century. It was adopted on June 14, 1992, at the Earth Summit in Rio de Janiero by 179 voting nations and is administered by the UN Commission on Sustainable Development.

algal bloom Rapid growth of phytoplankton algae in a body of water due to excess nitrogen and phosphorus. In the process of EUTROPHICATION, excess algae depletes the water's supply of dissolved oxygen and the ability of other organisms to exist in the environment. Algal blooms can lead to RED TIDES and DEAD ZONES and are often caused by pollution from agriculture and industry.

Arctic National Wildlife Refuge (ANWR) A 19-billion-acre region in northeast Alaska bordering Canada and completely within the Arctic Circle that likely has a substantial amount of recoverable oil and natural gas. As of 2006, exploratory drilling in the area was illegal.

Asian Brown Cloud A cloud of smog originating over the Indian subcontinent and extending into Mainland China, where it intensifies due to high levels of air pollution. When the cloud reaches the Pacific Ocean, it is carried by the jet stream to the West Coast of the United States and across the Midwest, where it may affect rainfall and drought cycles.

bagasse The residue generated by processing sugarcane into ETHANOL or sugar. It can be used as a source of ENERGY itself.

bioaccumulation See BIOMAGNIFICATION.

biodiversity The number of species and the number of variations within a species present in a given ECOSYSTEM. Wide-ranging biodiversity correlates with a healthy environment.

biodiversity hotspot A region known for its extensive BIODIVERSITY that is also facing destruction.

biomagnification The process of a substance entering the food chain at a low level and becoming concentrated when uptake is greater than excretion for a given organism. Thus, the substance moves higher in the food chain as larger animals consume smaller species. Pesticides such as DDT and PCBs and natural substances such as mercury and arsenic are especially prone to biomagnification because they do not break down in the environment. Biomagnification is sometimes used interchangeably with *bioaccumulation.*

biomass Same as biofuel. Plant or animal matter used as fuel, excluding coal and petroleum, which has been transformed through geological processes.

birthrate The number of births each year per 1,000 people in a given population.

Brundtland Report The popular name of the document produced by the *World Commission on Environment and Development* (WCED), which was chaired by Gro Harlem Brundtland. The 1987 report, titled "Our Common Future," defined sustainable development as development that "meets the needs of the present without compromising the ability of future generations to meet their own needs."

cap-and-trade A government-sanctioned, market-driven strategy to limit various types of pollution by mandating industrial emissions limits (a cap), but allowing companies who wish to exceed these limits to buy additional emissions permits from companies whose emissions are below their legal allowance (trade). Cap-and-trade programs have been used to address both air and water pollution.

carbon dioxide (CO_2) The chemical compound that is the primary greenhouse gas responsible for GLOBAL WARMING. As a gas, it exists naturally in the atmosphere and is generated by several natural processes, including fermentation and respiration. The burning of FOSSIL FUELS also releases significant amounts of carbon dioxide into the atmosphere. In high concentrations it is toxic.

carbon footprint A measurement of the carbon emissions from either an individual or a specific population, usually in tons per year, that is calculated by assessing how much CARBON DIOXIDE was generated by the person or group's consumption of goods and ENERGY.

carbon intensity The ratio of CARBON DIOXIDE emissions to economic activity; a measurement used to gauge ENERGY EFFICIENCY of a group, usually a country.

carbon monoxide (CO) An odorless, toxic gas emitted by internal-combustion engines and often used in manufacturing. Like CARBON DIOXIDE, it is a greenhouse gas that is naturally present in the atmosphere through volcanic activity and other natural processes.

carbon neutral The state of offsetting carbon emissions with practices that increase oxygen emissions, resulting in a state of carbon equilibrium. Carbon neutrality can be obtained by purchasing carbon offsets or planting trees and vegetation at a rate commensurate with carbon emissions.

carbon offsets The efforts to reduce, cancel out, or negate carbon emissions by a group or an individual by engaging in activities that absorb carbon emissions. Carbon offset actions include planting trees, using renewable ENERGY, or purchasing emissions trading credits.

carbon sequestration The process by which CARBON DIOXIDE is captured and pumped into underground reservoirs instead of being introduced into the atmosphere. Sequestration is one of the COAL industry's solutions to limiting emissions that contribute to global climate change.

carrying capacity The number of people the Earth can support without suffering extreme stress on NATURAL RESOURCES.

coal A FOSSIL FUEL in rock form, composed primarily of carbon and sulfur generated over millions of years from the remains of living matter. Coal is the world's main fuel source used to generate ELECTRICITY.

cogeneration (combined heat and power [CHP]) A technique to maximize ENERGY EFFICIENCY by using one power system to produce both heat and ELECTRICITY. CHP systems can be used in industry as well as by individual consumers.

conservation The practice of preserving the natural world by limiting use of resources and allowing ECOSYSTEMS to remain intact.

corporate average fuel economy (CAFE) standards Fuel efficiency requirements for automobiles, first established in the United States in 1975 in response to the OPEC oil embargo and consisting of miles-per-gallon requirements dependent on a vehicle's weight. Certain classes of heavy vehicles, including some pickup trucks, vans, and sport utility vehicles, are exempt from CAFE standards. The requirements are regulated by the National Highway Traffic Safety Administration (NHTSA) and Environmental Protection Agency (EPA).

crude oil A FOSSIL FUEL found in a liquid state in the Earth's crust, containing mostly hydrocarbons, sulfur, oxygen, and nitrogen. Crude oil is refined into different types of fuel oil, such as gasoline, jet fuel, and kerosene, as well as fertilizers, chemicals, and plastics. Same as *petroleum.*

dead zone An oceanic region characterized by low oxygen levels, or hypoxia, that disrupts or kills the normal marine ECOSYSTEM. Often caused by the process of EUTROPHICATION, in which excess nutrients (such as nitrogen and phosphorus) are introduced to the water through industrial pollution and agricultural runoff, leading to an algal bloom that suffocates the small organisms that serve as the food source for larger organisms. Dead zones tend to be seasonal and recur in the same areas annually; they range in size from less than a square mile to thousands of square miles.

deep ecology A philosophical form of ECOLOGY that emphasizes equality between all living species, giving humankind no special priority. Originated by Norwegian philosopher Arne Naess in 1972.

deforestation The process of clearing forested areas in order to claim the land for some other use, usually for agriculture or urban development. Deforestation leads to soil erosion, water pollution, floods, DESERTIFICATION, and other processes that upset the ecological balance of the region.

demographic dividend Economic growth that takes place when FERTILITY RATES fall and the number of working-age people coincides with a decline in youth dependency rates. The term is often used to describe India's workforce in the early 21st century.

demography The study of human populations.

desalination The process by which salt is taken out of water to make it fit for human consumption. Desalination can take place via reverse osmosis, forward osmosis, or several other processes and is often viewed as a solution to the water shortage problem in countries that lack access to large supplies of freshwater.

desertification Degradation of land in fragile ECOSYSTEMS, usually brought on by unsustainable agriculture and population growth in a given region.

diamond-water paradox A phenomenon of a free-market economy described by Adam Smith in *The Wealth of Nations* in which diamonds are not essential to life and yet are considered highly valuable, while water is essential to life and remains inexpensive and readily available. Also called the paradox of value.

distributed generation The process by which consumers who generate more ENERGY than they use can sell the surplus back to the grid. Often used in combined heat and power (CHP) systems.

doomsday argument The prediction of human EXTINCTION based on probability mathematics, given the number of people who have already been born. First proposed by Brandon Carter in 1983, the argument states that with 95 percent confidence the human race will be extinct within 9,120 years.

doubling time The period of time it takes for a population to double in size.

ecology The study of organisms and their environment.

ecological footprint The total area of land and water a given population requires in order to provide the ENERGY and resources they consume and to absorb the waste they produce. The footprint is a measurement used to illustrate sustainable and unsustainable consumption patterns among various peoples and countries.

ecological overshoot When a population exceeds the carrying capacity of its environment by consuming more land and water resources than the Earth can regenerate in a given time period; a primary indicator of unsustainability. Overshoot leads to a crash or die-off, such as those experienced by the ancient Mayans, Anasazi, or Viking settlers in Greenland.

ecosystem A region of plants and animal organisms that interact with their environment as an ecological unit.

ecotage/ecoterrorism Acts of vandalism, crime, and civil disobedience (often illegal) committed in an attempt to preserve the environment.

ecotourism (or ecological tourism) A form of ecologically and socially responsible travel that often involves immersion in the wilderness and minimal impact on the land. Stresses CONSERVATION and BIODIVERSITY.

electricity In terms of sustainable development, electricity is the conversion of electric ENERGY into other forms of energy, such as light, heat, or mechanical power. Electricity can be generated by many substances, but the majority of it is generated by COAL.

energy The capacity to do work.

energy efficiency The concept of obtaining the maximum amount of ENERGY from a source without wasting it.

energy security The ability of a country to obtain the ENERGY it requires to maintain and grow its economy without succumbing to vulnerabilities due to foreign affairs, infrastructure failure, terrorist acts, or any other form of disruption.

ethanol Alcohol that is used as a fuel alternative to gasoline. It is commonly produced from crops such as corn and sugarcane.

eutrophication The process whereby too many dissolved nutrients, such as nitrates and phosphates, are introduced into a body of water, resulting in an overgrowth of plant life and a depletion of dissolved oxygen necessary to sustain animal species.

extinction The dying out of all members of a particular species, resulting in a reduction of BIODIVERSITY.

famine Widespread hunger, illness, malnutrition, and starvation in a given area, often caused by economic and social factors that prevent people from obtaining necessary food and water.

fertility rate The average number of children born to each woman in the course of her life in a given region and time period.

flex-fuel vehicle A vehicle that can run on two different fuel sources, either because the vehicle contains two fuel-delivery systems or because different fuel types can be used interchangeably, such as a vehicle that can run on either gasoline or ETHANOL. Natural gas vehicles that can also run on gasoline are flex-fuel vehicles.

food independence The ability of a country to grow enough food to sustain its population without having to rely on exports.

fossil fuel Decayed organic material that has been transformed into hydrocarbons through the heat and pressure of the Earth's surface over a period of millions of years. The primary fossil fuels are COAL, oil, and NATURAL GAS.

fuel cell An electrochemical ENERGY conversion device in which a fuel and an oxidant are introduced into an electrolyte, creating a reaction that generates energy. In a proton-exchange membrane (PEM) fuel cell, hydrogen is the fuel, oxygen is the oxidant, and a proton-conducting polymer membrane is the electrolyte.

genetically modified food (GMF) Crops whose DNA has been genetically engineered to result in desirable traits, such as resistance to rotting, disease, lack of water, and heat, and which may result in higher yields. GM tomatoes were introduced in 1994, and since then soybeans, cotton, maize, canola, and rice have also been genetically modified.

geothermal power ELECTRICITY generated from the earth's heat; considered a renewable source of ENERGY.

global aging The phenomenon by which the average age in a given region or population increases. Global aging, especially in developed countries, is a function of low FERTILITY RATES and economic prosperity, among other factors. The implications of global aging are enormous—from economic problems caused by a shrinking workforce to social problems caused by the collapse of community and family networks.

global climate change Any sustained change in the temperature of the Earth's atmosphere and oceans. Includes both global cooling and GLOBAL WARMING.

global footprint See ECOLOGICAL FOOTPRINT.

global hectare A unit of measurement equal to a hectare, which is 10,000 square meters or 2.47 acres.

global warming A sustained increase in the temperature of the Earth's atmosphere and its oceans.

Great Leap Forward Mao Zedong's plan to modernize the People's Republic of China, which lasted from 1958 to 1962 and attempted to transform the nation from a peasant-dominated agrarian economy to a modern, industrialized economy. Agrarian reforms, droughts, and floods led to unsustainable agricultural practices and the deaths of an estimated 14 million to 43 million people.

green building The practice of using RENEWABLE RESOURCES and ENERGY efficient designs in construction. Green building has applications in many areas of the home, from site selection, heating/cooling and water systems, to maintenance, construction, and operation. Also known as sustainable building.

green energy ENERGY derived from renewable and non-polluting sources. Green energy includes wind, solar, geothermal, tidal power, biomass, and small-scale HYDROPOWER.

greenhouse effect The process by which sunlight enters the Earth's atmosphere and instead of bouncing off the Earth's surface and being reflected back into space, it becomes trapped by a layer of gases that do not permit the sunlight to pass through the atmosphere. The result is a warming of the atmosphere.

greenhouse gas Any of the substances in the atmosphere that contribute to the GREENHOUSE EFFECT. The main naturally occurring greenhouse gases are water vapor, CARBON DIOXIDE, METHANE, and OZONE. Industrially produced greenhouse gases include sulfur hexafluoride, nitrous oxide, hydrofluorocarbons, and chlorofluorocarbons.

Green Revolution As defined by Norman Borlaug in the 1960s, the Green Revolution refers to a series of technological and agricultural improvements in farming and food distribution that prevented widespread FAMINE in the latter half of the 20th century, particularly in countries that experienced a population surge.

groundwater Water that is obtained from underground aquifers via drilling or wells. If groundwater is extracted at rates that exceed an aquifer's ability to replenish itself, the wells may dry up, become too salinated for consumption, or become poisoned by arsenic.

hectare *See* GLOBAL HECTARE.

Hubbert curve A bell-shaped curve named after oil geophysicist M. King Hubbert, who developed it in the 1950s to demonstrate how oil production in the United States would peak in 1970, which it did.

hybrid vehicle A motor vehicle that combines two power systems, usually a gasoline-fueled internal combustion engine with a battery-powered assist. Hybrid vehicles get better gas mileage, are more ENERGY efficient, and less polluting than traditional motor vehicles.

hydrocarbons Chemicals containing molecules of carbon and hydrogen. They are the main component of FOSSIL FUELS.

hydrogen economy The as-yet-unrealized scenario in which a majority of a nation's ENERGY needs are met by hydrogen-generated fuels and ELECTRICITY, effectively replacing FOSSIL FUELS and other nonrenewable energy sources.

hydropower ENERGY captured from running water and used for another purpose. Waterwheels and paddleboats use hydropower; hydroelectric plants generate ELECTRICITY via turbines powered by dammed water.

hyperconsumption An excessive consumption of consumer goods and services that is far beyond what is necessary for survival and which contributes to unsustainability.

Jevons Paradox A phenomenon first observed by William Stanley Jevons and outlined in his 1865 book *The Coal Question*. Jevons noted that ENERGY efficiencies gained by James Watt's steam engine in England were cancelled out by the influx of additional steam engines that such efficiencies made possible.

Kuznets Curve A graph representing how economic inequality rises over time, reaches a peak, and then begins to fall as a function related to per capita income. Named for economist Simon Kuznets, it can be used to illustrate the disparity between poor, rural farmers and wealthier city dwellers, and by extension it provides an explanation for increasing migration and urbanization.

Malthusian catastrophe A situation in which unsustainable population growth leads to massive starvation and death, returning societies to a subsistence level of existence. Named after Thomas Malthus, who originated the idea of overpopulation.

megacity An urban area of 10 million people or more. As of 2005, 25 cities in the world qualified as megacities, most of them in underdeveloped countries. Megacities often feature high population densities, high levels of poverty, and a demand for resources that outstrips supply.

methane A greenhouse gas that is the most common naturally occurring hydrocarbon.

methane hydrate A frozen form of natural gas and water found in permafrost and underneath the ocean floor, which has the potential to become a significant fossil fuel resource in the future.

microcredit (also microfinance) Small loans, typically the equivalent of several hundred dollars, given to a group of three to five women for the purpose of fostering their economic freedom through small-scale enterprise. Microcredit programs in Bangladesh, India, and other underdeveloped nations have enabled hundreds of thousands of poor women to learn a trade, become literate in business methodology, and provide basic necessities for themselves and their families.

municipal solid waste (MSW) Trash and/or garbage; all waste generated by consumers including that which is later recycled or reused.

natural gas A fossil fuel in a gaseous state, consisting mainly of methane, but often with significant quantities of ethane, butane, propane, CARBON DIOXIDE, nitrogen, helium, and hydrogen sulfide.

natural resource A substance found on Earth that is valuable in its initial form. A natural resource can be renewable or nonrenewable. The natural-resource industries are frequently considered to be mining, petroleum extraction, fishing, hunting, and forestry.

negawatt power Represents ENERGY not consumed due to CONSERVATION and efficiency measures, or when the available supply is increased without a corresponding increase in infrastructure or power generation. Concept developed by energy expert Amory Lovins in 1989.

New Urbanism An urban planning and architectural design movement that arose in the 1980s and which seeks to create sustainable communities, prevent urban sprawl, and increase residents' quality of life through buildings and designs that encourage civic life and discourage automobile use and overconsumption.

nitrous oxide (N_2O) A colorless gas that occurs naturally in the atmosphere and that has anesthetic and analgesic properties. It is used in the medical and dental fields as laughing gas but it is also a powerful greenhouse gas, 296 times more powerful than CARBON DIOXIDE.

nonpoint source pollution Harmful substances that enter a body of water in small amounts from many locations, often due to agricultural and municipal runoff. Nonpoint source pollution tends to become highly concentrated in a watershed, often leading to RED TIDES, DEAD ZONES, and other detrimental phenomena.

nonrenewable resource A NATURAL RESOURCE that cannot be regenerated as quickly as it is consumed, making its continued use unsustainable. FOSSIL FUELS are nonrenewable, and other forms of ENERGY, including wood and nuclear energy, can also be nonrenewable if overharvested, such as in the case of old-growth rain forests and uranium mining.

nuclear power The controlled use of nuclear fission, using a radioactive isotope such as uranium-235, to provide ENERGY for ELECTRICITY and heat by creating a chain reaction that drives steam-powered turbines.

oil See CRUDE OIL.

oil sands Tarlike sands containing significant amounts of bitumen that can be refined into petroleum. Once thought to be too expensive to mine, oil sands are becoming a more feasible source of fossil fuel as supplies of easily extracted oil begin to dwindle.

oil shale Deposits of sedimentary rocks that contain bitumen and other organic material that can be distilled into oil. Lack of technology has prevented oil shale from becoming a source of recoverable oil.

Olduvai Theory A theory formulated in 1989 by Richard C. Duncan that uses statistics regarding world ENERGY production to suggest that industrialized civilization will have a lifespan of approximately 100 years, from roughly 1930 to 2030.

Organization of Petroleum Exporting Countries (OPEC) A cartel that includes (as of 2007) Algeria, Angola, Indonesia, Iran, Iraq, Kuwait, Libya, Nigeria, Qatar, Saudi Arabia, the United Arab Emirates, and Venezuela. Formed around 1960 and headquartered in Vienna, Austria, OPEC accounts for roughly 40 percent of world oil production and two-thirds of world oil reserves. Their goal is protect their interests in the international oil market, often by exercising price controls.

overpopulation In regard to human population on Earth, overpopulation is when the number of people exceeds the planet's carrying capacity.

oxyfuel technology A carbon emissions–reducing technique in which COAL is burned in an environment of pure oxygen, rather than air, which removes nitrogen from the emissions and makes it easier to store underground.

ozone (O_3) A molecule containing three oxygen atoms. At the Earth's surface, ozone is a health hazard and a primary component of smog.

ozone depletion The permanent destruction of the protective ozone layer in the stratosphere, due primarily to CFC and halon pollutants emitted into the atmosphere. Ozone depletion is associated with skin cancer and a reduction in marine levels of phytoplankton.

ozone hole The seasonal holes in the ozone layer over the North and South Poles, which allow harmful ultraviolet sunlight to enter the Earth's atmosphere.

ozone layer Part of the Earth's stratosphere, between 10 and 50 kilometers above Earth's surface, that contains a high concentration of O_3 and is responsible for preventing damaging ultraviolet light from reaching the Earth's surface.

Peak Oil The moment in history at which the world's production of oil will reach its highest point and begin its steady decline thereafter. Graphically depicted, Peak Oil resembles and is based on the bell curve developed by M. King Hubbert to illustrate the rise and fall of U.S. oil production.

petroleum See CRUDE OIL.

photovoltaic cell Often known as a *solar cell*, it is a device that converts photons from sunlight and sometimes from other light sources, such as lightbulbs, into ELECTRICITY.

point source pollution Substances introduced to a body of water from a specific location, either from large-scale dumping or an underwater pipe. Point source pollution is regulated under various local, regional, and national laws.

population The total number of a specific item.

population bomb As defined by Paul R. Ehrlich in *The Population Bomb* (1968), a population bomb refers to the combination of rapid population growth in a specific time or place, limited resources, and lack of willingness to deal with those limits.

population control The practice of limiting population growth, usually by lowering FERTILITY RATES and usually as an effort to curb poverty.

population density The number of people in a given area. Worldwide population density, given the amount of land on Earth, is 33 people per square mile.

population growth The change in a population over time.

population momentum The phenomenon by which a given population continues to grow even though fertility and BIRTHRATES are stagnant or falling. Reflects the fact that a majority of a population is of childbearing age, which will make the next generation larger than the previous generation. Population momentum explains why China's total population continues to rise, even though couples are restricted to having only one child.

population pyramid A graph that shows the distribution of age groups in a given population. Population, separated by gender, is charted on the X axis, with age charted on the central Y axis. Due to population growth, the graph usually resembles a pyramid, with the larger young population on the bottom and the sparser elderly population at the top. GLOBAL AGING has reversed this in some areas, making the graph much wider in the center.

post-consumer waste Usually meaning garbage, but technically refers to waste that is generated at the end of a consumer stream; that is, waste that was not generated in the production of subsequent goods to be consumed.

pre-consumer waste Garbage generated in the production of goods.

proton exchange membrane (PEM) fuel cell See FUEL CELL.

proven reserves A known quantity of a resource that can be feasibly recovered.

rain forest An ECOSYSTEM characterized by high rainfall and dense vegetation of broad-leafed trees that form a continuous canopy. Rain forests are known for their BIODIVERSITY and vulnerability to resource depletion.

red tide An algal bloom of a reddish color, resulting from the process of eutrification, that results in hypoxia (lack of oxygen), leading to an inhospitable environment for marine organisms. Common term for the algal blooms along the Florida coast and in the Gulf of Mexico.

renewable resource A natural source of ENERGY that cannot be used at a rate faster than it can be replenished; includes solar energy, wind, geothermal, water, and some forms of biomass.

resource curse The paradox in which countries that have vast reserves of NATURAL RESOURCES suffer economic problems despite the wealth created from their natural resources, often because they fail to diversify their economic base.

salination The process by which freshwater becomes salty and unfit for human consumption. Salination is often the result of WATER STRESS and depletion.

solar power Using the Sun's ENERGY for power. Solar power can be active, as when converted by photovoltaic cells to produce ELECTRICITY, or it can be passive, as in a greenhouse, where solar heat is used to warm air and grow plants.

sulfur dioxide (SO_2) A naturally occurring gaseous compound released by the burning of FOSSIL FUEL. It is a key component of ACID RAIN.

sustainable agriculture Farming practices enacted for the purpose of protecting arable land so it remains fertile. Sustainable agricultural practices include crop rotation, irrigation CONSERVATION, soil maintenance, and consideration of long-term economic factors. Sustainable agricultural practices typically do not include slash-and-burn techniques, excessive pesticide use, and monoculture (growing only one crop).

sustainable development Development that "meets the needs of the present without compromising the ability of future generations to meet their own needs." Concept first defined in "Our Common Future," the report of the United Nation's World Commission on Environment and Development in 1987.

sustainable energy Use of RENEWABLE RESOURCES to generate ENERGY that cannot be depleted and that will not harm the environment or contribute to global climate change. Sustainable energy includes wind and SOLAR POWER, WAVE POWER, tidal power, GEOTHERMAL POWER. It may include NUCLEAR POWER and BIOMASS.

tar sands See OIL SANDS.

tidal power See WAVE POWER.

tragedy of the commons The idea that resources available to everyone are protected by no one, in effect pitting individual interests against the common good. The tragedy of the commons has philosophical ramifications in regard to the water supply, the atmosphere, arable land, and other NATURAL RESOURCES.

United Nations An international organization founded in 1945 and dedicated to issues of international governance, human rights, social welfare, economic development, and security. As of 2007, the United Nations had 192 member nations and dozens of international programs and agencies, including the World Bank, that work to initiate peace and prosperity worldwide.

urban planning The practice of developing land according to community, local, and regional needs and plans. Urban or town plans can apply to specific buildings and also the landscape and infrastructure of an area in order to facilitate traffic flow, population density, commerce, and economic growth. Urban planning takes into consideration the resources available in a given area and exploits them accordingly. Lack of urban planning results in sprawl, slums, insufficient infrastructure, and resource problems.

urban sprawl Extensive suburban development spreading out from an urban core that often exacerbates traffic congestion through sparse land use and single-purpose developments, such as large residential neighborhoods and strip mall complexes. Urban sprawl can strain natural resources by eliminating arable land, encouraging DEFORESTATION, promoting hyperconsumption, requiring motor vehicle travel, and straining the power grid, water distribution, and sanitation systems.

water stress When demand for water outstrips supply. It can lead to SALINATION, pollution, depleted aquifers, and DESERTIFICATION.

wave power A renewable ENERGY form in which ELECTRICITY is generated by harnessing the cyclical energy of waves. Underdeveloped as an energy source, with much potential for expansion, particularly in certain geographical locations, such as the United Kingdom.

wind power ELECTRICITY generated from turbines that harness wind ENERGY.

Wise Use Movement A collections of groups and individuals who advocate for private, individual use of lands for recreation, development, and resource extraction instead of governmental controls. The movement, formed by conservative organizations and corporate entities, formed at the 1988 Multiple Use Strategy Conference in Reno, Nevada.

Index

Note: page numbers in **boldface** indicate major treatment of a subject. Page numbers followed by *f* indicate figures. Page numbers followed by *b* indicate biographical entries. Page numbers followed by *c* indicate chronology entries. Page numbers followed by *g* indicate glossary entries.

Index

Index

Index

Index

Index

O

Index

Index